Unveiling *the* Apocalypse

PROPHECY IN CATHOLIC TRADITION

Emmett O'Regan

Scripture quotations are from The Holy Bible, English Standard Version® (ESV®), copyright © 2001 by Crossway, a publishing ministry of Good News Publishers. Used by permission. All rights reserved.

Cover art: "The Last Judgment" by Jean Cousin the Younger (c.1595), Louvre Museum, Paris.
Photograph Copyright © Emmett O'Regan 2011

Published by Seraphim Press, Belfast.

ISBN: 978-0-9569558-0-7

Contents

List of Illustrations

Fig. 1 The Dome of the Rock
An image of the Dome of the Rock depicted in Phillip Baldensperger's *The Immovable East: Studies of the People and Customs of Palestine*, 1913.

Fig. 2 The Shepherd Children of Fatima

Fig. 3 Spectators of the Miracle of the Sun at the Cova de Iria, Fatima

Fig. 4 Illustration of the Ark of the Covenant

Fig. 5 Don Bosco's Dream of the Two Pillars
Basilica of Mary, Help of Christians in Turin

Fig. 6 Shepherd Children of La Salette

Fig. 7 The Coat of Arms of the House of Savoy
Courtesy of Flanker

Fig. 8 The Coat of Arms of Pope Leo XIII
Courtesy of Odejea
Creative Commons Attribution-ShareAlike 3.0 images

Fig. 9 The Coat of Arms of Pope Paul VI
Courtesy of Adelbrecht
Creative Commons Attribution-ShareAlike 3.0 images

Fig. 10 Illustration of arm *tefillin*
Taken from Picart, B. The Jewish Encyclopedia, 1725

Fig. 11 Arm and Head *tefillin*
Courtesy of Chesdovi,

Fig. 12 Total solar eclipse
Courtesy of Wuerzi
Creative Commons Attribution-Non Commericial-No Derivs 3.0 Unported License

Fig. 13 Location of the seven churches of Asia Minor and the 1999 Izmit earthquake
GNU Free Documentation License, Version 1.2

Fig. 14 Engraving of the 1833 Leonid Meteor Storm by Adolf Vollmy in 1889.
First published in the Adventist book *Bible Readings for the Home Circle*

Fig. 15 Path of totality of the 1999 solar eclipse
Courtesy of Fred Espenak – NASA/Goddard Space Flight Center.

Fig. 16 Curtiss Warhawk
Courtesy of the USAF

Fig. 17 Memphis Belle
Courtesy of the USAF

Fig. 18 Cumbre Vieja
Courtesy of NASA

Fig. 19 The projected course of the Cumbre Vieja mega-tsunami
Figure reproduced from Ward, S.N; Day, S. "Cumbre Vieja Volcano -- Potential
collapse and tsunami at La Palma, Canary Islands", *Geophysical Research Letters*
28, pp397–400. Copyright 2001 American Geophysical Union.
Reproduced/modified by permission of American Geophysical Union

Figs. 20-21 Images of the unexplained lights that appeared over the Coptic
Cathedral of St. Mark's in Assiut, August 2000.

Fig. 22 A photograph of one of the apparitions at Zeitoun, which first began to
occur in 1968.

Figs. 23-24 Photographs of an apparition above the Virgin Mary and Archangel
Michael Coptic church at Warraq, Cairo in December 2009.

Preface

Throughout the course of this book we shall discuss various prophecies, most of which are to found in the Bible, but also some which have been made in the centuries since Divine (Public) Revelation closed with the death of the last Apostle. It is therefore necessary to distinguish between such prophecies beforehand so as not to confuse the reader in relation to matters of faith.

The Magisterium of the Church sees in the texts of the Scriptures referring to eschatology[1] the reality of Public Revelation – a direct Revelation of God to humanity, which therefore makes this subject a matter of assent to faith. The Church however has left the exact definition of portions of Sacred Scripture related to the future of the Church open, as "...even if Revelation is already complete, it has not been made fully explicit; it remains for Christian faith gradually to grasp its full significance over the course of the centuries".[2] The true meaning of Sacred Scripture which has not yet been made fully explicit can only be defined through the Magisterium of the Church – i.e. the Bishop of Rome and the episcopacy together in communion with him.

Individual interpretations of Scripture, such as is presented in this book, are merely intellectual exercises – reflections which may or may not be correct, based solely on human reason. This sort of contemplation of Scripture can offer various different and often conflicting interpretations of the text based on personal experience, which is permitted on a purely intellectual basis as long as it does not impinge on areas which are contrary to faith and morals.

However the Church recognizes that throughout the ages, God communicates with believers on a personal level through various visions, apparitions and locutions, in what is known as private revelations. The prophecies of saints and visionaries outside of the Apostolic age fall into this category. A caveat of private revelations is that throughout the history of Christianity there have emerged many prophecies claiming to emanate from

---

[1] Throughout this book, the word "eschatology" will be used in its broader sense as relating to the period of the human history at the end-time leading up to and including the Last Judgment; rather than the original sense of the word still used in Catholic theology, which refers to human destiny and the four "last things" of death, judgment, heaven and hell. In Catholic theology, the word Greek word "eschatology" (from the Greek *eschata* meaning "last things") replaced the use of the Latin *De Novissimis*, and is primarily concerned with the afterlife. The other, more broad usage of the word includes the study of the historical events of the end-time, such as the final tribulation of the Church and the coming of the Antichrist etc. The word "eschatology" is often used in this sense instead of the word "apocalyptic", which since the 1980's has been used to refer to the literary genre of apocalyptic writings dating from around 200BC to AD200, rather than the sequence of events at the end-time.
The Miriam-Webster dictionary thus gives two separate definitions of the word "eschatology":
1: a branch of theology concerned with the final events in the history of the world or of humankind
2: a belief concerning death, the end of the world, or the ultimate destiny of humankind; *specifically*: any of various Christian doctrines concerning the Second Coming, the resurrection of the dead, or the Last Judgment.
[2] *Catechism of the Catholic Church* 66, (Vatican City: Libreria Editrace Vaticana, 1993)

this tradition which are actually spurious in nature. Such prophecies have often been confused by the faithful with genuine private revelations that have been recognized by the Church.

In his Theological Commentary on the Third Secret, Cardinal Ratzinger (now Pope Benedict XVI) provides a basis for distinguishing between such private revelations as follows:

> The criterion for the truth and value of a private revelation is therefore its orientation to Christ himself. When it leads us away from him, when it becomes independent of him or even presents itself as another and better plan of salvation, more important than the Gospel, then it certainly does not come from the Holy Spirit, who guides us more deeply into the Gospel and not away from it. This does not mean that a private revelation will not offer new emphases or give rise to new devotional forms, or deepen and spread older forms. But in all of this there must be a nurturing of faith, hope and love, which are the unchanging path to salvation for everyone.[3]

This potential for deception in messages claiming to be private revelations highlights the need for vigilance when attempting to discern their worth for the personal devotion of the believer. Even those private revelations which are considered genuine can in no way be considered on a par with the words of Sacred Scripture, since such communications are very often mixed with the personal conviction of the recipient. As Cardinal Ratzinger further states:

> Even in exterior vision the subjective element is always present. We do not see the pure object, but it comes to us through the filter of our senses, which carry out a work of translation. This is still more evident in the case of interior vision, especially when it involves realities which in themselves transcend our horizon. The subject, the visionary, is still more powerfully involved. He sees insofar as he is able, in the modes of representation and consciousness available to him. In the case of interior vision, the process of translation is even more extensive than in exterior vision, for the subject shares in an essential way in the formation of the image of what appears. He can arrive at the image only within the bounds of his capacities and possibilities. Such visions therefore are never simple "photographs" of the other world, but are influenced by the potentialities and limitations of the perceiving subject.[4]

With these caveats in mind, we can be assured that many positive elements can be drawn from those private revelations which lead us deeper towards the Gospel of Jesus Christ. Throughout the course of this book we will be considering the importance of various private revelations and the nature of their relationship with the eschatology of the Bible. In particular, we shall be focusing on the vision of the end-time as presented in the Book of Revelation – which Richard Bauckham quite aptly describes as "the climax of prophecy".[5] As such it will be necessary to outline a method of interpretation during the introduction, so that the reader may be better equipped to approach this monumental work.

---

[3] Ratzinger, J. "Theological Commentary" *The Message of Fatima* (Vatican City: Liberia Editrice Vaticana, 2000)
[4] Ibid.
[5] Bauckham, R. *The Climax of Prophecy* (London: Continuum, 1998)

Introduction

The Book of Revelation is undoubtedly the most enigmatic part of the Bible. Crossing over into a genre that has more in common with portions of the Hebrew Bible than the literature of the New Testament, Revelation is the pinnacle of ancient Judeo-Christian apocalyptic writing. It is quite justifiably regarded as the most difficult to understand of all the books of the Bible. Yet its seamless internal logic and complex development of diverse themes found throughout the Old Testament is a witness to its true nature as a work of unequalled genius.

The highly allegorical imagery of the Apocalypse and extremely subjective nature of its interpretation has left us with a legacy of conflicting theological and structural perspectives, and several differing views of the Apocalypse have been adopted by the mainstream Christian Churches. The Catholic Church has wisely left the interpretation of the Apocalypse open, and does not forward any single definitive explanation of this obscure text.[6] Unfortunately, other mainstream Christian sects have not been so prudent.

The interpretative approach which has found the widest attention in modern times has been that advanced by the American dispensationalist movement. As a result, popular conceptions of biblical end-time prophecy have become infused with strange theological concepts such as the Rapture and a future millennial reign of Christ on earth. Yet the eschatological model forwarded by this particular group is recognized by the majority of mainstream Christian denominations to be based on a distorted interpretation of Scripture, and holds no place in traditional Christian teaching.

A major contributing factor to the various misconceptions surrounding the Apocalypse is the way in which modern readers approach this highly controversial text.[7] If we come to read it with the presupposition that it conforms to the structural and chronological conventions of a regular book, then we have already made our first and greatest mistake. The Book of Revelation is most definitely not to be thought of as a chronologically linear, "A before B" type of narrative. In fact, it is one of the most complex and carefully crafted literary arrangements ever put together. The order in which the material is presented may at first seem convoluted and perhaps even baffling for some. But if we step back and analyse the work on a holistic basis, we are faced with a beautifully constructed literary masterpiece that is unparalleled in early apocalyptic literature.

Revelation takes us through a series of letters or oracles to the seven churches of

---

[6] See *Catechism of the Catholic Church* 66: "Yet even if [Divine] Revelation is already complete, it has not been made completely explicit; it remains for Christian faith gradually to grasp its full significance over the course of the centuries."

[7] S. Caldecott provides a brief, yet excellent guide to approaching the text of the Apocalypse in the CTS booklet *Companion to the Book of Revelation* (London: Catholic Truth Society, 2008).

Asia Minor to a vision of the throne room of God. From here we are whisked off on a journey that is both splendid and terrifying, full of hideous monsters, heroic endeavours and epic battles. We are taken from the very depths of despair in the persecution of the people of God and destruction of the world, through to the lofty heights of sublimity in the creation of a new heaven and a new earth and the resurrection of the dead to eternal life.

One of the most striking aspects of this spiritual odyssey is the recurring theme of judgment being meted out through a series of seven seals, trumpets and bowls. Where the series of seals ends in what seems to be a climactic scene of the dissolution of the cosmos, the trumpets begin, taking us through another sequence of judgement pronouncements, until that too arrives at the consummation of history. Along the way, the primary narrative of the septet sequences appears to be "interrupted" by some expansions on areas of interest to the author, such as the pursuit of the Woman by the Dragon, the martyrdom of the Two Witnesses, or the reign of the Beast; before we are led back again to the septet of bowl judgments and the continuation of the main story.

A comparative study of certain portions of Revelation, which acknowledges the similarities between the series of septets, has led to a modern scholarly consensus that the author has employed an extremely novel use of the literary device of recapitulation.[8] Recapitulation is a method used to draw emphasis on an area of particular importance to the author – an effect which the Apocalypse achieves splendidly. Each septet of seals, trumpets and bowls have underlying common themes which are then developed and expanded upon as the narrative moves forward, offering fresh insights into motifs that have been introduced earlier in the book. Thus a new dimension is given to each subject that is being recapitulated.

If we look at the trumpet plagues in chapters 8-9 for example, we can see that they are based on a typological arrangement of the ten plagues in the Book of Exodus. There are plagues of hail mixed with fire (8:7), water turning to blood (8:8), darkness (9:2) and locusts (9:3) – all of which are listed as the plagues sent by God against Egypt in Exod 7-12. If we turn to the bowl plagues in Rev 16, we can see that these also reflect the Exodus plagues. There are plagues of sores (16:2), water turning to blood (16:3-4), darkness (16:10), and frogs (16:13). So the bowl plagues of Rev 16 clearly recapitulate the trumpet plagues of Rev 8-9. But each time an event is recapitulated, a fresh new insight is added to that particular prophecy.

The Apocalypse's use of recapitulation extends well beyond these selected areas however. The battle of Armageddon for example is first introduced to us in Rev 16, but it is then recapitulated later in chapters 19 and 20. A scene showing the Last Judgment and consummation of history is given after the blowing of the seventh trumpet in Rev 11:18, but it also occurs again in 16:17 and 20:11-15. And the darkening of the Sun and Moon is mentioned explicitly in two separate passages – 6:12 and 8:12.

So it should be fairly obvious to the reader that there is no rigidly set form of chronological sequence to be found within the pages of the Book of Revelation. Instead we have a patchwork of events that have been complied without any regard for a regular,

---

[8] Although it must be noted that while the majority of scholars adhere to this position, there is always dissenting voices in such matters. For an overview of the conflicting positions on the structure of the Apocalypse and a staunch defence of the recapitulationist view, see Beale, G.K. *The Book of Revelation* (Carlisle: Paternoster, 1999), pp108-151

systematic temporal sequence. As the highly regarded Johannine scholar S.S. Smalley observes, the structure of Revelation should be considered to be arranged thematically rather than chronologically.[9] This fact forces us to adopt a totally different approach to the Apocalypse from that we would apply to a text which is chronologically linear in nature. Taking a linear approach to the Book of Revelation, as is adopted by many contemporary futurist interpreters, is wholly inadequate to such a structurally complex book.

Dispensationalists, who have heavily popularised many other misconceptions about the Apocalypse, have constructed a timeframe for the events of the eschaton based on an overly literal view of Revelation's chronology. According to this view, the beginning of the end-time will commence with the opening of the seven seals, and proceed forward from this point with the opening of seals, sounding of the trumpets, pouring of bowls, etc., all following each other in a neat, orderly sequence.[10] The major problem with such an approach is the subsequent development of an extremely unrealistic concept of the millennium in the Apocalypse.

Arguing from the chronological order of Revelation, dispensationalists believe that when Christ appears at the Second Coming, he will inaugurate the epoch of the millennium described in Rev 20. According to the dispensationalist viewpoint, Satan will be bound at this time for a period of a thousand years, during which time Christians will live and reign with Jesus in era of blissful peace. This rather strange eschatological concept which has been adopted by the hugely popular American dispensationalist movement is known as premillennialism – an idea which argues that a future millennial reign of peace will be inaugurated after the Second Coming of Jesus. In the pre-tribulational form of premillennialism, living and dead Christians will be immediately transported body and soul into heaven at the appearance of Christ at the Second Coming, in order to escape God's punishment of the unbelieving world in the coming Great Tribulation. A notion which is taken from an overly literal understanding of 1Thes 4:15-17. According to pre-tribulational dispensationalists, Christians will literally vanish instantaneously off the face of the earth, leaving the rest of the world to face the wrath of God in the great chastisement of humankind.

After the tribulation, dispensationalists believe that Christ will return to earth with the resurrected saints to establish the millennial reign on earth. During this age to come, Christ will reign on earth with his saints for a thousand years in a period of peace. Yet despite the enduring physical presence of Jesus, there will still be evil people skulking about on the outskirts of the Messianic realm, ready to rebel against Christ at the appointed time of Satan's release from his spiritual incarceration. According to this view, when the thousand years are finished, Satan will be released from his bonds to gather the evil nations for one last insurrection against Christ, and as a result will be ultimately defeated and thrown into the lake of fire.

Yet to the rational mind such a concept of future history is wildly disjointed. Something which belongs to the realm of fairy tales rather than the world of empirical science. This extremely peculiar attempt at establishing a timeframe for the eschaton is borne from a direct result of applying an overly literal interpretation of the chronology of

---

[9] Smalley, S.S. *The Revelation to John* (Downers Grove: IVP, 2005), p19

[10] See Hal Lindsey's immensely popular work *The Late Great Planet Earth* (Grand Rapids: Zondervan, 1970) for a typical dispensationalist take on the chronology of eschatological events.

the Apocalypse.

Another major factor that has led to the wide acceptance of such fantastic theological constructions is the continued refusal of certain fundamentalist Christian groups to believe in the teachings of modern science. Instead of obeying the very laws of physics He himself created, God is apparently quite happy to violate them at will. Astonishingly, some fundamentalist Christians have begun to argue against well-established modern scientific theories, simply because they appear to contradict the literal truth of the Bible.

The theory of evolution is roundly dismissed by scientific creationism, for example – a movement which holds that the creation story in the Book of Genesis is literally true, and that the earth was made over the course of seven days some six thousand years ago.[11] Creationists believe that the scientific findings concerning the geological age of the earth can be clarified by the notion of "catastrophism" – the events of Noah's flood churning up the strata of the earth's surface. According to creationists, the catastrophic event of the flood indiscriminately laid down layers of sediment that have since been mistakenly construed by scientists as having occurred gradually over billions of years. Thus the earth only *appears* to be billions of years old, and in the bizarre "reality" of the creationists the world only just sprung into existence several millennia ago. Fossils of extinct species such as the dinosaurs, are explained either as creatures who were not brought aboard the Ark and therefore perished during the Great Flood, or objects placed by the Devil to deceive humankind.

The theory of evolution is not the only universally accepted scientific paradigm questioned by fundamentalist Christians. Modern cosmology and the theory of general relativity have also been rejected by advocates of the literal truth of the Bible, in order to pave the way for the comeback of geocentricism.[12] This is despite the fact that the biblical passages used to support geocentricism (e.g. 1Chro 16:30; Isa 66:1; Psalm 104:5) are obviously couched in metaphorical language.

Such stubborn refusal to believe in modern scientific discoveries has led to a highly irrational mind-set among many modern Christians. But instead of fronting an apologetic for Christianity, this type of fundamentalism has proved detrimental to the faith by providing fodder for erudite atheistic writers such as Richard Dawkins.[13] To this new breed of anti-scientific Christians, a literal millennial reign of Christ at some point in the future is now no less believable than a literal Adam and Eve as the sole progenitors of the human race, or an Ark that could hold all the species of the world while a flood totally inundated the earth's surface. In this overly literal view of the primordial history detailed in the Bible, myth is presented as superior to history.

Yet this excessively literal concept of the message of the Bible is clearly deficient in the modern age. A mode of thought which is born of ignorance, rather than a rational contemplation of the figurative significance of Scripture. Once we recognize that the scenes depicted in the Book of Revelation will not be fulfilled literally, nor in the order of

---

[11] For a recent defence of Scientific Creationism see Batten, D. (Ed) *The Creation Answers Book* (Brisbane: Creation Book Publishers, 2007)

[12] See for example Gerardus Bouw's book *Geocentricity* (Cleveland: Association for Biblical Astronomy, 1992)

[13] See Dawkins, R. *The Blind Watchmaker* (London: Penguin, 1988), pp230ff

events described, then we are well on our way to understanding the book's true meaning. Indeed, the recapitulatory structure of the Apocalypse may in fact provide a vital key for interpretation.

As E.S. Fiorenza suggests, the structure of the Apocalypse is best conceived pictorially as a conical spiral[14] – a twisting recapitulatory configuration, which while driving the narrative forward, also reveals new insights into previously revealed information. So by holding thematically related portions of Revelation in juxtaposition, different passages that were initially thought to be independent can in fact complement each other. Therefore instead of passages such as the final revolt of Gog and Magog against Christ after the millennium in Rev 20 being considered as independent units that are to be distinguished from the battle of Armageddon in Rev 16 and the eschatological battle in Rev 19, we can safely affirm that all three passages in fact refer to the same event.[15] So instead of having just one account of the final war of humankind – we have three separate versions, all of which help to flesh out a fuller picture of the described event when viewed side-by-side as a sort of theological diptych or triptych. The same strategy can be applied throughout the Apocalypse, injecting individual prophecies with complimentary material, and leading to a fresh understanding of the text.

Another consideration that will impact our interpretation of Revelation is the presence of prophetic "layering". This concept takes into consideration the fact that some segments of the book have several different strata of meaning. If we look at the cycle concerning the Woman adorned with the Sun in Rev 12 for example, we can see there is an element of this story which reflects the nativity of Jesus. In an attempt to secure his own destiny, the Devil pursues the pregnant Woman and attempts to kill the Christ-child before his rise to power. But the Woman makes her escape from her oppressor and God provides her with a place of refuge in the desert. The parallels between this passage with Herod's slaughter of the innocents and the Holy Family's flight into Egypt are quite evident. Yet while there is obviously an element of this prophecy which remains rooted in past historical events, the author clearly feels that this story will have a renewed significance in the future.

As well as representing the Virgin Mary, the Woman adorned with the Sun also symbolizes the Church, which John predicts will be persecuted by Satan in the end-time tribulation (in the war of Satan against the Woman's other offspring). Scholars point out that an additional layer of meaning is contained in the flight of the Woman into the wilderness, which appears to be an allusion to the Israelite's wanderings in the desert after the Hebrew's exodus from Egypt.[16] So one aspect of this prophecy recounts a historical incident which belongs to the past; while on another level it also relates to an event which will come to pass in the future. For the author of the Book of Revelation, history is destined to repeat itself.[17]

---

[14] Fiorenza, E.S. "Composition and Structure of the Book of Revelation" *CBQ 39* (1977) p360. For a well-informed yet concise recent overview of the scholarly debate surrounding the structure of Revelation, see Tavo, F. "The Structure of the Apocalypse: Re-examining a Perennial Problem" *Nov T XLVII* (2005) pp47ff

[15] See for example G.K. Beale *The Book of Revelation* pp974ff

[16] See for example Morris, L *Revelation* (Leicester: IVP, 1987), p159

[17] One interesting example of biblical history repeating itself can be found in the 70AD destruction of the Herodian Temple by the Romans, which occurred on the 9th of the Jewish month of Av – the exact

The presence of layering is not confined to the Apocalypse however. Jesus' reference to Daniel's abomination of desolation in the Olivet discourse is another example of the stratification of biblical prophecy.[18] The vast majority of interpreters rightly conclude that Daniel's prophecy of the abomination of desolation was originally fulfilled by Antiochus IV Epiphanes' desecration of the Jerusalem Temple in 167BC. Yet Jesus clearly believed that this prophecy contained another dimension that would only be realized during the eschatological age.

When asked by the disciples what would be the signs of his Second Coming, Jesus pointed to the prediction of the abomination of desolation. In doing so, Jesus thus implied that the approximate time of his Parousia could be determined through careful scrutiny of this particular prophecy. So for Jesus, although Daniel's prophecy of the abomination was already fulfilled in the past, it would have another application at some point in the future.

At various stages in its history, the Early Church applied the prophecy of the abomination of desolation to different historical events. In the 1st century AD, it was thought to have been fulfilled in the destruction of the Herodian Temple in the year 70AD; and during the early 2nd century the erection of a temple dedicated to Jupiter on the Temple Mount by Hadrian in 135AD also seemed to fit the words of Daniel's prediction. For both sets of Christians, this would have been, and still is, a perfectly legitimate interpretation of the abomination of desolation. But given the fact that Jesus presented this prophecy in an eschatological context, Christians must also believe that its ultimate realization is to be found in events connected with the end of the age.

So there are at least three different facets to this prophecy – two of which occurred in the past, and one which will be fulfilled in the end-time. But which should be considered to be the "correct" interpretation? Should it be confined strictly to the past, or does it refer solely to the future? Is it purely symbolic of a situation that will always be faced by the Church? Or was this prophecy formulated to be able to communicate to believers in all ages?

Commentators have identified at least four major interpretive approaches to the Book of Revelation, all of which encompass the questions posed above:

The preterist Approach, which is generally forwarded by the majority of academics, holds that any interpretation of the Apocalypse must be read solely within the light of its own cultural milieu. The seer was concerned only with the situation faced by his community in the 1st century, and any interpretation must be restricted to this particular epoch. This approach has the benefit of highlighting the significance of the events and themes presented in Revelation to its original audience. The Apocalypse is very much a book of its day, and as is to be expected, a great part of this work is concerned with contemporary events. A major criticism of this approach however is that it does not take into account any futurist, eschatological aspect in the authorial intent of the book, which is of obvious importance to the Apostle.

---

anniversary of the destruction of Solomon's Temple by King Nebuchadrezzar of Babylon in 586BC. Both events are commemorated today in the Jewish fast day of *Tisha B'Av*. Many ancient peoples conceived of time as cyclic in nature, reflecting the pattern of the seasons. See R. Bolton's *The Order of the Ages* (San Rafael: Sophia Perennis, 2001) pp210ff for an in-depth metaphysical take on the cyclic nature of time. While Christians acknowledge that time is linear in nature and will eventually come to an end, it is possible that reflections of such cycles could ripple across this linear path.

[18] Matt 24:15

The idealist approach proposes that the Apocalypse should be understood symbolically as the age-old struggle between Good and Evil. As such, it contains timeless truths which are pertinent to the Church in any age. But this approach is recognized to be seriously deficient in its refusal to accept any historical setting or futurist intent for Revelation.

The historicist approach forwards the notion that the inspired prophecies of the Book of Revelation span the whole age of human history. The Cistercian abbot Joachim de Fiore is perhaps one of the most famous exponents of this approach, who claimed in the 12th century that the 1,260 days of the Apocalypse prophesied the events of the first 1,260 years of Western Christianity. Dispensationalists also adopt a similar approach for the letters to the seven churches in Rev 2-3, which they believe represent the seven ages of Church history.[19] However this view fails to appreciate the significance of the contents of the book for its original readers. And there is also a lack of consensus as to which historical events are prophesied.

The futurist approach has two distinct forms. The first is the view typified by classical dispensationalism, which holds that chapters 4-22 of the Apocalypse are concerned entirely with future events. According to dispensationalists, the events prophesied in the Book of Revelation will unfold in the order they are presented in the text. The second futurist approach, which G.K. Beale has dubbed "modified futurism",[20] is not as literal as dispensationalism, and does not adhere so rigidly to the chronological sequence of future events as corresponding to the exact order they are put down in the Apocalypse. Once again, a major caveat of the futurist approach is that it fails to take the book's historical setting into account, or the author's original message for his contemporary audience.

More recently, scholars have recognized the need to move beyond adhering to just one of the above positions too rigidly, and instead favour adopting an eclectic approach which changes to meet the specific needs of certain portions of the book.[21] This is essentially approach we shall adapt, but with an emphasis on the layering or stratification element of the prophecies of the Apocalypse. The Apocalypse speaks to its original 1st century audience on one level, while also transcending this immediate context to communicate with believers in every era, and in particular with those living at the end of the age. All of the above approaches can thus be catered for in the separate layers of meaning in the Book of Revelation.

The focus of our approach will be on the preterist, and above all the futurist positions, since while the author wished to convey a message relevant to readers in his own time, he also originally intended the Apocalypse to be a symbolic commentary on the events of eschatological age. But before we can attempt to recontextualize the

---

[19] J.P. Prevost offers a more convincing version of the historicist approach to the seven letters in his suggestion that they represent seven ages of the history of salvation. The first letter represents creation, with its reference to the Tree of Life (Rev 2:7), the second the ten plagues of Egypt in the Exodus story in the ten days of tribulation (Rev 2:10), the third the wilderness wanderings in the allusion to Baalam and Manna, and so on. For a fuller outline see Prevost, J.P *How to Read the Apocalypse* (London: SCM, 1991), pp76-77

[20] Beale, G.K. *The Book of Revelation* p47

[21] See Ibid. pp48-49. G.R Osborne, for example, takes a futurist approach to the Apocalypse, but still allows for a preterist interpretation. As Osborne succinctly argues, apocalyptic literature is "the present addressed through parallels with the future". *Revelation* (Grand Rapids: Baker Academic, 2002), pp21-22

contents of biblical prophecy for our own age, we must first understand what it meant to its original audience. Therefore at times we will switch from a preterist position to a futurist standpoint, in order to gain the best possible understanding of the original meaning of the text and its relationship to the present.

The other aspect of our approach, which holds that the Apocalypse follows a progressive recapitulatory structure and has no chronological order, also allows us to safely discard any notions of a future millennial reign of Christ, or the associated concept of a Rapture. The "Rapture" mentioned by Paul in 1Thes 4 should not be understood literally, but rather as a symbolic vision of the resurrection of the dead at the Last Judgment. Therefore this event should not be considered to take place in the physical realm, but on a plane beyond our current state of existence.

As for the idea of the millennial reign of Christ, we shall uphold the view of the amillennial position forwarded by St. Augustine in the 5th century – that there will be no literal future millennial reign of Christ on earth after his return at the Second Coming.[22] The millennium should rather be equated with the Kingdom of God in the teachings of Jesus, which was inaugurated with the ministry of Christ himself. Jesus stated that the binding of Satan (which the Apocalypse declares will happen during the millennium), had occurred through his own ministry. We can find some references to the binding of Satan in both the Gospels and in the Apocalypse:

> If I cast out demons by Beelzebul, by whom do your sons cast them out? Therefore they will be your judges. But if it is by the Spirit of God that I cast out demons, then the kingdom of God has come upon you. Or how can someone enter a strong man's house and plunder his goods, unless he first binds the strong man? Then indeed he may plunder his house. (Matt 12:27-29)

> Then I saw an angel coming down from heaven, holding in his hand the key to the bottomless pit and a great chain. And he seized the dragon, that ancient serpent, who is the devil and Satan, and bound him for a thousand years, and threw him into the pit, and shut it and sealed it over him, so that he might not deceive the nations any longer, until the thousand years were ended. After that he must be released for a little while. (Rev 20:1-3)

As we can see, there are some very close parallels between these two passages. Yet while dispensationalists place the binding of Satan as occurring at the millennial reign of Christ in the future, the above passage in Matthew clearly states that Christ had already bound Satan through his own ministry. So in its insistence that the millennial reign was inaugurated by the ministry of Jesus, it seems that the amillennial position is correct.

Yet there may also be a more literal dimension of the prophecy of the millennium that belongs to the past. St. Augustine is often regarded as one of the chief proponents of amillennialism, since he believed the millennium was to be found in the present age of the Church. But he also believed that this age would last for a literal amount of one thousand years – and that the millennial reign would end around the year 1000AD.[23]

There may be an element of truth behind the idea that the thousand year reign of Christ ended around the turn of the 1st millennium AD. The Great Schism between the Eastern Orthodox and Roman Catholic Churches occurred in the year 1054 – almost

---

[22] Augustine, *City of God* XX
[23] Ibid.

exactly a thousand years after the Apostolic Council in Jerusalem had first established Christian unity circa 50AD by settling the controversy over the circumcision of Gentile converts. Christ himself declared that if "a kingdom is divided against itself, that kingdom cannot stand" (Mark 3:24). So if this saying extends to the "kingdom" of Christianity itself, then the reign of Christ ended with the division of Christianity against itself at the time of the Great Schism – an event which stood against Jesus' prayer at Gethsemane the night before his crucifixion "that they may all be one" (John 17:21).

Now we have established the approaches we are to adopt during the course of our investigation of the various predictions of the Bible, we can attempt to use them to gain a fresh perspective on eschatological prophecy. By discarding an overly literal and chronologically linear perspective of the Apocalypse, we will discover that the prophecies contained in the Bible may be vastly more accurate than was previously thought. Startlingly, it appears that many of the prophecies contained in the Book of Revelation have already come to pass – including that of the number of Beast, with the remainder set to be fulfilled in the very near future.

We will begin our survey with a study into two of the most famous biblical prophecies of all – the prophecy of the return of the Jews to the land of Israel, and the prophecy of the abomination of desolation. As we shall see, it appears that these prophecies are intimately related, and by comparing both side-by-side, we can determine how the Book of Revelation may contain the exact date for the restoration of the land of Israel.

CHAPTER ONE

The Return to Zion

When the Israeli government eventually issued its formal declaration of independence in 1948, it was hailed by prophecy enthusiasts as one of the single most important fulfilments of biblical prophecy. The return of the Jews to the land of Palestine before the end of the world had been expected by apocalypticists for centuries. When the modern state of Israel in 1948 was created in the aftermath of World War II, it caused a considerable stir throughout various apocalyptic movements that still has far reaching consequences today. The realization of this much celebrated prediction gave fresh impetus to the pursuit of the interpretation of biblical prophecy for a whole new generation of Christians. Biblical end-time prophecy was no longer some foolish hope that had yet to prove itself in the distant future – it was unfolding before the eyes of believers in the present. What once could only be accepted as a matter of faith was now in fact becoming reality.

Before the tumultuous events of the early 20th century, the return of the Jews to the Holy Land had seemed unthinkable. The Jewish people were scattered throughout the world, with little or no political influence and a near complete lack of any form of central organization. Many of the European countries that played host to the diasporadic Jews had demonized them to such an extent that the Jewish people were almost universally regarded as a sub-human, parasitic band of conspirators bent on global domination. They could scarcely foster enough support to maintain their presence among the nations of Europe, let alone garner backing for a mass relocation to one of the most strategically important geographical sites in the world. Yet with a considerable degree of foresight, the return of the Jews to the Promised Land at the end of the age was expected by interpreters of biblical prophecy long before the restoration of the state of Israel had finally been realized in 1948.

What is even more astonishing is the fact that this event was only made possible after a series of remarkable circumstances resulting from the First and Second World Wars. Circumstances that could have in no way been envisaged by even the canniest of observers. By examining portions of Scripture that required the Jews to be in the Holy Land during the last days, commentators had anticipated this event well in advance of its actual fulfilment. Ever since the widespread dispersion of the Jewish people as a consequence of the failed revolts of the 1st and 2nd centuries AD, the Jews had turned to Scripture in order to reconnect their hopes of establishing a homeland for themselves once again in the land of Palestine. The Book of Deuteronomy had promised that if the Mosaic Torah was faithfully observed, God would gather his scattered people from their dispersion and bring them once again to the land of Israel:

And when all these things come upon you, the blessing and the curse, which I have set before you, and you call them to mind among all the nations where the LORD your God has driven you, and return to the LORD your God, you and your children, and obey his voice in all that I command you today, with all your heart and with all your soul, then the LORD your God will restore your fortunes and have compassion on you, and he will gather you again from all the peoples where the LORD your God has scattered you. If your outcasts are in the uttermost parts of heaven, from there the LORD your God will gather you, and from there he will take you. And the LORD your God will bring you into the land that your fathers possessed, that you may possess it. And he will make you more prosperous and numerous than your fathers. (Deut 30:1-5)

For the Jews, an eventual restoration of their national homeland was not merely an aspiration – it was an inevitability. The future Jewish restoration was an integral part of the promise laid down in the Abrahamic covenant in Gen 17, which would be established once again in the Messianic Age. Yet the prophecy of the return was not just the forlorn hope of a displaced nation desperately searching for comfort among the pages of its most revered text – it was a clear expectation of the writers of the Bible that the land of Israel would exist in the eschatological age.

Pre-twentieth century Christian interpreters had also picked up on this expectation, and recognized that the restoration of Israel would be one of the signs of the Second Coming of Jesus. A.W. Wainwright notes that Christians had expected the restoration of Jerusalem at the close of history long before the realization of this prophecy.[1] During the Middle Ages, for example, the crusaders believed that the prophecies concerning the eschatological restoration had indicated that Jerusalem would once again become a Christian city. The crusading armies felt that their presence in the Holy Land was divinely ordained by Scripture, and would hasten the occurrence of the Second Coming. However the medieval concept of replacement theology (supercessionism), which postulated that Christians had superseded Jews as the people of God, diminished the role of the Jewish people in this equation. Indeed for the vast majority of medieval Christian thinkers, the Jews held no significant eschatological role whatsoever. On the contrary, the continued existence of the Jewish people was considered to be somewhat of an embarrassment. The Messiah had already been revealed in the person of Jesus Christ, and by rights the Jewish people should no longer exist. The fact that the Jewish race continued as a separate entity seriously undermined the replacement theology championed by contemporary Christian theologians.

This prevailing worldview was to change in the 17th century, when a new wave of philo-Semitism (as opposed to anti-Semitism) had begun to find its way into millenarian interpretation. By combining passages of the Old Testament that seemed to predict the restoration of the land of Palestine to the Jewish nation, together with portions of the New Testament that appeared to indicate the future conversion of the Jewish nation, the millenarians had traced a new episode in the chronology of the eschaton. This particular belief quickly gained credence and was expounded by some of the most influential individuals of the 18th century. The British philosopher David Hartley (1705-1757), for example, believed that before the return of Christ, the Jews would return to Palestine and the Gospel would be preached to all nations.[2]

The conviction that the Jews would return to the land of Palestine at the end of the

---

[1] Wainwright, A.W. *Mysterious Apocalypse* (West Broadway: Wipf and Stock Publishers, 2001), p73
[2] Hartley, D. *Observations on Man, His Frame, His Duty and his Expectations*, (London: J. Johnson, 1801), 2:373-80

age was forwarded by the various prophetic movements from the 17th century forward. Groups such as the Ranters (an antinomian libertine sect) also predicted the return of the Jews to Palestine. One of their members even attempted to bring this prophecy into effect via his own intervention. John Robins travelled the length and breadth of England in an attempt to raise a standing army of 144,000 in order to wrest Palestine from Turkish control. Needless to say, these efforts were hopelessly in vain, and the aspirations of Robins, along with the Ranter movement as a whole, were extremely short-lived.

Thomas Brightman (1562-1607), one of the fathers of Presbyterianism in England, predicted that the promised future conversion of the Jews would occur between the years 1650 and 1695, which would eventually result in a revival of their nation in Palestine.[3] Sir Isaac Newton (1643-1727) is perhaps the highest profile pre-Restoration figure to have commented on this particular prophecy. Newton, who devoted most of his life to the study of Christian eschatology, had also picked up upon the Bible's promise of an end-time Jewish restoration. As S. Snobelen states, "For Newton … the return of the Jews would act as the ultimate evidence for the validity of biblical prophecy".[4] But unlike his contemporaries who envisaged the Jewish restoration nearer to their own time, Newton foresaw this event as being centuries in the future.

While the prediction of the return of the Jews to the Holy Land was mostly confined to the Protestant prophetic movements, it was also embraced by some of their Catholic counterparts. Jansenism (a branch of Catholicism that was condemned by several popes as heretical due to its strict teachings and Calvinistic approach to predestination) had spawned a prophetic sub-sect known as the Convulsionaries, one of whose number – Jacques-Joseph Duguet (d. 1733), predicted that the Second Coming would take place in the year 2000, after the return of the Jews to Palestine. By the end of the 18th century, the expectation of the re-establishment of a Jewish state in Palestine during the eschatological age had become a common theme in the interpretation of prophecy.

Restoration

For almost two thousand years the Jewish people had been left without a homeland, condemned to live a diasporadic existence among Gentile nations. Throughout the ages, the European countries that played host to the diasporadic Jewish communities often regarded their guests with open contempt. Separate religions within a state were rarely tolerated – they were widely considered to be a breeding ground of sedition. Loyalty to the state was proven by loyalty to the state religion. Any autonomous groups within the state could theoretically act outside the control of the local governments and undermine the prevailing political establishment. The religion of the

---

[3] Ball, B.W; Brill, E.J. *A Great Expectation - Eschatological Thought in English Protestantism to 1660* (Leiden: 1975), p117
[4] Snobelen, S. "'The Mystery of this Restitution of All Things'": Isaac Newton on the Return of the Jews', *Millenarianism and Messianism in Early Modern European Culture: The Millenarian Turn*, (Dordrecht: Kluwer Academic, 2001) p109

state was thus forcibly imposed on the populace as a matter of routine, and religious dissent was regarded as tantamount to treason. This was the climate faced by the diasporadic Jewish communities, who had constantly found themselves open to persecution from the state. During the Spanish Inquisition for example, Jews were forced by the local authorities to convert to Christianity under the threat of exile or death. Throughout Europe, Jews were forced to live in ghettos, and were prevented from attaining any of the most highly regarded jobs in medieval society. Instead, they were allotted those tasks which were deemed unsavoury or prohibited for Christians. Jobs such as tax collecting or money-lending.

Persecution of Jews was often instigated by members of the Church as well as the state. Priests and bishops would habitually charge Jews with the crime of deicide, labelling them as "Christ-killers". Drawing inspiration from controversial passages in the Gospels, such as Matt 27:25 ("His blood be on us and on our children!"), the Jews were deemed to be collectively responsible for the crucifixion of Jesus.[5] They were regularly open to xenophobic accusations, and falsely charged with committing a variety of heinous acts, such as deliberately facilitating the spread of the Black Death. "Blood libels" would often be brought against Jewish members of society, where they were accused of drinking the blood of Christian children in mockery of the Eucharist. Defamatory accusations such as these often led to open persecution, and anti-Jewish pogroms ensured that large numbers of Jews were either killed or exiled.

The Jews subject to the oppressive regimes of Europe developed a profound yearning for a homeland they could once again call their own. A place where they could be free of oppression from outsiders, and be able to practice their religion in peace and security. This longing was greatly intensified by the various persecutions directed against them, drawing a greater emphasis to their common aspirations, and by the end of the Middle Ages the key aims of the Zionist movement was already being fomented.

Although Zionism did not reach the stage of formal organization until the late 19th century, the ideology of the establishment of a sovereign Jewish state had existed from before the Maccabean wars of independence. The Jewish revolts of the 1st and 2nd centuries AD were early manifestations of this deep-seated desire, which had perpetuated itself from generation to generation. The prayer uttered by the European diasporadic Jews during the festivals of Yom Kippur and Passover – "Next year in Jerusalem" succinctly expressed the hope of a return to Palestine.

When Theodor Herzl founded the Zionist Organization in 1897, the Zionists decided that they would take it upon themselves to make this long standing dream a reality. Rather than having a primarily religious motivation, political Zionism was based on principles that were thoroughly secular in nature. The turbulent years of the 19th century had witnessed the rise of eugenics – a quasi-scientific form of racism which depicted Jews and other non-Aryans as inferior, almost sub-human races. As "a nation within a nation", Jews in particular were held with extreme suspicion by the general European populace. There was a common conspiratorial belief that the Jews of the world had clubbed together and united themselves under a common goal – total global

---

[5] An attitude which is systematically refuted by Pope Benedict XVI in his book *Jesus of Nazareth Vol. 2* (London: CTS, 2011).

domination. When *The Protocols of the Elders of Zion* were first published in Russia in 1903, they seemed to confirm the long held suspicions of anti-Semitic conspiracy theorists. These forged documents claimed to emanate from a secret cabal of Jews and Freemasons, and asserted that Jews were intent on world domination by controlling the worlds of finance and the media. By employing the use of black propaganda to persuade the masses of an all-encompassing Jewish plot against Western society, anti-Semitism was beginning to take a new and even more sinister form.

Widespread anti-Jewish pogroms had took hold in Russia after the assassination of Tzar Alexandar II in 1881, when it emerged that one of the revolutionaries, Gesya Gelfman, was of Jewish origin. The assassination was rumoured to be part of a Jewish plot to subvert the Russian monarchy. As an easily identifiable target historically regarded with suspicion, the Jews provided a catharsis for the bereaved Russian mobs. Thousands of Jewish homes and businesses were destroyed, leaving many families completely destitute. Jews were once again used as a means to vent the frustrations of a country eager to lash out in the throes of revenge.

These renewed outbreaks of anti-Semitism were not solely confined to Russia in the late 19th century. The Dreyfus Affair in France during 1894 had seen a wave of anti-Semitism arise in a nation that had been previously regarded as one of the most religiously tolerant countries in the world. When Alfred Dreyfus (a distinguished Jewish officer in the French army) was falsely accused of supplying the Germans with information on the development of French artillery technology, the ensuing scandal generated an anti-Semitic backlash in the media. As an Austrian journalist, Herzl was assigned to report on this case, and the anti-Semitism and injustice that the Dreyfus Affair exposed was to have a profound effect on his future development. In 1896, two years after these events, Herzl wrote his vastly influential work *The Jewish State*, before going on to found the Zionist Organization in 1897.

The Jewish people were beginning to recognize a need to establish their own homeland; a place where they could find shelter from the looming threat of genocide. As K. Armstrong notes, the Jewish "terror of annihilation was not of a moral or psychological void, but a realistic assessment of the murderous potential of modernity."[6] As the various European countries were increasingly adopting a menacing posture towards the Jewish people, the sense of urgency to establish a Jewish homeland rapidly gained momentum. Many Jews were beginning to feel that they could no longer afford to stand back and trust that God himself would lead the Jewish people back to the Promised Land through the intervention of his Messiah. They would have to take positive steps themselves to ensure that this goal could be brought into actualization.

There had already been some previous attempts to establish Jewish colonies in Palestine, sponsored by the Rothchilds and Montefiores in the late 1870s. The Jewish population of Palestine was further bolstered by an influx of immigrations at the behest of the Zionist movement, and Russian Jews seeking to escape the pogroms of the 1880s. While some Zionists seriously considered the possibility of establishing a Jewish state in Uganda, the vast majority saw the land of Palestine as the sole viable option.

The Christian belief in a future return of the Jews to the Holy Land contributed

---

[6] Armstrong, K. *The Battle for God* (London: HarperCollins, 2000), p149

greatly to the cause of Zionism. When Christian interpreters of prophecy began to develop Jewish sympathies during the Enlightenment, the hope of a return to the Promised Land made a significant step towards actualization. The Jewish people had found themselves a powerful and immensely influential ally in this new breed of "philo-Semites". The dream of a return of the Jews to Palestine had been highly romanticized in the West, particularly in English Protestant circles, and soon found favour in broader British culture. Eminent individuals ranging from Queen Victoria and King Edward VII, to Prime Ministers Lloyd George and Arthur Balfour supported the cause of the return of the Jews to the Holy Land. The favourable attitude of the British administration to the Zionist cause would have a considerable impact on the future development of the movement.

When the territories of the Middle East were being carved up among the Entente powers in the wake of the First World War, Palestine had been wrested from the control of the now defunct Ottoman Empire in 1918, and from 1920 onwards came under British mandate. In 1917 the Balfour Declaration was issued by the British government, which advocated the eventual establishment of a "national home" for the Jewish people in the land of Palestine. The Balfour Declaration announced that once under British mandate, the Jews would be permitted to immigrate to Palestine. And when the British did eventually take control of Palestine in 1920, the Jewish population began to surge dramatically.

After Adolf Hitler's Nazi party assumed power in Germany in 1933, the Jewish population saw another major influx when a flood of refugees began to pour into Palestine. But the Palestinian Arabs felt threatened by the sharp increase of Jews into their home territory, and began to stir up against this fresh swathe of immigrations. In order to appease the Palestinians, the British were forced to issue the MacDonald White Paper of 1939, which severely restricted further Jewish immigration.

When the full extent of the horrors of the Holocaust began to emerge in the aftermath of the Second World War however, an outpouring of sympathy for the plight of the Jewish victims began to take centre stage. As many Americans were only too aware, the USA itself had been partially culpable for the plight of the Jews in Europe, as the US government had done everything in its power to curb Jewish immigration into the country during the war, blocking yet another escape route from Nazi controlled Europe. Without the sanctuary that America could have provided, many Jews were needlessly slaughtered in the concentration camps of Eastern Europe. Something had to be done to make amends for the USA's contribution to the plight of the victims of the Holocaust and absolve the conscience of the American people. Given the emergence of this new zeitgeist, President Truman threw his substantial political clout behind the Zionist cause and helped to push the creation of a Jewish state in Palestine through the newly formed UN council.

After Britain announced its intentions of withdrawal in 1947, the UN voted for the partition of Palestine into separate Jewish and Arab states. On May 14th 1948, the Jewish leaders in Palestine established the state of Israel by issuing a declaration of independence. The prophecy of the return of the Jews to the Promised Land had finally reached fulfilment.

The Prophecy of the Return

The hope of a restored Israel resonated widely throughout prophetic interpretation and even transcended religious denomination. Both Christians and Jews alike had come to expect the fulfilment of the prophecy of the return. But what exactly was the scriptural grounding of this belief? There are many scriptural precedents which hint at an eschatological return of the Jews to the Holy Land. For example, some interpreters have suggested that Micah 5:1-3, which contains a well-known Messianic prophecy, implies that the chosen one (who, importantly for Christian theology, is described as pre-existent) will suffer rejection, and as a result he in turn rejects the children of Israel until their land is restored and the scattered remnant return:[7]

> Now muster your troops, O daughter of troops; siege is laid against us; with a rod they strike the judge of Israel on the cheek. But you, O Bethlehem Ephrathah, who are too little to be among the clans of Judah, from you shall come forth for me one who is to be ruler in Israel, whose origin is from of old, from ancient days. Therefore he shall give them up until the time when she who is in labor has given birth; then the rest of his brothers shall return to the people of Israel.

Ezekiel 38 states that in "the latter years" (a term which is synonymous with the biblical "end of days"), the scattered remnant would return to the mountains of Israel after a war and a long period of desolation, before being attacked in a battle which would precipitate Armageddon:

> In the latter years [Gog] will go against the land that is restored from war, the land whose people were gathered from many peoples upon the mountains of Israel, which had been a continual waste. Its people were brought out from the peoples and now dwell securely, all of them. (Ezek 38:8)

The language used here is undoubtedly eschatological in character, a fact which is bolstered even further by its affinities with Rev 20. In Rev 20:7-9, we are told that Gog and Magog would be gathered together by Satan to attack Jerusalem, in order to trigger the battle of Armageddon:

> And when the thousand years are ended, Satan will be released from his prison and will come out to deceive the nations that are at the four corners of the earth, Gog and Magog, to gather them for battle; their number is like the sand of the sea. And they marched up over the broad plain of the earth and surrounded the camp of the saints and the beloved city, but fire came down from heaven and consumed them...

This scene is set firmly in the future – specifically, during the last war of mankind before the Last Judgment. Therefore the above passage in Ezekiel 38, which foretells the ingathering of the exiles to the Holy Land, can only relate to an event that was expected to occur at the end of time.

The Book of Hosea also seems to have predicted an end-time restoration of Israel:

> For the children of Israel shall dwell many days without king or prince, without sacrifice or pillar,

---

[7] Haggith, D. *Prophets of the Apocalypse* (London: HarperCollins, 2001), p94.

without ephod or household gods. Afterward the children of Israel shall return and seek the Lord their God, and David their king, and they shall come in fear to the Lord and to his goodness in the latter days. (Hos 3:4-5)

The ingathering of the exiles is a common theme in Jewish prophetic literature. While the majority of this material relates to the restoration after the Babylonian exile, some portions appear to transcend this immediate context and anticipate the restoration of Israel at the end-time. For example Isaiah 66 describes the ingathering of the exiles in a context which is thoroughly eschatological in nature, mentioning both a judgment by fire and the creation of a new heaven and a new earth – both of which the Book of Revelation explicitly states would occur at the end of time:

> For behold, the LORD will come in fire, and his chariots like the whirlwind, to render his anger in fury, and his rebuke with flames of fire. For by fire will the LORD enter into judgment, and by his sword, with all flesh; and those slain by the LORD shall be many. "Those who sanctify and purify themselves to go into the gardens, following one in the midst, eating pig's flesh and the abomination and mice, shall come to an end together, declares the LORD. "For I know their works and their thoughts, and the time is coming to gather all nations and tongues. And they shall come and shall see my glory, and I will set a sign among them. And from them I will send survivors to the nations, to Tarshish, Pul, and Lud, who draw the bow, to Tubal and Javan, to the coastlands afar off, that have not heard my fame or seen my glory. And they shall declare my glory among the nations. *And they shall bring all your brothers from all the nations as an offering to the LORD, on horses and in chariots and in litters and on mules and on dromedaries, to my holy mountain Jerusalem,* says the LORD, just as the Israelites bring their grain offering in a clean vessel to the house of the LORD. And some of them also I will take for priests and for Levites, says the LORD. "For as the new heavens and the new earth that I make shall remain before me, says the LORD, so shall your offspring and your name remain. From new moon to new moon, and from Sabbath to Sabbath, all flesh shall come to worship before me, declares the LORD. "And they shall go out and look on the dead bodies of the men who have rebelled against me. For their worm shall not die, their fire shall not be quenched, and they shall be an abhorrence to all flesh. (Isa 66:15-24)

By comparing the above passage with Rev 20:7-21:1 we can establish that this particular reference to the ingathering of the exiles should be regarded as an eschatological event. The underlined verses above can be compared with their equivalents in Rev 20 below, which is unmistakably eschatological in character. And if we look at the segment in italics above, we can see that it speaks of the ingathering of the dispersed people of Israel to the holy city of Jerusalem, thus placing this ingathering of the exiles at the end of the age. Note that the events below closely follow the chronology outlined in Isaiah 66 – namely a judgment by fire and the creation of a new heaven and earth:

> And when the thousand years are ended, Satan will be released from his prison and will come out to deceive the nations that are at the four corners of the earth, Gog and Magog, to gather them for battle; their number is like the sand of the sea. And they marched up over the broad plain of the earth and surrounded the camp of the saints and the beloved city, but fire came down from heaven and consumed them, and the devil who had deceived them was thrown into the lake of fire and sulfur where the beast and the false prophet were, and they will be tormented day and night forever and ever. Then I saw a great white throne and him who was seated on it. From his presence earth and sky fled away, and no place was found for them. And I saw the dead, great and small, standing before the throne, and books were opened. Then another book was opened, which is the book of life. And the dead were judged by what was written in the books, according to what they had done. And the sea gave up the dead who were in it, Death and Hades gave up the dead who were in them, and they were judged, each one of them, according to what they had done. Then Death and Hades were thrown into the lake of fire. This is the second death, the lake of fire.

And if anyone's name was not found written in the book of life, he was thrown into the lake of fire.

    Then I saw a new heaven and a new earth, for the first heaven and the first earth had passed away, and the sea was no more.

This comparison helps us to confirm that the above passage in Isaiah relating to the return of the Jews to Israel is set during the eschatological age, rather than during the original return of the Jews to the Holy Land after the Persian king Cyrus' defeat of Babylon in 539BC.

Jesus' Prediction of the Eschatological Restoration

The greatest of the prophecies concerning the restoration of the land of Israel is considered to emanate from the lips of Jesus himself. Jesus was highly antagonistic towards the Temple establishment. The Gospels inform us that Jesus had repeatedly rebuked the Temple authorities and even set about "cleansing" the Temple of its resident money-changers in an open act of aggression. As G.N. Stanton notes, it appears that this action on behalf of Jesus was "an 'acted parable': a prophetic declaration of God's judgement on the Temple (and, by implication, on Israel as a whole)".[8] Stanton suggests that by examining the accusations of his opponents, we can determine that Jesus had used these actions to describe God's threat to bring destruction upon the Temple itself.[9] The Jewish leaders had profaned the Temple's sacred precincts and rejected the teachings of Jesus. As an act of Divine retribution for their rejection of the Messiah, Jesus showed through the use of symbolic action how the Jew's most revered holy site would be taken away from them and handed over to a Gentile nation.

However Jesus had a profound respect for the Temple itself, as was evidenced by his actions against the money-changers. It seems that Jesus believed that the Temple was imbued with a significance beyond its present external presence and application. By foretelling the future destruction of the Temple and recalling the Danielic prophecy of the abomination of desolation (Mark 13:1-2; 14-20), Jesus asserted that the Temple was itself a sign that could be used to predict the onslaught of the end-time.

When asked by his disciples how they were to recognize the coming of the last days, Jesus pointed to Daniel's prophecy of the abomination of desolation and suggested to his followers that they should look to the Temple Mount in order calculate the approach of the end-time. It is almost as if Jesus considered the Temple to be some sort of apocalyptic clock measuring the countdown to the apocalypse. Events that happened in the vicinity of the Temple Mount compound had a wider cosmic significance that reflected the situation on the heavenly sphere. By keeping a watchful eye on events unfolding on this relatively small area of land in the heart of Jerusalem, the vigilant would be able to determine when the Second Coming of Jesus was drawing near.

The significance of the Temple throughout salvation history cannot be over-emphasized. As well as being thought by Jews to embody the very heart and soul of the land of Israel, the Temple was considered to house the Shekhinah – the Divine presence

---

[8] Stanton, G.N. *Gospel Truth? New Light on Jesus and the Gospels* (Valley Forge: Trinity Press, 1995), p182

[9] Ibid. pp180-181

which was believed to reside over the Mercy Seat of the Ark of the Covenant. Jesus' own fate was intimately bound with the Temple, as his actions during the cleansing of Temple greatly contributed to the cause of his downfall and subsequent execution.[10] But these were not the actions of a madman bent on self-destruction. In castigating the Temple establishment, Jesus had conveyed an extremely important message in predicting the demise of the Jewish nation in Palestine.

Immediately before Jesus set out to meet his destiny at the cleansing of the Temple, the Gospel of Mark relates that a rather curious event took place. After leaving Bethany and making his way towards Jerusalem, Jesus came across a fig tree. As he was feeling hungry, Jesus decided to attempt to forage in the tree for some fruit. When he found the fig tree to be barren, he cursed it, saying "May no one ever eat fruit from you again." (Mark 11:14) After his cleansing of the Temple, Jesus and the disciples passed by the fig tree and saw that it was now withered to its roots (Mark 11:20). At first glance, these actions seem rather strange. Why would Jesus be so intolerant of an everyday fig tree, guilty of nothing more than not bearing fruit out of season? If we consider these actions to be yet another example of "acted prophecy" however, then they begin to make some sense.

Scholars are unanimous in determining this episode as an acted prophecy of judgment against the Temple.[11] As Jesus had cursed the fig tree in the immediate context of the cleansing of the Temple, his actions in the Temple invited the disciples to make a connection between both events. Like all of Jesus' parables, there is a hidden meaning beyond the immediate context of the narrative. It was not the humble fig tree that Jesus was cursing, but rather the symbol of the Temple establishment, and by wider implication the land of Judea itself. As well as symbolizing the Temple, the fig tree was a metaphor for the Jews living in the land of Palestine who failed to recognize their Messiah and bear the fruit of Christian faith. It was the Temple, along with the Jewish people living in Judea that would wither away.

Jeremiah uses language similar to Jesus' actions when speaking about the impending doom of the nation:

> Were they ashamed when they committed abomination? No, they were not at all ashamed; they did not know how to blush. Therefore they shall fall among the fallen; when I punish them, they shall be overthrown, says the LORD. When I would gather them, declares the LORD, there are no grapes on the vine, nor figs on the fig tree; even the leaves are withered, and what I gave them has passed away from them. (Jer 8:12-13)

Jesus would have been aware of this passage, and indeed may have had it in mind when acting out this parable. There are a number of similar motifs – that of the act of gathering, the non-productivity of fruits, and the withering of leaves. However this extract from Jeremiah contains a further illuminating insight – it explicitly states that as a result of this non-productivity, the nation would meet the fate of destruction. If Jesus was alluding to this passage in Jeremiah by performing his acted parable, then it would have been abundantly clear that he was symbolizing the future destruction of the Temple along with the rest of Jerusalem. As a result of the Jewish people's rejection of Jesus, the

---

[10] Stanton, G.N. *Gospel Truth? New Light on Jesus and the Gospels* p182

[11] See for example, Keener, C.S. *A Commentary on the Gospel of Matthew* (Grand Rapids: Eerdmans, 1999), pp503-505

Temple would be destroyed and the Jewish nation would no longer have a homeland in Palestine.

With this understanding of Jesus' acted parable of the fig tree still fresh in mind, we shall now turn to examine a key statement of Christ in his Olivet discourse concerning the approach of his Second Coming:

> And then he will send out the angels and gather his elect from the four winds, from the ends of the earth to the ends of heaven. From the fig tree learn its lesson: as soon as its branch becomes tender and puts out its leaves, you know that summer is near. So also, when you see these things taking place, you know that he is near, at the very gates. (Mark 13:27-29)

Given the prior emphasis on the judgment sign of the withered fig tree shortly beforehand in Mar 11:14, it seems likely that this event was intended to be connected to the above saying. If correct, these verses could then be interpreted as a direct reference to the restoration of a Jewish state before Jesus' Second Coming. The above passage from Mark's Gospel states that towards the end of time God would gather his "elect" (which in this instance would refer to the chosen people of Israel) who are scattered throughout the earth. Jesus then immediately turns from speaking of the ingathering of the exiles to elaborate further on this point by means of a parable. The withered fig tree, representing the Jewish nation in Palestine, would start to bud again in order to herald the imminent arrival of the Parousia after a period of desolation. When the ingathering of the exiles occurs, the followers of Jesus would know that his Second Coming was at hand.

Jesus had previously foretold the destruction of Jerusalem and its Temple, and the scattering of the Jewish people among the nations:

> But when you see Jerusalem surrounded by armies, then know that its desolation has come near. Then let those who are in Judea flee to the mountains, and let those who are inside the city depart, and let not those who are out in the country enter it, for these are days of vengeance, to fulfill all that is written. Alas for women who are pregnant and for those who are nursing infants in those days! For there will be great distress upon the earth and wrath against this people. They will fall by the edge of the sword and be led captive among all nations, and Jerusalem will be trampled underfoot by the Gentiles, *until the times of the Gentiles are fulfilled.* (Luke 21:20-24) (Emphasis added)

It is important to note here that by stating that the Gentile occupation is limited in duration – "until the times of the Gentiles are fulfilled", Jesus implies that after this time period the land would be restored to the Jewish people. The exact length of this period of desolation is given in the Book of Revelation as "forty-two months". As we shall see, by calculating this time span from the anchor cues provided in both the Gospels and the Apocalypse, we can successfully determine that there is an astounding degree of accuracy in this remarkable prediction. Before we turn to discuss how the Book of Revelation appears to provide us with the date of the restoration of Israel however, we should first look at the Bible's past track record for giving the exact dates of key events.

Daniel's Prediction of the Messiah

In what is recognized to be one of the most astonishingly accurate prophecies contained in the Old Testament, the Book of Daniel appears to predict the exact date of the ministry and death of Christ. In Dan 9, the archangel Gabriel attempts to reinterpret the figure of seventy years that was given by the prophet Jeremiah for the restoration of Israel, and reveals to Daniel that the seventy years given until the purification of the land must be understood as seventy weeks of years, that is seven *times* seventy years – a period equalling 490 years. If we study the exact wording of the passage below, we can see that it apparently gives a date for the death of the Messiah:

"Seventy weeks are decreed about your people and your holy city, to finish the transgression, to put an end to sin, and to atone for iniquity, to bring in everlasting righteousness, to seal both vision and prophet, and to anoint a most holy place. Know therefore and understand that from the going out of the word to restore and build Jerusalem to the coming of an anointed one, a prince, there shall be seven weeks. Then for sixty-two weeks it shall be built again with squares and moat, but in a troubled time. And after the sixty-two weeks, an anointed one shall be cut off and shall have nothing. And the people of the prince who is to come shall destroy the city and the sanctuary. Its end shall come with a flood, and to the end there shall be war. Desolations are decreed. And he shall make a strong covenant with many for one week, and for half of the week he shall put an end to sacrifice and offering. And on the wing of abominations shall come one who makes desolate, until the decreed end is poured out on the desolator." (Dan 9:24-27)

The "anointed one" in the above passage in the original Hebrew rendering is

משיח *moshiach* – the word from which "messiah" is derived. According to this passage, the Messiah would be "cut off" after a combined period of seven weeks and sixty-two weeks, or more simply a total period of sixty-nine weeks of years, or 483 years. The start point from which these sixty-nine weeks are to be calculated is stated as from the issuing of a decree to rebuild Jerusalem. It is generally agreed that the best possible fit for this decree is the edict issued by the Persian king Artaxerxes I. The Book of Nehemiah tells us that Artaxerxes sent an order in the twentieth year of his reign which officially endorsed the rebuilding of Jerusalem. He then commissioned his royal cupbearer, the Jewish prophet Nehemiah, to take charge of this task:

In the month of Nisan, in the twentieth year of King Artaxerxes, when wine was before him, I took up the wine and gave it to the king. Now I had not been sad in his presence. And the king said to me, "Why is your face sad, seeing you are not sick? This is nothing but sadness of the heart." Then I was very much afraid. I said to the king, "Let the king live forever! Why should not my face be sad, when the city, the place of my fathers' graves, lies in ruins, and its gates have been destroyed by fire?" Then the king said to me, "What are you requesting?" So I prayed to the God of heaven. And I said to the king, "If it pleases the king, and if your servant has found favor in your sight, that you send me to Judah, to the city of my fathers' graves, that I may rebuild it." And the king said to me (the queen sitting beside him), "How long will you be gone, and when will you return?" So it pleased the king to send me when I had given him a time. And I said to the king, "If it pleases the king, let letters be given me to the governors of the province Beyond the River, that they may let me pass through until I come to Judah, and a letter to Asaph, the keeper of the king's forest, that he may give me timber to make beams for the gates of the fortress of the temple, and for the wall of the city, and for the house that I shall occupy." And the king granted me what I asked, for the good hand of my God was upon me. (Neh. 2:1-8)

After Babylon was conquered by the Persian army under the leadership of Cyrus the Great in 539BC, the Persians adopted a policy of tolerance, and the Jewish exiles in Babylon were permitted to return to Jerusalem and rebuild the Temple. But while the Temple had been rebuilt under the leadership of Zerubbabel, Jerusalem itself had been badly neglected and the city still lay in ruins. Upon hearing the news of the terrible state of Jerusalem, Nehemiah, who held an official position in the Persian royal court, requested that the king allow him to return and rebuild the city. Artaxerxes granted Nehemiah's request in the twentieth year of his reign, and issued a decree to rebuild and restore Jerusalem – which is the start date for Daniel's sixty-nine weeks of years.

The twentieth year of the reign of Artaxerxes has been dated by historians to the year 445BC.[12] So if we calculate the aforementioned sixty-nine weeks (equalling a total of 483 years) from this date, the sixty-ninth week spans from the years 31 to 38AD – the period of the crucifixion of Jesus. So the Messiah who is "cut off" after the sixty-nine weeks could only be Jesus of Nazareth.

As we shall find out below, this is not the only deadly accurate long range prediction given in the Bible. While it might seem astonishing that the Bible could contain more than one long range prediction with such an incredible degree of accuracy, we shall see how it goes even further in giving the precise dating of the restoration of the state of Israel in 1948.

The 1,260 Years of Desolation

The prophecy of the abomination of desolation was presented by Jesus as a sign that would herald the approach of his Second Coming. But this is not the sole instance in the New Testament which alludes to Daniel's abomination of desolation. It can also be directly associated with chapter eleven of the Apocalypse. Rev 11:1-2 appears to contain a vital key to interpreting Jesus' prophecy of the abomination of desolation, and may even provide us with the exact date of the restoration of the state of Israel:

> Then I was given a long cane like a measuring rod, and I was told, 'Get up and measure God's sanctuary, and the altar, and the people who worship there; but exclude the outer court and do not measure it, because it has been handed over to gentiles -- they will trample on the holy city for forty-two months.

If we study the above passage, we can see that it states that Jerusalem would be given over to a Gentile nation at some point in the future. Here, the Gentiles are predicted to take possession of the Holy City for a period of "forty-two months", or as is given elsewhere in the Apocalypse, a period of 1,260 days (since forty-two months is the equivalent of 1,260 days). If we compare this passage with the above prophecy of Jesus in Luke 21:20-24, we can see that they both confine the Gentile invasion to a set period of time. So the limited duration of the Gentile occupation implies that a Jewish restoration would follow this takeover, and that the Holy Land would eventually be given back to the Jews. Indeed Dan 8:13 explicitly states that the sanctuary would be restored

---

[12] See for example LaSor, W.S; Hubbard, D.A; Bush, F.W. *Old Testament Survey* (Grand Rapids: Eerdmans, 1996), p561

to its "rightful state" after the period allotted to the Gentiles was completed:

> Then I heard a holy one speaking, and another holy one said to the one who spoke, "For how long is the vision concerning the regular burnt offering, the transgression that makes desolate, and the giving over of the sanctuary and host to be trampled underfoot?" And he said to me, "For 2,300 evenings and mornings. Then the sanctuary shall be restored to its rightful state. (Dan 8:13-14)

So by comparing the Book of Revelation with the Book of Daniel, we can determine that the period of the abomination of desolation, during which the Gentiles would occupy Palestine, would last for a total of 1,260 "days". After this preordained time period is finished, the Holy Land would then be given back to the Jews.

The forty-two months, or 1,260 days of the Apocalypse is also alternatively rendered as "a time, two times and half a time" – a term which is derived from the Book of Daniel.[13] This figure recurs repeatedly in the Apocalypse, and is of obvious importance to the author. Three and a half is one half of seven – the symbolic number of completion that dominates the text and structure of the whole book. Three and a half may therefore symbolize incompletion, or a sudden and abrupt ending. The "three and a half years" motif is lifted from the time-span the Seleucid ruler Antiochus IV Epiphanes had persecuted Jews in the second century BC. But it also has a partial background in the three and a half years of drought during the ministry of the prophet Elijah, and in Daniel's "time, times and half a time" period of 1,290 days.

Prophecy interpreters from the earliest days of Christianity onward have held that symbolic timeframes such as this can transcend their immediate context on a prophetic timescale. As early as the late 4th century AD, Tyconius had developed a number of rules of biblical interpretation. One of the most influential of these principles stated that in prophecy a day can mean a year or a month, and a year or a month can mean a day.[14] We can find an example of the differing uses of the days = years equation within the confines of Revelation itself. For example the "three and a half" or "time, times and half a time" motif, which is a period comprised of forty-two months or 1,260 days in Rev 11:2-3; 13:5 becomes three and a half "days" in Rev 11:9-11.

The day = year equation is a device used by the author to help obscure the true meaning of the text. By masking the literal meaning behind this simple device, the author could thus retain the cryptic style that was typically employed by the apocalyptists while still allowing scope for a precise fulfilment of the prophecy at hand. After all, it would hardly be prudent to disclose future events in explicitly clear language; lest the warning was either heeded and did not come into effect, or it became in effect a self-fulfilling prophecy. The apocalyptists used abstract images and symbolic numbers in order to help conceal the meaning of a prophecy until it had actually reached fulfilment. The words of the prophecy would only become apparent when the events had neared completion.

2 Pet. 3:8 is often quoted by prophecy enthusiasts to support the principle of lengthening or contracting time units:

> But there is one thing, my dear friends, that you must never forget: that with the Lord, a day is like

---

[13] Dan 7:25; 12:7

[14] Tyconius, *Liber Regularum* 6

a thousand years, and a thousand years are like a day.

With this scriptural precedent, interpreters have justified substituting prophetic "days" with "years". To cite but one example of this time expansion, the influential medieval abbot Joachim de Fiore (1135-1202) believed that the 1,260 "days" of the Apocalypse referred to the first 1,260 years of the age of the Church. For Joaichim, after the first 1,260 years of the Church were completed, a new dispensation of the Holy Spirit would be ushered in.[15]

Daniel's reinterpretation of Jeremiah's seventy year period to mean seventy "weeks of years" (discussed earlier in chapter 2) is another example of the smaller time unit = greater time unit equation. It is a simple yet effective way of obscuring the meaning of a text, and encourages the reader to approach it from multiple angles.

Now that we have established that the day = year equation is a legitimate principle in the interpretation of biblical prophecy, we can safely assert that the forty-two months or 1,260 "days" of Rev 11:1-2 can be also be interpreted to mean 1,260 years. With this method of interpretation kept firmly in mind, we can now search for an anchor point from which to secure this span of 1,260 years.

If we turn back to examine the words of the prophecy contained in Rev 11:1-2 in a little more detail, we can determine that when John prophesied that the Temple would be overrun by Gentiles, he was making a direct allusion to Daniel's abomination of desolation. By the time of Jesus, there was a widespread fear that the Temple precinct would be defiled once again in a manner similar to that experienced under the tyrannical rule of Antiochus IV Epiphanes. An anxiety which had been fed by the Roman occupation of Judea. The Roman authorities had adopted a changeable policy towards the Temple establishment. Some administrations would respect the autonomous governance of the Temple and the religious concerns of the Jewish people, while others were rather more insensitive.

When the Roman general Pompey captured Jerusalem in 63BC for example, he earned extreme consternation from the Jewish populace by entering the Holy of Holies in order to sate his curiosity on Jewish worship. Expecting to find at least some form of representation of the Jewish God, Pompey was perplexed to discover that this fiercely guarded sacred chamber contained nothing more than a few scrolls of religious text. Pompey's belligerent actions had caused outrage amongst the Jerusalemites, as Gentiles were strictly prohibited against entering the Temple district under pain of death. This infringement of Jewish law was a deeply humiliating experience for the Jewish people, and was worsened by the fact that the inner chamber of the Temple, or "Most Holy Place" could only be entered once a year by the High Priest on the Day of Atonement (Yom Kippur).[16] Pompey's actions would not easily be forgotten.

Upon his investiture of the kingship of Judea, Herod did little to allay the Jewish fears that the Temple would be further desecrated by the occupying Roman forces. Herod's attempts to placate his superiors by adorning the Temple gates with the standard of a Roman eagle provoked fury on the streets of Jerusalem. When a number of protestors attempted to forcibly remove the standard, they were captured, tried and

---

[15] *Liber Concordie novi ac veteris Testamenti.*
[16] See Josephus, *Wars*, I 7:6; cf. *Antiquities* XIV 4:4.

sentenced for execution by Herod.[17] These events only helped to confirm fears that another act of desecration on a scale similar to that perpetrated by Antiochus Epiphanes could occur at any time, and a new abomination of desolation would eventually be erected in the Temple complex.

By definition, the "abomination of desolation" refers to the erection of an object of worship contrary to the Jewish religion on the site of the Temple, thus profaning the holy place and rendering it desolate. Not, as some dispensationalists suggest, the future event of the Antichrist standing in the Most Holy Place of the Third Temple (which they predict will be built over or beside the Dome of the Rock in Jerusalem).[18]

We have a number of possible candidates for the future meaning (from John's perspective) of the "abomination of desolation". The first such possibility is the destruction of the Temple itself at the hands of the Roman army in 70AD. During the Jewish uprising of 66-70AD, the Zealot party had attempted to gain independence from Rome by ejecting the occupying Imperial army from Judea through the use of military force. This rebellion was to have disastrous consequences for the Temple.

In an attempt to put down the Jewish revolt once and for all, the Roman army, under the command of Emperor Vespasian's son Titus (who was later destined to assume his father's role as emperor), laid siege to Jerusalem in the spring of the year 70AD. As the siege progressed, the Romans were able to penetrate the city walls and take control of the northern part of the Upper City. However the heavily walled Temple compound provided an ideal defensive structure for the insurgents, and they retreated to the relative safety of the Temple precinct in order to make their last stand. In a final effort to eradicate the Zealots holed up in the Temple complex, a Roman legionary decided to set fire to the Temple building, despite express orders from Titus to preserve the sanctuary.[19] The ensuing conflagration consumed the building, and before long the holiest place in monotheism was engulfed in flames.

This event was an unmitigated disaster for Judaism. The Temple had been razed to the ground, never again to be rebuilt, spelling the beginning of the end for a Jewish national homeland in Palestine for nearly two thousand years. Jesus' prediction of the destruction of the Temple had finally been fulfilled.[20]

While we can garner enough evidence to suggest that the destruction of the Herodian Temple was at least a partial fulfilment of the prophecy of the abomination of desolation, it did not meet all the requirements stipulated in the Bible. The exact wording of the prophecy suggests that the abomination of desolation is some form of sacrilegious structure erected on the grounds of the Temple compound, rather than the destruction of the Temple itself:

So when you see the abomination of desolation spoken of by the prophet Daniel, standing in the holy place (let the reader understand), then let those who are in Judea flee to the mountains. (Matt 24:15-16)

---

[17] Josephus, *Wars*, I 33:2-4

[18] See for example Stewart, D; Missler, C. *The Coming Temple* (Orange: Dart Press, 1991)

[19] Josephus, *Wars* VI 4:3

[20] As he came out of the temple, one of his disciples said to him, "Look, Teacher, what wonderful stones and what wonderful buildings!" And Jesus said to him, "Do you see these great buildings? There will not be left here one stone upon another that will not be thrown down." (Mark 13:1-2)

The use of the Greek word εστος *hestos* (standing) suggests that the abomination is a literal object erected on the Temple Mount, and not just a metaphor for the state of destruction.

In the immediate aftermath of the First Jewish-Roman War, the only thing left standing on the Temple Mount was the scattered ruins of the once glorious Temple buildings. So while the Temple Mount was indeed desolate at this stage, there was not yet any actual abomination standing on the former site of the Holy of Holies. We must look elsewhere for the ultimate realization of Jesus' prophecy.

The next best contender for the fulfilment of the prophecy of the abomination of desolation is the erection of a temple dedicated to Jupiter on the Temple Mount circa 135AD. After the Temple was destroyed, the Romans set about clearing the Temple Mount complex by systematically levelling the ruins. The entire city of Jerusalem had been laid waste as a result of the siege of 70AD, and no efforts were made to rebuild until 130AD, when Emperor Hadrian proposed that a new city should be constructed on the ruins of the old. Hadrian made plans to erect a temple dedicated to Jupiter on the Temple Mount precinct – a proposal which caused outrage among the remaining Jews still living in Judea.

This proposed pagan temple was a major contributing factor to the Jewish uprising led by Simon Bar Kokhba in 132AD. Bar Kokhba was proclaimed as the promised messiah by the highly influential Jewish sage Rabbi Akiba, and won the support of many Jews who were perturbed by Hadrian's deeply antagonistic proposal. The Bar Kokhba revolt was to last for three years, until Bar Kokhba's death in 135. By the time this uprising was quashed, an estimated 580,000 people had been killed.[21]

In order to deter any future insurrections, Jerusalem was renamed Aelia Capitolina in honour of the emperor, and Jews were prohibited from entering the city walls. A genius of Hadrian and a statue of Jupiter were raised on the Temple Mount, and a temple dedicated to Venus was built nearby. Jerusalem, in its new incarnation as Aelia Capitolina, was now a thoroughly pagan city.

Although the construction of a temple to Jupiter on the Temple Mount may have provided another partial fulfilment of the prophecy of the abomination of desolation (especially to Christians and Jews living during this period), it does not fit all the conditions stipulated by the prophecy exactly. As we asserted previously, the Book of Revelation predicted that the duration of the period of the abomination of desolation would last for either a literal 1,260 days, or a symbolic 1,260 years. Hadrian's temple to Jupiter meets neither of these criteria, as it had only lasted until the reign of Emperor Constantine, who ruled between the years 312-337.

Constantine had converted to Christianity after his victory at the Milvian Bridge in 312 had elevated him to the status of sole emperor of the Western Empire. According to Eusebius, sometime before this pivotal battle against his arch-rival Maxentius, Constantine and his army witnessed a vision of a cross of light which appeared above the sun, bearing the Greek words Εν Τουτω Νικα – *En Touto Nika* "Conquer by This".[22] Constantine then had the labarum – the Christian Chi-Rho symbol, emblazoned upon the

---

[21] Cassius Dio *Roman History* 69:14.1
[22] Eusebius *Life of Constantine* I.28.

shields of his soldiers before their march to victory against Maxentius.[23]

In 324 Constantine managed to consolidate his position even further by disposing of the Eastern Emperor Licinius and assuming control over the entire Empire. With a Christian emperor at its helm, Jerusalem became a religious focal point for the entire Empire. Constantine set about demolishing the pagan temples of Jerusalem and replacing them with Christian shrines. Hadrian's temple of Jupiter was either destroyed or converted into a Christian shrine less than 200 years after its completion – far short of our desired figure of 1,260 years. So we must look elsewhere for a more enduring sacrilegious feature that stands on the site of the Temple sanctuary.

The best known and most permanent non Judeo-Christian structure on the Temple Mount is the Dome of the Rock (or *Qubbet as-Sakhra*), revered by Muslims as the third holiest shrine in Islam. Islamic tradition teaches that the prophet Muhammad experienced a miraculous night journey to Jerusalem on the back of the winged steed Buraq, where he ascended through the seven spheres of heaven above the site of the Temple.[24] The Dome of the Rock was constructed on the Temple Mount by Caliph 'Abd al Malik between the years 688-692 in order to commemorate Muhammad's night journey and to buttress the significance of Jerusalem for the world of Islam. Indeed Muhammad had originally instructed the *Ummah* to pray towards Jerusalem, before later shifting the focus of prayer towards the *Ka'aba* in Mecca after the Hijra in 622.

The *Qubbet as-Sakhra* still stands today, and is thought by many archaeologists to stand directly over the site that once housed the Holy of Holies of the First and Second Temples. At present, this is the only structure standing on the Temple Mount which could be classified as a desecration of sacred Jewish space. Could the Dome of the Rock be the abomination of desolation spoken of by both Daniel and Jesus?

While it may be somewhat inflammatory in today's sensitive political climate to assert that the presence of the Dome of the Rock on the Temple Mount is a religious aberration, we should still reserve the right to regard a non-Jewish, non-Christian building standing on a spot sacred to the shared Judeo-Christian heritage as a profanation of holy ground. As a monotheistic faith which traces its roots back to the prophet Abraham, Islam shares much in common with the Judeo-Christian tradition, and should therefore be held with the greatest of respect. However Christians, by the very nature of their beliefs, are nonetheless required to view Islam as a religion devoid of direct commission from God – unlike Judaism and Christianity. Consequently, it follows that this lack of divine sanction must be considered to extend to its religious buildings, particularly those constructed on sacred ground of such immense importance to Judaism and Christianity. Therefore Christians should be quite entitled to regard an Islamic structure on the site of Solomon's Temple as an "abomination", much in the same way that a Muslim would consider a Christian shrine built on the ground of the *Ka'aba,* or some other Islamic holy place to be sacrilegious.

Does this mean that we should side with the Christian and Jewish fundamentalists who call for the destruction or relocation of the Dome of the Rock to make way for the building of a Third Jewish Temple? The notion of destroying such a culturally

---

[23] Lactantius, *On the Deaths of the Persecutors*, 44.3-6
[24] Qur'an 17:1; Sahih Bukhari 9:93:608; Sahih Muslim 1:309

significant building, venerated by one of the world's greatest religions should be utterly reprehensible. Besides, such an act of open aggression is totally at odds with the pacifism that is so central to the teachings of Jesus.

This does not prevent us from interpreting the presence of the Dome of the Rock on a spiritual or symbolic level however. Spiritually speaking, there is still enough warrant to describe the Dome of the Rock as an "abomination of desolation". As the only permanent structure that has stood on the Temple Mount for any considerable length of time, the Dome of the Rock is arguably the best candidate for the ultimate fulfilment of the prophecy of the abomination of desolation. Its presence on the Temple Mount has ensured that no permanent Jewish or Christian worship has taken place on this sacred ground for over a thousand years. As far as Judeo-Christian worship is concerned, the Temple Mount truly is at present a place of desolation.

The prophecy of the abomination of desolation states that the area surrounding the Temple would be occupied by Gentiles either "until the times of the Gentiles are fulfilled" (Luke 21:24) or for 1,260 days/years (Rev 11:1-2). Since the destruction of the Second Temple, the only long term non-Judeo-Christian occupiers of the Holy Land have been pagan Rome and the various Muslim dynasties. Therefore the "Gentiles" of this prophecy can only refer to one of these two options. As we have already stated earlier, the occupation by pagan Rome was simply not long enough to meet the required criteria. The Muslim occupation on the other hand *is* of sufficient length, and as we shall see, maybe even *exactly* the right length.

Before the construction of the *Qubbet as-Sakhra*, the Temple Mount had remained desolate throughout the Roman and Byzantine periods. During the period of Muslim expansion after the death of Muhammad, Jerusalem was captured by Caliph Umar in 638. When Umar arrived on the Temple Mount, he was disgusted by the terrible treatment this sacred ground had been subjected to. The Temple Mount platform had become little more than a rubbish tip after the years of Byzantine rule, and lay strewn with waste. As part of a symbolic gesture of his intent to cleanse this sacred ground, Umar is said to have picked up a handful of dung and cast it over the platform wall.[25]

During their efforts to cleanse the site of these impurities, Umar's entourage eventually uncovered the *sakhra* – an area of exposed rock thought to be the summit of Mount Moriah, the rock upon which Abraham attempted to offer his son Isaac (or Ishmael, according to the Qur'an) as a sacrifice to Yahweh, and where the Ark of the Covenant was placed in the Holy of Holies in the Temple of Solomon. Umar forbade anyone from praying at the *sakhra* until it had been washed by three showers of rain, after which the holy place would be symbolically purified.

Following Umar's death in 644, plans were drawn up by his successor al-Malik to turn the *sakhra* into a rival for Mecca. Construction on the Dome of the Rock began in the year 688, fifty years after the Islamic conquest of Jerusalem. The building was modelled on existing Byzantine architecture, and was intended to rival the Jerusalem Christian shrines, such as the Church of the Holy Sepulchre, in grandeur. No expense was spared to transform this once barren site into a truly spectacular landmark that has dominated the topography of Jerusalem for over 1,300 years.

---

[25] Andrews, R. *Blood on the Mountain* (London: Weidenfeld & Nicholson, 1999), p188

If we note the year in which the construction of the Dome of the Rock began – 688AD, it is of considerable importance to the interpretation of this structure as the abomination of desolation that counting 1,260 years on from this date we arrive at the year 1948 – the date of the restoration of the state of Israel![26] Therefore just as the Book of Revelation suggests, there are exactly 1,260 years between the construction of the Dome of the Rock in 688 and the Jewish restoration in 1948.

The other biblical passages associated with the prophecy of abomination of desolation suggest that the start date for this time span should begin from when the desecrating influences of this structure were first established – the time when the Gentiles, or in this case the Arab Muslims, first started to trample on this holy place by busying themselves in construction of the Dome of the Rock – the only permanent structure to have stood on the Temple Mount since the destruction of the Second Temple.

The Book of Revelation states that the Temple Mount complex would be given over to the Gentiles for forty-two months – a length of time which may be symbolically interpreted as meaning 1,260 years. The limited duration of the Gentile occupation in this passage, along with Jesus' parallel statement in Luke 21:24, implies that the Jews would have their land restored after this period of occupation. Indeed the Book of Daniel, in which the prophecy concerning the abomination of desolation originated, openly states that after this allotted time span (which he, like John, refers to as "a time, two times and half a time"), sovereignty would be restored to the people of God:

> As for the ten horns: from this kingdom will rise ten kings, and another after them; this one will be different from the previous ones and will bring down three kings; he will insult the Most High, and torment the holy ones of the Most High. He will plan to alter the seasons and the Law, and the Saints will be handed over to him for a time, two times, and half a time. But the court will sit, and he will be stripped of his royal authority which will be finally destroyed and reduced to nothing. And kingship and rule and the splendours of all the kingdoms under heaven will be given to the people of the holy ones of the Most High, whose royal power is an eternal power, whom every empire will serve and obey. (Dan. 7:24-27)

And again in Dan 12:7, we are told that the shattering of the power of the holy people would come to an end after "a time, times and half a time":

> And I heard the man clothed in linen, who was above the waters of the stream; he raised his right hand and his left hand toward heaven and swore by him who lives forever that it would be for a time, times, and half a time, and that when the shattering of the power of the holy people comes to an end all these things would be finished.

So when combined, the above passages seem to predict that the restoration would take place after the Gentiles had trampled on the sanctuary for a period of "a time, times, and half a time", or 1,260 years – the exact amount of time between construction began on the Dome of the Rock in 688 to the creation of the modern Jewish state of Israel in 1948.

This is not the only astonishingly accurate facet of the prophecy of the abomination of desolation however. The Book of Daniel goes even further, and provides the exact date for when the abomination of desolation would be set up:

---

[26] 688 + 1260 = 1948

... from the time that the regular burnt offering is taken away and the abomination that makes desolate is set up, there shall be 1,290 days. (Dan 12:11)

Fig. 1 The Dome of the Rock in Jerusalem, which stands on the site of the Solomonic and Herodian Temples. Could this building be the "abomination of desolation" spoken of by the prophet Daniel?

In this passage, the prophet appears to provide a further hint at establishing the date of the "abomination of desolation". The prophecy states that the amount of time between the interruption of daily sacrifices performed at the Temple in Jerusalem to the erection of the abomination of desolation would be 1,290 "days". We should note here that Daniel's enumeration of 1,290 days is the inspiration behind Revelation's 1,260 days. Both figures represent the time span of three and a half years – "a time, times and half a time" or forty-two months. The differences between these figures can be explained by Daniel's use of a luni-solar calendar where 1,290 days could represent 3 and a half years,[27] whereas John used a solar calendar in which three and a half years was calculated as 1,260 days. However, as we shall see, this apparent discrepancy may provide us with a further insight into the prophecy of the abomination of desolation.

We have four possible choices for the period in which the daily sacrifices were interrupted:

The first is when Pharaoh Shishak I invaded Judah in 918BC and plundered the Temple in Jerusalem. Our second option is the first deportation of exiles to Babylonia by Nebuchadrezzar in 598-597BC, where once again the Temple was spoiled by the invading army. Thirdly, the destruction of the Temple by the forces of Nebuchadrezzar in 587BC could also be the event behind this prophecy. The fourth alternative may be found in Antiochus Epiphanes' desecration of the Temple between the years 168-164BC.

While the fourth option may provide us with the preterist context in this instance, we must look elsewhere for the eschatological interpretation – which the author explicitly states would be hidden within the confines of the text until "the time of the end". (Dan 12:9)

Prophetically speaking, the most significant events are contained within options two and three. The Babylonian exile is one of the most important periods of Israelite

---

[27] Goldingay, J.E. *Daniel* (Nashville: Word, 1989), p310

history, and left an indelible imprint upon the collective Jewish mind-set. Of these two options, the first deportation of Jews to Babylonia in 598-597BC should be the preferred choice, as the text itself seems to indicate a mere interruption of the daily sacrifices rather than a full blown destruction of the Temple. And strictly speaking, the years of Babylonian exile technically began in the year 598, given that the second deportation was only a later development in the same overall predicament. Both events are usually regarded as different stages of the same tumultuous era which began with the first rebellion against Babylon by King Jehoiakim.

In the late seventh century BC, Babylon had overthrown the Assyrian Empire under the leadership of Nabopolassar, and quickly became the dominant superpower of the Fertile Crescent. With the defeat of Egypt at the battle of Carchemish in 605, Babylon now assumed control over its tributaries in the Levant, including Judah. However when Babylon took the battle to Egypt in 601, both sides suffered heavy losses. With both Egypt and Babylon severely weakened, King Jehoiakim of Judah decided to make a bid for independence in 600 and withheld tribute from Babylon.

This course of action provoked the newly enthroned King Nebuchadrezzar of Babylon to plan an expedition against Judah as soon the Babylonians had recovered their losses. Nebuchadrezzar's forces then began to lay siege to Jerusalem in 598BC. Jehoiakim was killed during a preliminary raid of Babylonian-sponsored mercenaries against Jerusalem, leaving his son Jehoiachin to face the wrath of Nebuchadrezzar. Jehoiachin was forced to capitulate to the besieging Babylonian army, and the most prominent figures of Judah, including the king himself, were taken into captivity. Nebuchadrezzar then installed Jehoiachin's uncle, Zedekiah, as a puppet ruler.[28]

We know for certain that the daily sacrifices were interrupted at this time, as the Second Book of Kings tells us that the Temple was spoiled and completely stripped of its treasure – including the instruments used for ritual sacrifice:

> At that time the servants of Nebuchadnezzar king of Babylon came up to Jerusalem, and the city was besieged. And Nebuchadnezzar king of Babylon came to the city while his servants were besieging it, and Jehoiachin the king of Judah gave himself up to the king of Babylon, himself and his mother and his servants and his officials and his palace officials. The king of Babylon took him prisoner in the eighth year of his reign and carried off all the treasures of the house of the Lord and the treasures of the king's house, and cut in pieces all the vessels of gold in the temple of the Lord, which Solomon king of Israel had made, as the Lord had foretold. (2Kings 24:10-13)

The above incident appears to be the closest parallel to Daniel's anchor date concerning the interruption of daily sacrifices. Daniel states that the abomination of desolation would be set up 1,290 "days" after this event. If we calculate 1,290 years from 598BC then we arrive at the year 692AD – the date of the completion of the Dome of the Rock in Jerusalem! Therefore the time from the daily sacrifices were interrupted by the invasion of Nebuchadrezzar in 598-597BC to the completion of the Dome of the Rock in 692AD is a period of exactly 1,290 years! Could this be even further confirmation that the *Qubbet as Shakra* is the abomination of desolation spoken of by the biblical writers? The fact that the precise date of the construction of this building can be calculated from two independent aspects of the prophecy leaves little room for doubt. ✳

---

[28] See Anderson, B.W. *The Living World of the Old Testament* (Harlow: Longman, 1988), pp391ff for a brief historical overview of these events.

Conclusion

The insights discussed above add a powerful new dimension to the biblical prophecies which foretell the eschatological restoration of the Promised Land to the Jews. But does the prophecy of the return of the Jews to the Holy Land provide the modern state of Israel with the unequivocal support of God – as is suggested by some modern Christian Zionists? This opinion would be extremely difficult to maintain in the light of the actions of the Israeli government over the last six decades. For the most part, the Israeli's treatment of the Palestinian people since the creation of the state of Israel has been nothing less than deplorable. In Israel, the Jewish people had swiftly changed from the role of persecuted to becoming the persecutor itself. Instead of showing that their experience of the Holocaust would mean that they would never let a repeat of the horrors of ethnic polarization manifest itself again in outward acts of persecution, the Israelis have treated the Palestinian people with the same contempt that was once extended towards themselves.

During the lead up to the Israeli declaration of independence, there was a massive displacement of Palestinian Arabs throughout the land of Palestine, due to the Arab-Israeli war of 1948. The heavy fighting around Tel Aviv ensured that the area was quickly depopulated, and in the city of Haifa, Palestinians fled en masse after the Deir Yassin massacre left over a hundred dead. In the cities of Lydda and Ramla, the Israelis embarked upon a systematic expulsion of Palestinians from their homes to make way for Jewish colonists. A similar campaign of expulsion was also conducted in the Galilee. Overall, it is estimated that between 520,000-1,000,000 Palestinians were displaced in what is now known to the Arab population as the *nakba*, meaning "catastrophe".[29] The UN established permanent refugee camps in the Gaza strip, the East and West banks of Jordan, as well as in the Lebanon and Syria, for the majority of peasants affected by Israel's process of ethnic cleansing.

After the Six Day War of 1967, the Israelis had captured much of the territories that housed these refugee camps, including Gaza and the West Bank. As a result, there was another exodus of around 250,000 Palestinians that fled to the East Bank of Jordan. However around 900,000 Palestinians remained in Gaza and the West Bank, and now had to face Israeli rule. Since then, the Israeli government has persistently antagonized the Palestinians by engaging in a spate of reprisals for suicide bombings, killing thousands of innocent civilians in the process. The construction of the highly contentious West Bank barrier separating Israeli territory from Palestinian controlled land has also been deeply provocative, and is regarded by the Palestinians as an Israeli attempt at enforcing of policy of apartheid.

It is difficult to reconcile these actions with Divine providence whilst retaining some concept of theodicy. Should the Israeli government be effectively written a blank cheque, since the return of the Jews to the land of Israel is willed by God? While the reestablishment of the state of Israel during the 20th century is an event that is heavily

---

[29] *Encyclopaedia Britannica*

imbued with religious symbolism, it is hard to accept that the subsequent actions of the Israeli governments are also met with Divine approval.

The plight of the Palestinian people and America's support for Israel has played a significant role in the rise of Islamist terrorist groups. The existence of the modern state of Israel is potentially the single greatest destabilizing element in modern world politics, and has increased the rapidly widening division between the Muslim East and the Christian West. While we cannot fathom the moral issues and consequences of the creation of the modern state of Israel from our limited human perspective, it may yet play an even greater role in the events leading up to the Last Days. Somewhat ironically, the re-emergence of the nation that God had chosen to redeem the world through the coming of Christ could provide the catalyst for the future battle of Armageddon.

The 1,260 "days" of the Apocalypse appears to have been fulfilled in time-period between the construction of the Dome of the Rock on the site of the Temple Mount and the creation of the modern state of Israel. However its full significance may not be confined to this sole interpretation. It appears that another layer of meaning also lies behind this prophecy that has yet to unfold, which is related directly to the time of the end. The true nature of this final time-period has yet to reveal itself to us, but it is likely that this additional layer of meaning will be related to the "three and a half" component of this timespan, whether as a literal period of three-and-a-half years, or by shifting decimals, possibly 35 years. During this period, Revelation tells us that two religious figures will make a stand against the dominant anti-Christian world power, losing their lives in the process. But who are the Two Witnesses of Rev 11, and what exactly is their role in modern apocalyptic thought?

CHAPTER TWO

The Two Witnesses

The structure of the Book of Revelation has one of the most seemingly erratic plot arcs in the whole Bible. Chronologically speaking, the order of events is extremely convoluted, with many key scenes being recapitulated on a number of occasions. Digression is commonplace, and the book is frequently punctuated by liturgy. However there is a great deal of method belying this bizarre structure pattern. By recapitulating some of the pivotal moments of the book, the author is adding emphases to areas of importance, and at the same time allows them to be viewed from a totally different angle. In recapitulating certain scenes, the author compliments the previous instalment and adds new dimensions that were previously absent.

The Apocalypse can be broken into several distinct self-contained units or "acts" and "intervals", with the focus constantly shifting between the earthly and heavenly spheres. On a holistic overview of Revelation, the most important of these acts is to be found in chapters 11-13 – a portion of the Apocalypse which is often referred to as the "Divine Drama". Indeed its positioning at the centre of the Apocalypse is no accident. In the ancient world the climax of a book was traditionally placed at the middle instead of the end of a work. By giving the climax a central positioning, ancient authors sent a clear signal that this was the focal point of the story, and gave themselves ample space for tying up loose ends and informing the readers of fate of the protagonists after the chief event.[1]

The narrative of the Divine Drama opens with an account of the ministry of the Two Witnesses. The Witnesses are presented by the Apocalypse as eschatological prophets send by God to reinvigorate the Church at the encroachment of the end time. They are described as prophets in the classical style of the Old Testament, possessing many of the attributes of their biblical predecessors. After they complete the task of prophesying to the nations, we are told that the Two Witnesses will be overpowered and killed by the Beast (interestingly, the name "Antichrist" does not occur in the Book of Revelation, and appears only in the Johannine epistles) in what we can only assume is a reference to the great eschatological persecution of the Church predicted so frequently in the Bible. Then, after the "three and a half days" are finished, we are told that the Witnesses would be resurrected from the dead before ascending into heaven:[2]

---

[1] The employment of this literary device or structural form is known as a "chiasm", a word derived from the cross shaped Greek letter Chi – χ. For a more detailed study of this device see for example McCoy, B. "Chiamus: An Important Structural Device Commonly Found in Biblical Literature" *CTS Journal 9* (2003)

[2] However this 'resurrection' need not be a literal return from the dead of two future apocalyptic figures. Revelation's narrative often makes leaps between the heavenly and earthly spheres. So the 'resurrection' of the Two Witnesses may actually refer to their resurrection in the heavenly realm at the Last Judgement, rather than a literal, physical return from the dead.

But I shall send my two witnesses to prophesy for twelve hundred and sixty days, wearing sackcloth. These are the two olive trees and the two lamps in attendance on the Lord of the world. Fire comes from their mouths and consumes their enemies if anyone tries to harm them; and anyone who tries to harm them will certainly be killed in this way. They have the power to lock up the sky so that it does not rain as long as they are prophesying; they have the power to turn water into blood and strike the whole world with any plague as often as they like. When they have completed their witnessing, the beast that comes out of the Abyss is going to make war on them and overcome them and kill them. Their corpses lie in the main street of the great city known by the symbolic names Sodom and Egypt, in which their Lord was crucified. People of every race, tribe, language and nation stare at their corpses, for three-and-a-half days, not letting them be buried, and the people of the world are glad about it and celebrate the event by giving presents to each other, because these two prophets have been a plague to the people of the world.' After the three-and-a-half days, God breathed life into them and they stood up on their feet, and everybody who saw it happen was terrified; then I heard a loud voice from heaven say to them, 'Come up here,' and while their enemies were watching, they went up to heaven in a cloud. Immediately, there was a violent earthquake, and a tenth of the city collapsed; seven thousand persons were killed in the earthquake, and the survivors, overcome with fear, could only praise the God of heaven. (Rev 11:3-13)

When we examine the text in a little more detail, there appears to be a link between the Two Witnesses and the eschatological outpouring of the Spirit prophesied in scripture. According to Joel 2:28-29, the period of the outpouring of the Spirit is a time of renewal for the Church – an era which will precede the battle of Armageddon:

And it shall come to pass afterward, that I will pour out my Spirit on all flesh; your sons and your daughters shall prophesy, your old men shall dream dreams, and your young men shall see visions. Even on the male and female servants in those days I will pour out my Spirit.

The eschatological outpouring of the Spirit is depicted by the biblical writers as a new Pentecost which revives the Church from a state of apostasy. The "Great Apostasy" – a mass exodus from the Christian faith at the approach of the end-time, was prophesied by the writers of the New Testament. In 2Thes 2:3-12, St. Paul stated that the Second Coming would not happen until a widespread apostasy of the Church has taken place:

Let no one deceive you in any way. For that day will not come, unless the rebellion comes first, and the man of lawlessness is revealed, the son of destruction ....

2Tim 3:1ff describes the prevailing attitude of general humanity at the end-time:

But understand this, that in the last days there will come times of difficulty. For people will be lovers of self, lovers of money, proud, arrogant, abusive, disobedient to their parents, ungrateful, unholy, heartless, unappeasable, slanderous, without self-control, brutal, not loving good, treacherous, reckless, swollen with conceit, lovers of pleasure rather than lovers of God, having the appearance of godliness, but denying its power.

Jesus also revealed that a period of apostasy would foreshadow the event of his Second Coming:

And then many will fall away and betray one another and hate one another. And many false prophets will arise and lead many astray. And because lawlessness will be increased, the love of many will grow cold. But the one who endures to the end will be saved. (Matt. 24:10-14)

Likewise, 1Tim. 4:1-3 also predicted that there would be a departure from the faith "in later times" – a phrase which is equated with the end-time:

Now the Spirit expressly says that in later times some will depart from the faith by devoting themselves to deceitful spirits and teachings of demons, through the insincerity of liars whose consciences are seared, who forbid marriage and require abstinence from foods that God created to be received with thanksgiving by those who believe and know the truth.

Since the rise of British empiricism in the 17th century, there was an increasing trend amongst western intelligista to adhere to deism, agnosticism or atheism, rather than belief in a revealed God. Empiricism then opened up the way for its philosophical derivatives, such as subjectivism, existentialism, logical positivism and relativism. These beliefs then filtered down to the masses through the auspices of the secular media and quickly became entrenched due their egocentric appeal. But as the very antithesis of theism, these beliefs have resulted in today's mass exodus from the Christian faith.

Belief in a revealed God (theism), teaches that God is not merely some unmoved mover who created the universe then left it to its own devices, never again to intervene in worldly affairs. Theism holds that the God of creation chose to reveal Himself to humanity at certain key stages to guide the development of humankind and steer it towards a set path in the Divine plan. A God who is immanent in the world, while also at the same time transcending it. The Christian form of theism teaches that the ultimate Revelation of God came in the person of Jesus Christ – the incarnation of the Word of God.

Theism requires the believer to follow a strict ethical code that can sometimes be at odds with the personal desires of the adherent. Atheism, agnosticism and deism on the other hand have no such limitations; and those who subscribe to these worldviews are not encumbered by a moral code contrary to their own volition. In this scenario, ethics are determined by the individual alone and not dictated by guidelines left by an external supernatural force.

Since Charles Darwin published his *Origin of Species* in 1859, thus undermining the previously powerful Teleological Argument (a philosophical argument which states that we can determine the existence of God due to an apparent element of design in the universe), atheism has been promulgated with evangelical zeal by its adherents. We only need to look at the writings of Richard Dawkins to get an idea of the fervour with which modern atheism is espoused.[3]

The public response to the proponents of atheism has been generally favourable, mostly due to the "conscience searing" appeals of a self-determined moral code. As a result of the proliferation of atheism by the secularizing forces of the world's governments and media, there has been a substantial weakening of faith in the Christian religion. Millions of baptized Christians throughout the world have departed from the faith and embraced atheism or agnosticism instead. The spiritual vacuum left in the wake

---

[3] See for example his most famous work, Dawkins, R. *The Blind Watchmaker*, or the most recent espousal of his atheist ideology in *The God Delusion* (London: Transworld, 2006) For a perceptive theistic critique of Dawkins' work see McGrath, A. *Dawkins' God* (Oxford: Blackwell, 2005), or *The Dawkins Delusion?* (London: SPCK, 2007), by the same author.

of this apostasy has been filled by the "consumer religion" of the New Age movement, which allow individuals to adopt or discard beliefs to suit their personal whims. Over the past forty years Church attendance has plummeted at an incredible rate. Where pews were once thronged to capacity, there are now ever increasing vacant spaces separating the few remaining faithful who have made the effort to express their devotion to the Sabbath. This age, more than any other, fulfils the prophecy of the "Great Apostasy".

It is into this unbelieving world that the Book of Revelation tells us will step forth two prophets, moulded in the classical style of antiquity. In a final act of Divine grace, the task of these end-time prophets is to attract as many believers possible back into the Christian fold before the Second Coming of Jesus and the Last Judgment of humankind. Many other eschatological prophecies of the Bible foretell that an outpouring of the Spirit would restore faith once again before the end of the world. Could this eschatological outpouring of the Spirit be instigated by God's last messengers to humankind?

The Bible appears to suggest that the ministry of the Two Witnesses will effect one last resurgence of the Christian faith before the end-time. As a result of this ministry, which will serve as a Second Pentecost, millions will be converted to the Christian faith. The reunification of Christianity after the reconciliation of the Eastern Orthodox Church with Rome was a common theme in various Christian prophecies from the High Middle Ages onwards.[4] Later, after the events of the Reformation in the 16th century, prophecies concerning this spiritual renewal would also include a reunification with the Reformed Churches as well.[5]

Prophecies found in the New Testament promise that before the end of the world, the Jews would be converted to Christianity. Indeed the future conversion of the Jews has since become a key component in Christian eschatology. In his letter to the Romans, St. Paul foretells that the Jewish people would eventually accept Jesus as the promised Messiah:

> I want you to understand this mystery, brothers: a partial hardening has come upon Israel, until the fullness of the Gentiles has come in. And in this way all Israel will be saved, as it is written, "The Deliverer will come from Zion, he will banish ungodliness from Jacob"; "and this will be my covenant with them when I take away their sins." (Rom 11:25-27)

The "fullness of the Gentiles" mentioned above appears to be an allusion to Matt 24:14, which states that the Gospel will be preached to all the nations before the arrival of the end-time:

> And this gospel of the kingdom will be proclaimed throughout the whole world as a testimony to all nations, and then the end will come.

According to the end-time chronology given in the Bible, the event of the Gospel being preached in all nations appears to coincide with the spiritual revival at the approach of the eschaton. So by alluding to Matt 24:14 in his letter to the Romans, Paul seems to

---

[4] See Reeves, M. *The Influence of Prophecy in the Later Middle Ages* (Notre Dame: University of Notre Dame Press, 1993), pp397-399
[5] See for example the various prophecies of the future conversion of England below.

have associated the future conversion of the Jews with the Gospel being preached to all nations and the final revival of Christianity during the end time. The Jews would be converted after the spread of Christianity throughout the world has brought in the "fullness of the Gentiles". A teaching which is upheld in the *Catechism of the Catholic Church*:

> The glorious Messiah's coming is suspended at every moment of history until his recognition by "all Israel", for "a hardening has come upon part of Israel" in their "unbelief" toward Jesus. St. Peter says to the Jews of Jerusalem after Pentecost: "Repent therefore, and turn again, that your sins may be blotted out, that times of refreshing may come from the presence of the Lord, and that he may send the Christ appointed for you, Jesus, whom heaven must receive until the time for establishing all that God spoke by the mouth of his holy prophets from of old." St. Paul echoes him: "For if their rejection means the reconciliation of the world, what will their acceptance mean but life from the dead?" The "full inclusion" of the Jews in the Messiah's salvation, in the wake of "the full number of the Gentiles", will enable the People of God to achieve "the measure of the stature of the fullness of Christ", in which "God may be all in all".[6]

The biblical idea of the future conversion of the Jews was expanded upon by the early Church fathers. St. Augustine of Hippo (354-430AD) for example, wrote that before the end time arrives, the Jews would be converted to Christianity under the auspices of Elijah (Elias). In doing so, Augustine connected this future Christian restoration with the Two Witnesses of Rev 11:

> After admonishing them to give heed to the law of Moses, as he foresaw that for a long time to come they would not understand it spiritually and rightly, he went on to say, "And, behold, I will send to you Elias the Tishbite before the great and signal day of the Lord come: and he shall turn the heart of the father to the son, and the heart of a man to his next of kin, lest I come and utterly smite the earth." It is a familiar theme in the conversation and heart of the faithful, that in the last days before the judgment the Jews shall believe in the true Christ, that is, our Christ, by means of this great and admirable prophet Elias who shall expound the law to them.[7]

Although the identity of the witnesses of Rev 11 has often been disputed, there is a broad consensus that the prophecies concerning the return of the prophet Elijah is the major source of inspiration for both of these individuals. Just as 1 and 2 Kings tells us that Elijah had the ability to shut up the heavens for three and a half years (1Kings 17:1), and call down fire from the sky in order to consume his enemies (2Kings 1:9ff), the Two Witnesses are also endowed with similar attributes:

> And if anyone would harm them, fire pours from their mouth and consumes their foes. If anyone would harm them, this is how he is doomed to be killed. They have the power to shut the sky, that no rain may fall during the days of their prophesying.... (Rev 11:5-6)

In the New Testament, the role of Elijah was portrayed as that of a restorer – a figure who would prepare the way for the coming of the Messiah. For example in Matt 17:11, Jesus stated that "Elijah does come, and he will restore all things." Elijah would lead the people back to the roots of their faith in preparation for the coming of the Messiah. John the Baptist was confirmed by Jesus as having fulfilled the role of the promised coming of Elijah – the "voice of one crying in the wilderness: Prepare the way

---

[6] *Catechism of the Catholic Church* 674
[7] Augustine, *City of God* XX:29

of the Lord; make his paths straight." (Matt 3:3).

The restorative mission of Elijah before the end-time was first foretold in the Book of Malachi, which can be dated to the mid-5th century BC:

> Behold, I will send you Elijah the prophet before the great and awesome day of the LORD comes. And he will turn the hearts of fathers to their children and the hearts of children to their fathers, lest I come and strike the [earth] with a decree of utter destruction. (Mal 4:5-6)

This belief was significantly developed upon during the intertestamental period, and by the time of Jesus, the doctrine of the future coming of Elijah was already well established.[8] The role of the future Elijah as a restorer figure was inspired by the original mission of the ancient Israelite prophet. In the First and Second Books of Kings, Elijah was called by God and allotted the task of re-establishing the religion of Yahweh in the apostate land of Israel. Under the influence of the Phoenician princess Jezebel, who was married to Ahab the King of Israel, the Baal cult had been widely proliferated throughout the Northern Kingdom. The practice of the Baal religion was so pervasive during this time-period that Elijah had begun to despair that there was no one left in Israel who had not capitulated to the ubiquitous Canaanite religion. However Yahweh allayed these concerns, informing him that there were seven thousand faithful Israelites who had not bowed down to Baal. Yahweh then gave instructions to Elijah on how he was to re-establish the true religion in the land of Israel, which he would accomplish with the help of Elisha of Abelmeholah. (1Kings 19:14ff). By performing the instructions given to him by God, Elijah thus effected the restoration of the religion of Yahwism, bringing the Israelites back into the worship of their ancestors.

While the Two Witnesses of Rev 11 seem to be a predominant allusion to restorative mission of Elijah and Elisha in 1 and 2 Kings, the New Testament suggests that this second "Elisha" role also contains echoes of a Moses-like figure. As well as containing abilities attributed to Elijah, Rev 11 also states that the Two Witnesses will have powers that are usually associated with Moses – "they have power over the waters to turn them into blood and to strike the earth with every kind of plague, as often as they desire" (Rev 11:6). Indeed much of the plagues in Revelation have been grafted from the plagues of Exodus.[9]

There are a number of various other indications that the identity of the second witness should be equated with Moses. The Book of Deuteronomy had declared that God would raise up a prophet like Moses in the future.

---

[8] However we should also take note that before the Christian era these prophecies were firmly eschatological in tone, expecting the arrival of Elijah, as well as the Messiah, to happen prior to the "Day of the Lord". It was only during the Christian period that the coming of Elijah and the Messiah was disassociated with the end-time (although not completely, as the scholarly findings on "inaugurated eschatology" in the ministry and teaching of Jesus have shown).

[9] For example, the plague of fire and hail in Rev 8:7 (cf. Rev 16:8-9, 21) is lifted from the plague of fire and hail in Exod 9:23ff. The plagues of water turning to blood in Rev 8:8, 11:6 and 16:3-4 is taken from Moses turning the Nile to into blood in Exod 7:17ff. The plagues of darkness in Rev 8:12, 9:2 and 16:10 is influenced by the plague of darkness in Exod 10:21ff. The plague of locusts in Rev 9:3 relates to the locust plague of Exod 10:12ff. The plague of sores in Rev 16:2 is a reference to the sores inflicted upon the Egyptians in Exod 9:9. The demonic frogs of Rev 16:13-14 is an allusion to the plague of frogs in Exod 8:5ff. See Beale *The Book of Revelation* pp808-812

The LORD your God will raise up for you a prophet like me from among you, from your brothers-
it is to him you shall listen. (Deut. 18:15)

This passage led to an early belief that a second Moses figure would appear on the
prophetic stage of Israel. This is evidenced by the questions put to John the Baptist by
the priests and Levites in John's Gospel:

And this is the testimony of John, when the Jews sent priests and Levites from Jerusalem to ask
him, "Who are you?" He confessed, and did not deny, but confessed, "I am not the Christ." And they asked
him, "What then? Are you Elijah?" He said, "I am not." "Are you the Prophet?" And he answered, "No."
So they said to him, "Who are you? We need to give an answer to those who sent us. What do you say
about yourself?" He said, "I am the voice of one crying out in the wilderness, 'Make straight the way of
the Lord,' as the prophet Isaiah said." (Now they had been sent from the Pharisees.) They asked him,
"Then why are you baptizing, if you are neither the Christ, nor Elijah, nor the Prophet?" (John 1:19-25)

The above passage illustrates the early belief of three separate eschatological
figures – the Messiah, Elijah, and another figure mysteriously referred to as "the
Prophet". This figure, known at this stage simply as "the Prophet", was regarded by first
century Jews as the Moses-like prophet promised by the Book of Deuteronomy. As the
eminent Johannine scholar D.A. Carson notes, "The promise of a prophet like Moses who
would speak the words of God (Deut. 18:15-18) was early taken to refer to a special end-
time figure...."[10] John 1:19-25 thus shows that the Apostle was aware of the tradition of
a second Moses figure by the time he wrote his Gospel.

Therefore it seems that the second Moses figure would have been a prominent
figure in John's Apocalypse, and the identification of the second witness with Moses is
just as valid as that of "Enoch". The synoptics inform us that Moses and Elijah appeared
to Peter, James and John during the Transfiguration of Jesus (Matt. 17:1-8; Mark 9:2-8;
Luke 9:28-36). If the Apostle John did go on to write the Apocalypse, as there is good
reason to believe, it is highly likely that this event would have had a profound impact on
his later thought.[11] The appearance of Moses and Elijah during the Transfiguration may
have been incorporated into John's understanding of the Two Witnesses by the time he
wrote the Apocalypse.

Suggestions for identifying the Two Witnesses as Elijah and Enoch are primarily
based on the Bible's separate accounts telling how these two prophets were translated
bodily into heaven (Gen 5:24; 2Kings 2:11). According to those who adopt a literal
interpretation of the Book of Revelation, these ancient prophets will physically return
from heaven during the last days in order to prepare the way for the Second Coming of

---

[10] Carson, D.A *The Gospel According to John* (Grand Rapids: Eerdmans, 1991), p143
[11] It is beyond the scope of this book to discuss in detail the question of authorship of the Apocalypse. It
should suffice to say that there is still a good case for attributing authorship to the Apostle John, as well as
common authorship with the Fourth Gospel and Johannine epistles. The three share similar phrases and
theological emphases not found anywhere else in the New Testament, such as Jesus as the Divine Logos –
the Word of God (cf. John 1:1-3; 1John 1:1-3; Rev 19:13). The main argument against common authorship
– differences in style and the use of Greek between the Fourth Gospel and the Apocalypse, can be
explained by John's use of an amanuensis. Furthermore, there is more than enough evidence, both internal
and external to substantiate the claim for common authorship of the Johannine literature of the Bible. For a
more detailed presentation of the case for apostolic authorship see Carson, D.A *The Gospel According to
John*, pp68-81; cf. Smalley *Thunder and Love* (Milton Keynes: Nelson Word, 1994), pp35-40.

Jesus.[12] This notion fails to take into consideration the fact that the writers of the New Testament had identified John the Baptist as Elijah however. For them, Elijah did not make a literal return from his heavenly abode. Rather, Elijah was considered to be a role that was assumed by the person of John the Baptist. Moreover, John the Baptist's fulfilment of this role was not understood as a reincarnation of the ancient prophet himself (since belief in reincarnation is rejected by Christian teaching), but rather as his spiritual successor. For example in Luke 1:17, Zechariah states that his son had come in the "spirit and power of Elijah", rather than being an actual reincarnation of the 9th-century BC prophet. This passage shows us that the Two Witnesses will be individuals who will come in the spirit and power of Elijah and Moses/Enoch, rather than being actual physical reappearances or reincarnations of these prophets of antiquity.

Now that we have absorbed a brief understanding of the original meaning of the Two Witnesses of Revelation, we are thus presented with the problem of attempting to identify the role of these individuals for our own age. As we noted earlier, many interpreters of eschatological prophecy quite justifiably equate our present situation with the "Great Apostasy" foretold in the Bible. If correct, this would thus suggest that we are on the threshold of the coming of the Two Witnesses – a pair of individuals styled after Elijah and Moses who will come to revive the flagging Church from its current state of decline. According to the Book of Revelation, these apocalyptic figures will face open opposition to their restorative mission, and meet the ultimate fate of martyrdom.

But how are we to identify these individuals when they eventually do appear? Is there a possibility that we can discover their identity by examining other prophecies that deal with this subject? By holding the various prophecies of the future persecution of the Church found in the officially approved prophecies of Fatima and La Salette in juxtaposition with some important snippets of information to be gleaned from various other predictions, we can establish that the identity of at least one of the Two Witnesses is to be equated with a Roman Catholic pontiff.

The Angelic Pope

The association between the Two Witnesses and a leader of the Roman Catholic Church is hinted at in prophetic literature dating from the Middle Ages to the present, in the related concepts of an "Angelic Pope" and a "martyr-pope". The idea of an Angelic Pope arose in the middle of the 13th century, first appearing in a prophecy quoted by Roger Bacon (c.1214-92), the English Franciscan friar celebrated for his advocacy of empiricism and contribution to the modern scientific method.[13]

According to medieval apocalypticism, the Angelic Pope would restore order to

---

[12] Lindsey, H. *There's a New World Coming* (Grand Rapids: Zondervan, 1974), p162
[13] See Roger Bacon's *The Third Work* and *The Compendium of Study*, cited in McGinn, B. *Visions of the End* (New York: Columbia University Press, 1979), pp190-191. The prophetic kernel for the Angelic Pope can be traced back even further however, to Joaichim of Fiore's ideas on the role of the papacy beginning at the close of the "second age", and in early pseudo-Joachite literature such as the *Commentary on Jeremiah*.

the Church during the last days and purge it of corruption. He would usher in a period of spiritual revival, winning over vast amounts of converts, including the Jews, and heal the rift with the Eastern Orthodox Church caused by the Great Schism of 1054.

The prophecy of the *pastor angelicus* – the Angelic Pope, was set against the backdrop of a time when the temporal power of the papacy all too often attracted power-hungry individuals open to corruption. The hopes for a truly holy pontiff who would reject worldly leanings were piqued with the election of Pietro da Morrone, a saintly Benedictine hermit, to the papacy in 1294. The chair of St. Peter had been vacant for two years and three months since the death of Nicholas IV, and tensions were running high among the cardinals to elect a new pope. Morrone, who was well-known to the cardinals as a deeply holy individual, had warned that God would inflict vengeance upon the Church if they did not elect a pope within four months. A unanimous decision was then reached that since no other suitable candidate could be found, Morrone should ascend the papacy to forestall this promise of Divine retribution.

The reluctant hermit took the name Celestine V, but clearly overwhelmed by the position he had unwillingly been bestowed, Celestine abdicated the papacy five months after his election and was subsequently imprisoned by his successor Boniface VIII. Failing to live up to the lofty expectations that were heaped upon him, Celestine died in captivity within a year of his imprisonment. But his humble and austere example would provide the future template for the Angelic Pope.

The prophecies of the reign of the Angelic Pope were often entangled with that of the Last Emperor or Second Charlemagne. It was foretold that these two great leaders would work together to help revive the flagging Christian faith at the end of the age.

In medieval prophetic literature the Angelic pope and Last Emperor gradually assumed attributes accorded to the Two Witnesses of Rev 11. A clear association between the Two Witnesses of the Book of Revelation and the Great Monarch can be found in the writings of Adso, a tenth century Christian monk. Adso, who wrote an apocalypse at the request of Queen Gerberga of the Franks around 950, stated that the Last Emperor would die on the Mount of Olives in Jerusalem before the coming of the Antichrist:

> Some of our learned men say that one of the kings of the Franks will come in the last time will possess anew the Roman empire. He will come at the last time and will be the last and the greatest of all rulers. After he has successfully governed his empire, at last he will come to Jerusalem and will put off his sceptre and crown on the Mount of Olives.[14]

Despite subtle connotations linking the Angelic Pope with one of the Two Witnesses in medieval prophecy, none of these predictions foretell a destiny of martyrdom for the Angelic pontiff. This is odd indeed, since the primary focus of Rev 11 is the martyrdom of the Two Witnesses.[15] Instead, we find a number of prophecies of a

---

[14] McGinn, B. *Visions of the End* p86. The legend of the Last Emperor can be traced back to Pseudo-Methodius, writing around 660AD. Pseudo-Methodius foretold that the "king of the Romans" would lay down his crown on Golgotha after the rise of the Antichrist. See Ibid. p76. This location in Jerusalem later changed to the Mount of Olives by the time of Adso, possibly in order to strengthen the allusion to the Two Witnesses of Rev 11.

[15] In fact the modern term "martyr" is derived from the Greek word for "witness" μαρτυς *martys*.

martyr-pope who immediately precedes the coming of the Angelic Pope. One of the
earliest of such prophecies can be traced back to the *Commentary on Jeremiah* – a
pseudo-Joachite work dating to around 1240:

> The future migration will indeed be worse than the former one because it will be arrogant,
> although not harder. Therefore Peter will be crucified, the pope will be killed, and according to the doctors,
> the conventual sheep and their subjects will be scattered at the death of the pastor. I do not know if it will
> be after three days or three years that the Good Shepherd and Leader of the House of Israel will arise,
> because there is no passage concerning anyone being in charge during this space. Therefore, perhaps the
> Church will lack a ruler when Pilate rules as Antichrist with the support of the Jews, that is, grasping
> traitors. The Christian people and even the pope will either actually be killed or will be afflicted in spirit.[16]

Fatima

Among the various other well-known prophecies concerning a future martyr-
pope, the Third Secret of Fatima is undoubtedly the highest profile. The revelation of the
Third Secret of Fatima was one of the most eagerly anticipated events in the history of
the Catholic Church during the twentieth century. Deliberately hidden from the public by
the Vatican hierarchy for over fifty years, the contents of the Third Secret were the
subject of much speculation among both the clergy and laity. The fact that its disclosure
was intentionally withheld by the Vatican helped to surround the Third Secret with an
aura of mystery, leading to ever bolder and wilder claims about the apocalyptic nature of
its central message. Indeed Fatima has since become one of the most important spiritual
events in the history of the Catholic Church, and has directly influenced the policy
making of almost every subsequent pope.[17]

The events surrounding the original revelation of the secrets of Fatima to three
Portuguese shepherd children in 1917 are just as interesting as the contents of the secrets
themselves. The most famous occurrence at Fatima – the miracle of the Sun, was
witnessed by thousands of individuals, including the secular media, putting it among the
best testified accounts of a miracle ever recorded.

On 13th May 1917, three children were tending sheep at the Cova da Iria fields
near the hamlet of Aljustrel, a mile outside the village of Fatima in central Portugal. As
is common among modern Marian apparitions, including Lourdes and La Salette, the
recipients of the visions were still flushed with the innocence of youth. Lucia Santos was
the eldest child at ten years of age, while her cousins Francisco and Jacinta Marto were
aged eight and seven respectively.

The children had been instructed by their parents to repeat the Rosary during their
daily duties in order to help protect the flock. Being devout children, they obligingly
accepted the importance of the Rosary, and would say it every day after lunch. As they
were reciting their prayers at the Cova da Iria, the children claimed to have been startled

---

Although it did not acquire its present sense until after the Apocalypse was already written.

[16] See McGinn, B. *Visions of the End* pp189-190

[17] As he reigned for only three months before his premature death in 1979, Pope John Paul I did not live
long enough to show the influences of Fatima on his papacy. But he was known to be a devotee of Fatima,
having visited the shrine itself and spoken to Lucia directly.

by a sudden flash of light. They were puzzled to see lightening on such a fine day, as the sky was cloudless and there appeared to be no sign of a thunderstorm. Nonetheless, the children's instincts told them to make towards home for shelter. A second flash drew their gaze to above a small holm-oak tree, where they saw a Lady dressed in brilliant white. Lucia conversed with the Lady, who requested that the children return to the Cova da Iria on the 13th of each month for the next six months.

Lucia was reluctant to relate this experience with others, and asked Jacinta and Francisco to keep the matter to themselves. Jacinta, being the youngest, could not contain her excitement however, and proceeded to tell her family of the events at the Cova with childlike fervour. Her story was met with immediate scepticism from her family and neighbours, but soon found itself spread round their hometown of Aljustrel nonetheless.

Fig. 2 The Shepherd Children of Fatima – Jacinta and Francisco Marto and Lucia Santos in 1917

By the time the next scheduled visit of the lady to the children arrived on 13th June, a small crowd had gathered at the Cova to witness the spectacle. However the Lady was only visible to the children; and as always, only Lucia and Jacinta could hear her speak. When asked by Lucia would she take the children to heaven, the Lady replied that she would take Jacinta and Francisco soon, but that Lucia would have to stay a while longer to make her message known to the world. As the Lady was talking to the children, those present at the scene reported that they could hear a faint buzzing noise. And when the apparition departed from the Cova the second time, some of the witnesses stated that they could see a small cloud rise from above the holm-oak before heading backwards towards the east and disappearing into the horizon.[18]

Fame of the apparition quickly spread around the neighbouring villages, and soon the whole mountain range surrounding the village was buzzing at the news of these events. When the time came round for the next visit on the 13th July, pilgrims from all over the countryside were flocking to Fatima. A crowd of several thousand had gathered in the fields around the Cova da Iria, waiting for the Lady's next visitation. The cloud

---

[18] De Marchi, J. *The True Story of Fatima* (St. Paul: Catechetical Guild Educational Society, 1956)

was seen once again by the crowds hovering over the small tree, accompanied by the buzzing sound. However while the crowds could only see a faint swirl of mist, the children claimed to have seen the Lady quite clearly, and described her as being adorned with dazzling apparel which appeared to shine like the Sun.

During this apparition, the Lady told the children that she would perform a great miracle during her last visit in October as a confirmation to the crowd of her appearances. She then showed the children a frightening vision of hell, which Lucia would later reveal in her Third Memoir, written in 1942, as the First Secret:

> Our Lady showed us a great sea of fire which seemed to be under the earth. Plunged in this fire were demons and souls in human form, like transparent burning embers, all blackened or burnished bronze, floating about in the conflagration, now raised into the air by the flames that issued from within themselves together with great clouds of smoke, now falling back on every side like sparks in a huge fire, without weight or equilibrium, and amid shrieks and groans of pain and despair, which horrified us and made us tremble with fear. The demons could be distinguished by their terrifying and repulsive likeness to frightful and unknown animals, all black and transparent. This vision lasted but an instant. How can we ever be grateful enough to our kind heavenly Mother, who had already prepared us by promising, in the first Apparition, to take us to heaven. Otherwise, I think we would have died of fear and terror.[19]

The second part of the secret warned that God was about to chastise the world for its sins; but stated that this dreadful fate could be avoided if the world would consecrate itself to the Lady's Immaculate Heart:

> You have seen hell where the souls of poor sinners go. To save them, God wishes to establish in the world devotion to my Immaculate Heart. If what I say to you is done, many souls will be saved and there will be peace. The war is going to end: but if people do not cease offending God, a worse one will break out during the Pontificate of Pius XI. When you see a night illuminated by an unknown light, know that this is the great sign given you by God that he is about to punish the world for its crimes, by means of war, famine, and persecutions of the Church and of the Holy Father. To prevent this, I shall come to ask for the consecration of Russia to my Immaculate Heart, and the Communion of reparation on the First Saturdays. If my requests are heeded, Russia will be converted, and there will be peace; if not, she will spread her errors throughout the world, causing wars and persecutions of the Church. The good will be martyred; the Holy Father will have much to suffer; various nations will be annihilated. In the end, my Immaculate Heart will triumph. The Holy Father will consecrate Russia to me, and she shall be converted, and a period of peace will be granted to the world.[20]

Years later, Lucia stated that the second part of the secret predicted the immanence of the end of the Great War, and that another worse war would break out during the pontificate of Pius XI.[21] She felt that the prophecy of the night illuminated by an unknown light, which the Lady said would herald the beginning of the other, more deadly war, was fulfilled by the great aurora borealis of Jan 25th 1938. This low-altitude red aurora, which could be seen throughout Europe, was caused by an unusually intense

---

[19] De Jesus, L. *Fatima in Lucia's Own Words* (Fatima: Postulation Centre, 1976), p108

[20] Ibid. pp108-109

[21] Pius XI died in February 1939 however – some eight months before the German invasion of Poland (the point most historians recognize as the start of the war). This apparent anomaly can be explained by the occurrence of the great aurora during the pontificate of Pius XI, which Lucia considered to be the heavenly announcement of the start of the war. One of the main preludes to the war took place just two months after the appearance of the great aurora, when the German army annexed Austria during the Anschuluss of March 1938. This marked the beginning of Germany's expansionist policy which would ultimately result in the outbreak of the war a year and a half later.

solar storm. In London, the reddish lights were mistakenly thought to be the result of a large blaze, and fire engines were scrambled throughout the city in search of its source. Similar incidents were reported throughout Europe and much of North America. Two months later, German troops marched into Austria, setting Germany on a course that would ultimately lead to the Second World War.

The second part of the secret of Fatima is also thought to have predicted the collapse of the Soviet Union in 1991, after Pope John Paul II apparently fulfilled Our Lady of Fatima's request by giving a blessing to the world in 1984. However critics have contended that the request was not carried out as specified, since Russia was not explicitly mentioned in this blessing.[22] And while the communist Soviet Union did collapse, Russia still has not converted to Catholicism. The Eastern Orthodox Church is still the most dominant religion in Russia. So the Second Secret's promised conversion of Russia is most likely a reference to the prophecy of the reconciliation of the Roman Catholic and Eastern Orthodox Churches under the auspices of the Angelic Pope.

When the time came round for the Lady's next visit on 13th August, the whole of Portugal had heard of the apparitions at Fatima, including its anti-clerical government. In 1910 Portugal had become embroiled in a revolution which eventually led to the abolition of the monarchy. As the Church had previously sponsored the Portuguese monarchy, it was regarded by the Republican government as a relic of the old order. The Church's influence threatened the existence of the Republican state and divided the allegiances of its civilians. As such, the Republican government adopted a policy of anti-clericalism and embarked on an aggressive campaign of secularism. The state sponsored media heaped scorn upon all aspects of religion, and the events at Fatima were satirised with particular glee.

As the apparitions at Fatima managed to attract such a huge following, the local government felt it had to step in to curb the growth of this fledgling movement. Arturo Santos, the mayor of Vila Nova de Ourem, also known as "the Tinker", was the chief administrator over the county to which Fatima belonged, and decided that he would have to personally intervene to quash this new superstition. He summoned Lucia, together with her father, to the Town Hall in Ourem for questioning, but was frustrated by the girl's unwillingness to cooperate. The Tinker resolved that more robust tactics would have to be employed to disrupt the children's following.

As the children were making their way to the Cova da Iria on 13th August for their next encounter with the lady, the Tinker insisted that he would take the children there by carriage. But the mayor's intentions were rather more dubious. He took the children against their will and brought them to his house at Ourem instead, hiding them under a rug so they could not be seen by the passing pilgrims who were making their way to the place of the apparitions.

Back at the Cova, the crowd had gathered as usual when they learned that the children had been kidnapped by the mayor. Their anger was interrupted by a thunderclap, and once again the cloud appeared over the holm-oak. Witnesses reported seeing spectacles which have since been reported at the sites of other Marian apparitions, such as the colours of the rainbow, which reflected around the Cova and bounced off

---

[22] See Kramer, P. (Ed.) *The Devil's Final Battle* (The Missionary Association: Terryville, 2002), pp vii-xv

peoples' faces. The leaves of the trees also appeared to turn into flowers.

After these phenomena had abated, the crowds' focus was once more drawn back to the plight of the children. For the next two days the youths were interrogated by the mayor and his officials, who were determined to extract from them the details of the Lady's secret. The children were transferred to the public jail where the Tinker decided to use psychological torture in order to obtain the desired information. He threatened to place the children in a vat of boiling oil, and they were taken off one by one by the prison guards. Despite believing the Tinker's conviction to carry out these threats, the children steadfastly refused to divulge their secret. The mayor's actions had proved fruitless, and the populace was threatening to rise up against him. So the children were released on the 15th of August and brought back to Fatima.

The Lady appeared to the children again in an unscheduled visit on 19th August at a different location – a field called Valinhos near Aljustrel. This apparition was to compensate for the children's failure to appear at the Cova on the 13th due to the mayor's intervention. The Lady repeated her promise to perform a miracle in October, but said that it would have been even greater if the children had not been taken against their wishes to Ourem. Again, the children were instructed to come to the Cova da Iria on the 13th of the following month.

The crowds, estimated at around 30,000, assembled again at the Cova on the 13th September. This time they were accompanied by Church officials, who came to observe and record the events for themselves. Among them was Canon Manuel Formagio, a representative of the exiled cardinal-patriarch. Many witnesses to the events in September claimed to have seen a luminous orb float down to rest on the holm-oak, before disappearing again into the east. Others reported seeing a rain of small, ethereal white flowers that could not be caught. However it is clear from Canon Formagio's statement that these visions were subjective, as he himself did not see any phenomena during this occasion other than a slight darkening of the Sun. But of the thousands of eyewitnesses who did behold the visions, all of them reported to have experienced the same phenomena.[23]

The Lady's promise to work a miracle on the 13th October was now widely known throughout Portugal, and the size of the crowd when the appointed day arrived reflected this expectation. Estimates of the number of attendance to the final apparition range from 50,000-100,000; with 70,000 being the generally accepted figure. The secular media were also present, with the aim of capturing the moment when the children's promised miracle turned out to be a resounding failure. But their attendance proved counter-productive to their intended purpose, and instead would provide a totally objective testimony to the events that followed. The reports of the secular newspapers complimented rather than debunked the claims of the faithful, and helped to corroborate the evidence supplied by the thousands of other witnesses.

The children were waiting in the rain for the Lady to arrive, but began to grow uneasy when she had failed to appear at her usual time around noon. There had been fears among some of the relatives for the children's safety. If the miracle failed to materialize, there was a chance that the crowd would grow angry and seek to vent their frustrations on the children. These concerns soon subsided however, as shortly after

---

[23] De Marchi, J. *The True Story of Fatima*

1pm, Lucia asked Jacinta to kneel down – the Lady was coming.

On this final appearance, the Lady requested a chapel to be built in her honour at the Cova, and told the children that the war would soon be over. As soon as the children indicated that the Lady was taking her leave, the rain stopped and the dark clouds suddenly parted. Lucia cried out "Look at the Sun!". The children themselves claimed to have seen a vision of the infant Jesus and St. Joseph blessing the people, as well as a vision of the Lady in the form of Our Lady of Sorrows and of Mt. Carmel. But the crowd saw something altogether different from the children.

The miracle of the Sun at Fatima is one of the most well documented and widely witnessed miracles the world has ever known. People from every walk of life were present at the scene, believers and unbelievers unlike – including reporters for several secular newspapers such as the pro-government journal *O Seculo*. The Sun was just past its zenith in the afternoon and there was no cloud obscuring it, leaving its full dazzling radiance to be seen by the crowd. Yet while prolonged direct eye-contact with the Sun usually causes severe retinal damage, it could now be gazed at without so much as straining the eyes of the observers. It then appeared to spin and emit strange colours that were reflected on the crowds and surrounding environment. The Sun then began to "dance" in the sky, before detaching itself from the firmament and sweeping down in a menacing gesture, terrorizing the thousands of onlookers who thought the end of the world was at hand. The clothes of those gathered which had been soaked by rain only moments earlier were now completely dry.

The anticlerical journal *O Seculo* reported the following:

> At that moment a great shout went up, and one could hear the spectators nearest at hand shouting: "A miracle! A miracle!" Before the astonished eyes of the crowd, whose aspect was biblical as they stood bareheaded, eagerly searching the sky, the sun trembled, made sudden incredible movements outside all cosmic laws – the sun "danced" according to the typical expression of the people. [24]

The other newspapers, such as *O Dia* cited below, described the miracle of the Sun in similar terms:

> The grey mother-of-pearl tone turned into a sheet of silver which broke up as the clouds were torn apart and the silver sun, enveloped in the same gauzy grey light, was seen to whirl and turn in the circle of broken clouds. A cry went up from every mouth and people fell on their knees on the muddy ground ... [25]

Dr. Domingos Pinto Coelho, an eminent eye specialist writing for another Portuguese newspaper, *Ordem*, gives the following account:

> The sun, at one moment surrounded with scarlet flame, at another aureoled in yellow and deep purple, seemed to be in an exceedingly fast and whirling movement, at times appearing to be loosened from the sky and to be approaching the earth, strongly radiating heat. [26]

---

[24] Cited in De Marchi, J. *The True Story of Fatima*
[25] Ibid.
[26] Ibid.

Fig. 3 Some of the witnesses of the miracle of the Sun at Fatima watching the vision as it occurred on 13th October, 1917.

It must be stressed that although these visions could be seen by the vast majority of those present, they were primarily of psychological, rather than physical origin. Two women told an investigator that they did not see any unusual phenomena at all. However the cases of individuals who saw nothing that day were extremely isolated and the events at Fatima remain beyond any satisfactory scientific explanation. The most common scientific explanation offered is that the crowd had experienced mass hypnosis. But there could not have been any prior form of suggestion by the children, as no one knew what form the promised miracle would take. Another factor used to argue against mass hypnosis is the fact that the same solar phenomena were witnessed by the staff and children of a school in the town of Alburitel, which was around eleven miles away. The author and poet Alfonso Viera testified that he too could see the events from his own home, which was even further away than the school – at a distance of around 24 miles.

The theories proposed by sceptics that attempt to attribute the events at Fatima as unusual weather phenomena are somewhat inadequate. Even if we could put the miracle of the Sun down to a freak meteorological occurrence (despite that there are no known weather conditions which match the effects described by the thousands of witnesses), the fact that the children had been promised a miracle at this precise time would make the phenomenon a miracle in itself.[27] But given that some people did not see the visions, we can conclude that the events had a primarily subjective, rather than objective existence.

It seems that the miracle was caused by a mass hallucination of supernatural origin. The fact that some of those present claimed not to have seen anything at all supports the conclusion that the miracle of the Sun was subjective. But it also had effects which could be felt in the external world, as is attested by the fact that the witnesses' rain-sodden clothes were dried instantaneously.

After a period of investigation lasting thirteen years, the events at Fatima were officially accredited as "worthy of belief" by the Roman Catholic Church on 13th October 1930. As foretold by the Lady, Francisco and Jacinta's lives were cut tragically short. They succumbed to the influenza epidemic of 1918. Francisco died in 1919 and Jacinta soon after in 1920. Their bodies were exhumed in 1935 and 1951 as part of the canonization process. While Francisco's body had decomposed, Jacinta's body, like the other great Marian visionary, St. Bernadette Soubirous of Lourdes, was found to be

---

[27] As is pointed out by S. L. Jaki in *God and the Sun at Fatima* (New Hope, KY.: Real View Books, 1999)

miraculously incorrupt. The children made their first steps towards sainthood when they were beatified by Pope John Paul II on May 13th 2000.

The Third Secret

Lucia survived her cousins as promised, and entered a convent in 1925, before going on to join the Carmelite order in Coimbra, Portugal during 1948. She was to remain at this location until her death on 13th February 2005 aged 97. Lucia revealed the first two secrets in her Third Memoir in 1941 in order to help the beatification process for Jacinta and Francisco, but was reluctant to commit the Third Secret to writing at this early stage. During a bout of illness in 1944 which was feared could claim her life, Lucia wrote down the Third Secret at the orders of the Bishop of Leira and enclosed it in a sealed envelope for safekeeping. She stated that it should not be revealed until after 1960, as by that stage this part of the secret would be better understood.

However when Pope John XXIII opened Lucia's sealed envelope in 1959, he decided not to reveal the contents of the Third Secret to the public, stating that the Third Secret did not refer to the years of his pontificate. When the date set by Sr. Lucia for the secret's release had passed without it being made public, speculation began to grow around the nature of its contents. Rumours were circulating that the Pope had turned white when he first read the secret, fuelling fears that it spoke of an impending Third World War. A threat which seemed only too real during the height of the Cold War and the danger posed by the Cuban Missile Crisis of 1961.

When the Third Secret was eventually released on 26th June 2000, it became clear that it was centred around the martyrdom of a pope. There was a mixed reaction to the interpretation offered by the Vatican's official document *The Message of Fatima*. In an attempt to link the vision with the assassination attempt on John Paul II on 13th May, 1981, Cardinal Sodano had announced during the beatification ceremony of Francisco and Jacinta on 13th May 2000 that the "bishop dressed in white" in the vision was "apparently" killed. The fact that the assassination attempt occurred on the anniversary of the first apparition seemed to make sense of this understanding. As did the Pope's claims to have seen a banner of Our Lady of Fatima in the crowd as he fell, stating that he felt it that his life was saved by "a mother's guiding hand".

But when the full text was released just over a month later, it became evident that the pope in the vision was killed *outright*, not "apparently killed". Moreover the "bishop dressed in white" in the vision was slain by a number of assailants, not a lone gunman. Therefore the pope the children saw in this vision could not have been John Paul II. This fact can easily be ascertained from the original words of the Third Secret given below in full:

I write in obedience to you, my God, who command me to do so through his Excellency the Bishop of Leiria and through your Most Holy Mother and mine.

After the two parts which I have already explained, at the left of Our Lady and a little above, we saw an Angel with a flaming sword in his left hand; flashing, it gave out flames that looked as though they would set the world on fire; but they died out in contact with the splendor that Our Lady radiated towards him from her right hand: pointing to the earth with his right hand, the Angel cried out in a loud voice: 'Penance, Penance, Penance!'. And we saw in an immense light that is God: 'something similar to how people appear in a mirror when they pass in front of it' a Bishop dressed in White 'we had the impression that it was the Holy Father'. Other Bishops, Priests, men and women Religious going up a steep mountain, at the top of which there was a big Cross of rough-hewn trunks as of a cork-tree with the bark; before reaching there the Holy Father passed through a big city half in ruins and half trembling with halting step, afflicted with pain and sorrow, he prayed for the souls of the corpses he met on his way; having reached the top of the mountain, on his knees at the foot of the big Cross he was killed by a group of soldiers who fired bullets and arrows at him, and in the same way there died one after another the other Bishops, Priests, men and women Religious, and various lay people of different ranks and positions. Beneath the two arms of the Cross there were two Angels each with a crystal aspersorium in his hand, in which they gathered up the blood of the Martyrs and with it sprinkled the souls that were making their way to God.[28]

There are several inconsistencies between Cardinal Sodano's interpretation and the actual words of the vision, making this "official" interpretation somewhat deficient. However it has been noted that in his theological commentary in the *Message of Fatima* document, Cardinal Ratzinger was careful not to fully endorse Cardinal Sodano's limitation of the secret solely to the 1981 assassination attempt.[29]

We shall discuss later how there was perhaps an ulterior motive for the Vatican's presentation of this oddly fitting interpretation. For now it should be sufficient to assume that one of the main reasons the Vatican forwarded this understanding of the prophecy was because it safely relocated the words of the secret to a past event. If the official line was to interpret the assassination of the pope in the vision as already having achieved fulfilment in the past, then the prophecy of the Third Secret is unfalsifible, and the Church's approval of the Fatima cult is beyond reproach. Yet if we are to give proper credence to this prophecy, then we have to concede that its ultimate fulfilment lies at some point in the future.

A closer examination of the text of the Third Secret highlights its affinities with another major prophecy contained in the New Testament – that of the eschatological persecution of the Church. Sr. Lucia has stated on record that the Third Secret was related to chapters 8-13 of the Apocalypse – a segment of the book which is predominantly concerned with the future persecution of the Church.[30] The theme of religious persecution can be seen most prominently in chapter 12 of this portion of the Book of Revelation, which traditional Catholic interpretation also links with the Great Apostasy. Here the Woman adorned with the Sun (who besides the Virgin Mary, also symbolically represents the Church) is pursued by the great Red Dragon, which symbolizes the Devil.

The Dragon sweeping a third of the stars from the sky is usually interpreted in the light of Rev 12:9-10, which describes the fall of Satan from heaven, along with the angels who had joined him in rebellion. But it has also been interpreted in traditional Catholic teaching as the Devil leading one third of the clergy into apostasy.[31] This verse thus connects the final persecution of the Church with the prophesied Great Apostasy at the eschaton – an association already made apparent in the *Catechism of the Catholic*

---

[28] Congregation for the Doctrine of the Faith, *The Message of Fatima* (Vatican City: Libreria Editrace Vaticana, 2000)

[29] Boudreaux, R. "Catholic Church Unveils 'Third Secret of Fatima'" *LA Times* (27th June 2000)

[30] De la Sainte Trinite, M. *The Whole Truth About Fatima Vol III* (Buffalo: Immaculate Heart Publications, 1990), p533

[31] See for example Kramer, H.B. *The Book of Destiny* (Rockford: TAN, 1955), p280

Church:

Before Christ's second coming the Church must pass through a final trial that will shake the faith of many believers. The persecution that accompanies her pilgrimage on earth will unveil the "mystery of iniquity" in the form of a religious deception offering men an apparent solution to their problems at the price of apostasy from the truth. The supreme religious deception is that of the Antichrist, a pseudo-messianism by which man glorifies himself in place of God and of his Messiah come in the flesh.

The Antichrist's deception already begins to take shape in the world every time the claim is made to realize within history that messianic hope which can only be realized beyond history through the eschatological judgement. The Church has rejected even modified forms of this falsification of the kingdom to come under the name of millenarianism, especially the "intrinsically perverse" political form of a secular messianism.

The Church will enter the glory of the kingdom only through this final Passover, when she will follow her Lord in his death and Resurrection. The kingdom will be fulfilled, then, not by a historic triumph of the Church through a progressive ascendancy, but only by God's victory over the final unleashing of evil, which will cause his Bride to come down from heaven. God's triumph over the revolt of evil will take the form of the Last Judgement after the final cosmic upheaval of this passing world.[32]

The theme of persecution can be seen elsewhere in the portion of the Apocalypse specified by Sr. Lucia, in the martyrdom of the Two Witnesses detailed in Rev 11. The main content of chapter 11 of the Apocalypse is recapitulated in chapter 12, shedding further light on the subject of the future persecution of the Church. We are told that both the ministry of the Two Witnesses and the sojourn of the Woman adorned with the Sun in the wilderness take place during the 1,260 "days" of the Apocalypse, which suggests they take place in the same time-frame. Both chapters also have the common theme of persecution and martyrdom as a backdrop, with the Woman adorned with the Sun being pursued by the great Red Dragon and the Two Witnesses suffering martyrdom at the hands of the Beast.

In its presentation of them as Elijah-style restorer figures, Rev 11 implies that the promised spiritual revival or outpouring of the Holy Spirit at the Second Pentecost is inaugurated by the ministry of the Two Witnesses. Rev 12:14 also appears to allude to this spiritual renaissance. During the flight of the Woman adorned with the Sun (who in one aspect represents the Church) from the pursuing Red Dragon, she is saved from her predicament by being gifted "the two wings of the great eagle" to help her escape to the place of sanctuary prepared for her in the wilderness:

And when the dragon saw that he had been thrown down to the earth, he pursued the woman who had given birth to the male child. But the woman was given the two wings of the great eagle so that she might fly from the serpent into the wilderness, to the place where she is to be nourished for a time, and times, and half a time. (Rev 12:13-14)

Given the parallel themes of persecution in chapters 11 and 12 of Revelation, it seems highly likely that the two "wings" of Rev 12:14 is a masked reference to the Two Witnesses of Rev 11. So a possible interpretation of this verse could be that the Woman/Church is saved from the Devil's main instrument of attack – the spread of apostasy, by the intervention of the Two Witnesses. The two "wings" help to fend off this offensive and provide shelter for the Church during the course of her plight.

---

[32] *Catechism of the Catholic Church* 675-677

Verse 15 goes on to recapitulate the above passage in order to add a different perspective, and informs us that the Dragon spewed a great flood out of his mouth that threatened to overwhelm the Woman/Church:

> The serpent poured water like a river out of his mouth after the woman, to sweep her away with a flood.

The "flood" represents the threat of apostasy and persecution to completely destroy the Church. But then something completely unexpected happens. The earth comes to the Woman's aid and swallows up the deluge:

> But the earth came to the help of the woman, and the earth opened its mouth and swallowed the river that the dragon had poured from his mouth. (Rev 12:16)

If we are to follow our interpretation to its logical conclusion, then this must be another prediction of the prophesied spiritual revival, which occurs here after the Woman is given the help of the two "wings"/Witnesses. The earth responds to the call of the Two Witnesses in the form of conversion, and the threat presented by the Devil to totally overwhelm the Church with a flood of apostasy thus subsides.

Now that we are armed with these insights into chapters 8-13 of the Apocalypse – the portion which Sr. Lucia said was specifically related to the Third Secret, we can continue our analysis of the content of the vision. The central focus of the vision of the Third Secret revolves around the martyrdom of the "Bishop dressed in White" – an obvious reference to the pope. The fact that the contents of the Third Secret (including the reference to the martyrdom of a pope) is to found in chapters 8-13 of the Book of Revelation invites us to draw a comparison with the major theme of martyrdom in this portion of the text – namely that of the Two Witnesses, who are killed at the behest of the Beast that rises from the bottomless pit.

Indeed there a number of similarities which connect the Third Secret to Rev 11. The pope of the vision is killed in a city with a hill, at the top of which is a "large cross". A description which sounds remarkably like Jerusalem, which situated atop the Judean hills, was the location of Golgotha – the place of Christ's sacrificial death. This would thus explain the reference to the "large cross" in the vision; and the pope's Via Dolorosa-like journey to the summit of the "steep mountain". This image is a striking parallel to Rev 11, where the Two Witnesses are overpowered by the Beast and killed "in the main street of the great city known by the symbolic names Sodom and Egypt, in which their Lord was crucified." (Rev 11:8) As we can see from the latter half of this passage, the place where "their Lord was crucified" is an unmistakable reference to Jerusalem.

The fact that Lucia described the city as half in ruins may reflect the situation of the Church at this time, which as the "Heavenly Jerusalem" and Bride of Christ in Rev 20-21, is half in ruins due to the Great Apostasy.

The conclusion to the Third Secret, where the two angels gather up the sacrificial blood of the martyrs into crystal aspersoria[33] and sprinkle it over souls making their way to heaven, recalls the act of atonement performed by the Aaronite high priest, as is

---

[33] Liturgical tools used in Catholic Mass to sprinkle holy water.

outlined in Lev 16. Here, the sacrificial victim's blood is ordered to be sprinkled on the Mercy Seat of the Ark of the Covenant during the Day of Atonement:

> And he shall take some of the blood of the bull and sprinkle it with his finger on the front of the mercy seat on the east side, and in front of the mercy seat he shall sprinkle some of the blood with his finger seven times. Then he shall kill the goat of the sin offering that is for the people and bring its blood inside the veil and do with its blood as he did with the blood of the bull, sprinkling it over the mercy seat and in front of the mercy seat. Thus he shall make atonement for the Holy Place, because of the uncleannesses of the people of Israel and because of their transgressions, all their sins. (Lev 16:14-16)

The sin offerings of Lev 16 on the Day of Atonement has is compared in Christian thought to the vicarious sacrifice offered by Christ on the cross. The two angels depicted at the close of the Third Secret may thus represent the two cherubim that adorned the Mercy Seat of the Ark of the Covenant with outstretched wings.

Fig. 4 The two cherubim that adorned the Mercy Seat of the Ark of the Covenant – do the two angels described in the Third Secret represent these cherubim?

If we look back to Rev 11, it also closes with a vision of the Ark seated in the heavenly temple, after the resurrection of the Two Witnesses:

> Then God's temple in heaven was opened, and the ark of his covenant was seen within his temple. There were flashes of lightning, rumblings, peals of thunder, an earthquake, and heavy hail. (Rev 11:19)

The similarities are simply too hard to ignore. There must be an intended point of comparison. As well as alluding to the Ark of the Covenant, the two angels of the Third Secret may be a veiled reference to the Two Witnesses in their resurrected form.

If we look at the table below, we can get a better overview of the amount of parallels between the Third Secret and Rev 11:

Third Secret	Revelation 11
Theme of Martyrdom: The pope is killed by a group of soldiers.	Theme of Martyrdom: The Two Witnesses are killed by the Beast. (Rev 11:7-10)
Location: A city with a cross at the top of a mountain.	Location: The place the Lord was crucified (Jerusalem)
Conclusion: In an allusion to the Ark of the Covenant in Lev 16, two angels sprinkle blood on souls making their way to heaven.	Conclusion: A vision of the Ark of the Covenant is seen in the heavenly Temple.

It seems that the Third Secret implicitly attempts to identify a future pontiff with one of the Two Witnesses of the Apocalypse. We shall now turn to consider some of the other prophecies of a future martyr-pope in an attempt to draw further parallels to this hypothesis.

The "Two Pillars" of St. John Bosco

A perhaps more direct link between the future assassination of a pope and the Two Witnesses of Rev 11 can be found in the prophetic writings of St. John Bosco (1815-1888). St. John Bosco (or Don Bosco as he is sometimes affectionately known) had experienced a series of prophetic dreams throughout his life, which he later wrote down for posterity. In one of the most famous of these dreams, known as "The Two Pillars", Don Bosco recounts how he experienced a dream in which the Catholic Church was symbolized as a great ship. Many interpreters have noted how this dream appears to have predicted the occurrence of the First and Second Vatican councils.[34] The dream tells of two meetings on the ship during the midst of a storm – which has been interpreted as the tumult of secularism and apostasy which has threatened to overwhelm the Church in the modern age.

> The supreme commander on the big ship is the Sovereign Pontiff. He, on seeing the fury of the enemies and the evils among which his faithful find themselves, determines to summon around himself the captains of the smaller ships to hold a council and decide on what is to be done. All the captains come aboard and gather around the Pope. They hold a meeting, but meanwhile the wind and the waves gather in storm, so they are sent back to control their own ships.
> There comes a short lull; for a second time the Pope gathers the captains together around him, while the flag-ship goes on its course. But the frightful storm returns.[35]

Don Bosco narrated this vision in 1862, six years before Pope Pius IX convoked

---

[34] See for example, Socci, A. *The Fourth Secret of Fatima* (Fitzwilliam: Loreto Publications, 2009) p62
[35] Bacchiarello, J. (Ed) *Forty Dreams of St. John Bosco* (Rockford: TAN, 1996) pp206-208.

the First Vatican Council in 1868.[36] The interruption of the first council in the dream prophesied the suspension of the First Vatican Council after the capture of Rome by the House of Savoy in 1870.   Note that after the second council in the dream, Don Bosco states that "the ship goes on its course", which seems to be a prediction of its successful completion.   It is only after the ship has safely embarked on the course set at this meeting that the storm returns.

Then after the second council had concluded in his dream (which would be after 1965 – the year which the Second Vatican Council closed), Don Bosco prophesies an era of tribulation, followed by a period of revival.   Then in the midst of this renewal a pope is assassinated:

> The Pope stands at the helm and all his energies are directed to steering towards those two columns, from the top of which and from every side of which are hanging numerous anchors and big hooks, fastened to chains.
>
> All the enemy ships move to attack it, and they try in every way to stop it and to sink it: some with writings or books or inflammable materials, of which they are full; others with guns, with rifles and with rams. The battle rages ever more relentlessly.   The enemy prows thrust violently, but their efforts and impact prove useless.   They make attempts in vain and waste all their labor and ammunition; the big ship goes safely and smoothly on its way.   Sometimes it happens that, struck by formidable blows, it gets large, deep gaps in its sides; but no sooner is the harm done than a gentle breeze blows from the two columns and the cracks close up and the gaps are stopped immediately.   Meanwhile, the guns of the assailants are blown up, the rifles and other arms and prows are broken; many ships are shattered and sink into the sea.   Then, the frenzied enemies strive to fight hand to hand, with fists, with blows, with blasphemy and with curses.
>
> All at once the Pope falls gravely wounded.   Immediately, those who are with him run to help him and they lift him up.   A second time the Pope is struck, he falls again and dies.   A shout of victory and of joy rings out amongst the enemies; from their ships an unspeakable mockery arises.
>
> But hardly is the Pontiff dead than another Pope takes his place.   The pilots, having met together, have elected the Pope so promptly that the news of the death of the Pope coincides with the news of the election of the successor.   The adversaries begin to lose courage.[37]

This dream has a number of parallels to the Third Secret of Fatima.   The theme of a pope being killed by a group of aggressors is the first and perhaps most obvious. However it may also contain links with Rev 11.   A recurring theme in this dream is the presence of two enormous pillars or columns jutting up out of the sea.   One was associated with devotion to the Immaculate Virgin, while the other was related to the Consecrated Host.

We may be able to establish a connection between the two pillars in this dream with the Two Witnesses.   Previously in Don Bosco's dream, one of the pillars had a placard at its feet, with the words *Auxilium Christianorum* – "Help of Christians".   This title, usually bestowed upon the Virgin Mary, is evocative of a prophecy concerning the "Great Monarch" or "Second Charlemagne" which gives the Last Emperor the symbolic name "Help From God".

> The fifth period of the Church, which began circa 1520, will end with the arrival of the Holy Pope and of the powerful Monarch who is called "Help From God" because he will restore everything. (Venerable Bartholomew Holzhauser 1613-1658)[38]

---

[36] Ibid. p205
[37] Ibid. pp208-209
[38] Holzhauser, B. *Interpretatio Apocalysis usque ad cap. XV, v. 5* (Bamberg: 1784)

Could there be an intentional link here between the pillar named "Help of Christians" and Ven. Holzhauser's Great Monarch, who was symbolically named "Help From God"?

Fig. 5 A painting of St. John Bosco's dream of the Two Pillars in the Basilica of Mary, Help of Christians in Turin

The placard at the other pillar contained the words *Salus Credentium* – "Salvation of the Faithful". This is the tallest and most prominent of the two columns in Don Bosco's dream. This difference in stature seems to denote that the first pillar, which symbolizes the "Help from God" given in the person of the Great Monarch, is inferior to the second column which represents the Angelic Pope.

As we noted earlier, the Angelic Pope and the Great Monarch came to be associated with the Two Witnesses of the Apocalypse in medieval prophecy. If the pillars of Don Bosco represent the Angelic Pope and the Great Monarch, then they would also correspond to the Two Witnesses.

There are a number of other parallels between the dream of the two pillars and the ministry of the Two Witnesses. The motif of a restorative wind coming from the two pillars to help repair the damage the ship/Church sustained during the tempest of rebellion recalls the prophecy of the spiritual revival or Second Pentecost, which as we have already suggested will be inaugurated by the Two Witnesses after the current age of the Great Apostasy.

The death of the pope in this dream, like that of the Two Witnesses, is met with rejoicing and jubilation on the behalf of the antagonists, recalling the scene in Rev 11:9-10:

> For three and a half days some from the peoples and tribes and languages and nations will gaze at their dead bodies and refuse to let them be placed in a tomb, and those who dwell on the earth will rejoice over them and make merry and exchange presents because these two prophets had been a torment to those who dwell on the earth.

Don Bosco's prophetic dream of the two pillars and the Secrets of Fatima both suggest that the future assassination of a pope is connected to the Two Witnesses of Rev 11. They also appear to predict the coming of a new Pentecost – Don Bosco with the healing wind of the two pillars restoring the battered ship, and the Secret of Fatima with its promise of the conversion of Russia and triumph of the Immaculate Heart of Mary.

Predictions of a spiritual renewal and the assassination of a pope can also be found in the message of another famous Marian apparition, which has only recently come to light in 2002. The content of the secrets of La Salette have been the subject of much controversy for over 150 years. But amazingly, their recent discovery has shown how both the prophecies of La Salette and those of Fatima have independently converged on the same themes of the assassination of a pope and a great spiritual revival. What makes it all the more striking is the fact that the Third Secret could not have relied upon the secret of La Salette as a major source, since the latter was concealed in the files of the Vatican Secret Archives until the turn of the millennium.

The Secrets of La Salette

On the 19th of September, 1846, two shepherd children, Melanie Calvat and Maximin Giraud, were tending herds around the mountaintop village of La Salette, near Grenoble, France. Melanie, who was fifteen at the time, along with Maximin, eleven, claimed to have witnessed a sudden apparition of "a beautiful lady", sitting on the top of a heap of stones, weeping bitterly. Melanie and Maximin claimed that they did not immediately recognize the woman as the Virgin Mary, and would only come to this conclusion at a later stage.

The Lady called out to the children and beckoned them to draw nearer, so she could convey a message of "great news". She spoke to them first in French, then in Patois – their local dialect, telling them of her disappointment at the sins of the people. The Lady warned them of an impending famine resulting from the failure of potato crops (which occurred throughout Europe, with particularly calamitous results for the population of Ireland, between the years 1845-1849). After announcing some warnings and misgivings that were to be made public, the Lady then divulged a secret to each of the children. First to Maximin, who could hear the Lady's words while Melanie saw only her lips move. And when the Lady spoke to Melanie, Maximin in turn could not hear. So both children claimed to have been unaware of the other's secret.

For five years, the children steadfastly refused to reveal any of the contents of their secrets, despite being constantly pestered, bribed and threatened by members of the laity. When Pope Pius IX requested that he should be provided with a copy of the Lady's message in 1851 however, Melanie and Maximin agreed that they would commit their secrets to writing on the condition that it would be for the Pontiff's eyes alone. The secrets were then duly passed on to the Vatican. After Pius IX had read the letters, some of those present later stated that the Pope was visibly moved. The children's letters were then consigned to the Holy Office Secret Archives, were they were to remain buried for almost a hundred and fifty years.

Fig. 6 Maximin Giraud and Melanie Calvat – the shepherd children of La Salette, in 1846

After a period of investigation and a number of miraculous cures associated with the event, the Church gave official recognition to the apparition of La Salette in 1851, accrediting it to be "worthy of belief". However the Bishop of Grenoble issued a declaration in 1855, stating that the mission of the shepherd children ended in their communication of the vision along with the secrets, and the legacy of La Salette was now in the hands of the Church.

During the years after the apparitions, Melanie entered a convent near Grenoble and took up a lifelong religious vocation. She attempted to establish her own religious order – the Order of the Apostles of the Last Days for males and the Order of the Mother of God for females, the rule of which she claimed was given to her directly by the Lady herself. But she was met with opposition from local Church leaders. From 1860 onwards, Melanie began to draw up "reworked" versions of the secret of La Salette, which diverged considerably from the content of the original secret written down in 1851. The most famous of which told how the Rome would eventually lose the faith and become the seat of the Antichrist. The Holy Office did not lend its backing any of the later versions of the Secret of La Salette, and her work published in 1879 under the title of "Apparition of the Blessed Virgin on the Mountain of La Salette" was eventually placed on the Index of Prohibited Books.

Needless to say, this dispute sent out conflicting messages to the Catholic laity. On one hand the Church had appeared to grant the apparitions of La Salette unwavering commitment, declaring it to be "worthy of belief", and on the other it appeared to be opposed to the later ministry of one of the visionaries.

When the original letters the children had sent to Pius IX were finally unearthed by Fr. Michel Corteville in 1999, they showed the extent to which Melanie's later material differed from the original secrets. Buried in the Vatican Secret Archives for more than a century, these secrets were presumed by many to have been lost forever in the library's cavernous recesses. Fr. Corteville discovered the secrets of La Salette in 1999 during the course of his research, and together with the famous mariologist Fr. René Laurentin, published both the original secrets for the first time in 2002 in their book *Découverte du secret de la Salette* (*The Discovery of the Secrets of La Salette*). Now that the original secrets had been rediscovered, a comparison could be made between the content of Melanie Calvat's later writings of 1873 and 1879, and her original version of 1851.

These newly discovered secrets were quite different from the original officially approved material. The brevity of the original secrets in comparison to Melanie's later writings is perhaps the most telling feature that her later work was an expansion of the original. Melanie's later version of the secret was comprised mostly of material which expanded on the original message.[39]

J.M.J.

Secret which the Blessed Virgin gave me on the Mountain of La Salette on September 19, 1846

Mélanie, I will say something to you which you will not say to anybody:
The time of the God's wrath has arrived!
If, when you say to the people what I have said to you so far, and what I will still ask you to say, if, after that, they do not convert, (if they do not do penance, and they do not cease working on Sunday, and if they continue to blaspheme the Holy Name of God), in a word, if the face of the earth does not change, God will be avenged against the people ungrateful and slave of the demon. My Son will make his power manifest! Paris, this city soiled by all kinds of crimes, will perish infallibly. Marseilles will be destroyed in a little time. When these things arrive, the disorder will be complete on the earth, the world will be given up to its impious passions. The pope will be persecuted from all sides, they will shoot at him, they will want to put him to death, but no one will not be able to do it, the Vicar of God will triumph again this time. The priests and the sisters, and the true servants of my Son will be persecuted, and several will die for the faith of Jesus-Christ. A famine will reign at the same time. After all these will have arrived, many will recognize the hand of God on them, they will convert, and do penance for their sins. A great king will go up on the throne, and will reign a few years. Religion will re-flourish and spread all over the world, and there will be a great abundance, the world, glad not to be lacking nothing, will fall again in its disorders, will give up God, and will be prone to its criminal passions. [Among] God's ministers, and the Spouses of Jesus-Christ, there will be some who will go astray, and that will be the most terrible. Lastly, hell will reign on earth. It will be then that the Antichrist will be born of a Sister, but woe to her! Many will believe in him, because he will claim to have come from heaven, woe to those who will believe in him! That time is not far away, twice 50 years will not go by. My child, you will not say what I have just said to you. (You will not say it to anybody, you will not say if you must say it one day, you will not say what that it concerns), finally you will say nothing anymore until I tell you to say it! I pray to Our Holy Father the Pope to give me his holy blessing.

Mélanie Mathieu, Shepherdess of La Salette, Grenoble, July 6, 1851.

J.M.J.+[40]

There were no references to Rome becoming the seat of the Antichrist in this version of Melanie's secret, as had been expected. Instead, like the secrets of Fatima, Melanie's secret spoke of a future persecution of both the Church and the pope, and a period of spiritual renewal under the auspices of the "Great Monarch".

It is interesting to note that unlike the outright killing of a pope in the Third Secret

---

[39] Although it could be argued that the full revelation of the message was given over time, as is the case in the experiences of other mystics. For example Sr. Lucia continued to receive visions of Jesus and Mary long after the apparition of Our Lady in October, 1917.
[40] Cited in Bourmaud, D. "Discovery of the Secrets of La Salette: A Book Review" *Newsletter of the District of Asia* (2003)

of Fatima, the above account of the persecution of a pope does appear to foreshadow the assassination attempt of John Paul II in 1981. The pope of Melaine's secret survives the attempt on his life. However it seems that this event should be distinguished from the prophecy of the actual assassination of a future pontiff. Instead the secret given to Maximin appears to allude to this as a separate event:

> On September 19, 1846, we saw a beautiful Lady. We never said that this lady was the Blessed Virgin but we always said that it was a beautiful Lady. I do not know if it is the Blessed Virgin or another person. As for me, I believe today that it is the Blessed Virgin. Here is what this Lady said to me:
> "If my people continue, what I will say to you will arrive earlier, if it changes a little, it will be a little later. France has corrupted the universe, one day it will be punished. The faith will die out in France: three quarters of France will not practice religion anymore, or almost no more, the other part will practice it without really practicing it. Then, after [that], nations will convert, the faith will be rekindled everywhere. A great country, now Protestant, in the north of Europe, will be converted; by the support of this country all the other nations of the world will be converted. Before all that arrives, great disorders will arrive, in the Church, and everywhere. Then, after [that], our Holy Father the Pope will be persecuted. His successor will be a pontiff that nobody expects. Then, after [that], a great peace will come, but it will not last a long time. A monster will come to disturb it. All that I tell you here will arrive in the other century, at the latest in the year two thousand."

> Maximin Giraud
> (She told me to say it some time before.)
> My Most Holy Father, your holy blessing to one of your sheep.
> Grenoble, July 3,1851.[41]

Maximin's secret also foretells a spiritual renaissance and the future persecution of a pope. After he depicts the persecution of the pope however, Maximin goes on to speak of his replacement by a successor. This would imply that the oppressed pontiff on this occasion would die as a result of the persecution, as he now needs to be replaced. Here too, the prophecy of the Second Pentecost is intertwined with the persecution of a pope. Maximin's secret begins with a reference to the Great Apostasy, before going on to predict a spiritual revival, which will begin with the conversion of a "Protestant country in the north" – a clear reference to England. Maximin foretells that the conversion of England will be the catalyst for the spiritual renewal or Second Pentecost.

The Conversion of England

A few other well-known prophecies foretell the future conversion of England. Perhaps the oldest prophecy concerning a future re-evangelization of England can be attributed to St. Edward the Confessor, who was the penultimate Anglo-Saxon King reigning from 1042 to 1066.[42] The fact that it was made five hundred years before England's departure from the Catholic Church makes it all the more remarkable. According to contemporary reports, St. Edward claimed to have been visited by the

---

[41] Ibid.

[42] The earliest version of this prophecy can be found in the manuscript *Vita Ædwardi Regis,* an anonymous work dated to around 1067 which was commissioned by Queen Edith, the wife of Edward the Confessor. See Barlow, F. (ed.), *Life of King Edward* (New York: Thomas Nelson, 1962), p xxxii

spirits of two pious monks upon his deathbed in 1066, who revealed to him the future destiny of his beloved country:

> The green tree which springs from the trunk
> When thence it shall be severed
> And removed to a distance of three acres
> By no engine or hand of man
> Shall return to its original trunk
> And shall join itself to its root
> Whence first it had origin
> The head shall receive again its verdure
> It shall bear fruit after its flower
> Then shall you be able for certainty
> To hope for amendment [43]

This meaning of this prophecy remained obscure for the next five hundred years, until the separation of the Church of England from Roman Catholicism in 1534 during the reign of King Henry VIII. With the benefit of hindsight, we can determine that the only logical interpretation of this prophecy is that the "separation of the green tree from its parent stem" was the Church of England's rejection of papal supremacy and break with the Catholic Church under King Henry VIII. When the persecution of the Catholic Church in England began to subside in 19th century, contemporary English Catholics upheld that the distance of "three furlongs" that the "green tree" would be separated from its parent stem should be taken to mean the duration of three centuries. The prominent Catholic convert Ambrose Lisle Phillipps quoted a version of this prophecy upon the return of the Catholic hierarchy to England in 1850 after a three hundred year absence, signalling that the saintly king's prediction had come to fruition.[44]

Inspired by the momentous political shifts in his home country, Blessed John Henry Newman also anticipated the renewal of Catholicism in England in his famous 'Second Spring' sermon of 1852.[45] The hopes of the re-conversion of England to Catholicism was a common theme in European prophecy circles, and several well-known variants were in circulation by the 19th century.

A prophecy of the conversion of England attributed to St. Malachy places the event well after the 19th century:

> Ireland will suffer English oppression for a week of centuries, but will preserve her fidelity to God and His Church. At the end of that time she will be delivered, and the English in turn must suffer severe

---

[43] See Luard, H R. (Ed.) *Lives of Edward the Confessor* (London: 1858), p285

[44] Although the version of this prophecy that Phillipps quotes differs from the original on a few points: "The extreme corruption and wickedness of the English nation has provoked the just anger of God. When malice shall have reached the fullness of its measure, God will, in His wrath, send to the English people wicked spirits, who will punish and afflict them with great severity, by separating the green tree from its parent stem the length of three furlongs. But at last this same tree, through the compassionate mercy of God, and without any national (governmental) assistance, shall return to its original root, reflourish and bear abundant fruit." (*Catholic Encyclopaedia*) There is no anachronistic mention of 'England' in the original prophecy, since England did not exist as a nation before the Norman conquest. It seems that an explanatory prologue has been appended to the prophecy at some point after its original composition, suggesting it circulated separately as a wider tradition in medieval English folklore.

[45] Newman, J.H. *The Second Spring* (1852)

chastisement. Ireland, however, will be instrumental in bringing back the English to the unity of Faith.[46]

The week of centuries is usually taken to date from the Norman conquest of Ireland in the late 12th century to the creation of the Irish Free State in 1922. The "serious chastisement" may be interpreted as England's involvement in the First and Second World Wars, which led to the deaths of hundreds of thousands of British servicemen and thousands of civilians. Yet, if this prophecy is correct, then the conversion of England must lie at some point in the future, since it places the event as occurring sometime after the creation of the Irish Free State in 1922.

There are a number of possible scenarios explaining the involvement of Ireland in the prophesied future conversion of England. One of the major influences behind this prophecy appears to be the role of early Irish missionaries in the re-evangelisation of Western Europe after the collapse of the Roman Empire in 476. The loss of the social and political infrastructures provided by the Roman government saw Christianity slide into decay in the western half of the Empire. Irish missionaries such as St. Columbanus and St. Columba of Iona helped to re-establish Christian monasteries and centres of learning in Britain and mainland Europe, insuring the continuation of the religion in the West. This prophecy appears to hint that this particular moment in history is destined to repeat itself, in a foreshadowing of events to come.

The prophecy of Ireland's role in the conversion of England may refer to the influx of Irish immigrants into Britain during the famine years, bringing with them the religion of their homeland. This infused the country with a fresh influx of believers to boost the overall number of Catholics, and helped to spread the faith amongst the poor working class families of England. It may also be a partial reference to role played by the Irish politician Daniel O'Connell in the Catholic Relief Act of 1829, which facilitated the return of the Roman Catholic hierarchy to England in 1850.

The prophecy of the future conversion of England also recalls the tradition of that nation's titular role as the "Dowry of Mary". This particular tradition, which is associated with St. Edward the Confessor and Our Lady of Walsingham (a Marian apparition in Norfolk, England, dating back to 1061), contains connotations of England presented as a wedding gift to Christ, the eschatological Bridegroom:

> Let us rejoice and exult and give him the glory, for the marriage of the Lamb has come, and his Bride has made herself ready; it was granted her to clothe herself with fine linen, bright and pure" (Rev 19:7-8)

Here the Bride is the Church, which has made itself ready for the Bridegroom through the purification of the Second Pentecost. As a result of this purification process, the Church is figuratively allowed to dress herself in pure, virginal linen.

Another of the various prophecies foretelling the future conversion of England was made by a German priest, Ven. Bartholomew Holzhauser (d.1658): "After

---

[46] The *Catholic Encyclopaedia* states that "This prophecy is said to have been copied by the learned Dom Mabillon from an ancient manuscript preserved at Clairvaux, and transmitted by him to the martyred successor of Oliver Plunkett." Jean Mabillon was a French Benedictine monk and scholar who edited the works of St. Bernard of Clairvaux, publishing them in 1667. So he may have discovered this document while researching the works on St. Bernard.

desolation has reached its peak in England, peace will be restored and England will return to the Catholic faith with greater fervour than ever before...."[47] Like the prophecy of Maximin's secret, Holzhauser also states that the spiritual revival will be effected through the conversion of England: "... by the support of this country all the other nations of the world will be converted".

The future conversion of England seems a greater possibility now than at almost any other stage in the five hundred years since the English Reformation. Many Anglicans are seriously disaffected with the Church of England hierarchy's increasingly vacillating stance to the pressures of secularism. Much to the dismay of many traditional Anglicans, the Church of England has been capitulating to modern secular values for the past twenty years, with many bishops allowing decidedly un-Christian practices such as the ordination of female priests and bishops and the toleration of homosexual relationships.

The incursion of these secular values into a previously traditionally conservative Christian sect highlights the dangers to the cohesiveness of an organised religion without a single supreme voice of authority. Conservative Anglicans yearning to practice a more authentic form of Christianity are increasingly drawn towards the assurances of Roman Catholicism – a fact that has not went unnoticed by the Vatican. In 2009, Pope Benedict XVI issued an apostolic constitution facilitating the transition from Anglicanism to full communion with Rome, allowing entire Anglican branches, such as the Traditional Anglican Communion, to enter into unity with the Holy See.

The constitution declared that Anglicans wishing to convert to Roman Catholicism would be able to retain Anglican liturgy and tradition, and keep a certain degree of autonomy.[48] In 2010, a "first wave" of five Church of England bishops announced that they would be converting to Catholicism, creating the Personal Ordinariate of Our Lady of Walsingham in January 2011, bringing hundreds of Anglican parishioners into the Catholic fold with them.

We can be sure that many more will follow if the Anglican Church continues on its path of capitulation to modern secular values.

The "Glorious Olive" of St Malachy

Another piece of prophetic "evidence" which can be used to determine the identity of the Two Witnesses can be found among the famous list of popes traditionally thought to have been compiled by St. Malachy. This widely renowned 12th century Irish saint has been attributed authorship to one of the most famous prophetic writings outside of the Bible. Whilst on pilgrimage to Rome, St. Malachy is said to have compiled a list of 112 Latin mottoes, each containing a reference concerning each of the popes from his own day down to the end of the world. Many of these prophecies have proved to be startlingly accurate, particularly since the beginning of the modern era.

The prophecies of St. Malachy have been accorded a great deal of significance in

---

[47] Holzhauser, B. *Interpretatio Apocalypsis usque ad cap. XV, v. 5*

[48] Benedict XVI, *Anglicanorum Coetibus* (Vatican City: Libreria Editrace Vaticana, 2009)

recent times, as the motto which corresponds to the present pope – Benedict XVI, is the penultimate name on this list, and there is only one more pope left on the list after the incumbent pontiff. If correct, then this leaves us with the frightening prospect that the end-time will occur at some stage during the pontificate of the next pope.

Interest in the prophecies of St. Malachy usually peaks around the time of a papal conclave, when commentators attempt to speculate on who will assume the role of the next pontiff by comparing the details of the frontrunners with the relevant Latin motto. However each of the mottoes are typically vague, and the connection linking them to the corresponding pope is not always immediately obvious. For example, sometimes the motto is interpreted to allude to a family coat of arms, or the name of a place where the pope lived or was stationed during their ministry. Therefore this would make pre-empting the election of a pope from the prophecies of St. Malachy alone extremely difficult indeed.

Maelmhaedhoc Ó Morgair (1094-1148), better known to us as St. Malachy, was the archbishop of Armagh and primate of the Catholic Church in Ireland during the early 12th century. He was also a close friend of the famed St. Bernard of Clairvaux, with whom he stayed during his first pilgrimage to Rome in 1140. St. Malachy fell sick while at Clairvaux as he set out on a second pilgrimage to Rome, and died in St. Bernard's arms on 2nd November 1148. St. Bernard wrote a biographical memoir of the saint's life – *The Life of Malachy*. Although this work states that Malachy was endowed with the gift of prophecy, no mention is made of his prophecies of the popes. This glaring omission is but one of the arguments used to question the veracity of the claim that these prophecies were indeed written by the medieval Irish bishop.

According to the tradition behind the prophecies of the popes, the saint had received a vision while he made his pilgrimage to Rome in order to petition Pope Innocent II for pallia for the Sees of Cashel and Armagh. During his stay in the Eternal City, Malachy is said to have fallen into a trance-like state, in which he saw a great list unfolding before him containing 112 mottoes that referred to each of the popes (as well as some antipopes) from Celestine II (d.1144), down to the end of time. He then committed this list of names to writing and gave the document to Pope Innocent II. This work was subsequently lost however, supposedly buried in the Vatican archives until it was rediscovered around the year 1590. St. Malachy's prophecies were then published for the first time in 1595 by the Benedictine historian Arnold Wion, in his book *Lignum vitae*.

The major source of contention for the authenticity of these prophecies of St. Malachy is the fact that the mottoes are more accurate for the popes on the list prior to the date of its "discovery" circa 1590. The list shifts from being chiefly comprised of straightforward links to the corresponding popes prior to the publication date, to a disproportionately higher amount of vague connections after they first appeared in 1595. The names of the popes on the list before 1590 have straightforward connections to corresponding pontiff, while after this date some of the interpretations made to conform to the related pontificate appear to be more contrived. This would render the pre-1590's predictions to be *vaticinium ex eventu* (prophecy after the event).

Another factor used to argue against the authenticity of the prophecies attributed to St. Malachy is the fact that various lists of a similar nature were also enjoying popularity during the Middle Ages. A series of symbolic pictures of future popes falsely attributed to Joachim de Fiore entitled *Vaticinia de Summis Pontificibus* (Prophecies of the Supreme Pontiffs) were in circulation during the same general time period.[49]

A similar work, the *Vaticinia Michaelis Nostradami de Futuri Christi Vicarii ad Cesarem Filium* (Prophecies of Michel Nostradamus on the Future Vicars of Christ to Cesar his son, or *Vaticinia Nostradami* for short) – a series of eighty watercolour images of future popes, also emanates from this era. The *Vaticinia Nostradami*, or "Lost Book of Nostradamus", was discovered in 1994 by the Italian journalist Enza Massa. A library card attached to the original manuscript in the *Biblioteca Nazionale Centrale di Roma* by Carthusian monks claims that these images were made by Nostradamus, which he then bequeathed to his son Cesar.[50] The card goes on to state that the manuscript was brought to Rome by Cesar in order to be donated to Cardinal Maffeo Barberini, the future Pope Urban VIII (r.1623-1644). It then found its way into the National Central Library of Rome where it was subsequently buried for over three hundred years.

Since this type of document was much in vogue during the late Renaissance, taken together with the fact that there are a greater number of prophetic "hits" prior to its publication date of 1595; it is argued that St. Malachy's list of popes should be dated to the late 16th century.[51] However the prophecies attributed to St. Malachy continues to remain of interest to prophecy enthusiasts, as many of the predictions made for the popes after 1590 have also proven to be incredibly accurate. This would suggest that, whether they were written by Malachy or not, whoever wrote these phrases does appear to have been endowed with the gift of prophecy.[52]

It is beyond the scope of this work to list all of the post-publication phrases attributed to St. Malachy that are considered to contain a degree of accuracy. However it should be worthwhile to contemplate some of the more noteworthy instances. Among the most highly esteemed of the post-16th century prophecies of Malachy is the motto which corresponds to the pontificate of Pius IX – *Crux de cruce*, "Cross from a cross". The first cross in this motto has been taken by interpreters as a symbol of suffering, while the second is construed as a reference to the coat of arms of the Italian House of Savoy, which bears a large white cross on a red background.[53] Interpreted in this fashion, the phrase has thus been taken to mean "suffering caused by the cross [of Savoy]".

King Victor-Emmanuel of the House of Savoy annexed the Papal States in 1870, bringing the temporal authority of the papacy over central Italy to an end. As a result of these actions, the papacy was left without official sovereignty until the signing of the Lateran Treaty, which led to the creation of the Vatican City State in 1929.

---

[49] See Reeves, M. *The Influence of Prophecy in the Later Middle Ages* pp453-462

[50] Although it is highly unlikely that these are genuine works of Nostradamus.

[51] Although we will acknowledge this later dating of Malachy's list as the most likely theory and that the titular "Malachy" may be a pseudonym for someone writing in the late 16th century; for the sake of simplicity we shall continue to refer to the list as belonging to "St. Malachy".

[52] As is argued by John Hogue in his book *The Last Pope* (Shaftesbury: Element Books, 2000) which should be consulted for a more in-depth analysis of the prophecies of St. Malachy

[53] Hogue, J *The Last Pope* pp230-238

Fig. 7 The coat of arms of the House of Savoy

Another much vaunted post-Wion prophecy in Malachy's list is that concerning Leo XIII (r.1878-1903). The phrase relating to this pontiff is *Lumen in caelo* – "a light in the sky". This prophecy is said to have been fulfilled in the fact that Leo XIII's rather striking coat of arms contains a heraldic representation of a comet.

Perhaps one of the most accurate predictions made by any of the prophecies of St. Malachy is the motto associated with the pontificate of Benedict XV (r.1914-1922): *Religio depopulata* – "Religion Depopulated". The reign of Pope Benedict XV, which began at the outbreak of the First World War, would also witness the Bolshevik Revolution in 1917 and rise of the militantly atheistic Soviet Union in 1922, as well as the Spanish flu epidemic of 1918.

Fig. 8 The papal coat of arms of Pope Leo XIII.

The Soviet Union adopted an aggressive policy of suppression towards religion of any kind, basing its principles on the Marxist ideology that religion was an opiate for the masses. According to Marx, religion kept humanity steeped in an illusory sense of contentment that hindered it from realizing its full potential. When the Soviet Union began to implement Marx's reactionary ideals against religion as a matter of government policy, it would cause one of the greatest mass apostasies from the Christian religion in history. Christians were deterred from practicing their faith either through open persecution or through state sponsored anti-religious propaganda. The Marxist-Leninist strain of Communism would eventually spread beyond the borders of the Soviet Union, taking root in Maoist China, Vietnam, North Korea, Loas and Cuba. The end result of the crusade against religion that began during the pontificate of Benedict XV would ensure that one half of the world's population would live under atheistic regimes from 1950 to 1990.[54]

The prophecies of St. Malachy have proved to score a number of other "hits" during the twentieth century, with the mottoes for popes John XXIII (r.1958-1963), Paul VI (r.1963-1978) and John Paul II (r.1978-2005) all proving to contain a degree of accuracy. The phrase for John XXIII, *Pastor et nauta* – "a shepherd and sailor" is particularly apt for this pope, as before he ascended papal throne, Cardinal Angelo Roncalli was the patriarch of Venice – a city famed for its maritime culture. Paul VI's motto *Flos florum* – "flower of flowers" is fulfilled by his coat of arms, which bears three *fleurs-de-lis*.

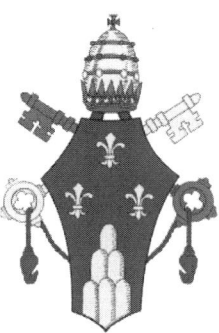

Fig. 9 Papal coat of arms of Pope Paul VI

The phrase ascribed to John Paul II, *De labore solis* – "from the labour of the Sun", is another particularly striking prediction, as Karol Wojtyla was born during a partial eclipse of the Sun on 18th May 1920, and was buried on the day of partial solar eclipse on 8th April 2005.

The phrase attributed to Benedict XVI, *De gloria olivae* – "From the glory of the olive", has already been hailed as another accurate prediction by St. Malachy aficionados, as there is a link in Catholic tradition between the name "Benedict" and the word "olive". Before Cardinal Joseph Ratzinger took over the reins of the papacy as Benedict XVI in April 2005, some prophecy watchers predicted that the successor to John Paul II would come from the Benedictine order of the Olivetans.[55] When Cardinal Ratzinger adopted the papal name Benedict XVI, this was seen by some to bridge the connection. However

---

[54] McGrath, A. *The Twilight of Atheism* (London: Rider, 2004) p67
[55] For example Geoffrey Ashe states in his work *The Book of Prophecy* (London: Orion, 1999), which was published well before the election of Benedict XVI, that "*Gloria Olivae* … might apply to a pope from a branch of the Benedictines called Olivetans." p125

it appears that we should look elsewhere for the real fulfilment of this prophecy.

If we study the prophecies of St. Malachy in a little more detail, we may note that towards the end of the list the mottoes become distinctly more apocalyptic in tone. The pairing of the phrases "From the Half Moon" (for Pope John Paul I) and "From the Labour of the Sun" recall the astronomical phenomena described by Jesus and the prophets as accompanying the arrival of the last days.

> Immediately after the tribulation of those days the sun will be darkened, and the moon will not give its light, and the stars will fall from heaven, and the powers of the heavens will be shaken. (Matt. 24:29)

The eschatological overtones in the phrase *De Labore Solis* are inescapable, as the term "labour of the Sun" is a direct reference to the birth pangs of the Woman adorned with the Sun in Rev 12.

> And a great sign appeared in heaven: a woman clothed with the sun, with the moon under her feet, and on her head a crown of twelve stars. She was pregnant and was crying out in birth pains and the agony of giving birth. (Rev 12:1-2)

The epilogue to St. Malachy's prophecies concerning the reign of the pope who will succeed Benedict XVI is thoroughly apocalyptic in character, and describes the final persecution of the church, the destruction of Rome, and the Last Judgment.

> In the final persecution of the Holy Roman Church there will reign Peter the Roman, who will feed his flock among many tribulations; after which the seven-hilled city will be destroyed and the dreadful judge will judge the people.

Amongst this cluster of apocalyptic imagery towards the end of Malachy's list, we would expect the motto relating to Benedict XVI to be similarly imbued with eschatological symbolism. Indeed it seems that the phrase *Gloria Olivae* – "the glory of the olives" does have such significance. This phrase recalls the words of the Apocalypse concerning the Two Witnesses, who are described as "the two olive trees and the two lamp stands that stand before the Lord of the earth." (Rev 11:4). If this prophecy is intended to reference this passage in the Book of Revelation, then it would equate the current pope, Benedict XVI with one of the Two Witnesses – one of the two "olive trees" described in the Apocalypse. So does St. Malachy list of popes suggest that Pope Benedict XVI is the martyr-pope foretold in Catholic prophetic tradition? If so, how could such an event come to take place? And what would be the motivation for the assassination of Benedict XVI?

The pope has long been a symbol of hatred for Muslim extremists. For many Islamists, the conflict between the Crusaders and Saracens during the Middle Ages is not a sad and brutal episode confined to history; it is an on-going process still relevant to the modern age. Some groups continue to envisage the pope as the symbolic figurehead of the Christian West, and as such, the leader of the modern Western "crusade" against Islam. We need only to look at the al Qaeda plot to assassinate John Paul II during his visit to the Philippines in 1995 to gain an idea of this sort of "crusader" mentality.

Pope Benedict XVI exacerbated the Islamists' contempt for the papacy during a lecture delivered in Regensburg on September 12, 2006. During the now infamous

Regensburg Address, the Pope incurred the anger of Muslims around the world by citing the Byzantine Emperor Manuel II Paleologus (1350-1425) in a critique of the Islamic concept of *Jihad* (literally "struggle", but most often interpreted as "holy war"). The Pope quoted Paleologus' words: "Show me just what Muhammad brought that was new, and there you will find things only evil and inhuman, such as his command to spread by the sword the faith he preached."[56]

Although the Pope had made clear that these words were Manuel II Paleologus' and not his own, his quote was taken out of context with the rest of his speech and was soon widely circulated around the Islamic media. Needless to say, this twisted interpretation of the Pope's lecture did not endear the newly elected pontiff to the wider Muslim world. The reality behind this furore was that the media's presentation of the Pope's words was actually a distortion of the central message of the speech – which was a call for greater dialogue between Christianity and Islam.

Pope Benedict's lecture was met with a response that was the complete antithesis of the actual content of his message. Protesters took to the streets in various Arab countries and sporadic rioting soon followed, forcing the Pope into issuing a clarification of his statement, which was appended to the official Vatican document. Although the clarification of his lecture helped to quell many moderates, it was rejected outright in other quarters. *Fatawa* were issued by Sheikh Abubukar Hassan Malin of the Supereme Islamic Courts Council in Somalia and the Lashkar-e-Toiba in Pakistan, urging Muslims to kill the Pope for his blasphemous remarks against the Prophet Muhammad. Two Somali gunmen murdered an elderly Italian nun in reprisal for the Pope's comments; and in a spate of attacks against Christians in Iraq, an Assyrian Christian priest was kidnapped and beheaded. This episode only helped to reinforce the extremist's anti-Western polemic and to further polarize the division between the papacy and Islamic fundamentalism.

On 20th March 2008, Osama bin Laden accused the re-publication of the images involved in the 2006 Danish cartoon row of being part of a new crusade against Islam involving Pope Benedict XVI. Bin Laden warned of a "severe" reaction in Europe to this decision, which caused an outrage among Muslims during the original controversy in 2006. Could this speech be a threat against the Pope? Given the current political climate, Benedict XVI, more so than any other pope before him, is a prime target for assassination by Muslim extremists.

If the papal prophecies of St. Malachy connect the current pope, Benedict XVI, with the Two Witnesses of Rev 11 and the martyr-pope of Catholic tradition, then according to this prophecy a great spiritual renewal of the Church will begin during the reign of Benedict XVI, who may then go on to join the ever-increasing list of Christian martyrs.

---

[56] "Lecture of the Holy Father: Faith, Reason and the University Memories and Reflections" (Vatican City: Libreria Editrice Vaticana, 2006). The quote which caused the furore originally appeared in "*Dialogue Held With A Certain Persian, the Worthy Mouterizes, in Anakara of Galatia*" written in 1391.

Conclusion

By comparing the various prophecies we have studied above, we have seen how the idea of the martyrdom of a pope connected with a spiritual revolution appears to be a universal theme in Catholic prophecy. The prophecies of Fatima, La Salette, St. Malachy, St. John Bosco and the Angelic Pope all point towards this event, which also ties in with the biblical prophecies of the Second Pentecost/eschatological outpouring of the Spirit, the ministry of the Two Witnesses and the Great Apostasy. The main complimentary segments of these individual prophecies can be summed up below as follows:

Joel 2:28; Acts 2:17:
Eschatological Outpouring of the Spirit – commonly interpreted as a spiritual reawakening at the End-time.

Malachi 4:5-6
Elijah will come before the day of Judgement to "turn the hearts of fathers to their children and the hearts of children to their fathers, lest I come and strike the land with a decree of utter destruction."

Matthew 24:14
"And this gospel of the kingdom will be proclaimed throughout the whole world as a testimony to all nations, and then the end will come."

Book of Revelation:
Rev 5:6 mentions "The seven spirits of God [= Holy Spirit] sent out into all the earth", which is equated with the outpouring of the Spirit. Ministry and martyrdom of the Two Witnesses – symbolically referred to as "Olive Trees". It is implied that the Two Witnesses will inaugurate the eschatological outpouring of the Spirit/spiritual revival.

Angelic Pope (Various):
Angelic Pope and Great Monarch will bring about a spiritual revival before the coming of the Antichrist.

Secrets of Fatima:
Assassination of a pope. Promised conversion of Russia and triumph of the immaculate heart of the Virgin Mary.

St. John Bosco:
Wind coming from "two pillars" to restore the ship/Church (which may allude to the ministry of the Two Witnesses and spiritual revival). Assassination of a pope after the Second Vatican Council.

Secrets of La Salette:
Period of apostasy before a spiritual revival. Conversion of "a Protestant country in the north". Persecution and implied death of a pope.

Malachy's List of Popes:
De Gloria Olivae "Glory of the Olives"– reign of Benedict XVI. Implies a connection with the two olive trees or Two Witnesses of Rev 11.

What could be the principal cause of this great social upheaval? What event could spawn a worldwide religious revival and the martyrdom of the persons responsible for bringing it about? As we have already discussed, the present age is widely acknowledged by interpreters of biblical prophecy to be the era of the Great Apostasy foretold to take place before the end of the world. Religion in the once-Christian West is in a state of rapid decline, and atheism, agnosticism and deism are currently the dominant theistic worldviews of the modern era. At present, the trend towards these modes of thought seems irreversible. The world's secular governments and state media endorse belief systems such as atheism and agnosticism in order to curb dissonance with nationalistic dogma and ensure allegiance to the state over organized religion.

Non-theistic beliefs have enjoyed enormous popularity in the modern era due to their innate ability to cater to its adherents' self-interests, allowing them to personally define their own moral code. The prevalence of such belief systems has led to the widespread acceptance of moral relativism. As Ivan Karamazov was led to conclude in Fyodor Dostoevsky's *The Brothers Karamazov*, in the absence of God, anything is permissible. By shifting away from moral absolutism in their rejection of religion, atheism and agnosticism (which logically lead to moral subjectivism) allow the individual to define their own ethical code without the threat of any judgment in the afterlife. These spiritual worldviews perfectly square with the increasing prominence of hedonism in modern culture, leaving many people instantly drawn to belief systems which best suit their own lifestyle choices. The emerging prominence of these secular philosophies has led to the creation of a consumer society for religious beliefs, where individuals can "shop" for a spirituality that fits with their own preferred tastes.

Without the belief in a revealed Deity, the religious void which Jean-Paul Sartre described as the "God-shaped hole in human consciousness" has been filled with beliefs that mesh with the liberty offered by moral relativism, such as New Age mysticism and the associated resurgence of astrology and occult magic. By pandering to the appeals of egocentricity, atheism, agnosticism and deism have lasting popular appeal; and short of Divine intervention, they will not easily be displaced. It would require a major miraculous event, eclipsing even that of Fatima, to inspire such a spiritual revolution in the modern age. And if the Catholic Church it is to gain the massive amounts of conversions foretold by numerous prophecies, this miracle would have to be associated in some way with Catholicism.

The prophecies of the re-conversion of the West and the Last Emperor contain parallels with the conversion of the Roman Empire to Christianity under the auspices of Constantine. And just as the destruction of Rome took place shortly after the Empire's conversion to Christianity, so too will the modern world collapse after the gift of the Second Pentecost.

We are left to ponder a crucial question concerning this future spiritual renaissance – why are the Two Witnesses who spearhead this new religious impetus met with such opposition and hostility as is described in the Apocalypse? The Book of Revelation tells us that the Two Witnesses are killed by "the beast that comes out of the Abyss" – an event which is alluded to in the various other prophecies concerning the martyr-pope, and the medieval prophecies which hold that the Angelic Pope and Great Monarch will be succeeded by the Antichrist.

This reaction of open hostility suggests that the Two Witnesses will be in direct opposition to the current anti-religious sentiment which will eventually pave the way for the coming of the Antichrist. It also suggests that the spiritual renewal will not be universal, and that a substantial number of people will still refuse to embrace the one true faith. Rather, the Second Pentecost will be reserved for those whose hearts are already open to it – the teachers of falsehood will no longer be able to deceive the elect (Matt 24:24), but the evil-doer will still do evil, while the righteous will go on to do what is right (Rev 22:10). The spiritually-minded will be drawn back to the true path towards God, but evil people will still find ways to persist in their disbelief, and one can only expect that they will treat this new religious revival with great indignation.

As a result of this opposition, the Apocalypse predicts that the Two Witnesses will be killed by their adversaries. But what will these eschatological prophets do or preach that would cause so much upset? How in the midst of a spiritual revival could they be met with such hostility that their deaths are met by widespread rejoicing? What could cause so much unpopularity?

The Book of Revelation tells us that these religious leaders will stand in opposition to the rule and system of the Antichrist. It seems that at least part of this diabolic system is already in existence in the modern age, and its denouncement has the potential to create such a polarization between believers and unbelievers. As we shall see in the next chapter, there is good reason to believe that the prophecy concerning the number of the Beast has already reached fulfilment in the age of social-communications technology. And if this technology was condemned by the Catholic Church, it could have some major repercussions throughout the world...

CHAPTER THREE

The Worldwide Web of Deceit

The passage concerning the number of the Beast is for many the pivotal moment of the Book of Revelation. This, perhaps the most well-known of all the prophecies of the Bible, has captured the imaginations of countless millions. As well as being a central component of Christian end-time belief, the prophecy of the number of the Beast has provided an endless source of inspiration for fiction writers and film makers alike. The key to the number of the Beast's resonance with popular culture lies in the intrigue behind its cryptic meaning. It lays each of us down with a personal challenge – calling us decipher the puzzle for ourselves, and find the true meaning behind this elusive text. Find the man whose name matches up to this number and you have found the Antichrist himself...

However the task of attempting to identify the Antichrist through various calculations of the names of eminent historical figures has proved to be one of the most elaborate wild-goose chases of history. Accusations have ranged from the more obvious choices to the positively ludicrous. Each of the varying methods that have been employed in order to discern the identity of the Antichrist have continuously failed to produce any findings worthy of credence outside of a 1st century AD context. Attempting to verify the identity of the Antichrist in advance is an approach that is much too speculative to be in any way reliable. There are simply too many people and too many variables involved, making it virtually impossible to use the number of the Beast to be able to establish the identity of the Antichrist in advance. This aspect of the prophecy will only be able to be ascertained in retrospect, if indeed it does has such an application beyond the 1st century. Therefore, instead of searching for *whom* this number may refer, it would be a decidedly more effective approach to focus on to *what* it may refer to.

While there have been many excellent surveys of the Apocalypse by both the most erudite of scholars and the sharpest amateurs, sadly, some of the most popular interpretations of the number of the Beast have emanated from paranoid radicals and apocalyptic cults with rather extreme ideas. Such groups have discredited any serious attempts to study possible futurist applications of this aspect of biblical prophecy. As a consequence, any effort to equate the number of the Beast with an approximate fulfilment in modern times is usually met with either cynicism or ridicule. Repeated attempts to identify the contemporary meaning of this prophecy have been made *ad nauseam*. A situation which has only helped to desensitize a usually open minded public, turning even the most impartial observer into a hard-nosed sceptic.

However we should not let this factor deter mainstream Christians from examining an important part of their belief system. The conviction that the eschatological prophecies contained in the Bible will someday come to pass is a central tenet of the Christian faith. As such, the prophecy of number of the Beast is as much a part of Christian belief as any other scripturally authoritative passage of the New Testament. It is as equally valid an eschatological belief as say, the doctrine of the Second Coming of Jesus, or the General Resurrection of humanity at the Last Judgment.

During the course of the present chapter, we will examine the prospect that the prophecy concerning the number of the Beast may have already achieved fulfilment in the relatively recent past, albeit in a rather unexpected manner. The idea that this infamous eschatological prophecy could have come to fruition unbeknownst to the vast majority of the world's population may prove difficult to believe for the more sceptical observer. And rightly so. After all, it seems impossible to imagine how so many God-fearing Christians could be inadvertently duped into accepting such a blasphemous "boundary-marking" device. Surely there would have been some warning signs to ward the Christian elect away from this devilish scheme?

Yet the Book of Revelation does not suggest that there would be any immediately perceptible warning signs to alert believers to the fulfilment of this prophecy. If it had occurred in an overtly conspicuous or literalistic manner, with 666 being industrially stamped on the forehead or palms of every living human, then it would be difficult to imagine that it would be accepted as passively as is described in the Book of Revelation. Surely some sort of resistance would be expected. Yet no form of revolt against this tyrannical scheme is spoken of in the Apocalypse. It implies that people across every social and religious denomination will accept this "number" in order to engage in any form of economic transaction, and that they would do so without any form of hesitation:

Also it causes all, both small and great, both rich and poor, both free and slave, to be marked on the right hand or the forehead, so that no one can buy or sell unless he has the mark, that is, the name of the beast or the number of its name. (Rev 13:16-17)

There is no indication of any reluctance on behalf of the people. Nor is there any refusal to participate, as would be expected from suspecting Christians. The only way an event of this magnitude could come into realization would be if a great deal of subtlety was involved. It would require deception rather than coercion. Indeed Revelation states time and again that a strategy of deceit is used to mislead the inhabitants of the earth into accepting the mark of the Beast (Rev 13:14; 18:23; 20:3, 8, 10). Rev 19:20 explicitly elaborates that deception is the primary means used to effect the willing cooperation of the inhabitants of the earth:

And the beast was captured, and with it the false prophet who in its presence had done the signs *by which he deceived those who had received the mark of the beast* and those who worshiped its image.

If the earth's inhabitants were aware of this ploy, then it is only logical to assume that Christians would refuse to participate in any such act imbued with Satanic connotations. The Book of Revelation therefore implicitly suggests that everyone will remain ignorant of the situation until they have already accepted the use of the number as an inescapable aspect of daily living. Christians and non-Christians alike will be unwitting participants duped into accepting a "number" as an essential means of commerce.

Some modern interpreters of the eschatological prophecies of the Bible have forwarded the suggestion that the use of microchip technology will somehow be involved in the implementation of the prophecy of the mark of the Beast.[1] According to this hypothesis, people will be implanted with a RFID chip that in some way bears the number of the Beast, possibly contained in a barcode, in a similar manner to how modern pets are micro-chipped. These microchips will apparently be required in order to participate in any form of economic transaction. In this scenario, the chips will be injected under the skin of the palm or forehead, supposedly for the perfect ambient temperature conditions generated in these areas.

There are a number of serious objections to the above interpretation of the mark of the Beast however. An operation on this scale could hardly be described as subtle. We would need to postulate a Satanic conspiracy so pervasive that it would require the cooperation of virtually all the world's governments, civil servants and law enforcement agencies. With so many people involved in this global-wide conspiracy, it would be impossible to keep such a diabolical scheme hidden from public knowledge. Suspicions would be aroused from the very outset, prompting numerous investigations that would eventually expose the true implications of accepting such a procedure. If everyone was aware of the Satanic character of these microchip implants, they would have to willingly embrace the mark despite being fully aware of the spiritual consequences involved.

Such a proposition cannot be sustained once we take a more rational approach to the fulfilment of this prophecy. Are we really supposed to expect that millions of devout Christians would engage so readily in such an overly elaborate diabolic plot? That the world's governments would set aside years of conflict and petty squabbling, only to unite under the banner of Satanism, and then attempt to implement one of the world's best known prophecies in a so brazenly transparent fashion? The only conceivable way that the number of the Beast could become a reality is if it was executed in a manner so inconspicuous that we could be using it right now without even realizing. Its mass acceptance by the world's population would necessitate it to be done in a way that is not immediately palpable. To this end, it seems that these objectives have already been met.

Before we can explore the futurist aspect of this prophecy any further, we must first turn to examine how it was understood in its original setting. By attempting to put ourselves inside the mind of the author, we might better understand any meaning it may provide for us today.

Gematria – the Original Meaning of 666

Scholars are unanimous in maintaining that Rev 13:15-18 is firmly set within the social, political and economic backdrop against which the book was written. The mark of the Beast mirrors the seal which God places on his followers elsewhere in the Bible, including Revelation itself. (Exod 13: 9, Deut 6: 8, Ezek 9: 4, Rev 7: 2-4). Most theologians feel that the number of the Beast is an allusion to the name of a figure contemporaneous with John, and have formulated many compelling theories as to whom

---

[1] Based largely upon Mary Stewert Relfe's book *When Your Money Fails* (Montgomery, AL.: Ministries, 1981), commentators gradually shifted from credit cards, to barcodes and then to RFID chips to explain how people may be made to use the number of the Beast. See Haggith, D. *Prophets of the Apocalypse* (London: HarperCollins, 2001) pp118-120 for an example of this belief.

this number refers. It is beyond the scope of this work to present a comprehensive list of all the suggestions put forward throughout the years, but it will be worthwhile to take the time to note a few of the most convincing explanations.

By far the most popular solution offered is that the number of the Beast is the numerical equivalent of the name Nero Caesar. As the first emperor to persecute Christians, Nero was the prototype for all would be Antichrists, and would have strongly figured as the chief antigonist for the Johannine Christians. Scholars have shown how Nero is perhaps the most likely candidate behind John's cryptic reference to the Beast. It will prove helpful for our own purposes to elaborate on how the name of this maniacal emperor equates with the number of the Beast.

The process of equating the name of Nero with the number of the Beast involves the use of gematria,[2] a popular form of word-play that derived from the fact that letters of various ancient alphabets were also used as numerals. One of the most widely attested usages of number symbolism in ancient Judaism, gematria (a Hebrew word thought to be derived from the Greek γεομετρια *geometria* – geometry) was a system widely used in ancient esoteric religion which assigned a numerical value to a word. Before the revolutionary innovation of decimals in the separate Hindu-Arabic numeral system we use today, the substitution of letters for numbers was prevalent throughout almost every ancient language. A common and still widely used example of this technique can be found in the use of Roman numerals. But while Roman numerals used only seven letters of the Latin alphabet as number symbols, every letter in the Hebrew alphabet was used in its numerical system. Therefore each letter in a Hebrew word also held a numerical equivalent.

The numerical value of a word was calculated by adding together the value of each letter. Thus the Hebrew word חי *chai*, meaning life, had the numerical value of 18 (ח = 8) + (י = 10) = 18. This imbued the number 18 with a symbolical significance for Jews. The number 18 is considered lucky in Judaism to this day, and during births, Bar and Bat Mitzvahs, and weddings, it is common for monetary gifts to be given in multiples of 18.

Gematria focuses on the interrelationship between letters words, and phrases, and associates words with the same numerical value on a symbolic level. Words with equal numerical value were considered to lend an insight into the shared properties and characteristics of the words involved. The most common use of early gematria was concerned with determining the symbolic value of people's names. But it was also used as a hermeneutical tool by ancient biblical commentators. A Jewish text dated to between 200-500AD known as the *Haggadah* contains 32 hermeneutical "rules" used for interpreting scripture, which are known as the 32 *Middot*. Rule 29 of the 32 *Middot* is the use of gematria – a fact which shows how seriously this process was taken in ancient Judaism.[3]

The early rabbis sought to find new depths in sacred Scripture by carefully studying every minutiae of the text, including the numerical value of words. The process

---

[2] The word gematria is used specifically for the Jewish practice of this form of cryptography. The Greek version of this type of numerology is known as isopsephy.

[3] See Strack, H.L. Stemberger, G. *Introduction to the Talmud and Midrash* (Edinburgh: T.&T. Clark, 1991) pp95-98

of gematria assumes that the numerical equivalence behind such words are the product of God's design. Since the spoken Word was the agent through which God created the world, each letter of the Hebrew alphabet was considered to represent a creative force in itself. Hebrew was considered by esoteric Judaism to be the original Edenic language spoken by mankind before the confusion of languages at the building of the tower of Babel (Gen 11:1-9). For Jews, Hebrew was the language of God Himself, and therefore the language through which the world was created.

It was thought that the numerical equivalence between words was more than mere coincidence. Numerical equality pointed to a bond between words that transcended normal means of deduction. For Jewish mystical adepts, numerically equated words were purposefully linked by the divine intellect at the moment of creation, and were waiting to be discovered and explained. So passages of Scripture were fastidiously studied by Jewish mystics searching for further illumination on sacred texts by finding and comparing numerical equivalences.

Numbers with apparent spiritual overtones recur throughout the Bible. The great flood lasted forty days, the Israelites spent forty years wandering in the wilderness, Elijah travelled for forty days and forty nights to reach Horeb, and Jesus fasted for forty days in the desert. The number seven held a similar if not greater importance to the biblical writers, and nowhere is this more prevalent in the Book of Revelation. We have seven trumpets, seven seals, seven bowls, seven churches, seven spirits of God. Upon a literary analysis, scholars have even determined to varying degrees that Revelation's very structure has been arranged to conform to this number.

The ancient Jewish rabbis took particular interest in attempting to find esoteric meanings behind names and numbers in the Torah. For example, in Gen 32:5 when Jacob said "I have lived with Laban", the Rabbis discovered that the numerical equivalent of Laban is 613, which in turn was thought to symbolise the 613 precepts of the Mosaic Law. So "I have lived with Laban" then took on the new meaning of "I have lived according to the Mosaic Law". This form of textual manipulation was thus used by the Rabbis as evidence that the pre-Exodus patriarchs had intuitively obeyed the same Law that was revealed to Moses on Mt. Sinai.

The later use of gematria in the Kabbalah (an esoteric form of Jewish mysticism developed during the Middle Ages in the *Zohar*, which claims to have its roots in the teachings of Rabbi Shimon Bar Yorchai in the 2nd century AD) assigned a spiritual value to each number. For instance, 10 is considered to be the number of perfection, as it is represented by the Hebrew letter י (yodh), the first letter of the divine tetragrammaton

יהוה (Yahweh). Seven – the number of days of creation, was considered to be the number of completion. As the number six fell just short of the number of completion, it was considered to be the number of imperfection. Man was created on the sixth day, illustrating his imperfect nature. Thus 666, the number of man, was the superlative form of imperfection, and the person this number represented was the personification of imperfection itself.

This fascination with numerical order and sequence in the Torah would later give rise to the notion of a "Bible code" in some strains of Judaic thought, which suggests that every major event from the past, present and future is encoded within the pages of the

Pentateuch.[4]

The practice of gematria was not exclusive to ancient Judaism and early Christianity however. The earliest attested usage of gematria can be found on an inscription dedicated to King Sargon II of Assyria (727-707BC), which states that the king built the wall of Khorsabad 16,283 cubits long in order to correspond with the numerical value of his name. So it is thought that the origins of gematria may be traced back to Mesopotamia.

Gematria was also widely used throughout the ancient Mediterranean through the use of the Greek language. Like the Hebrew and Aramaic alphabets, the Greek alphabet also used each of its constituent letters to represent numerals. So the Greek language could also convert words into a numerical equivalent. The usage of this practice in Greek was known as isopsephy.[5]

It is contested whether the Jewish practice of gematria was influenced by the Greek isopsephy, or whether it found its way into Hebrew usage earlier through Mesopotamia.[6] Despite these scholarly uncertainties, the use of isopsephy is known to be of considerable antiquity. There are many references to this Greek form of gematria on historical record, many of which predate Christianity. A reference to isopsephy is thought to lie behind a traditional oral teaching attributed to Pythagoras, which states "What is most wise? Number or that which gives names to things?"[7] Deissmann cites two graffiti written in Greek found in the ruins of Pompeii illustrating the use of this practice which read "I love her whose number is 545 [ΦΜΕ]," and "the number of her honourable name is 45 (or 1035)".[8]

Philo of Alexandria shows knowledge of isopsephy in his Questions and Answers on Genesis:

> Why does God say, "Sara thy wife shall not be called Sara, but Sarra shall be her name?" Here again some foolish persons may laugh at the addition of one single letter, that is to say, of a hundred, for in Greek characters the letter r [P] means a hundred; but if they jest in this way they are foolish, as being unwilling to behold the inward merits of things and to cleave to the footsteps of truth; for that element, r, which is here thought of merely as the addition of one letter, is the parent of all harmony, making things great instead of small, general instead of particular, and mortal instead of immortal; since Sara, when called Sara with one r, is interpreted "thy princedom," but with two r's, Sarra, "princess."[9]

There is little doubt that gematria shaped the Early Christian form of number symbolism. An early example on the impact of gematria on Christianity can be found in the Sibylline Oracles. The surviving Sibylline Oracles are pseudonymous works attributed to the famed ancient Greek prophetesses known as the Sibyls, and are not to be confused with the now lost Sibylline Books of Roman history. Although they profess to be a collection of prophetic utterances dating from the pre-Christian era, in reality they

---

[4] See for example Drosnin, M. *The Bible Code* (London: Orion, 1997), or Satinover, J. *The Truth Behind the Bible Code* (London: Sidgwick & Jackson, 1997).

[5] See appendix II for the Greek numerical system.

[6] For example Keith Barry argues that the use of gematria in the Middle East developed from the Greek usage of isopsephy during the process of Hellenisation after the conquests of Alexander the Great. Barry, K. *The Greek Qabalah* (York Beach: Weiser, 1999), ppxiii-xiv; 21.

[7] Aelian *Varia Historica* 4.17; cf Iamblichus *Vita Pythagorica* 82

[8] Deissmann, cited in Aune, D.E. *Revelation 6-16* (Dallas: Word, 1997), p772

[9] Philo *Questions and Answers* III.53

were largely composed of mixed sources including strong Jewish and Christian influences, and are usually dated to around 150-180AD. The Jewish and Christian elements of the Sibylline Oracles provide an invaluable insight into apocalyptic thought during the Early Church.

The Sibylline Oracles demonstrate that the process of gematria/isopsephy was known and used by Christian writers by at least the mid to late second century AD. One of the oracles hints as to how the name of Jesus in Greek (ΙΗΣΟΥΣ) adds up to 888.[10] (I = 10) + (H = 8) + (Σ = 200) + (O = 70) + (Y = 400) + (Σ = 200) = 888:

Four vowels, and two consonants in him
Are twice announced; the whole sum I will name:
For eight ones, and as many tens on these,
And yet eight hundred will reveal the name
To men insatiate; and do thou discern
In thine own understanding that the Christ
Is child of the immortal God most high.

Another even earlier Christian use of isopsephy may be found in the Epistle of Barnabas, which is dated to between 70-130AD. Here, the author of Barnabas interprets the number 318 found in Gen 14:14 as a symbolic reference to Jesus and the cross. The number 18 symbolises the numerical value of the first two Greek letters of Jesus' name – iota and epsilon, being added together. The 300 symbolises the cross, since it is represented in Greek by the cruciform letter tau:

Learn fully then, children of love, concerning all things, for Abraham, who first circumcised, did so looking forward in the spirit to Jesus, and had received the doctrines of three letters. For it says, "And Abraham circumcised from his household eighteen men and three hundred." What then was the knowledge that was given to him? Notice that he first mentions the eighteen, and after a pause the three hundred. The eighteen is I (=10) and H (=8) -- you have Jesus -- and because the cross was destined to have grace in the T he says "and three hundred." So he indicates Jesus in the two letters and the cross in the other. He knows this who placed the gift of his teaching in our hearts. No one has heard a more excellent lesson from me, but I know that you are worthy.[11]

The above interpretation may reflect the author's knowledge of a similar Jewish tradition concerning the symbolic value of the number 318 in Gen 14:14. In the Babylonian Talmud, the numbering of Abraham's servants at 318 was gematria for Eliezer, the servant of Abraham, as the sum of the Eliezer in Hebrew was 318.[12]

$$\text{אליעזר} \quad (eli\text{'}zer)$$
$$(\text{א} = 1) + (\text{ל} = 30) + (\text{י} = 10) + (\text{ע} = 70) + (\text{ז} = 7) + (\text{ר} = 200) = 318$$

The earliest instance of Christian gematria can be found within the pages of the New Testament itself, in the Book of the Apocalypse. As D. E. Aune notes, a majority of scholars feel that the use of gematria lies behind the original meaning of the number of

---

[10] *Sib. Or* 1:395-400
[11] *Epistle of Barnabas* 9:7-9 Trans Kirsopp Lake
[12] *b. Ned.* 32a

the Beast.[13] The Book of Revelation explicitly states that the number 666 is the "number of a man" – which is hard to interpret in any other light than the numerical equivalent of a person's name.

Even the earliest Christian commentators understood that gematria would have to be applied to solve the riddle of the number of the Beast. Ireneaus, writing around 180AD, speculated that the name behind the number of the beast could be the Greek word ΛΑΤΕΙΝΟΣ *Lateinos* – which referred to the Roman Empire.[14] The numerical value of *Lateinos* yields the total 666 (Λ = 30) + (A = 1) + (T = 300) + (E = 5) + (I = 10) + (N = 50) + (O = 70) (Σ = 200) = 666.

Irenaeus also suggested the names Evanthas and Tietan as possible fits for the number 666. The word ΕΥΑΝΘΑΣ *Evanthas* is of obscure origin. It may be the name of a person contemporaneous with either John or Irenaeus who has been subsequently lost to history. The name TEITAN was also forwarded by the first commentator on the Book of Revelation, St. Victorinus of Pettau,[15] and is thought to be either a reference to the Titans of Greek mythology, or to Titus, the Roman general who destroyed the Temple in 70AD before becoming emperor in 79.

Therefore it is clear that even the earliest commentators on the Apocalypse understood that the riddle behind the number of the Beast could be solved through the use of gematria or isopsephy. It is only through the use of this method that the true interpretation of the number of the Beast can be revealed.

Many scholars feel that the original name behind the number of the Beast was that of the Roman Emperor Nero. This theory is perhaps the most plausible explanation for the preterist understanding of this cryptic reference. As the first Roman Emperor to persecute Christians, Nero would have been viewed by John's audience as the ultimate blueprint for the physical incarnation of evil.

During the month of July in 64AD, the Great Fire had engulfed Rome, destroying two entire districts of the city. Many lives were lost in the conflagration, and thousands left homeless. Naturally, there was a great deal of public anger concerning this event, and the Roman populace were searching for someone or something to vent their rage. Rumours were circulating that Nero had razed the city in order to create a *tabula rasa* – a blank slate that would enable him to implement his ambitions for a complete urban regeneration of the Empire's capital. As a means of exculpating himself, the Emperor attempted to pin the blame on the newly emerging Christian sect, which had already begun to attract suspicion from certain quarters of Roman society.[16] There were whisperings of the group being associated with cannibalism and incest, stemming from a misunderstanding of the celebration of the Eucharist and Christianity's emphasis of "brotherly love". As a recently formed group surrounded by an aura of distrust, the Christian movement had provided Nero with the perfect scapegoat.

---

[13] Aune, D.E. *Revelation 6-16* p771

[14] Ireneaus *Adv. haer.* 5.30.3

[15] See Victorinus, *Commentary on the Apocalypse*

[16] A view which was held by Tacitus: "But all human efforts, all the lavish gifts of the emperor, and the propitiations of the gods, did not banish the sinister belief the conflagration was the result of an order. Consequently, to get rid of the report, Nero fastened the guilt and inflicted the most exquisite tortures on a class hated for their abominations, called Christians by the populace." *Annals* XV.44.2-3 Trans. Stevenson, J. *A New Eusebius* (London: SPCK, 1987), pp2-3

With an ideal patsy positioned to absorb any censure for the burning of Rome, the ruthless emperor was free to press ahead with his coveted building project.[17] A new palace was constructed in the midst of the ruins of the old city, and rumours began to circulate that Nero had intentionally started the fire as a means for this specific purpose. In order to divert attention away from himself, the Emperor inaugurated the first official persecution of Christians by the state, a position held by Rome that was to recur intermittently over the course of the next two hundred years. Tacitus, a Roman historian writing circa 112AD, describes the level of brutality administered by the empire in dealing with the Christians:

> Accordingly, an arrest was first made of all who confessed; then, upon their information, an immense multitude was convicted, not so much for the crime of arson, as of hatred of the human race. Mockery of every sort was added to their deaths. Covered with the skins of beasts, they were torn by dogs and perished, or were nailed to crosses, or were doomed to the flames. These served to illuminate the night when daylight failed. Nero had thrown open his gardens for the spectacle, and was exhibiting a show in the circus, while he mingled with the people in the dress of a charioteer or drove about in a chariot. Hence, even for criminals who deserved extreme and exemplary punishment, there arose a feeling of compassion; for it was not, as it seemed, for the public good, but to glut one man's cruelty, that they were destroyed.[18]

There is a particularly strong tradition that Ss. Peter and Paul were executed during the Neroian persecution. After the Apostolic Council at Jerusalem circa 50AD, Peter undertook a lengthy missionary journey that would eventually lead him to Rome. According to the apocryphal account contained in *Acts of Peter* 37-39, the Apostle requested to be crucified upside-down in a final act of humility, as he felt that he was not worthy enough to emulate the glorious sacrificial death of his master. D.A. Carson notes that although the later accounts of Peter's death contained in the largely fictitious *Acts of Peter* "are too remote and too infected with legendary accretions to be reliable", the fact that some victims were indeed crucified upside-down is independently affirmed by the Roman historian Seneca.[19]

A more dependable source can be found in Tertullian, who writing about 212AD, also attests that Peter was crucified, although no mention is made of this being in any way other than the more conventional method of crucifixion.[20] An even earlier reference to the martyrdom of Peter can be found in the writings of Pope St. Clement of Rome, dating back to circa 96AD.[21] However the earliest and most authoritative account of Peter's death is contained in the Fourth Gospel, when after the Resurrection, Jesus informed the Apostle of the fate that lay in store for him:

---

[17] Most of the early historians, such as Suetonius and Cassius Dio attribute blame for the fire to Nero. (See Suetonius *Life of Nero* 38; Cassius Dio *Roman History* LXII.16) Some modern historians, such as W.H.C. Frend, contend that Nero may have originally attempted to shift the culpability onto the Jews, who then transferred the guilt onto the rival Christian sect. See Frend, W.H.C. *The Early Church* (London: SCM Press, 2003), p31

[18] Tacitus, *Annals*, XV.44.2-8. Trans. Stevenson, J. *A New Eusebius* pp2-3

[19] Carson, D.A. *The Gospel According to John* (Grand Rapids: Eerdmans, 1991), p680 cf. Seneca, *Consolation to Marcia* 20

[20] Tertullian, *Scorpiace* 15

[21] 1 *Clement* 5:4 "There was Peter who by reason of unrighteous jealousy endured not one not one but many labors, and thus having borne his testimony went to his appointed place of glory." (Translated by J.B Lightfoot.)

"Truly, truly, I say to you, when you were young, you used to dress yourself and walk wherever you wanted, but when you are old, you will stretch out your hands, and another will dress you and carry you where you do not want to go." (This he said to show by what kind of death he was to glorify God.) (John 21:18-19)

Therefore the available evidence suggests that Peter was crucified as a direct result of the persecution initiated by Nero. The Emperor's responsibility for the martyrdom of the leader of the apostles would not have been quickly forgotten by the Johannine church.

The accounts of the death of St. Paul are equally shrouded with obscurity. According to the Book of Acts, Paul was brought to Rome to stand trial for causing a disturbance at the Temple in Jerusalem.[22] As a citizen of the Roman Empire, Paul was accorded with certain rights, including that of a judicial hearing at the capital. Acts tells us that after a long and arduous journey to Rome in the custody of an imperial legion, Paul was incarcerated in the city for two years. However at this point of the narrative Acts comes to an abrupt ending and no mention is made of the Apostle's subsequent fate.[23] This rather sharp conclusion has suggested to some conservative theologians that Paul was in fact still alive at the time the Book of Acts was written, giving the extremely early date of pre-62AD for the composition of the Luke-Acts corpus.[24]

It is often disputed whether Paul was executed during the Neroian persecution or at some stage before it. Many feel that he was executed as a result of the trial at the end of the two year period mentioned in Acts 28:30 (c.62AD), before the outbreak of the persecution. The Early Church traditions assert that his death was a direct result of Nero's plot against the Christians in 64AD.[25] Whatever the truth of the matter, the fact remains that in either scenario Paul would have stood trial conducted under the ultimate authority of Nero, who reigned from 54-68AD. As such, the Emperor was widely held to be personally responsible for his death. Fortunately for Paul, his form of capital punishment was slightly more humane than the grisly and purposefully prolonged means of execution that awaited his brethren. As a Roman citizen, Paul would have been conferred with the mercifully quick and relatively pain-free death of decapitation.[26]

Given Nero's attempt to dissolve the fledgling Christian movement, and his personal involvement in the deaths of two of its most prominent leaders, it would not be surprising if the author of Revelation had sought to identify the vilified Emperor as the prototype or precursor of the Antichrist. Indeed it seems that in all likelihood, Nero is the most obvious source of reference for the number of the Beast, as the combined evidence

---

[22] Acts 21:26ff

[23] Acts 28:30-31

[24] See for example Marshall, I.H. *Luke* (Carlisle: Paternoster, 1978), p35

[25] E.g. Eusebius, *Church History* III 1.2

[26] We should note here an alternative account of the fate of Paul which maintains that the Apostle escaped to Spain. This is largely based on Rom 15:24 and Clement's report that Paul had preached to "the limits of the west" (*The First Epistle of Clement to the Corinthians*, 5:5–6). However the archaeological discovery of an early Christian sarcophagus bearing the Latin inscription "Paul, saint, martyr" during an excavation of the Roman Basilica St Paul's Outside the Walls in 2002, appears to confirm the tradition that this was his last resting place. The Roman Emperor Constantine had built a small basilica to accommodate pilgrims to St Paul's tomb around the year 320. In 390, Emperor Theodosius encased the Apostle's remains in a stone sarcophagus (which was recovered during the excavations of 2002) and extended the original building. However this building was destroyed by an earthquake in 433, and during renovations the sarcophagus was buried and covered with a marble tombstone, where it remained hidden until its recent discovery.

weighs heavily in his favour. One of the best indicators that points us towards this conclusion is the fact that when "Caesar Nero" is transliterated from the Greek Καισαρ Νερον (*Kaisar Neron*) into Hebrew, we get the spelling קסר נרון; which as we can see from the table below, totals up to the diabolic sum of 666:

א	aleph	1	ל	lamedh	30
ב	beth	2	מ	mem	40
ג	gimel	3	נ	nun	50
ד	daleth	4	ס	samekh	60
ה	he	5	ע	ayin	70
ו	waw	6	פ	pe	80
ז	zayin	7	צ	sadhe	90
ח	heth	8	ק	qoph	100
ט	teth	9	ר	resh	200
י	yodh	10	ש	sin	300
כ	kaph	20	ת	taw	400

Reading from left to right, as is the case in any Semitic form of writing, we can break down the calculation as follows: (ק = 100) + (ס = 60) + (ר = 200) + (נ = 50) + (ר = 200) + (ו = 6) + (נ = 50) = 666.

This proposal is subject to a number of criticisms however. The letters have to be tweaked slightly to achieve the figure 666. The proper Hebrew spelling for Caesar is usually קסיר, not קסר, and the extra י (yodh) would take the total up to 676. This has cast doubt on whether *Kaisar Neron* is the authentic interpretation behind the number of the Beast. Yet an Aramaic document recently discovered at Wadi Murabba'at has been used to support the Nero theory. This manuscript also leaves out the י (yodh) in the transliteration of the name Caesar, giving the possibility of a commonly used variant spelling.[27] Also, the Latinised version of the name "Nero Caesar" which leaves out the Greek case ending *n* (ו when transliterated into Hebrew), gives the sum of 616. This discrepancy could then be used to explain why in some ancient manuscripts the number 616 is used in place of 666.[28] Although, another possibility is that this variation may be explained as a deliberate attempt to link the beast with Caligula (12-41AD). Caligula's

---

[27] As is shown by Aune in his commentary, p770.

[28] Although we should note that the number 666 is considered by scholars to be the original rendering of the number of the Beast, as it is attested to by the vast majority of the earliest extant manuscripts. See Aune, D.E. *Revelation* 6-16 p722 n.18c. Cf. Beale, G.K. *The Book of Revelation* p719 n.298

name in Greek, Γαιος Καισαρ (*Gaios Kaisar*) also adds up to 616.[29]

The association between Nero and the number of the Beast has (along with Rev 17: 10-11) been used as evidence for John's belief in the *Nero redivivus* legend. The deaths of the most tyrannous of rulers, as well as individuals held in great reverence, are often difficult for the public to wholeheartedly accept. We can find a modern example of such a phenomenon in the widely credited rumour that Hitler had survived the war and was living incognito somewhere in South America. The aura of menace surrounding such individuals is often hard to dispel, and the fear generated around them persists even after their demise. Another example can be found in the Iraqi people's refusal to believe that Saddam Hussein's dictatorial regime was permanently disposed of after the invasion by America and its allies in 2003. Before his arrest and subsequent execution, many Iraqis thought that the despot would be eventually restored to power.

At the opposite end of the spectrum, the deaths of popular figures, such as Elvis Presley and the Ethiopian emperor Haile Selassie were equally held in denial by their most ardent followers. The numerous sightings of Elvis reported after his death has become a long standing joke in the media; while the Rastafarian movement is still adamant that the assassination of the Ethiopian king did not actually take place, and that Selassie will one day return to fulfil his messianic role and lead the African people back to their homeland in a new exodus.

People within the Roman Empire found the suicide of Nero similarly hard to accept. The widespread notoriety of the Emperor had been deeply engrained upon the public imagination, and manifested itself in a reluctance to accept the reality of his death. It was almost as if the Empire's subjects were too afraid to hope that the tyrant was gone for good, lest they were caught unawares on Nero's unexpected re-emergence. A belief had developed that he was hiding in Parthia and would soon return to seize back his empire at the lead of an army of Parthian invaders. Towards the end of the 1st century, when the likelihood of Nero's return from hiding as a living person began to fade (as by this stage he would have been unfeasibly elderly), a new belief took its place, which foretold that he would rise from the dead leading a mighty horde of undead soldiers to take back his rightful dominion.

The possibility that the number of the Beast was used by John to allude to Nero need not infer that he believed in a literal fulfilment of the *redivivus* myth however. As G.R. Osborne states:

> Just as God fashioned the woman, dragon, and child vision (12:1-6) after the Apollo legend and so on, so he fashioned the vision of the beast after the Nero legend. Neither is true, but the form becomes a "redemptive analogy" to tell the readers that what they knew as legend would become history.[30]

Nero provided the perfect template on which to model the future coming of the Antichrist. Like Antiochus Epiphanes before him, the Emperor was arrayed with all the exemplary characteristics of the spirit of the Antichrist. Nero, as the first world emperor to persecute Christians, displayed all the necessary attributes of any potential future physical incarnation of the Devil, and as such proleptically symbolised the final leader in

---

[29] $(\gamma = 3) + (\alpha = 1) + (\iota = 10) + (o = 70) + (\varsigma = 200) + (\kappa = 20) + (\alpha = 1) + (\iota = 10) + (\sigma = 200) + (\alpha = 1) + (\rho = 100) = 616.$

[30] Osborne, G.R. *Revelation* pp496-497

history to persecute the people of God. As we have already discussed, a cyclic concept of time where past events reverberate out into the future is a classic trait of ancient prophetic thought.

Another intriguing aspect of "the name of the beast or the number of its name" (Rev 13:17), is that it also has a more straightforward, literal interpretation. The lexical form of the Greek word for "beast" used here is θηριον (*therion*), which when

transliterated into Hebrew gives תריון. Using the table above to determine the numerical value of *therion* in Hebrew, we can thus see that the Greek word for beast literally gives the number 666.[31] This wordplay was in all probability intended by the author, and provides further evidence that while John may have been writing in Greek, he was still thinking in his original Semitic mother tongue.

The interpretation of the "mark" of the Beast as an essential means of commerce is sometimes regarded by preterists to fit the 1st century context as a brand or a tattoo that was given to the participants of emperor-worship. In Roman society it was considered seditious not to pay homage to the state gods, and the only exemption offered in this compulsory practice was extended towards the Jews. The Romans held deep respect for the religions of antiquity, but they had little tolerance for new cults that would not pay homage to the state in an open act of worship.

When it became clear that Christianity was a religion in its own right and not merely a sub-sect within Judaism, the exemption offered towards Christians was retracted, and many were compelled to make sacrifices to the state gods in order to demonstrate their loyalty to the Emperor. When some Christians refused to comply with these stipulations, persecution ensued in the form of imprisonment, corporal punishment, or even public executions in the local amphitheatres. During the later Decian persecution, those who did submit to the authorities and participated in the sacrifices towards the state gods were given a certificate acknowledging they had done so, and were allowed to continue to believe in whatever they wished.

Although there is no evidence of the practice of branding by the Romans in this instance, it was used elsewhere in the Hellenistic world. Ptolemy Philopater I (217BC) forced Jews to be registered in a census, and after they had taken part in the registration process he ordered for them to be branded with the ivy leaf sign of Dionysian worship.[32]

The "branding" with the figure of 666 is a concept unique to the Book of Revelation. The number 666 is heavily imbued with religious symbolism.[33] It parodies the use of the number seven in the Apocalypse, which occurs repeatedly throughout the book (seven trumpets, seven seals, seven bowls, seven spirits, etc.). Seven was considered to be the number of completion, and was often associated with divinity. God made the world in seven days, and seven is the number of the Sabbath. As six falls short of this number, it signifies incompleteness. It also stands in contrast with the number of Jesus' name – 888. Eight is the beginning of a new era, after the completion of seven.

---

[31] (ת = 400) + (ר = 200) + (י = 10) + (ו = 6) + (נ = 50) = 666.

[32] 3 Macc. 2:28-29

[33] For an excellent concise treatment of religious number symbolism see Caldecott, S. *Beauty for Truth's Sake* (Grand Rapids: Brazos, 2009), pp53-71. A fuller treatment of number symbolism in the Bible can be found in J.J. Davis' book *Biblical Numerology* (Grand Rapids: Baker, 1968). See also Bullinger, E.W. *Number in Scripture* (New York: Cosimo Classics, 2005)

Male children are circumcised on the eighth day to begin their new life in the covenant.

666 stands for the unholy trinity of the Devil, the Beast and the False Prophet, and in a grotesque form of mimicry, apes the number of the Holy Trinity – 777. It symbolises yet another of Satan's failed attempts to imitate God in order to acquire divine attributes for himself. In attempting to attain godly perfection, the Devil always comes up short.[34]

The use of parody by the antagonists of Revelation is a common theme found throughout the book. Indeed the Apocalypse is almost dualistic in certain respects. Nearly every major character is paired by an antithetical replication of itself. The figure of the Lamb for example, is one of the book's most dominant images; but Rev 13:11 contains a description of a diabolic "anti-Lamb" which speaks like a dragon. Although the author uses similar imagery to depict both characters, the contrast between the two could not be more apparent.

Antithetical parallelism is a pattern that recurs throughout Revelation's central narrative.[35] The Apocalypse's exposition of a triune Godhead in the throne room vision of chapters 4-5[36] is countered by the "anti-trinity" of the Dragon, Beast and False Prophet in the latter portion of the book. One of the seven heads of the sea-beast (which in turn mirrors the seven-fold nature of the Holy Spirit in Rev 1:4; 3:1; 4:5 and 5:6) appears to be fatally wounded, but by parodying the resurrection of Jesus, the wound is miraculously healed.

The whore-city of Babylon in Rev 17 acts as a foil for the bride-city of Jerusalem in Rev 21. This deliberate contrast by the author is further heightened by the fact that the function of the bride-city is to supplant the corrupt whore-city.[37] And just as the servants of God are sealed upon the forehead in Rev 7, the followers of the Beast are similarly branded with the mark of the Devil. This passage is directly influenced by the act of the sealing of saints elsewhere in the Bible. In Deut 6:8, the Israelites are commanded to keep God's words bound to their hands and foreheads as an outward sign of their fidelity. In anticipation of Christian symbolism, Ezekiel 9 also contains a reference to the marking of the Jewish faithful upon their foreheads with the cross-shaped paleo-Hebrew letter *taw* so that they may be protected from the onslaught of divine retribution. The seal upon the foreheads of the servants of God is understood by the author of Revelation to be that of the Divine name (Rev 14:1), just as the followers of the Beast are marked by the number of its name.

So how exactly are modern Christians meant to interpret this infamous biblical passage? How can it possibly have any significance beyond its immediate context? Christians are asked to believe that the words contained in this passage will one day

---

[34] The theme of Satan's ambition to usurp the throne of God and his subsequent failure appears elsewhere in Scripture, in Isaiah 14.

[35] For an in-depth study of antithetical parallelism in the Apocalypse see the collective works of Prof. Gordon Campbell, such as: "L'Apocalypse de Jean. Une Lecture Thematique", *Excelsis* (2007); "Antithetical Feminine-Urban Imagery and a Tale of Two Women-Cities in the Book of Revelation." *Tyndale Bulletin* 55.1 (2004), pp81-108

[36] God, the Lamb and the sevenfold spirit all share centre stage; with the Lamb and God even sharing the throne itself. This has been recognised as an attempt by the author to show that each of the persons of the Godhead share the same divine essence, and that they are in fact co-equal.

[37] See Campbell, G. "Antithetical Feminine-Urban Imagery and a Tale of Two Women-Cities in the Book of Revelation." *Tyndale Bulletin* 55.1

become reality. But the literal framing of this prophecy seems too obvious a concept to be able to come to completion. If any governmental body attempted to implement such a device that was integral to participating in commerce (never mind a concerted global effort involving *every* government), surely it would be immediately recognized and rejected by the common public... Or would it?

If this prophecy was executed in a manner that diverged from the common perception of the form of the mark of the Beast, then there is every chance that it could escape the suspicion of the general populace. What if the mark of the Beast was not a literal brand or mark that was permanently worn in the receiver's hands or foreheads, but an external object that was only used occasionally? And what if this object was perceived to be an essential part of modern life – an item that was not only extremely useful for conducting business, but also fashionable as well? As we shall see, it seems that this situation has already risen.

Before we can establish how the prophecy of the mark of the Beast may have come to completion in the recent past, we must first determine how the prophecy of the number of the Beast has been fulfilled, and how it may in fact be staring at us in the face every hour of our waking lives.

The True Meaning of 666?

The triple letter abbreviation for the worldwide web – www, is ubiquitously present in almost every aspect of daily life. Each time we switch on the television we are bombarded by website addresses directing us to the homepage of various advertisers. Likewise, every time we open a newspaper or magazine we are directed to corporate websites which offer a fuller range of services and product details. All of them beginning with three simple letters. Three letters that are to be seen everywhere we look – www. If this threefold repetition of letters could be found to some way represent the threefold digits of the number of the Beast, then the letters www could perhaps provide us with the ultimate fulfilment of this prophecy.

It certainly seems impossible to engage in commerce without being associated in some way with the internet. Every business, from the greatest to the smallest, heavily depend on the worldwide web as a key interface point between themselves and the consumer. Corporate websites are a necessary advertising requirement for every major multinational business, and a large proportion of financial transactions are now conducted over the internet. Even minor companies are increasingly making use of the internet's marketing potential. It just takes a quick glance around any urban area to see website addresses emblazoned across vans and lorries of local tradesmen, retail outlets and various other entrepreneurial enterprises. We are faced with a similar situation upon opening the commercial section of any telephone directory.

Website addresses can be found on the packaging of almost every product we buy, from potato crisps to lawnmowers, from shampoo bottles to vacuum cleaners. It seems almost impossible to buy or sell anything that hasn't got the letters www displayed upon the external wrapping. Even package-free goods, such as fruit, are still associated in some way with the internet, whether via the brand they are sold under, or through the supermarket that sells them. And unlike say money for example, which differs from country to country, the internet is truly a global phenomenon. So the internet already appears to fulfil at least one aspect of the prophecy of the number of the Beast. The part which foretold that it would become an essential component of commerce: "*so that no one can buy or sell unless he has the mark, that is, the name of the beast or the number of its name*".

But it may be objected that the same thing could apply to numerous features of commerce – no one can buy or sell anything without a telephone number on it, or without barcodes. However, the internet provides us with a second, more convincing characteristic that fulfils this, the most important aspect of the prophecy of the number of the Beast. The curiously regimented letters www attract some attention themselves, and immediately throw up a host of questions. What are they for? If they appear at the start of every website address, does this not render them completely superfluous? Could we not just leave them off and get the same result? Another peculiar characteristic is the uniformity of each of the letters: www – a regimented sequence which seems almost contrived in nature. A uniformity which recalls the threefold repetition of digits in the number 666. Indeed it is in this respect that they present the most frightening prospect – could they in some way actually represent the "number" of the Beast? If the letter w could in some way be equated with the number 6, then would the letters www not provide us with the ultimate fulfilment of the prophecy of the number of the Beast? It just so happens that the letter w can be equated with the number 6, and not by some overly convoluted abstract engineering, but in the original language of the author of the Book of Revelation.

As we have already discussed, each of the letters of the Hebrew/Aramaic alphabet have a numerical equivalent. Since scholars have already determined that the author's native language was most probably Aramaic,[38] it is easy to presume that whatever he saw in his vision may have had some connection with Semitic wordplay.[39] We may also assume that any present application must also in some way involve the substitution of Hebrew letters for their numerical equivalent. If we look at the table below, we can see that the Hebrew counterpart for the letter w is ‏ו‎ (*waw*), which in turn represents the number six. So when transliterated into Hebrew www (‏ווו‎) equals 6-6-6.

---

[38] R.H. Charles for example, concluded that the book's many solecisms, Semitisms and grammatical irregularities shows that while the writer wrote in Greek, he was actually thinking in Hebrew. *A Critical and Exegetical Commentary on the Revelation of St. John Vol 1* (Edinburgh: T&C Clark, 1920), clii

[39] As is evidenced by the numerical value of the Greek word for beast – *therion*, which we have already seen totals up to 666 when transliterated into Hebrew. But even if the Apostle had the defunct Greek letter digamma in mind for the number six, this would still lead us to the same conclusion. Digamma was originally called *wau* in the archaic Greek alphabet, and was derived from the Semitic letter *waw*. The Greek letter digamma had dropped out of usage in Koine Greek, but survived in the numerical system. It is still pronounced and transliterated as w. So even though it may not be quite as obvious as it is in Hebrew, www still equals 6-6-6 in the Greek language.

א	’	1		ל	l	30
ב	b, v	2		מ	m	40
ג	g	3		נ	n	50
ד	d	4		ס	s	60
ה	h	5		ע	‘	70
ו	w	6		פ	p	80
ז	z	7		צ	ts	90
ח	ch	8		ק	q	100
ט	t	9		ר	r	200
י	y	10		ש	s	300
כ	k	20		ת	t	400

It may be immediately objected from a critical perspective that the letters do not actually total up to the number six hundred and sixty six, but merely represent the separate figures six-six-six. In Hebrew this number is *shesh me'oth sheshim washesh*, and is represented by the diverse characters תרסו.[40] However we may respond to this criticism by highlighting the fact that the author intended this number to be understood symbolically. It is a cryptic reference to "*the number of a man*", maybe even referring to the Roman Emperor Nero. As we have already seen, scholars achieve the calculation of Nero's name only by going through a complicated bilingual mathematical process. Our equation of www with six-six-six is a lot more straightforward. Besides, the number of the Beast is more popularly known as six-six-six rather than six hundred and sixty six; and could have been understood in this manner even by a first century Jewish Christian from Palestine. As the prominent American New Testament scholar C.S. Keener points out: "Although the coincidence would not have been as obvious in ancient Mediterranean numeric systems as it is today, ancients using base ten would not miss the significance of the threefold repetition of sixes."[41]

Even though the uniform appearance of the digits 666 would not have become immediately apparent until the invention of the decimal system in the 7th century AD, it would have been evident that the number could be broken down to three consecutive units containing the word *shesh* (six). We can see the repetition of the basic root word for six in its Hebrew rendering *shesh* me'oth *sheshim* wa*shesh* (six hundred and sixty six). Therefore achieving 6-6-6 from www is highly simplistic even by 1st century AD

---

[40] M. Oberweis suggests that these letters recall the use of the Hebrew word תרסו "you should destroy". Oberweis, M. "Die Bedeutung der neutestamentlichen 'Raetzelzahlen' 666 (Apk 13:18) und 153 (Joh 21:11)." *Zeitschrift fur die neutestamentliche Wissenschaft 77* pp226-241. If this is correct, then it may also be a partial allusion to the "angel of the bottomless pit" in Rev 9:11, whose name is given in Hebrew and Greek as "the destroyer".

[41] Keener, C.S. *Revelation* p355

standards. There is no need to delve into advanced calculus in order to determine this equation – it is instantly attainable through a short and logical process. This is in dramatic contrast to many of the obscure and complex attempts to equate 666 with names such as Adolf Hitler or Ronald Reagan. The number 666 was applied to Hitler during the Second World War by a theory which used the equation A =100, B = 101, C =102, etc.[42] Using this method the name "Hitler" adds up to 666. The former American President was famously singled out because along with a number of other coincidences linking him with the number 666, his first middle and last names – Ronald Wilson Reagan, all had six letters, giving six-six-six. Both of these attempts were transparently hare-brained, yet believed by many people to be true.

So it is perhaps more than a little ironic that an extremely simple approach such as that presented above provides us with the closest match to the original words of the prophecy. But there is another facet to the prophecy of the number of the Beast we still have to take into consideration – the fact that it is supposed to be placed on people's hands or foreheads in its guise as the mark of the Beast. How do we reconcile this prediction with the fact that the letters www do not appear to have been appended to anyone's hand or forehead? While on the surface it may seem that this part of the prophecy has yet to be fulfilled, there is a very real possibility that it has in fact already happened. In order to find out what the prophecy of the mark of the Beast really predicts, we must first turn back to discover its original meaning.

The "Mark" of the Beast

If the true futurist meaning of the number of the Beast is to be found in the recurring consecutive letters www, then we must square this hypothesis with the fact that the Book of Revelation tells us that the mark of the Beast would be worn in the hand or forehead. There is at present no requirement for anyone to be branded with www in order to participate in any form of commerce, and it would be ludicrous to propose that such a scheme could be implemented in the future. Similarly, any plans to inject microchips bearing website addresses under the skin of the hand or forehead would attract too much attention to go unnoticed. People would soon suspect that something was awry and a swift public backlash would be expected. Any plot that attracts suspicion from the outset is doomed to failure.

The only possible way a machination as elaborate and controversial as the mark of the Beast could come to fruition is through an extremely subtle process. So we should attempt to find an alternative explanation for the mark of the Beast, one which will provide us with a different concept to that of a physical "branding" or "sealing". To do so we must return to further examine the original words of the prophecy, and discover the real idea behind this particular portion of the Apocalypse.

During prayer services in Judaism from at least the intertestamental period onwards, many devout Jews wore small portions of Scripture (usually the *shema* of Deut 6:4, along with three other passages) kept in leather boxes known as *tefillin* in Aramaic,

---

[42] See Wainwright, A.W. *Mysterious Apocalypse* p175

which are today commonly known by the Greek word "phylactery". Due to a literal interpretation of Deut 6:8: "You shall bind [the commandments] as a sign on your hand, and they shall be as frontlets between your eyes", phylacteries are worn upon the arms and foreheads of practicing Jews during prayer services. Some well-preserved *tefillin* dating back to before the 1st century were among the finds uncovered during the archaeological excavations at Qumran after the discovery of the Dead Sea Scrolls.

Jesus himself mentions the practice of wearing phylacteries in his condemnation of the excesses of some of the Pharisees in Matt 23:5:

> They do all their deeds to be seen by others. For they make their phylacteries broad and their fringes long, and they love the place of honor at feasts and the best seats in the synagogues and greetings in the marketplaces and being called rabbi by others. (Matt 23:5-7)

Indeed practising members of Orthodox Judaism still follow this custom, and phylacteries are mostly worn during weekday morning prayer services.

As C.S. Keener points out, it is almost certain that Jesus himself would have practiced the custom of laying *tefillin*.[43] The same could also be said of his disciples. As a practicing Jew, the Apostle John would have worn phylacteries at some point in his life. Therefore given that Rev 13:16 contains such strong echoes of Deut 6:8, the image of a phylactery must have been foremost in mind when John wrote of the mark of the Beast in the Apocalypse. But in Revelation the Jewish tradition of wearing phylacteries becomes inverted, and is incorporated into the author's trademark signature of antithetical parallelism.[44] In a blatant act of mimicry, the divinely-ordained *tefillin* are transformed into the diabolical mark of the Beast.

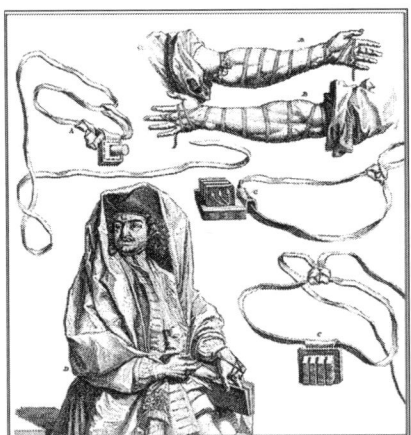

Fig. 10 In order for observant Jews to escape accusations of flamboyancy, a "hand" *tefillin,* is actually strapped to the upper arm and covered with clothing.

---

[43] Keener, C.S *A Commentary on the Gospel of Matthew* (Grand Rapids: Eerdmans, 1999), p542
[44] See Osborne, G.R. *Revelation* p517, who states: "It is likely that John and his readers would see the mark of the beast as a parody of [the Jewish custom of wearing phylacteries]."

Another physical aspect of phylacteries which perhaps completes their parody by the number of the Beast is the fact that they are marked on two opposite sides with the Hebrew letter ‏שׁ‎(shin) ,which looks remarkably similar to the letter w in the modern Latin alphabet.[45]

Fig. 11 A head *tefillin* sporting the Hebrew letter ‏שׁ‎

The presence of the Hebrew letter shin on the head phylactery represents the first letter of the name ‏שׁדּי‎ (Shaddai) – one of the names used for God in the Torah. The other letters which form the name Shaddai – ‏דּ‎ *daleth* and ‏י‎ *yod*, are formed by the knots that are used to tie the *tefillin* to the body. This practice recalls the name of God written upon the foreheads of the followers of the Lamb in Rev 14:1:

> Then I looked, and behold, on Mount Zion stood the Lamb, and with him 144,000 who had his name and his Father's name written on their foreheads.

And just as phylacteries contain a hidden reference to the name of God, so too does the mark of the Beast contain a hidden reference to the name of the Antichrist.

When we take these numerous parallels into account, it thus becomes evident that the events depicted in Rev 13:16 are a direct parody of the Jewish custom of wearing *tefillin*. However there are a few notable differences between the way the respective marks or seals are conferred upon each of these opposing sides in the Apocalypse. The followers of the Lamb are sealed with the name of God on their foreheads as a reward for their faithful actions (Rev 14:1-5), whereas those who receive the mark of the Beast are unwitting participants, swindled into accepting the mark through deception (Rev 19:20).

Now that we have established that the Jewish practice of laying *tefillin* was one of the major influences behind Rev 13:16, we can gain an important insight into what its physical appearance would resemble today. The mark is not a brand or a tattoo permanently adorned by its recipients – it is an external box-shaped object that is temporarily "worn" by the receiver. If the letters www are indeed to be equated with the

---

[45] There are actually two shins on a head *tefillin* – one on each side. But one of the letters has an extra arm in order to denote the four biblical passages that are contained in the *tefillin*.

number 666, then in today's terms, the mark of the Beast would be a box-shaped device which is both "worn" on the hand, and which at the same time is associated in some way with the use of the internet. It just so happens that the all-pervasive event of the internet-enabled mobile phone provides us with a frighteningly accurate modern equivalent of the "anti-phylactery" depicted by the seer of Revelation.

The use of mobile phones in both the developed and developing countries of the world has grown exponentially over the past decade. According to Wireless Intelligence, there are currently some five billion mobile phone connections worldwide, with analysts predicting that this figure is set to increase to six billion by the year 2012.[46] Although this figure does not comprise the entirety of the earth's population of 6.9 billion (since some of these connections are no longer in use and include individuals with more than one connection), it still comes frighteningly close. Mobile phone use has even broken into in the Third World market, with a large percentage of the population of the developing world owning a mobile phone. Even credit or debit cards cannot lay claim to this level of ubiquity.

There is also the possibility that payments through smartphones could replace that of credit or debit cards.[47] *First Data*, a major American payment processing company, have developed Near Field Communications (NFC) chip technology that can be included in mobile phones to pay for transactions instead of traditional credit or debit cards. This is done by tapping the phones against store pay-points.[48] In March 2011, this technology was successfully rolled out by NXP, allowing smart-phone owners to make small transactions – such as paying at fast food outlets and ticket sales counters, without the need for a PIN. This easy payment process may prove attractive to the billions of mobile phone owners worldwide – three quarters of whom will have direct access to this technology by the year 2015.[49]

NFC technology is partly based on another project sponsored by Bill Gates, which allows the millions of "unbanked" people throughout the Third World access to a bank account through the use of mobile phones, allowing for the safe deposit and transfer of money.[50] The vast majority of the inhabitants of the Third World are mostly deprived of banking capabilities, leaving them open to targeting by thieves. The already widespread use of mobile phones throughout the Third World provides a unique readymade infrastructure for electronic banking, where payments can be made to individuals through their handsets rather than as lump cash payments through a local branch. So payment through mobile phones has the potential to become a truly global phenomenon. If these future financial applications for smart-phones are successful in displacing the use of credit and debit cards, they may further explain how people will be compelled to use the mark of the Beast to engage in commerce.

While the Apocalypse declares that the False Prophet will cause *everyone* (Gk. παντας *pantas*) to receive the mark, it does not state that every person will unquestionably accept this obligation, or that it would be enforced under the threat of

---

[46] Anon. "Over 5 billion mobile phone connections worldwide" *BBC News* (9th July 2010)

[47] James, J. "Are Smartphones taking over credit card payments?" *Credit Karma Blog* (6th August 2010)

[48] Ham, S. "GO-Tags May Replace Cash and Credit Cards" *Bloomberg Businessweek* (28th August 2008)

[49] Cowan, R.B. "NXP Says Demand for NFC Chips to Soar" *Reuters* (11th May 2011)

[50] Biggs, J. "Bill Gates wants to help the Third World with cellphone banking" *Crunchgear* (2009)

punishment for those that refuse to comply. Instead, the information provided by the original text implicitly suggests that the people of the world are duped into receiving the mark.

Perhaps the best way of deceiving people to this effect would be to foster a false sense of dependency concerning the mark – to convince people that they cannot function to their utmost abilities without its presence to help them through the drudgery of daily life. Exactly the sort of reliance that the modern person feels for their mobile phone.

Since the introduction of WAP (Wireless Application Protocol) technology in 1999, mobile phone users have been able to access the internet directly through their handset. Now all but the most basic of devices are WAP enabled as standard. So we have a direct link between the usage of the letters www and a hand-held device that could be considered to be the modern equivalent of an "anti-phylactery", in the guise of the internet-enabled mobile phone. If we are to affirm that the birth of the internet was the fulfilment of the prophecy of the number of the Beast, then the prophecy of the mark of the Beast – where the number of the Beast is worn in the hand, could not have been fulfilled until the event of the internet-enabled mobile phone. Indeed, in the not too distant future, the use of internet enabled mobile phones may also provide an explanation for the Apocalypse's assertion that the "number" of the Beast, or "anti-phylactery", can be worn upon the forehead.

In 2006, a South Korean company known as Kowon Technology, launched a range of "anti-glance" personal LCD TV glasses in response to the surge in demand for TV streamed to mobile phones. Inspired by the annoyance of other people glancing over the viewer's shoulder to catch a glimpse of the latest action on TV, Kowon Technology developed a head-mounted display unit that allows the user privacy of content. This device consists of a pair of glasses with two 4.8 x 4.2 mm, 320 x 240 LCD panels in front of each eye, which provide the user with the illusion of a 32" TV screen hovering at the distance of two metres away from the face. This innovation thus helps to solve one of the most regularly complained about features of mobile TV – the insufficiently small viewing screen.

Although LCD TV glasses are perhaps too bulky at present to attract a wide demographic in the west, it is foreseeable that future wireless, slim-line versions of the device will be indistinguishable from normal sunglasses, thus rendering their appearance as socially acceptable and maybe even as a desirable fashion accessory. This potential may yet ensure that TV glasses will be a future craze in the technology market. External appearances aside, the sheer practicality of LCD TV glasses should guarantee their future success, as they could help to revolutionize portable personal computing. Devices such as smartphones and tablet computers look set to replace the laptop pc as the ultimate portable computing device. With the increasing miniaturization of technology and the rise of smartphones, the need for an everyday laptop as a means of surfing the internet has become redundant. However there remains some limitations to the smartphone – the screen size available on a truly pocket-sized device such as a mobile phone renders it inadequate for the purposes of portable computing equipment. Large amounts of text need to be visible and readable on-screen at any given time in order for it to be truly efficient as a personal computer. This problem is easily solved by the ability to use LCD TV glasses with the handset, which can be used to meet the large screen prerequisite that would enable the smartphone to become the ultimate portable handheld personal computing device.

There is a current trend among purveyors of technology to advance the integration of household and portable gadgetry into one compact and easy-to-use format. The very nature of the mobile phone as an essential, pocket-sized piece of kit that can easily be carried at all times, ensures that it provides the best support for the integration of technology into one handheld device. Indeed, we are presently witnessing the incorporation of digital camera, video camera, television, internet gateway and gaming device into the already cumbersome list of the mobile phone's utilities. The large screen requirement demanded by mobile TV and pocket-sized portable personal computers should ensure that a slimmed down version of the LCD TV glasses will become an everyday item in the near future. Dr Michio Kaku, a leading theoretical physicist and futurist, predicts that a slim-line version of computerized TV glasses will soon have widespread popular use over the course of the next few years.[51]

This future possibility may help to solve the apparently peculiar condition set down by Rev 13:16 that the "mark" of the Beast could also be worn upon the forehead. To gain a better description of what this mark will look like, we must again turn to Exod 13:16, Deut 6:8, 11:18 which are among the major influences behind this particular portion of the Apocalypse. Deut 6:8 states that the commandments should be worn by the followers of Yahweh as a visible sign of the covenant, instructing they are to be bound to the hand, or worn as *totapoth* between the eyes. Although the true nuance of the word is not fully conveyed by some of the available translations,[52] the Hebrew word *totapoth* is generally interpreted as "frontlet bands" – namely a band like adornment worn around the forehead as a head *tefillin*. Could a future application of devices such as LCD TV glasses be used to explain how the mark of the Beast will be worn upon the forehead as a parody of the Jewish practice of wearing head *tefillin*?

So by comparing the text of Deut 6:8 with Rev 13:16, we have found that the imagery lying behind the two verses is not that of a tattoo or brand permanently stamped upon the forehead or hand, but rather some sort of device that is worn externally, and only temporarily. The mark of the Beast is actually an antithetical parallelism of the ancient Jewish practice of wearing phylacteries.

The Apocalypse states that the False Prophet would cause the people of the earth to receive the mark of the Beast in order to parody the *tefillin* worn by the followers of Yahweh. Could the invention of internet-enabled mobile phones and the future use of LCD TV glasses be the ultimate fulfilment of this parody?

If we accept that WAP technology provides the best available answer as to how the number of the Beast could be worn in the hand, then the Book of Revelation may warn of a future cancer epidemic related to mobile phone use. The Apocalypse foretells that those who receive the mark of the Beast will be inflicted with a grave and agonising disease:

> So the first angel went and poured out his bowl on the earth, and harmful and painful sores came upon the people who bore the mark of the beast. (Rev 16:2)

---

[51] Dr. Kaku expressed these views in the first part of his documentary series *Visions of the Future*, which was first aired on BBC4 on 5th November 2007.

[52] The various English versions of the Bible render *totapoth* as the rather vague and archaic translation "frontlets", which does not immediately conjure the image of a band-like adornment to those who are not familiar with the term.

Could there be a connection between the terrible sores inflicted upon the bearers of the mark of the Beast and the possible side-effects of using mobile phones? From the earliest days of their use, there has been a major concern that the electromagnetic radiation in mobile phones could cause certain types of cancer. Concerns of a similar nature have been proven correct in the past – the impact of cigarette smoke on physical health being the most well-known example. The danger posed by mobile phone usage stems from the possibility that the electromagnetic field (EMF) produced by such devices could cause abnormalities in healthy cell tissue, resulting in the spread of cancer. Some highly credible scientific research has shown how the EMFs emanating from power lines can cause an increased risk of childhood leukaemia.[53] And there is a serious concern that the long term effects of mobile phone use or living nearby a base station could produce similar, if not worse effects.

The EMFs emitted by mobile phones are able to penetrate the human skull up to two inches into the brain, with the thinner bone density of children making them particularly susceptible to this type of radiation. There have been concerns that if these microwaves interfered with the development of cell tissue they could promote irregular growth and eventually culminate in the spread of cancerous cells. Nonetheless, the risks involved in mobile phone use have been downplayed by many of the world's governments and health agencies. Most of these sources insist that the EMFs produced by mobile phones and base stations are too weak to pose any danger. Several reports have stressed that the combined available research suggests that there are no immediate links between mobile phone use and the development of cancer; but have conceded that they must defer further judgment until they are able to assess the long term effects. One such long term report was published in late 2006, involving a twenty year study of over 420,000 mobile phone users. This research, conducted by prominent Danish scientists, has concluded that there was no increase in the risk of various cancers associated with mobile phones in the long term.[54]

These results have managed to allay the concerns of many critics and have been hailed as a major breakthrough by the scientific community. But there are still some sceptics who refuse to accept that the EMFs generated by mobile phones are harmless. Dr. George Carlo, the former head of the Wireless Technology Research (WTR) program, is perhaps the highest profile outspoken critic to contest these results. The WTR, fronted by Carlo, was commissioned by the Cellular Telecommunications Industry Association (CTIA) in 1993 to investigate the effects of mobile phones on the human body, which continued to run until 2000. The CTIA expected the WTR to produce findings that would debunk speculation that mobile phones could pose a serious health risk. However the WTR's findings were deeply embarrassing for the CTIA, including results such as evidence of genetic damage, a doubling in the risk of a rare brain cancer, and a correlation between the site of tumours and the place where mobile phones are held

---

[53] Draper, G; Vincent, T; Kroll, M.E; Swanson, J. "Childhood cancer in relation to distance from high voltage power lines in England and Wales: a case-control study" *British Medical Journal vol. 330* (June 2nd 2005) p1290
[54] Schüz, J; Jacobsen, R; Olsen, J.H; Boice, J.D; McLaughlin, J.K; Johansen, C. "Cellular Telephone Use and Cancer Risk: Update of a Nationwide Danish Cohort". *Journal of the National Cancer Institute 98* (December 2006) pp1707–1713.

against the head. Subsequently, attempts were made by the industry to shut down the WTR and bring further research under tighter control; and steps were taken discredit Carlo himself.

In a book co-authored by Carlo in 2001, he details the results of his findings as head of the WTR and maintains that the cell phone industry has so far managed to successfully suppress incriminating data exposing a link to cancer.[55] Astonishingly, Carlo further claimed that John Boice and Joe McLaughlin (the epidemiologists behind the Danish report into long term mobile phone use published in 2006) had approached him while he was still head of the WTR for funding of this exact study. Carlo claims that Boice and McLaughlin misinterpreted the WTR's objectives, and reportedly offered to manipulate the results of the study to show the industry in a favourable light. After this proposal was rejected by the WTR, Boice and McLaughlin proceeded to pitch their idea to the industry, which was eager to get them on side. Carlo thus suggests that the Danish study was in fact artificially engineered by the industry in an attempt to invalidate the fears surrounding prolonged mobile phone use.[56]

Carlo's claims are not to be taken lightly. As a high ranking industry insider, he is privy to an amount of information that an investigative journalist could only dream of. He is himself a trained epidemiologist, and the founder of a non-profit health and safety organization; making him uniquely qualified to speak of the dangers of mobile phone usage. If his claims involving a cover-up by the mobile phone industry are correct, then the implications that follow could be disastrous. While the long term effect of prolonged mobile phone usage is still unknown, if the matter is not further scrutinized by impartial, independent observers, followed by the dissemination and implementation of protective measures, then we could be facing a major cancer epidemic within the next twenty years.

Indeed there are some startling parallels in this case with furore surrounding the impact of tobacco intake on smokers' health. When details began to emerge establishing a connection between cigarette smoke and lung cancer, the tobacco industry attempted to stifle this information and prevent it from entering the public arena. They too fronted an "independent" research organization as a sop to public fears – the Council for Tobacco Research (CTR). But the CTR's real objectives were to provide disinformation and divert attention away from the dangers of smoking. So Carlo's claim about the Danish study being a PR coup is not without precedent in the world of industry.

If a long term link between mobile phones and the development of cancer turns out to be correct, then Revelation's depiction of "horrible, malignant sores" appearing on those who have received the mark of the Beast may forewarn us of an impending cancer epidemic related to mobile phone use.

Never again in the course of human history will there arise another set of circumstances which fulfils the required criteria for the prophecy concerning the number of the Beast so exactly. The letters www can be equated with the number 666 through a simple process of transliteration into the Hebrew or Aramaic language and then ascertaining their numerical value. These letters, which act as the embodiment of the

---

[55] Carlo, G; Schram, M. *Cell Phones: Invisible Hazards of the Wireless Age* (New York: Carroll & Graf Publishers, Inc., 2001)
[56] Carlo, G. "Dr. George Carlo's Response to the Danish Study", *Safe Wireless Initiative* (2006)

internet, are presently associated with a device that is temporarily worn in the hand, much like a modern version of the phylacteries worn by Jews contemporary with John; and which the Apostle himself may once have worn. There is also the future possibility that this device can be worn on the forehead, in the shape of LCD TV glasses, thus explaining the Apocalypse's prediction that the mark of the Beast can also be worn on the forehead.

No one in the modern world can buy or sell without being someway associated, either primarily or secondarily, with the use of the internet or mobile phones; and there is the future possibility that this technology will be incorporated into electronic banking in the same way we use credit cards today. These new forms of media have quickly become a staple for modern industry, and even the most basic of businesses consider them to be essential marketing tools. They are also used by well over half the world's population – explaining the Book of Revelation's contention that no-one would be able to buy or sell without the mark or number of the Beast. To round off the prophecy, there is a very real threat that the use of mobile phones presents a serious health risk which corresponds with the Apocalypse's warning that those who receive the mark of the Beast would be inflicted with "terrible sores".

Taken together, the combined evidence that suggests the number and mark of the Beast is to be equated with the internet and internet ready mobile phones is quite formidable. The criteria for this case are summed up in table form below:

Biblical Criterion	Modern Equivalent
The mark will be on the hand or forehead, and be similar in appearance to phylacteries. (Rev 13:16)	Mobile phones are, by their very nature, a handheld device. Use of LCD TV glasses could explain the mark being alternatively located on the forehead.
No one can buy or sell without the mark or the number of the Beast. (Rev 13:17)	No one can buy or sell anything that is not in some way associated with the internet or the use of mobile phones. There is the future possibility that mobile phones will replace the use of credit cards.
The mark is cryptically referred to as the number 666. The true hidden meaning of this number can be discerned by those who possess sufficient knowledge. (Rev 13:18)	Once transliterated into Hebrew, the letters www have the numerical equivalent of 6-6-6.
Wearing the mark of the Beast ultimately results in the bearer being inflicted by a grievous disease. (Rev 16:2)	Some research indicates that prolonged usage of mobile phones may eventually result in users developing various cancers.

Christians are obliged by an assent of faith to believe that the words of the Book of Revelation will someday come to pass – an obligation which extends to the prophecy of the mark of the Beast. If we do not accept that the letters www are connected to the prophecy of the number of the Beast, should we then wait for another future event that will meet the criteria specified in Rev 13:16-18 even more exactly? The only way it could correlate with the words of the Apocalypse more closely is if we are to posit a completely literal fulfilment of this prophecy, along with a literal fulfilment of the rest of the book. If we insist on towing this line however, then our expectations will never be met. A literal Beast with seven heads is not going to emerge from a literal sea and insist on everyone being branded with the literal number 666.

Christians have long recognized the need for such prophecies to be interpreted figuratively rather than literally. The equation of the letters www with the number of the Beast is one such figurative interpretation, but one which at the same time remains rigorously faithful to the wording of the original text. The chances of another situation arising where a central aspect of the world's commerce can be directly linked with the number 666 through a simple process consistent with first century Jewish-Christian thought patterns is, quite frankly, verging on the impossible. We are therefore compelled to assess our current circumstances in light of these facts.

The above conclusions inevitably leads us to ask what are the spiritual consequences of the continued use of the internet and internet ready mobile phones? This question is ultimately left for the Church to decide, if it does eventually concur that we can establish a link between the internet and the number of the Beast. For the time being, we can only guess what spiritual harms are posed by such media.

The sociological dangers of the internet and mobile phones have already been perceived by some prominent members of the Catholic hierarchy. The director of the Vatican press office and spokesman for the Holy See, Fr. Federico Lombardi, has spoken out on how the compulsive nature of the internet and mobile phones can degrade the interior spiritual lives of believers by distracting them from prayer:

> "There is an interior and spiritual dimension of life that must be guarded and nourished. If it is not, it can become barren to the point of drying up and, indeed, dying... Reflection, meditation, contemplation are as necessary as breathing. Time for silence - external but above all internal - are a premise and an indispensable condition for it... In the age of the cell phone and the internet it is probably more difficult than before to protect silence and to nourish the interior dimension of life. It is difficult but necessary.
> For believers, in this dimension prayer, dialogue with God is developed, life in the spirit, which is more important that physical life itself. Jesus told us not to fear those who can kill the body as much as the one who can destroy our soul."[57]

Archbishop Vincent Nichols, the Catholic primate of England and Wales, highlighted one of the most subtle and perhaps most sociologically dangerous aspects of the internet. During an interview with the *Sunday Telegraph*, the Archbishop of Westminster warned how the impersonal nature of the internet and mobile phones has had a detrimental effect on key social skills which could result in a negative overall change in core human behaviour.

> "I think there's a worry that an excessive use or an almost exclusive use of text and emails means that as a society we're losing some of the ability to build interpersonal communication that's necessary for living together and building a community. We're losing social skills, the human interaction skills, how to read a person's mood, to read their body language, how to be patient until the moment is right to make or

---

[57] Lombardi, F. "Don't Let Wi-Fi Leave Your Prayer Life Dry" *Zenit* (23rd Nov 2008)

press a point.

> Too much exclusive use of electronic information dehumanises what is a very, very important part of community life and living together. Facebook and MySpace might contribute towards communities, but I'm wary about it. It's not rounded communication so it won't build a rounded community... If we mean by community a genuine growing together and a mutual sharing in an interest that is of some significance then it needs more than Facebook.
>
> Among young people often a key factor in them committing suicide is the trauma of transient relationships. They throw themselves into a friendship or network of friendships, then it collapses and they're desolate. It's an all or nothing syndrome that you have to have in an attempt to shore up an identity; a collection of friends about whom you can talk and even boast. But friendship is not a commodity, friendship is something that is hard work and enduring when it's right."[58]

While the internet has many features which must be lauded, such as the provision of easy access to a broad array of learning, it also has an enormous potential for harm. Because the web is beyond censorship, it has become saturated with images of unspeakable acts of violence as well as the most depraved forms of pornography. Needless to say, exposure to such images can be seriously detrimental to the development of corruptible minds.

The internet has provided paedophiles with a vast library of illicit material, while chat rooms are used by perverts to target and groom their victims. It contains websites dedicated to features such as how to commit suicide, or for the glorification of anorexia. It can detail how to make explosives or deadly poisons from common household ingredients. Terrorists find the web to be an indispensable propaganda tool. Here they can spout their warped ideologies to the masses, spreading sedition through lies and disinformation along the way.

Mobile phones have a similar capacity for misuse. Indeed mobiles have become one of the most commonly used mediums of viewing illicit material, with even schoolchildren being able to share graphic images of sex or violence downloaded from the internet with their fellow classmates through Bluetooth technology. Mobile phones are also responsible for the widespread craze of "happy-slapping", in which video footage of innocent bystanders being attacked, or youngsters being bullied, is recorded on handsets for amusement. These scenes are then regularly posted on social networking websites so they can be viewed by the general public. And there is also the more recent problem of "sexting", where young people share explicit images of themselves or sexual partners taken on mobile phones with friends.

The sociological dangers of the internet and the medium of mobile phones do not end here however. Nicholas Carr has shown how the internet is changing the very way we read and absorb information.[59] The long term effects of such radical changes in society are extremely difficult to gage, but even now we are witnessing that such changes in basic human behaviour are already taking place. The loss of face to face interaction in social communication has quickly led to a decline in inhibitions, were taboos are frequently broken down in the lack of physical company. We can only speculate on how these new media will alter the future course of sociological development.

---

[58] Nichols, V. cited in Wynne-Jones, J "Facebook and MySpace can lead children to commit suicide, warns Archbishop Nichols" *The Telegraph* (1st Aug 2009)
[59] Carr, N. "Is Google Making Us Stupid? What the Internet is doing to our brains." *The Atlantic* (2008)

Taken in this regard, the internet and mobile phones may indeed prove to be "tools of the Devil". Every positive aspect of the internet can be counteracted by an equal or worse negative element. In most respects, use of the internet is no more "evil" than the use of other technology, such as telephones or TV. But the fact that this technology provides unfettered access to every conceivable act of human depravity escalates it potential for corruption. Maybe if it was more effectively regulated from its inception it would not have received such a negative appraisal, and from a religious viewpoint, could be put alongside other modern technological developments. Now that we are aware of a link between this technology and one of the most important prophecies of the Apocalypse, we are forced to address the implications of its use by the Christian faithful.

New World Order?

So how did this famous prophecy come to be fulfilled so exactly? We are left with three possible answers:

The first, which will be extensively appealed to by atheists and non-Christians alike, is that the equation of www with 666 has occurred by random chance. While this option may initially prove attractive for some, the odds that these three letters (which happen to be intimately bound with modern commerce) could be directly transliterated into the numerical equivalent of 666 in the mother-tongue of the author of the Apocalypse could occur by chance is veritably astronomical.

Secondly, Christians could assert that these circumstances have been brought into effect through supernatural forces. They have been allowed to take place in accordance with God's Divine plan for the redemption of humanity and to usher in the Second Coming of Jesus.

The third alternative could also be used by atheists and non-Christians, but can also appeal to Christians. As www matches the number 666 so neatly, we are left with the nagging suspicion that this central dynamic is in fact manmade. That it may in fact be an artificial construct manipulated to conform to the words of the prophecy contained in Rev 13:16-18 – either by some covert and influential Satanic cult, or by a shadowy secret society.

The "New World Order" hypothesis presented by many Christian Fundamentalists and members of the anti-government far-right movement is one of the most prolific conspiracy theories in popular culture. Today, many Christians believe that the prophecy of the mark of the Beast will be implemented by a secret cabal of Satanists who are part of a vastly influential secret society known as the Illuminati. According to the New World Order conspiracy theorists, the ultimate goal of the Illuminati is to establish a one-world government that will be presided over by the Antichrist.

While some aspects of the New World Order conspiracy theory is grounded in intriguing fact, such as the existence of Bilderberg Group and the Bohemian Club, most of its conclusions are drawn from circumstantial evidence and pure speculation. So the postulated survival of the Illuminati down to the present is by no means conclusive. Until any concrete evidence comes to light in regard to the continued existence of the

Illuminati, we must suspend any judgment on the actual reality of this organisation.

Moreover, the belief that a small group of society's elite shapes world events has another, deeply sinister side to it. Many anti-government extremist groups in America have become dangerously militant as a result of this conspiracy theory. The Oklahoma bomber Timothy McVeigh for example, is but one such extremist whose motivations were influenced by the belief that the American government had been overtaken by Satanic global elitists. Indeed, rural North America is strewn by pockets of anti-government extremists prepared for open aggression against their own government.

Even more disturbingly, the New World Order conspiracy theory is one of the driving forces behind the anti-Western polemic of Islamic fundamentalism. The actions of the American government against the Arab world is seen by Islamist groups such as Al Qaeda as the fruits of the pro-Zionist global elite. Islamists believe the Illuminati New World Order conspiracy to be very real indeed; and even use the intrigue behind this theory as a propaganda tool with which to gain new recruits. The Satanic character of this fabled international cabal adds a strong religious dimension to their *Jihad* against the godless West. Not only do the Islamists perceive themselves as fighting against America and its Western allies in order to help preserve the Islamic faith and facilitate its growth; but they imagine themselves to be engaged in a struggle against the very armies of Satan.

When we also take the anti-Semitic tendencies of this all-encompassing conspiracy theory into consideration, we can see how such beliefs are extremely inflammatory. The insinuation of a secret Jewish plan for complete control of the world has been used to stoke the fires of anti-Semitism throughout the centuries. It took its ultimate form in the promulgation of the *Protocols of the Elders of Zion*, and the use of this tract as part of the Nazi's anti-Jewish propaganda. Even though the promotion of such beliefs ultimately resulted in the Holocaust, they are still widely circulated by racist groups and certain "Christian" organizations throughout the world. And now these beliefs have found a new resurgence in the hate-filled speeches of popular Islamist clerics.

If the belief in the Illuminati is used to such negative effects, then it can only be discouraged. Especially in the absence of any concrete evidence to prove its continued survival to the present. It is inevitable that such beliefs will continue to persist however. The various individuals and organisations that might insist on establishing a connection between the Illuminati and the letters www, must remember that Christians are urged to temper their beliefs both with rationalism and with pacifism. They should also keep in mind the instructions of the First Epistle of St. Peter concerning authorities – even those we do not agree with:

> Be subject for the Lord's sake to every human institution, whether it be to the emperor as supreme, or to governors as sent by him to punish those who do evil and to praise those who do good. For this is the will of God, that by doing good you should put to silence the ignorance of foolish people. Live as people who are free, not using your freedom as a cover-up for evil, but living as servants of God. Honor everyone. Love the brotherhood. Fear God. Honor the emperor. (1Pet. 2:13-17)

Antagonism, no matter how frustrating or provocative, must be met passively, as the only legitimate Christian means of protest is one of non-aggression. If there is a coming tribulation, then we must look to the example of the early Christian martyrs, who fearlessly went to the most agonizing deaths imaginable, while at the same time forgiving those responsible for their torment.

According to the New World Order conspiracy theory, the Illuminati will establish a single economic system which will fulfil the prophecy of the number of the Beast. So it is not hard to predict that these same conspiracy theorists will point to groups such as the Illuminati as the ultimate cause of the letters www being deliberately constructed to correspond with the prophecy of the number of the Beast. But how far can we really take this theory? Is it really rational to propose that a significant proportion of the world's political and economic leaders are part of a Satanic cabal intent on enslaving humanity?

While associations such as the Order of Skull and Bones, Bilderberg Group, Bohemian Club, etc. are undoubtedly real; the existence of a more shadowy institution pulling the strings behind these organizations remains in the realm of conjecture. Even if a group such as the Illuminati does exist in the modern day, it is perhaps overly paranoid to believe that it is comprised chiefly of Satan worshippers intent on fulfilling the prophecy of the number of the Beast. Is it really rational to presume that such a large amount of people in the highest positions of power in the world would willingly attempt to introduce a Satanic plot of such vast scope?

Besides, how the phrase "worldwide web" came to be coined and abbreviated to form www is well documented.[60] Sir Tim Berners Lee, the inventor of the internet, is the sole person responsible for the coining of the phrase "worldwide web". Berners Lee is a respected academic noted for his brilliance, humility and charitable nature, not some avowed Satanist or puppet of an elitist secret society intent on bringing the prophecy concerning the number of the Beast into realization. Besides, the real aims of Freemasonry – the separation of church and state and the secularization of society, have already been accomplished, inducing the state of mass apostasy the Church is currently enduring today. We are therefore forced to conclude that the prophecy of the number of the Beast has been fulfilled of its own accord, rather than due to the involvement of some shadowy Satanic organization.

If we cannot sustain the opinion that the phrase "worldwide web" was coined to purposefully fulfil the prophecy concerning the number of the Beast, we are left with only two possibilities. Either the equation www = 666 is simply a random coincidence that just so happens to fulfil all the criteria outlined in Rev 13:18; or it is the realization of an ancient prophecy that has occurred via supernatural intervention. While the former option will be the choice of preference for many who wish to eschew belief in the Christian religion, the odds against this happening by blind chance is simply too vast to retain any reasonable degree of plausibility. The latter choice appears to be the only reasonable conclusion.

While we have argued above that the prophecy of the number of the Beast has come about of its own accord, the Book of Revelation does seem to suggest that the mark of the Beast would be brought about by the actions of a human being – the forerunner to the Antichrist. This person is identified in Rev 13 as the False Prophet. So how are we to reconcile both of these views? Could a person have been responsible for implementing the prophecy of the mark of the Beast without knowing the consequences of their actions?

---

[60] See for example Tim Berners-Lee's own account of the origins of the acronym www in his book *Weaving the Web: Origins and Future of the World Wide Web* (London: Orion, 1999).

If we examine the pages of the Apocalypse in greater detail, we can establish that the prophecy of the forerunner to the Antichrist may already belong to the past. And while in a roundabout way he is indeed responsible for the birth of the internet, it was not through any intentional plan of his own. Rather he is simply the person who sets in motion a chain of events which have led to our current predicament. In order to fully establish the identity of the False Prophet, we must first turn back to the pages of the Bible in order to discern the signs of the times. It is only once we do so that we can positively ascertain who this individual really was.

CHAPTER FOUR

Signs of the Times

The Bible states at a number of key junctures that God would announce the beginning of the eschatological age through the occurrence of a number of signs. When the disciples asked Jesus "what will be the sign of your coming and of the close of the age?" (Matt 24:3), Christ responded by listing a series of events that would warn of the approach of the Last Judgment – the so-called "signs of the times".

One such sign given by Jesus we have already discussed in some detail in chapter one – the eschatological restoration of Israel. Another of the signs foretold by Jesus in the Olivet discourse is a succession of wars, (which once transposed into the modern age, was most probably fulfilled by the First and Second World Wars), and rumours of wars (the threat posed by the Cold War?). These will not bring about the end by themselves however – they are merely signs of the beginning of the end:

> And you will hear of wars and rumors of wars. See that you are not alarmed, for this must take place, but the end is not yet. For nation will rise against nation, and kingdom against kingdom, and there will be famines and earthquakes in various places. All these are but the beginning of the birth pains. (Matt. 24:6-8)

A final persecution of the Church and the Great Apostasy are among the other signs given in the Olivet discourse, as is the prophecy of the Gospel being preached to all nations – which we have argued is a reference to the Second Pentecost:

> Then they will deliver you up to tribulation and put you to death, and you will be hated by all nations for my name's sake. And then many will fall away and betray one another and hate one another. And many false prophets will arise and lead many astray. And because lawlessness will be increased, the love of many will grow cold. But the one who endures to the end will be saved. And this gospel of the kingdom will be proclaimed throughout the whole world as a testimony to all nations, and then the end will come. (Matt. 24:10-14)

One of the signs mentioned, which can be found throughout both the Old and New Testaments, is that of the eschatological darkening of the heavenly bodies:

> Immediately after the tribulation of those days the sun will be darkened, and the moon will not give its light, and the stars will fall from heaven, and the powers of the heavens shall be shaken. (Matt. 24:29)

These signs are repeated time and again throughout the Bible, and are obviously of great importance to the biblical writers. But what exactly are these signs? And how are we meant to determine that they have been fulfilled in modern times? As we shall see below, by examining the Book of Revelation's use of these signs, we may be able to link these portents with some other prominent eschatological events – such as the date of the eschatological fall of Satan and the implementation of the prophecy of the mark of the Beast.

The Sixth Seal

By examining the positioning of the eschatological darkening of the heavenly bodies in relation to other similar portions of the Apocalypse, we may be able to connect these events with the fall of Satan and the prophecy of the mark of the Beast. If we can establish such a link, then as a relatively rare combination of astronomical events, the darkening of the sun and moon and the falling of stars are concrete physical signs which would allow us to attach a definite date to these other prophecies.

The narrative of the mark of the Beast in Rev 13 is an antithetical parallelism of a previous event in the Apocalypse. Earlier in the Book of Revelation, after the opening of the sixth seal in 6:12, the martyrs are sealed upon the forehead with the name of God:

> Then I saw another angel ascending from the rising of the sun, with the seal of the living God, and he called with a loud voice to the four angels who had been given power to harm earth and sea, saying, "Do not harm the earth or the sea or the trees, until we have sealed the servants of our God on their foreheads." (Rev 7:2-3)

The fact that this occasion is parodied later in the Apocalypse – at the "sealing" of the inhabitants of the earth with the mark of the Beast, invites us to associate and contrast both events. In making this connection, the Book of Revelation seems to suggest that both occurrences are unfolding at the same moment in time. As is often the case in ancient religious literature, macrocosmic heavenly events are reflected on earth in microcosm. This same basic concept can also be found in the Apocalypse. For example the opening of the seven seals in heaven is reflected on earth as a series of omens or calamities. But this time the events in the heavenly sphere are reflected on earth as a diabolical mirror image. In an attempt to mimic the actions of God and thus assume the divine persona, Satan imitates the sealing of the martyrs by deceiving the inhabitants of the earth into accepting the mark of the Beast. It is therefore implied in the text that both events occur simultaneously, each to counter the effects of the other. So if the act of divine sealing and the inauguration of the mark of the Beast coincide together at the same moment in time, then chronologically speaking, the occurrence of the mark of the Beast must take place at the opening of the sixth seal.

If both events occur at the same time, as the text itself suggests, then since the sealing of the martyrs in Revelation is marked by the astronomical phenomena at the opening of the sixth seal, it may be possible to date the exact occurrence of the prophecy concerning the number of the Beast. So by examining the portions of the Apocalypse that deal with the theme of the sealing of the saints, we can shed extra light on the prophecy of the mark of the Beast.

Immediately after the narrative in Rev 13 where the sea-beast compels everyone to receive its mark on their right hand or forehead, we are confronted with a heavenly vision of the 144,000 martyrs in Rev 14:1:

Then I looked, and behold, on Mount Zion stood the Lamb, and with him 144,000 who had his name and his Father's name written on their foreheads.

In a purposefully crafted contrast with the earth-dwellers who have received the mark of the Beast, this vision shows that the name of God and the Lamb is written on the foreheads of the heavenly martyrs. This is clearly intended to mirror the mark of the Beast. But as we mentioned previously, the sealing of the saints first occurred earlier in chapter seven of the Apocalypse, immediately after the opening of the sixth seal in Rev 6.

The sealing of the 144,000 is part of the sequence of events that unfold after the opening of the sixth seal. The first set of events was the eschatological darkening of the Sun and Moon and falling of stars followed by an earthquake. The second set takes place in heaven, with the sealing of the saints reflecting the diabolical form of "sealing" which is taking place on earth. Each of the events are grouped together in the same textual unit of the sixth seal, which suggests they unfold at the same point in time.

The eschatological astronomical phenomena herald on earth the occasion of the sealing of the martyrs in heaven. But they also are also the harbinger of the fulfilment of the mark of the Beast. Therefore we should look at the phenomena that occur at the opening of the sixth seal in order to establish if there was any similar events which took place in the recent past to coincide with developments in the internet or mobile phones. If we do find any such signs, this would be further tangible physical evidence that the prophecy concerning the mark of the Beast has indeed came to fruition.

We can narrow the confines of our search even further if we restrict it to one of the most obvious time periods – that of the introduction of the WAP technology which enabled internet access through a mobile handset. Since this was the first time that internet technology was integrated into a handheld device, it should also be considered to be the first time anyone could truly be said to have the number of the Beast "in their hand", as the prophecy of the mark of the Beast stipulates. The only way the letters www could be said to be worn in the hand as a phylactery-type device is in the creation of the internet-enabled mobile phone.

We are thus provided with a firm anchor date, as the Nokia 7110 – the world's first WAP enabled mobile phone, went on sale in November 1999. This is the earliest possible date that the prophecy of the mark of the Beast could be said to have reached fruition. So we should now turn to investigate whether there were any interesting astronomical phenomena in and around this general time period that could correspond to the eschatological astronomical phenomena at the opening of the sixth seal. As it happens, the years 1999-2000 provided a veritable bumper harvest of celestial omens.

Before we discuss these events any further, we must first turn back to Rev 6:12-13 in order to discern what exactly the text is describing. After the opening of the sixth seal we are told that there was a violent earthquake, the Sun becomes darkened, the Moon turns blood-red and stars fall from the sky:

"When he opened the sixth seal, I looked, and behold, there was a great earthquake, and the sun became black as sackcloth, the full moon became like blood, and the stars of the sky fell to the earth as the fig tree sheds its winter fruit when shaken by a gale." Rev 6:12-13

Throughout the Bible, the prophetic sign *par excellence* of the immanence of the end-time is the darkening of the Sun and Moon. This motif is to be found time and again in the writings of the prophets in connection with the end of days.[1] It also features prominently in Jesus' eschatological discourse in the synoptic Gospels, as well as in the Book of Acts and Revelation itself.[2] While some scholars maintain that this passage refers to the dissolution of the cosmos at the end of time, it is generally agreed that another, more mundane explanation is the primary inspiration behind its interpretation.[3]

The most obvious impression one gets from the statement that "the sun became black as sackcloth" is that the author is describing a total solar eclipse. Solar eclipses and other astronomical phenomena were widely regarded as prodigies in the Greco-Roman world, and were thought to foretell impending disasters or sudden changes in world history.[4] Jewish writers also shared this belief, and Flavius Josephus reported that such signs had heralded the destruction of Jerusalem.[5]

Fig. 12 A photograph of the Sun in totality. The author of the Apocalypse described such an event as the Sun becoming "black as sackcloth".

The description of the Moon turning to blood is recognized to be an allusion to a lunar eclipse.[6] During a total eclipse of the full Moon, the Moon becomes enveloped by the earth's shadow and is completely deprived of light from the Sun. The Moon only remains visible to the naked eye through light from the sun being reflected off the earth's atmosphere, making it appear a deep red-orange or "blood" colour. This also explains why in the Gospels of Mark and Matthew, the Moon is simply "darkened" rather than turning blood red; since both events relate to one and the same event (Mark 13:24; Matt. 24:29).

The account of the stars falling to Earth is a quite explicit reference to a meteor shower, and as such should not require any further explanation. So the events depicted in

---

[1] Joel. 2:3; Isa. 13:10, 24:23; Eze. 32:7; Amo. 8:9
[2] Mar. 13:24 = Mat. 24:29 = Luk. 21:25; Act. 2:20, Rev. 6:12, 8:12
[3] See Smalley, S.S. *The Revelation to John* who following R.H. Charles for example, suggests that the writer "knows that the end is not yet and there is more to follow." p168
[4] See Aune, D.E. *Revelation 6-16* p413-419
[5] Josephus. *Wars* 6.288-310
[6] Smalley, S.S. *The Revelation to John* p167.

Rev 6:12-13 that portend the actualization of the prophecy concerning the number of the Beast at the opening of the sixth seal can be briefly described as an earthquake, a lunar eclipse, a total solar eclipse and a meteor shower.

As S.S. Smalley suggests, what is being described here is not the end of the world itself, it is rather a representation of cosmic events that signal the temporal tribulations which will precede it.[7] They are a sign that the period of the end-time has begun, rather than a description of the end of the world itself.

Individually, each of these events occur on a regular enough basis. We can expect an event such as a total eclipse of the Sun to be visible from somewhere in the world on an almost yearly basis, and lunar eclipses often occur twice a year. In the case of solar and lunar eclipses, each of these phenomena can be witnessed in certain parts of the globe and not in others. This is because of the position of the earth's axis in relation to the Sun or Moon. An eclipse visible to a viewer in Canada will not necessarily be observable to an onlooker in India.

The visibility of a total eclipse of the Sun has even further constraints, and can only be observed from the "path of totality" – a strip of land only just over 110km across, running along a trajectory which follows the setting of the Sun. So while a total solar eclipse can only be viewed in a narrow band, this band can stretch for thousands of miles, traversing continents along the way. As a total eclipse is confined to such a narrow strip of land, the time between the event being seen in any one place can be up to a hundred years apart. For many, a total solar eclipse is a once in a lifetime experience. This fact can help to substantially reduce the probability that such an event can coincide together with the other incidents described in Rev 6:12-13 on a regular basis.

If we restrict ourselves to a single place as well as a certain time period, we can further reduce the odds of such phenomena occurring concurrently. Therefore it should be necessary to establish some controls, and limit our search for the occurrence of these events to be centred on a certain position. For the sake of conformity with the Scriptures, we are compelled to confine the location of these events to somewhere in the Middle East or Near East – the land which the Bible was foremost concerned with. We should also restrict ourselves to with a year of the release of the first internet ready mobile phone – as this was the first time the letters www (which equal 666) could truly be said to have been applied phylactery-like to a person's hand, thus fulfilling the prophecy concerning the mark of the Beast. Now that these structures are in place, our search can begin.

As the total solar eclipse of 11th August 1999 was the final major astronomical event of the second millennium, it was a much-hyped affair. Solar and lunar eclipses have been ascribed with a certain mystical importance since the dawn of civilisation. But this occasion was made all the more important by its occurrence at the very turn of the millennium. Anticipation concerning the millennium had reached fever-pitch by the year 1999, and this eclipse was accorded with especial importance. This major astronomical event was perfectly timed to coincide with the turn of the second millennium, and as such symbolically drew it to a close. For anyone searching for a celestial omen to mark this important event, the 1999 solar eclipse fitted the bill exactly. It also occurred within three months of our prescribed date of November 1999 – the release date of the first WAP enabled mobile phone and fulfilment of the prophecy of the mark of the Beast. If

---

[7] Ibid. pp168-169

the prophecy of the mark of the Beast was heralded by the eschatological astronomical phenomena described in the Bible, then this event is the best possible explanation for the prophesied darkening of the Sun.

The 1999 solar eclipse also meets another of our criteria, as one of the best places from which this event could be viewed was in Northern Turkey. The Book of Revelation was originally addressed to seven churches in Asia Minor – which is presently located within the borders of modern Turkey.[8] Asia Minor was the adopted home of the Apostle John, who according to tradition, journeyed to Ephesus sometime after the Resurrection.[9] So this locale would have particular relevance for the author of the Apocalypse, who was a long term resident at Ephesus before his exile to Patmos. Indeed, a concentration of the eschatological signs given in the sixth seal of Revelation seem to have been centred on the site of ancient Asia Minor.

As we mentioned earlier, solar eclipses were often regarded in antiquity as omens of impending catastrophe. The ancients would look on such events with dismay rather than wonder. Unfortunately, the solar eclipse of 11th August 1999 did in fact turn out to be a harbinger of evil for the inhabitants of North-Western Turkey. On 17th August 1999 – just six days after the eclipse, a major earthquake, measuring 7.5 on the Richter scale, struck the city of Izmit, killing over 17,000 people.

Lying on the North Anatolian fault, Turkey is no stranger to seismic activity. But the devastation caused by this earthquake was particularly severe, as it had struck in a heavily populated region. Coupled with the fact that the earthquake was of an exceptionally high magnitude, the death toll was the worst Turkey had seen in sixty years. For the people of North-western Turkey, the 1999 eclipse really was a portent of catastrophe.

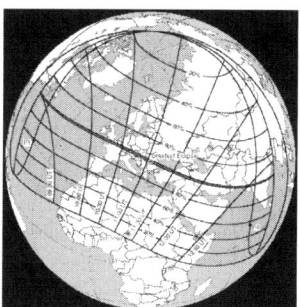

Fig. 13 The middle line shows the narrow path from which the 1999 total solar eclipse could be seen. This route passed through Turkey near the location of the 1999 Izmit earthquake, which followed just days later. The darker area is the region from where the event could be seen as a partial eclipse.

---

[8] See Rev 1:4

[9] According to Roman Catholic tradition, the Apostle John travelled to Ephesus with Mary, the mother of Jesus, where the Blessed Virgin was to live out her remaining years before her death and assumption into heaven. According to a variant Eastern Orthodox tradition, John remained with Mary in Jerusalem until her death before making his way to Ephesus later in life. Both accounts are based on John 19:26-27, where before his death on the cross, Jesus asks the Beloved Disciple to take Mary as his adopted mother. While these traditions may differ as to when and with whom John first travelled to Ephesus, both link the Apostle with this specific location.

These were not the only events in this short time period that aligns with our proposed criteria however. There were two other separate events that took place around this same general time period that may have fulfilled the "falling stars" aspect of the prophecy of Rev 6:12-13. When the 1999 solar eclipse occurred on the 11th August, it took place during the peak of the annual Perseid meteor shower. So two of the astronomical signs prophesied in Rev 6:12-13 – the darkening of the sun and the falling of stars, appear to have coincided in this same short space of time.

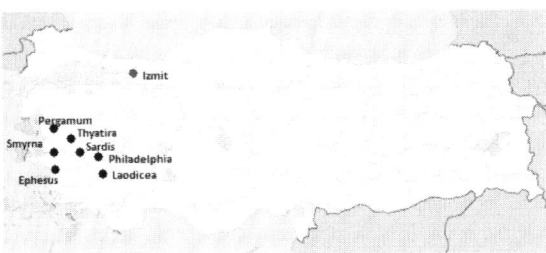

Fig. 14 The location of the 1999 earthquake in Izmit, Turkey, not far from the original location of the seven churches of Asia Minor and the path of the 1999 total eclipse.

The Perseids are known for providing the most regularly consistent display of shooting stars, and along with the Leonids are the most celebrated meteor showers among stargazers. The Perseids are caused by debris left behind the tail of the comet Swift-Tuttle, which passes close to the Earth once every hundred and thirty years. This debris then burns up in the atmosphere when the Earth passes through the meteor belt left behind in the comet's wake. The effects this material burning up upon entry into the Earth's atmosphere can be seen from the surface as the fiery streaks of light that the ancients referred to as "falling stars". The Perseid meteor shower takes place over a number of days during the summer, peaking this time on 12th August. So this famous meteor shower could be seen on the very night of the total solar eclipse on 11th August 1999.

Another, perhaps even better possible fulfilment of the prophecy of the apocalyptic "falling stars" may have taken place during the Leonid meteor storm of mid-November 1999. The Leonid meteor showers are caused by the comet Tempel-Tuttle, but are not usually as active as the Perseids, which are the most regular in terms of visibility. But once every 33 years, at the perihelion of Tempel-Tuttle, they produce a "meteor storm", which are vastly more prolific than meteor showers. Meteor storms can produce thousands of meteors an hour, as opposed to just the few every hour provided by meteor showers. The Leonid meteor storm is the most spectacular such event that can be seen from Earth, and is affectionately known among astronomers as "The King of Meteor Showers".

The Leonids provided one of the most spectacular meteor storms in recorded history, when in 1833 the night-skies of North America were illuminated with the light of thousands of meteors every minute. The Great Leonid Meteor Storm of 1833 was so intense many onlookers thought that the end of the world was at hand.[10] Some estimates have put the 1833 storm as high as over one hundred thousand an hour.[11]

The Leonid meteor storm is not always as prolific as this particular instance, and the next comparable occurrence was not seen again until 1966. Yet each 33 year cycle of meteor storms are still vastly more productive than regular meteor showers. The most recent return of the Leonid meteor storm peaked on 17th November 1999, and although this time the storm was not quite as impressive as its 1833 and 1966 antecedents, it still produced a rate of up to 200 per minute at its peak when viewed from the Sinai Peninsula.[12]

Fig. 15 The most famous depiction of the 1833 Leonid Meteor Storm is an engraving by Adolf Vollmy in 1889. This engraving, which was published in the Adventist book *Bible Readings for the Home Circle*, was based on an earlier painting by the Swiss artist Karl Jausin. It is likely that the Apocalypse's description of "a third of the stars" falling from the sky refers to an event such as this.

Instead of just one year with a significant meteor storm on Tempel-Tuttle's return as is usually the case, several notable Leonid storms were seen throughout 1998-2002. But as the comet passes, the Leonids fade in intensity, and no more Leonid meteor storms of a similar magnitude are expected until the comet's next visit around the year 2032. Therefore the Leonid meteor storm would also meet our conditions, as this peaked during the very hub of our time restrictions – the exact month of the release of the first WAP phone in November 1999. And one of the best places from which this event could be viewed was in Western Asia – including Turkey itself.

We have now found at least three of the signs which the Apocalypse foretold would herald the fulfilment of the prophecy of the mark of the Beast – a solar eclipse, an earthquake, and either a meteor shower during the eclipse or a rarer meteor storm at the very time of our prescribed date. The only other sign stipulated in Rev 6:12-13 we have yet to find is that of a lunar eclipse. And again, we have not one, but two to choose from.

If we were to depart from the geographical confinement of our above search

---

[10] See Rogers, S. Cited in "The Great Leonid Meteor Storm of 1833" *Nasa Science News* (1999)
[11] See Fazekas, A. '2009 Leonid Meteor Shower: "Strong Outburst" Expected' *National Geographic News* (2009)
[12] Frost, M. *Desert Storm: The 1999 Leonid Meteor Shower* (1999)

restrictions, then there was a partial lunar eclipse visible in parts of America and Australia on 28th July 1999 – two weeks before the solar eclipse of 11th Aug 1999. But partial eclipses do not give the Moon a blood red hue, and this eclipse was not visible over the Near or Middle East. However if the term "the Moon turned to blood" could be used to describe any lunar eclipse, this would give us a remarkably tight clustering of events. The fact that Jesus' Olivet discourse states that the Moon "will not give its light", rather than turning blood red, could be used to support this argument.

But if we want to follow our restrictions more closely, then on 21st January 2000 – two months after our anchor date of November 1999, Europe experienced the spectacle of a total lunar eclipse, giving the moon a characteristically blood-red appearance. This event could also be seen from the area where the other events were concentrated – in North-Western Turkey.

All of the criteria specified in Rev 6:12-13 occurred within a few months of our proposed anchor date, and all were centred on the same general location – the area to which the Book of Revelation was originally addressed. The solar eclipse took place three months before our anchor date of November 1999 during a meteor shower, followed soon after by a large earthquake. Then a meteor storm, which takes place once every 33 years, peaked during the exact month of the anchor date – November 1999. Two months later there was a total lunar eclipse which turned the Moon blood-red.

The fact that these events all took place in the same general time period and all could be witnessed within the same geographical location, coinciding with the fulfilment of the prophecy of the mark of the Beast, cannot be put down to mere coincidence. There are simply too many factors involved to dismiss these as pure chance occurrences. But there is another significant aspect of this prophecy not mentioned in the Apocalypse. The prophecy contained in Rev 6:12-13 is based on the earlier sayings of Jesus in the Gospel writings, and can thus be further supplemented by the Olivet discourse.

In his eschatological discourse on Mount Olivet, Jesus foretold that the darkening of the Sun and Moon and the falling of stars would be followed by a great sign visible in the sky – the sign of the Son of Man:

> Immediately after the distress of those days the sun will be darkened, the moon will not give its light, the stars will fall from the sky and the powers of the heavens will be shaken. And then the sign of the Son of man will appear in heaven. (Matt 24:29-30)

Incidentally, a remarkable celestial event did indeed take place after the occurrence of the above events, which we have suggested were fulfilled in the year 1999. On 5 May 2000 – six months after our anchor date, there was an alignment of the planets Mercury, Venus, Mars, Jupiter and Saturn with the Sun, Moon and Earth. Such events are extremely rare, occurring only once every fifty years or so. Then, three weeks later, on 31 May 2000 there was a "great conjunction" of the planets Jupiter and Saturn. Such an event takes place every 18-20 years, with the next occurrence due in December 2020.

Some commentators have posited that the story of the original "sign of the Son of Man", the Star of Bethlehem, was based on a similar event – a triple conjunction of the planets Jupiter and Saturn in the year 7BC, followed by a massing of the planets Jupiter, Mars and Saturn in the constellation Pisces in 6BC.[13] If this is correct, then a planetary

---

[13] Johannes Kepler first made the suggestion in 1614 that the Star of Bethlehem was a triple conjunction of Jupiter and Saturn, followed by the appearance of a 'new star' or supernova, much like the one he had

alignment such as the one that took place in the year 2000, followed weeks later by the great conjunction of Jupiter and Saturn, could well have been the "sign of the Son of Man" spoken of by Jesus, or at the very least a foreshadowing of events to come. The fact that this event occurred in the same general timeframe as phenomena correlating to that described in Rev 6:12-13, and also in accordance with supplementary material found in the Olivet discourse, pushes the odds even further up the scale of improbability.[14]

The fulfilment of prophecy in the Bible is often connected with the occurrence of celestial omens. The aforementioned Star of Bethlehem is but one example of the relationship between prophecies and omens in the ancient world. As is the eschatological astronomical phenomena which herald the beginning of the end-time. But there are many other such signs depicted in the Book of Revelation which accompany earthly events. Indeed Jesus himself expressly stated that astronomical events would figure heavily in the run up to his Second Coming:

> There will be great earthquakes and in various places famines and pestilences. And there will be terrors and great signs from heaven. (Luke. 21:11)

If we are to take this statement seriously, then we are prompted to attempt to find other such phenomena which are related to moments in history that have been interpreted as the fulfilment of prophecy in the recent past. As we shall see, there appears to be quite a few of these key events that seem to be marked by heavenly portents – occurring either almost simultaneously, or within a few months of each other.

Wormwood

The nuclear disaster at Chernobyl is perhaps one of the most heavily popularized modern events which appear to have been foretold in the Apocalypse. Some commentators have pointed to the fact that the name "Chernobyl" has possible etymological connections with the word "wormwood".[15] The name "Chernobyl" is rooted in the Ukrainian word *chornobyl*, which refers to the *Artemisia vulgaris* or Mugwort. The Mugwort is also known as "common wormwood" and is closely related to the *Artemisia absinthium* – the type of plant mentioned in the Apocalypse.[16] If this is the case, then the events at Chernobyl can be directly linked to the sounding of the third trumpet in Rev 8:10-11:

> The third angel blew his trumpet, and a great star fell from heaven, blazing like a torch, and it fell on a third of the rivers and on the springs of water. The name of the star is Wormwood. A third of the waters became wormwood, and many people died from the water, because it had been made bitter.

---

observed himself in 1604. (Kepler, J. *De vero anno quo aeternus dei filius humanam naturam in utero benedictae Virginis Mariae assumpsit*)

[14] We should note here that Adrian Gilbert also places the occurrence of the sign of the Son of Man during the turn of the millennium, in his book *Signs in the Sky* (London: Corgi, 2001) Although for reasons quite different from our own. There was also what is known in astrological terms as a "grand cross alignment" in this same time period.

[15] See Schemann, S. "Chernobyl Fallout: Apocalyptic Tale" *New York Times* (25th July 1986)

[16] The type mentioned in Revelation is Αβσινθος (*Absinthos*)

The fallout of radioactive material from the Chernobyl accident was spread throughout Europe by contaminated rain clouds. Indeed the effects of this radioactive material could be detected throughout most of the northern hemisphere. As well as rainfall, radioactive material was transported by the surrounding rivers, particularly the Pripyat and the Dnieper, rendering the immediate vicinity extremely hazardous. Radiation is still leached into the waterways from the contaminated soil, particularly during times of flooding in the exclusion zone.

... it fell on a third of the rivers and on the springs of water.

The radiation cloud thrown up by the Chernobyl accident spread radioactive material around the world – one third of the Earth's surface would be a very close estimation. On a more local level, 70% of the radiation fell in Belarus, contaminating one-fifth of the country's agricultural land.[17]

... many people died from the water, because it had been made bitter.

Consumption of the contaminated water at Chernobyl seriously affected human health. There has been an alarming increase of cancer and birth defects in the Ukraine since the meltdown first occurred in 1986. Overall, the nuclear disaster at Chernobyl is estimated to have been responsible for over 90,000 deaths, with that figure set to rise over the coming decades.

These facts can all be used to account for most of the words of the prophecy contained in Rev 8:10-11; but the mention of the falling star seems at first to present us with an enigma. The exact wording of the phrase in Rev 8:10-11 seems to detail the characteristics of a comet: "a great star fell from heaven, blazing like a torch". The Roman author Pliny described a particular type of comet as "torches".[18] If we note the timing of the Chernobyl accident, it may be of some relevance that the disaster occurred in the same general time period of the last appearance of Halley's Comet. On its most recent visit to the inner solar system, Halley's Comet was visible in the night skies during January to April in 1986, coinciding with the date of the Chernobyl disaster which took place on 26 April 1986. Comets were also feared in ancient literature as harbingers of doom – an apprehension which appears to have been substantiated in this particular instance.

The correlation of this combination of events with the prophecy of Rev 8:10-11 is either an amazing coincidence, or it constitutes another fulfilment of the words of the Apocalypse. We cannot easily put the Chernobyl/wormwood etymological link, combined together with the fact that the disaster occurred directly after the appearance of Halley's Comet, down to yet another example of apocalyptic coincidence. The Wormwood passage of the Book of Revelation further shows how earthly events are reflected in the heavens as astronomical signs in the eschatological prophecies of the Bible.

---

[17] Rainsford, S. "Belarus cursed by Chernobyl" *BBC News* (26th April 2005)
[18] Pliny *Hist. nat.* 2.22.90; 2.25.96

The Rise of the Locusts

We can find another case of astronomical phenomena heralding the fulfilment of prophecy elsewhere in the Apocalypse. In Rev 9 a celestial omen takes place before the rise of the demonic locust swarm from the abyss:

> And the fifth angel blew his trumpet, and I saw a star fallen from heaven to earth, and he was given the key to the shaft of the bottomless pit. He opened the shaft of the bottomless pit, and from the shaft rose smoke of a great furnace, and the sun and air were darkened from the smoke from the shaft. Then from the smoke came locusts on the earth, and they were given power like the power of scorpions. (Rev 9:1-3)

Clearly the author of Revelation attaches a great deal of significance to such heavenly portents. They are used to introduce several key scenes and characters. Immediately prior to the appearance of the locusts in Rev 9:3 we are told that a star had fallen to earth and unlocked the abyss, out of which a horde of strange hybrid-creatures emerge. The falling star is directly connected to the emergence of the locusts on earth, and acts as an introductory device announcing their arrival on the world stage.

The identity of the locusts of the Apocalypse has been a matter of speculation for centuries. Many of the demonic creatures depicted in the Book of Revelation are composed of the body parts of various animals, much akin to the fantastical creatures of contemporary Greek, Egyptian and Mesopotamian mythology, such as the Chimera, Sphinx or Shedu. However unlike the Chimera-esque beasts of Rev 9:17ff, the locusts of Revelation seem to have no direct parallel to any other hybrid creatures of classical mythology.

Rev 9:3 tells us that the shaft of the abyss was opened by a star falling to earth. Falling stars in apocalyptic literature are widely acknowledged to represent the descent of demonic beings to earth.[19] On a more literal level, this passage seems to refer to a meteor or asteroid impact. Since newsworthy events of this nature are exceptionally rare, it should not be hard to identify once we establish what event the locusts of Revelation symbolize.

If we break down the description of the locusts given in Rev 9:7-10 we should be able to determine the reality behind the symbols. We can then proceed from that point to attempt to discern whether there were any notable meteorite impacts in around this general time frame, as the Apocalypse suggests:

> In appearance the locusts were like horses prepared for battle: on their heads were what looked like crowns of gold; their faces were like human faces, their hair like women's hair, and their teeth like lions' teeth; they had breastplates like breastplates of iron, and the noise of their wings was like the noise of many chariots with horses rushing into battle. They have tails and stings like scorpions, and their power to hurt people for five months is in their tails. (Rev 9:7-10)

---

[19] Scholars are divided over whether it is an angelic or demonic being in this particular instance. For example some, such as Smalley tend to see the actions of a divine agent here (Smalley *The Revelation to John* p225), while others such as Beale identify the falling star as a diabolic entity (Beale *The Book of Revelation* pp491-493). Although it must be said that Beale presents the best case in this matter.

Some modern prophecy commentators have suggested that the locusts could represent attack helicopters.[20] Indeed the equation of these creatures with modern aircraft seems to be worthy of some merit in a futurist interpretation of the Apocalypse. Rev 9:1-11 is directly influenced by the Book of Joel, where in chapter 2 verse 5, we are told that the prophet had a vision of monstrous locusts that "leap on the tops of the mountains". Locusts were universally feared amongst the agrarian societies of the ancient Mediterranean. A locust plague can completely decimate crops, stripping vast areas of agricultural land completely bare. This level of devastation would inevitably result in famine throughout the surrounding affected areas. Since these pests are equipped with the power of flight, they could arrive quite unexpectedly, swarming in to destroy everything in their wake before remorselessly moving on to the next destination. In this respect, locusts do appear to have some affinities with military aircraft (at least on a metaphorical level).

The Apocalypse gives a prolonged and detailed description of these demonic locusts, allowing us to garner a wealth of data from which to infer a hypothetical connection with modern aircraft. Obviously we should not expect an overly literal fulfilment of this prophecy. The only way this description can make sense to a modern reader is if we try to recontextualize it by comparing it to similar images in our own environment. And military aircraft seems to present us with the best modern day equivalent of the hybrid locust creatures described in the Book of Revelation. But while commentators such as Hal Lindsey finds similarities between these "locusts" and attack helicopters, perhaps we can find a better comparison by drawing parallels with military airplanes – particularly those used in the Second World War. We shall break down the similarities as follows:

"*In appearance the locusts were like horses prepared for battle*" – the locusts are analogous to war-horses, which were the ancient world's military equivalent of an armoured vehicle. As locusts have the power of flight, we could state with some justification that these particular locusts were like flying war-horses – or recontextualizing this image for the modern reader: "flying tanks".

"*They had breastplates like breastplates of iron*" – this aspect is perhaps the easiest for the modern reader to relate to, as all aircraft are composed of a metal outer shell.

"*The noise of their wings was like the noise of many chariots with horses rushing into battle.*" – Again, this is a rather accurate description of the rumblings made by modern airplanes when roaring overhead.

"*Their faces were like human faces*" – If we think of a pilot's head being visible from the cockpit, then this would provide an adequate solution to this element of the locusts' description.

"*Their teeth were like lions' teeth*" – many military aircraft are adorned with distinctive artwork which could explain a feature such as this. Harking back to the Second World War, one of the most iconic images to be emblazoned upon American fighter planes, such as the Curtiss P-40 Warhawk, is that of shark's teeth nose art around the underside of the front of the airplane.

---

[20] Lindsey, *There's a New World Coming* pp138-139. See also Haggith, *Prophets of the Apocalypse* pp219-220

Fig. 16 A Curtiss P-40 Warhawk with "shark's teeth" nose art.

The tradition of painting aircraft with distinguishing symbols may also account for the locusts "having hair like women's hair". American military airplanes often had "Petty Girls" as nose art, featuring cartoon pin-ups of scantily-clad women with long flowing hair. Some versions of the Curtiss Warhawk had their nose painted yellow around the propellers, which could explain the locusts having "*on their heads were what looked like crowns of gold*".

Moreover, the locusts of Revelation possess an attribute usually only found in creatures such as scorpions – they are armed with inbuilt weaponry, or "stings"; just as military aircraft are equipped with inbuilt weaponry. The use of the scorpion as a simile in this instance is especially apt, since its attack mechanism is more akin to a ranged weapon than the sting of a wasp or bee. A scorpion is equipped to "launch" its sting towards its target, rather than stabbing at it directly. When viewed in the light of these comparisons, the above description does seem to bear a striking resemblance to military aircraft. If John had been granted a vision of such future events, he could only have attempted to explain them through the imagery of his own 1st century AD context. In this respect, the description is actually quite remarkable.

Fig. 17 The famous *Memphis Belle* American bomber, with typical "Petty Girl" nose art.

Now we have found the best possible fulfilment of the prophecy of the locusts for the modern age, we are thus enabled to search for the astronomical event that the Apocalypse foretells would herald their arrival. If a major meteor impact occurred around the same time as the invention of military airplanes, this would fulfil the exact sequence of events given in Rev 9:1-5. As it so happens, one of the most remarkable extra-terrestrial impacts in recorded history unfolded during in June, 1908. An event which coincided with the creation of the first military aircraft.

The Tunguska incident has intrigued scientists and enthusiasts of the unexplained alike over the course of the last two centuries. Many alternative theories have been formulated in an attempt to explain the events that took place in this remote part of the Siberian wilderness. At around 7:30am on 30th June 1908, a colossal explosion estimated at 15 megatons detonated five miles above the Earth's surface, flattening everything within a 2,000km² radius. The blast was visible to eyewitnesses 500 miles away, and the over the next few days the night skies were illuminated by the vaporized gases that had dissipated into the atmosphere.

The most curious aspect of this incident is that no traces of extra-terrestrial debris were ever found at the site, as is usually the case in a meteoroid or asteroid impact. This led some commentators to conclude that the explosion was caused by the airburst of either a fragment of a comet, which is composed primarily of ice and dust; or a low density asteroid, which would have vaporized in the Earth's atmosphere.[21] Could this event have heralded the rise of the "locusts" from the abyss?

Less than three months after the Tunguska incident, in the September of 1908, an event took place which would eventually result in the birth of the first military aircraft. In February 1908, the Wright brothers had signed a $25,000 contract with the US Army to develop a machine capable of sustained flight. The army would buy an airplane from the brothers under the conditions that they could demonstrate that the machine could be flown along with a passenger and pilot for the duration of at least an hour at an average speed of 40mph.

Orville Wright began the US Army trials on 3rd September 1908 at Fort Myer, Virginia, where he demonstrated his machine's power of flight to an open audience. The brother's previous attempts had been shrouded in secrecy, so this was the first time the general public had witnessed such a spectacle. Prior to this uniquely pivotal moment, the concept that a heavier-than-air machine could be capable of powered flight had seemed impossible. But now the Wright brothers had proved beyond doubt that man was capable of taking to the air in a machine made of heavy materials.

The first trials were extremely successful, and Orville broke several records in the opening demonstrations. But this smooth start would soon be marred by a tragic accident. Two weeks later, Lt. Thomas E. Selfridge (who was appointed by the army to travel with Orville as a passenger) was killed when a split propeller sent the machine into a nosedive. Lt. Selfridge became the first person to die as a result of an airplane crash and Orville was left badly injured. The delivery of the flying machine to the US Army would now have to be postponed until the following summer. After his recovery, Orville

---

[21] In 1930 Harlow Shapley was the first astronomer to suggest that the event was caused by a comet. More recently, a team of Italian researchers led by Dr. Luigi Foschini forwarded evidence that the explosion was caused by a low density asteroid. See "Probable asteroidal origin of the Tunguska Cosmic Body" *Astronomy and Astrophysics* (2001)

made a few more demonstrations of the machine before the army finally accepted it as the world's first military airplane on 2nd August 1909, naming it *Signal Corps Airplane No. 1*. The brothers received an additional $5,000 bonus for exceeding the original 40mph specification. The smoke of Tunguska had barely settled before the first "locust" had flown forth on the Earth's horizons.

The reference to the locusts not being allowed to harm anyone for five months in Rev 9:5 is rather more problematic. If we consider the "months" here to rather represent a period of five years, then it could refer to the first use of the airplanes in military attacks during the First World War in 1914. No one was actually killed by the attack of a military airplane until five years after the Wright brother's plane was formally accepted by the US Army.

The Horsemen of the Apocalypse

If the locusts represent the birth of modern military aircraft, could they also have symbolized the onslaught of the two world wars? The unleashing of the locusts is described by the Apocalypse as being the first of three "woes" that are to befall the inhabitants of the earth. If the first woe represented the invention of military airplanes during the Great War, then it may be that this event was a way of symbolizing the war itself. In this case the first woe would represent the First World War, which was characterized by the invention of airplanes. But what does the second woe refer to?

The first woe has passed; behold two woes are still to come. Then the sixth angel blew his trumpet, and I heard a voice from the four horns of the golden altar before God, saying to the sixth angel who had the trumpet, "Release the four angels who are bound at the great river Euphrates." So the four angels, who had been prepared for the hour, the day, the month, and the year, were released to kill a third of mankind. The number of the mounted troops was twice ten thousand times ten thousand; I heard their number. And this is how I saw the horses in my vision and those who rode them: they wore breastplates the color of fire and of sapphire and of sulfur, and the heads of the horses were like lion's heads, and fire and smoke and sulfur came out of their mouths. By these three plagues a third of mankind was killed, by the fire and smoke and sulfur coming out of their mouths. For the power of the horses is in their mouths and in their tails, for their tails are like serpents with mouths, and by means of them they wound. The rest of mankind, who were not killed by these plagues, did not repent of the works of their hands nor give up worshipping demons and idols of gold and silver and bronze and stone and wood, which cannot see or hear or walk, nor did they repent of their murders or their sorceries or their sexual immorality or their thefts. (Rev 9:12-21)

If the first woe refers to the First World War, then it would be tempting to equate the second woe with the Second World War. This can be done by comparing the second woe with a similar passage in Daniel that seems to have foretold the events of World War Two. As we noted earlier in chapter one, the Book of Daniel appears to have predicted the restoration of the land of Israel after the "Little Horn" makes war against the "saints" of the Most High:

"Then I desired to know the truth about the fourth beast, which was different from all the rest, exceedingly terrifying, with its teeth of iron and claws of bronze, and which devoured and broke in pieces and stamped what was left with its feet, and about the ten horns that were on its head, and the other horn that came up and before which three of them fell, the horn that had eyes and a mouth that spoke great things, and that seemed greater that its companions. As I looked, this horn made war with the saints and prevailed over them, until the Ancient of Days came, and judgment was given for the saints of the Most High, and the time came when the saints possessed the kingdom. "Thus he said: 'As for the fourth beast, there shall be a fourth kingdom on earth, which shall be different from all the kingdoms, and it shall devour the whole earth, and trample it down, and break it to pieces. As for the ten horns, out of this kingdom ten kings shall arise, and another shall arise after them; he shall be different from the former ones, and he shall put down three kings. He shall speak words against the Most High, and think to change the times and the law; and they shall be given into his hand for a time, times and half a time. But the court shall sit in judgment, and his dominion shall be taken away, to be consumed and destroyed to the end. And the kingdom and the dominion and the greatness of the kingdoms under the whole heaven shall be given to the people of the saints of the Most High; their kingdom shall be an everlasting kingdom, and all dominions shall serve and obey them.' (Dan 7:23-27)

If we accept that this prophecy relates to the restoration of Israel after the Second World War (as we suggested earlier in chapter one); then it follows that the "Little Horn" which persecutes the "saints" could only be Adolf Hitler. Daniel's Little Horn is part of the entity represented by the fourth beast with ten horns, and makes war against the "saints of the Most High". The Aramaic word קדישין *Qadishin*, translated here as "saints", literally means "holy ones" and refers specifically to the Jewish people. The Little Horn prevails over the Jews until his kingdom is taken away, and dominion is restored to the "holy ones" of God. This reference to an end-time persecution of the Jewish people before dominion is restored to them could only refer to the events surrounding the Holocaust.

In this scenario, the fourth beast's ten horns might represent the ten nations of the Axis powers of the Second World War – Germany, Italy, Japan, Hungary, Romania, the Slovak Republic, Bulgaria, Yugoslavia, Croatia and Thailand. The three kings subdued by the fourth beast would therefore symbolize the three main Allied nations – the USA, Great Britain and Soviet Russia. These three kings are depicted earlier in the Book of Daniel in the vision of the four beasts. The three kings were represented by the three beasts that preceded the fourth beast with ten horns:

"I saw in my vision by night, and behold, the four winds of heaven were stirring up the great sea. And four great beasts came up out of the sea, different from one another. The first was like a lion and had eagles' wings. Then as I looked its wings were plucked off, and it was lifted up from the ground and made to stand on two feet like a man, and the mind of a man was given to it. And behold, another beast, a second one, like a bear. It was raised up on one side. It had three ribs in its mouth between its teeth; and it was told, 'Arise, devour much flesh.' After this I looked, and behold, another, like a leopard, with four wings of a bird on its back. And the beast had four heads, and dominion was given to it. After this I saw in the night visions, and behold, a fourth beast, terrifying and dreadful and exceedingly strong. It had great iron teeth; it devoured and broke in pieces and stamped what was left with its feet. It was different from all the beasts that were before it, and it had ten horns. I considered the horns, and behold, there came up among them another horn, a little one, before which three of the first horns were plucked up by the roots. And behold, in this horn were eyes like the eyes of a man, and a mouth speaking great things. As I looked, thrones were placed, and the Ancient of days took his seat; his clothing was white as snow, and the hair of his head like pure wool; his throne was fiery flames; its wheels were burning fire. A stream of fire issued and came out from before him; a thousand thousands served him, and ten thousand times ten thousand stood before him; the court sat in judgment, and the books were opened. I looked then because of the sound of the great words that the horn was speaking. And as I looked, the beast was killed, and its body destroyed and given over to be burned with fire. As for the rest of the beasts, their dominion was taken away, but their lives were prolonged for a season and a time. (Dan 7:2-12)

If the four beasts of Dan 7 represent the main players in the Second World War, then we are left with the puzzle of determining which beast symbolizes which country. We have already equated the fourth beast with the Axis powers, so this leaves us to identify the other three with their respective counterparts. An obvious choice for the bear in a futurist interpretation of Daniel is that of a reference to Russia, since it is that country's national symbol. We can find even more evidence to support this hypothesis if we dissect this passage a little further. The extract states that the bear is standing "up on one side", which is often taken to indicate that the bear is raised up on its hind legs ready to attack. The bear has three ribs in its mouth, which compel it to "devour much flesh". These "ribs" are most likely another representation of the "three kings". If we are to maintain that this episode relates to the Second World War in its futurist, eschatological interpretation, then the three ribs would be a reference to what historians have dubbed the "Big Three" – Winston Churchill, Franklin Roosevelt and Joseph Stalin.

During the Second World War, there were major conferences attended by the Big Three, during which comprehensive strategies and post war policies were thrashed out. The Big Three conferences were held in Tehran, the capital of Iran, and Yalta, a Crimean city in southern Ukraine – territories which were then occupied by Soviet Russia. Could this explain how the "three ribs" were in the "mouth" of the bear? The ribs' exhortation to "arise, devour much flesh", may thus be interpreted as a reference to the immense loss of life as a result of the war in the Eastern Front, and the free license given to Russia by the other Allied leaders during the Big Three conferences. The war on the Eastern Front was by far the bloodiest theatre in the Second World War, resulting in the deaths of over 5 million Axis forces and over 8 million Russian military personnel, as well as around 18 million civilian deaths. A comparison with the losses of the other two major Allies, 382,000 on the British side and around 400,000 on the American, helps to put these figures into perspective.

If the bear symbolizes Russia, then we should look to see if any of the other beasts can be compared to the other two major Allied nations – the USA and the United Kingdom. The most notable characteristics of Daniel's third beast is that it has four wings and four heads and "dominion was given to it". But what exactly is this dominion over? While the text does not elaborate on this point, it would be easy to assume that the dominion given to this beast is that of the Holy Land. Ancient Israel was often a vassal territory of the surrounding superpowers, including Egypt, Assyria, Babylonia and Persia. It would be natural for the reader to assume that the dominion referred to here was that over the land of Palestine. As we noted earlier in chapter one, from the years 1920 to 1948, Palestine was under British mandate. Therefore Daniel's third beast may symbolize the United Kingdom. Interpreted in this fashion, the four heads would symbolize the four countries that comprise the UK – England, Scotland, Wales and Northern Ireland, and perhaps the wider British Empire by association.

We can only equate America with the first beast by a process of elimination, as there does not seem to be any immediately obvious parallels between the two other than the eagle's wings – the eagle being the national symbol of America. Daniel's first beast undergoes a metamorphosis, changing from a ferocious lion into a human figure with human sentiments. This may symbolize the United States' transformation from a slave-holding nation to a state favouring emancipation. The eagle's wings would then perhaps represent the two opposing sides of the United States – the slave-holding southern states that would become the Confederacy during the Civil War, and the slave-free north that would become the Union. The lion changes into a man only after these opposing sides are removed and the country then once again stood as a united whole.

This interpretation of Daniel's four beasts, while somewhat speculative, can be used to tie in with the restoration of Israel after the appearance of the beasts in this vision. The fourth beast with the ten horns persecutes the saints of the Most High and fights against the other three beasts. The heavenly court then sits in judgment and the fourth beast is destroyed. The kingdom, or dominion, (which is most likely the same dominion that was given to the third beast – that over the land of Palestine) is then taken from the other three beasts and given to the saints of God. The three other beasts are allowed to continue for another while, until the coming of the Son of Man with the clouds of heaven.

So what bearing does the above interpretation of Dan 7 have on the second woe of the Apocalypse? The second woe of Revelation is set in motion by the release of four angelic beings, whose mission is apparently to destroy a third of humankind. But what do these four angelic beings represent? Could they be associated with the four beasts of Dan 7? As G.K. Beale points out, the fact that these angels were held in captivity suggests that they are in fact demonic beings.[22] This episode is comparable to the narrative of the four other demonic spirits of the Apocalypse – the four horsemen of the Apocalypse. Could the second woe recapitulate the opening of the first four seals of the Apocalypse and the release of the four horsemen?

The four angels of Rev 9:14 are presented in a manner which suggests they have already been introduced to the reader. As D.E Aune observes: "That the phrase "the four angels" is articular suggests either that it refers back to the four angels standing at the four corners of the earth in 7:1... or that it refers to a group of four angels that the author assumes are familiar to his readers."[23] There are a number of similarities between the four horsemen and the four angels of Rev 9:14 which infer that they relate to one and the same group – both sets are evil spirits, four in number, and both come to bring war to the earth. There is also the shared theme of mounted cavalry. Both of their missions entail destroying a large proportion of humanity – the horsemen of chapter six are charged to destroy a quarter of the people (Rev 6:8), while the horsemen of chapter nine are commissioned to kill a third (Rev 9:15).

There also appears to be a connection between the four angels/horsemen of the Apocalypse and four beasts of Daniel. If we examine the relationship between the four horsemen with the four living creatures, we can determine that the horsemen appear to be an antithetical parallelism of the living creatures. The four living creatures of Revelation are the four cherubim in the throne room of the heavenly temple, and are a combination of the heavenly creatures depicted in Ezek 1:5-11 and Isa 6:2. The four horsemen are summoned by the four living creatures after the breaking of the first four seals, and are portrayed as demonic counterparts to the heavenly cherubim.

The four beasts of Daniel are also presented as a demonic corruption of the four cherubim of the heavenly throne room. If we compare the descriptions of the two sets of creatures, particularly with Daniel's first beast, we can see that they are remarkably similar:

---

[22] Beale, G.K. *The Book of Revelation* p506
[23] Aune, D.E. *Revelation 6-16* p536

Four Living Creatures	Four Beasts of Daniel
First creature is like a lion	First beast is like a lion
Third creature is like a man	First beast is made to stand like a man
Fourth creature is like an eagle	First beast has eagle's wings
All six creatures have wings	Leopard and Lion have wings

The imagery of both sets of creatures is derived from the artwork of ancient Mesopotamia, where hybrid mythological beasts were composed of the body parts of several animals.[24] Winged sphinxes and lions were commonplace in the throne rooms of ancient Assyria and Babylonia, and would have been familiar to both Ezekiel and the author of Daniel. So the inspiration behind the living creatures and Danielic beasts are drawn from this common source.

We can also draw some parallels between the attributes of the four horsemen of the Apocalypse and Daniel's four beasts:

Four Horsemen of the Apocalypse:	Four Beasts of Daniel:
First rider is given a crown	Daniel's third beast is given dominion
Second rider makes men slay one another	Second beast is commanded to devour much flesh
Fourth rider is named death and hell follows him	Fourth beast is terrifying and destroys everything in its wake

If the four angels of the second woe are to be equated with the four horsemen of the Apocalypse, as well as the four beasts of Dan 7, then a quite sizeable portion of the apocalyptic literature of the Bible would be devoted to providing a prophetic commentary on the Second and First World Wars. Given that these episodes of modern history are unparalleled in the scope of evil perpetrated by human beings against one another, it should perhaps be expected that events with the historical magnitude of the two World Wars would have been prophesied in the Bible. Human beings have always inflicted evil upon one another, but never before was this manifested on such a colossal scale. By the end of 1945 almost 100 million people had been killed at the hands of their fellow man in the combined losses of both wars.

The crime of genocide ascended to a whole different level during the course of the Second World War when it was conducted on an industrial scale against Europe's Jewish population. Given its symbiotic relationship with the Jewish people, it would be hard to

---

[24] Osborne, G.R. *Revelation* pp233-235

accept that the Bible would omit any mention of such wholesale slaughter of the Jews. Could we really accept the prophetic legitimacy of the Hebrew Bible if it neglected to foretell a Jewish race-specific disaster on the scale of the Holocaust?

If we are correct in our above hypothesis that the eschatological meaning of the "Little Horn" foretold in the book of Daniel was fulfilled in the person of Adolf Hitler, we are left to question the exact nature of this role in relation to the Antichrist. The Danielic Little Horn is usually interpreted in Christian eschatology as being a reference to the future coming of the Antichrist. But if our hypothesis that Dan 7 refers to the Holocaust, Second World War and the restoration of Israel; and that the Little Horn is a representation of Adolf Hitler, do we then have to conclude that Hitler was the ultimate fulfilment of the prophecy of the Antichrist? Not necessarily. As we shall see, there is another role described in the Apocalypse that tells of a precursor to the Antichrist, much in the same way John the Baptist was the forerunner of Jesus.

The False Prophet

The Book of Revelation foretells that a forerunner to the Antichrist would appear on the stage of human history during the eschatological age in the person of the "False Prophet". Could Hitler have fulfilled this precursory role? The False Prophet is presented by the Apocalypse as a part of the unholy trinity, along with the Dragon and the Beast. He is referred to by name a number of times in the Book of Revelation, in 16:13; 19:20 and 20:10. But it is in verses 13:11ff that the False Prophet plays his most important role, under the guise of the beast from the earth:

> Then I saw another beast rising out of the earth. It had two horns like a lamb and it spoke like a dragon. It exercises all the authority of the first beast in its presence, and makes the earth and its inhabitants worship the first beast, whose mortal wound was healed. It performs great signs, even making fire come down from heaven to earth in front of people, and by the signs it is allowed to work in the presence of the beast it deceives those who dwell on earth, telling them to make an image for the beast that was wounded by the sword and yet lived. And it was allowed to give breath to the image of the beast, so that the image of the beast might even speak and might cause those who would not worship the image of the beast to be slain. (Rev 13:11-15)

The False Prophet is depicted in Revelation as an "anti-Elijah" type figure who makes the paths straight for the coming of the Antichrist. The fact that the False Prophet mimics Elijah's greatest miracle – calling down fire from heaven, invites us to draw comparisons between the two: "It performs great signs, even making fire come down from heaven to earth in front of people" (Rev 13:13). The main purpose of this passage is symbolic, and is used to show that the role of the False Prophet is to prepare the way for the coming of the Antichrist. As such it is probably is not meant to be understood in any literal sense.

The imagery of the land-beast of Rev 13 is taken from Dan 8, which predicted among other things, the reign of Alexander the Great (d.323BC), the division of the Macedonian Empire, and the Jewish persecution of Antiochus IV Epiphanes (d.164BC). But as it possesses some of both beasts' shared attributes, the Apocalypse's land-beast appears to be an amalgam of Daniel's ram and goat. The ram with the two horns in

Daniel is a passive character which is quickly destroyed and represents the kingdoms of Media and Persia. Although the land-beast is most similar to this creature in looks, it is more similar in nature to the goat of Dan 8, from which arises the tyrannous "Little Horn".

The Apocalypse repeats here its typical composite use of disparate Old Testament imagery by combining Daniel's ram and goat into a single corporate image. The Book of Revelation often assimilates the apocalyptic imagery of the Old Testament, adding new prophetic emphases through its synthesis of this material. There are many examples of the Apocalypse combining the imagery of various parts of the Hebrew Bible. As we mentioned above, the four living creatures of Revelation are an amalgam of the cherubim and seraphim of Ezek 1:5-11 and Isa 6:2-3. The living creatures in Ezekiel each have four faces – that of a man, a lion, an ox and an eagle, and each have four wings. In the Book of Isaiah, the seraphim have six wings and chant the trisagion – "Holy, holy, holy is the LORD of hosts; the whole earth is full of his glory!" The Apocalypse combines both these passages to form its own spin on the living creatures. Ezekiel's cherubim now each have a single face – one of a lion, one of an ox, one of a man, and one of an eagle. But instead of having four wings as in Ezekiel, they now have the six wings of Isaiah's seraphim and chant a new version of the trisagion – "Holy, holy, holy is the Lord God Almighty, who was and is and is to come!" (Rev 4:8)

Another example can be found in the Book of Revelation's presentation of the four beasts of Daniel as the sea-beast in Rev 13:1-2. Instead of the four separate creatures – a lion, a bear, a leopard and a beast with ten horns, we have a single corporate leopard-like entity with ten horns, the feet of a bear and the mouth of a lion. So just as the description of the sea-beast/Antichrist given in Rev 13:1-2 is a combination of the four beasts of Dan 7, so too is the land-beast/False Prophet a fusion of the creatures of Dan 8. By combining the beasts of Dan 8 to form the False Prophet, the Apocalypse is implicitly suggesting that we can find supplementary material to compliment this character in Daniel's vision of the ram and goat. When we turn back to Daniel, we find that the vision of the ram and the goat concerns the same individual as in chapter 7 – the infamous "Little Horn" who persecutes the Jews before the restoration of Israel. So the Little Horn of Daniel is one and the same as the False Prophet of the Apocalypse.

With this fresh understanding of Dan 8 now fresh in mind, we should now re-examine this chapter to see if it can shed any further light on the person of the False Prophet. The angel Gabriel interpreted this vision of the goat's Little Horn to Daniel as follows:

> And at the latter end of their kingdom, when the transgressors have reached their limit, a king of bold face, one who understands riddles, shall arise. His power shall be great – but not by his own power; and he shall cause fearful destruction and shall succeed in what he does, and destroy mighty men and the people who are the saints. By his cunning he will make deceit prosper under his hand, and in his own mind he shall become great. Without warning he shall destroy many. And he shall even rise up against the Prince of princes, and he shall be broken – but by no human hand. (Dan 8:23-25)

The scholarly consensus correctly maintains that the preterist meaning of the Little Horn of the book of Daniel is to be found in the reign of Antiochus IV Epiphanes.[25] Yet as we have discussed before, very often in the history of salvation the past contains

---

[25] See for example, Goldingay, J.E. *Daniel* (Nashville: Word, 1989), pp174ff

echoes of events that are to take place in the future. The events of the past appear to follow some sort of Divine blueprint of the events that will unfold in the eschaton. So accepting that Antiochus Epiphanes was the primary, preterist meaning behind the Little Horn of Daniel should present little difficulties. But Dan 8:17 explicitly states that this vision also has an eschatological dimension: "Understand, O son of man, that the vision is for the time of the end." So there is an additional eschatological meaning behind the story of the Little Horn, or Antiochus Epiphanes, who Revelation suggests foreshadows the person of the False Prophet. Therefore by examining the life and actions of Antiochus IV, we can gain an idea of the central qualities of the False Prophet.

After the premature death of Alexander the Great in 323BC, his vast empire was divided between four of his generals, with Syria falling under the control of the Seleucid kings and Palestine under the Ptolemies. In 198BC, the Seleucid king Antiochus III wrested control of Palestine from Ptolemy V, which was then passed on to his son Antiochus IV Epiphanes. Epiphanes was a brutal overlord, and subjected the Palestinian Jews to a vicious campaign of Hellenization. Nicknamed Epimanes ("madman" – a pun on the Greek *epiphanes*, meaning "illustrious"), Antiochus IV attempted to impose Hellenism on Palestine as a means of unifying it with the rest of the Seleucid empire.

After a brief rebellion in Jerusalem, Epiphanes seized the Holy City while returning from a campaign in Egypt and slaughtered many of its inhabitants. He established a permanent garrison of Syrian soldiers in Jerusalem and prohibited the practice of Judaism on pain of death.[26] While some Jews capitulated to Epiphanes' demands and apostatized, many remained steadfast and were mercilessly cut down. Antiochus IV attempted to establish the worship of Greek gods by setting up an altar to Zeus in the precinct of the Temple Mount (the original "abomination of desolation" mentioned by Daniel). Much to the disgust of the Jews, pigs were sacrificed on the Temple altar in a deliberate act of desecration.

These provocations were not taken lightly be the inhabitants of Judea, and ultimately provided the catalyst for the Jewish revolt led by the Maccabees. Under the leadership of Judas Maccabeus, the Jews eventually drove the Seleucids from Jerusalem and established Jewish sovereignty in Judea that would last for over a hundred years. After successfully ousting Seleucid rule in Judea, the Maccabees then set about cleansing the Temple of its desecration, inaugurating the Jewish festival of Hanukkah.

The False Prophet of the Apocalypse appears to be modelled after an individual who had achieved notoriety for his ferocious persecution of Jews. Does this suggest that the eschatological False Prophet would also be a persecutor of the Jewish people? The portrait of Antichous IV as a persecutor of the Jews is surely his most enduring image, and it is most likely that it is this aspect of his life and actions that would be adopted by the future incarnation of this role in the person of the False Prophet. If so, then Adolf Hitler would be the ultimate fulfilment of the prophecy of the False Prophet. Hitler perfectly emulated his second century BC precursor in many ways. Just as the Seleucid ruler embarked on a severe Jewish persecution during the 2nd century BC, so this latter day Antiochus Epiphanes would undertake the greatest persecution of the Jews in history. If Hitler was anticipated proleptically by any other historical character, then it could only

---

[26] 1 Macc. 1:57

be by Antiochus IV Epiphanes.

But we have so far overlooked the most important aspect of the role of the False Prophet. The Apocalypse states that it is the land-beast/False Prophet who is responsible for the implementation of the prophecy of the mark of the Beast:

> Also it causes all, both small and great, both rich and poor, both slave and free, to be marked on the right hand or forehead, so that no one can buy or sell unless he has the mark, that is the name of the beast or the number of its name. (Rev 13:16-17)

Could Hitler really have been the primary cause of the development of the worldwide web? The answer is, in a roundabout way, yes. Like the First World War before it, the Second World War provided an urgent need for the development of new technologies that otherwise may not have not been converged upon for several decades. World War Two has been identified by many modern historians as the ultimate catalyst for the modern digital age. Without the frenetic arms race brought on by this conflict and the resultant hastening of scientific development that it had induced, modern technology would have advanced at a much slower pace. The nations involved in the conflict entered into a state of total war, where all available resources including civilian duties and scientific research, were concentrated solely on the war effort.

The Manhattan Project's development of the Atomic bomb is undoubtedly the most significant and dangerous outcome of the war, but there were major technological breakthroughs across many different areas. Aircraft technology was significantly improved during the war, and inventions such as radar and sonar enabled vastly greater detection abilities in both the air and sea. Other innovations developed during the war included the rocket technology that would later result in the space age, and the creation of the world's first computers.

The early precursors to modern computers, such as the German Z3 (1941), the British Colossus (1944), and the Harvard Mark I (1944), were built in direct response to the needs and conditions set by the Second World War. The Z3 was the first general purpose digital computer, and was developed by the Germans to aid construction of aircraft, while the Colossus computer was devised by the British to help decipher messages encrypted by the Germans using the Lorenz SZ40/42 machine. The Harvard Mark I, which is widely regarded as the true forerunner of modern computers, was created by the US Navy for ballistic and gunnery calculations during the war. Without the accelerated circumstances and pressure of the Second World War, the computer age would not have advanced at such an incredible rate and we would not possess the same advanced technology we have today.

So by invading Poland and instigating the Second World War, the actions of Hitler indirectly led to the development of the first computers, which would inevitably result in the global network known as the worldwide web. Therefore this "False Prophet", who is the forerunner to the Antichrist, could be said to have caused the inhabitants of the world to be "marked" with the number of the Beast by causing the Second World War and consequently accelerating the development of computer technology.

The interpretation of Hitler as the False Prophet prophesied by the Bible could also be used to explain the variant dating for the coming of the Antichrist in the secrets of La Salette. The dating of Melanie's secret for the arrival of the Antichrist was 100 years after 1846, as opposed to Maximin's date which stated that "a monster" would come to disturb the peace at the end of the millennium:

> Lastly hell will reign on earth. It will be then that Antichrist will be born of a sister, but woe to her! Many will believe in him, because he will claim to have come from heaven, woe to those who will believe in him! That time is not far away, twice 50 years will not go by.[27]

Melanie speaks of a forerunner to the Antichrist in the later non-Church authorised version of her secret:

> 'A forerunner of the antichrist with his troops from several nations will fight against the true Christ, the only Savior of the world; he will spill much blood, and will want to annihilate the worship of God in order to make himself be looked upon as a God. The earth will be struck all kinds of plagues [in addition to pestilence and famine which will be general;] there will be wars until the last war, which will then be made by the ten kings of the antichrist, which kings will have all one same design and will be the only ones who will rule the world. Before these arrive, there will be a type of false peace in the world; one will think only about amusing oneself; the wicked will deliver themselves over to all kinds of sin, but the children of the holy Church, the children of the faith, my true imitators, will grow in the love of God and in the virtues which are dear to me.'[28]

Although we cannot consider Hitler to be *the* Antichrist (who is prophesied to assume control at the time of the end) he was an antichrist-type figure. Perhaps the greatest antichrist-type figure besides the Antichrist himself. 1John 2:18 speaks of "many antichrists"; and as part of the unholy trinity, the False Prophet could be considered to be the most important antichrist figure apart from the Antichrist himself. The 100 years for the coming of the Antichrist given in Melanie's secret began in 1846, and is just within the above timeframe for Hitler. The German dictator killed himself towards the end of the war in 1945, so the period of twice fifty years did not go by – it stopped just short at ninety-nine years, which would be a rather accurate prediction for the death of Hitler. In this interpretation of Melanie's secret, the statement "Antichrist will be born of a sister" could refer to the fact that Hitler was born to Klara Hitler – a devout Roman Catholic, as an alternative explanation to the usual conception that the Antichrist would be born to a nun.

If we accept that Hitler was the fulfilment of the prophecy of the False Prophet, we are thus faced with two problems. The first is that the Apocalypse introduces the sea-beast/Antichrist first, which on a cursory reading seems to suggest that the Antichrist appears first, and is then followed by the False Prophet who uses his power to support the Antichrist's regime. But as we have stressed time and again, the Book of Revelation regularly flouts chronological convention in its recapitulatory framework. His placing as first in the sequence may reflect a hierarchy of importance rather than chronological order. The fact that the land-beast is presented in an anti-Elijah role to prepare the way for the coming of the Son of Perdition implicitly suggests that the False Prophet precedes the Antichrist.

---

[27] Bourmaud, D. "The Discovery of the Secrets of La Salette: A Book Review", *Newsletter of the District of Asia*

[28] See Gouin, P. *Sister Mary of the Cross: Shepherdess of La Salette Melanie Calvat* (New Jersey: The 101 Foundation, 1968)

A second problem arises from the Apocalypse's description of the sea-beast as being the entity with the ten-horns, rather than the False Prophet, which would conflict with our assertion that the False Prophet is Daniel's beast with ten horns (which we argued is the ten nations of the Axis powers). However these similar attributes can be reconciled in a passage in the Apocalypse where we are told that as an act of homage to its master, the False Prophet constructs an idol fashioned in the image of the sea-beast:

> ...by the signs that it is allowed to work in the presence of the first beast it deceives those who dwell on earth, telling them to make an image for the for the beast that was wounded by the sword and yet lived. And it was allowed to give breath to the image of the beast, so that the image of the beast might even speak and might cause those who would not worship the image of the beast to be slain. (Rev 13:14-15)

So the ten nations of the Axis powers may foreshadow another alliance of nations under the Antichrist in the future.

Holocaust

If the Book of Daniel predicted the Jewish Holocaust, can we find any further references to this terrible moment of history in the Book of Revelation? We have previously attempted to demonstrate how the second woe of the Apocalypse may have contained a prediction of World War II. So if there was any reference to the mass extermination of the Jews to be found in the Apocalypse, it would most likely be located in the portion of the book dealing with the second woe:

> So the four angels, who had been prepared for the hour, the day, the month and the year, were released to kill a third of mankind. The number of mounted troops was twice ten thousand times ten thousand; I heard their number. And this is how I saw the horses in my vision and those who rode them: they wore breastplates the color of fire and of sapphire and of sulfur, and the heads of the horses were like lions' heads, and fire and smoke and sulfur coming out of their mouths. By these three plagues a third of mankind was killed, by the fire and smoke and sulfur coming out of their mouths. (Rev 9:15-18)

At first, interpreting this passage as a prediction of World War II seems to present us with a number of problems. A third of mankind was not killed during the Second World War, nor were there two hundred million mounted troops involved in this global conflict. But when we turn to the original Greek of the Apocalypse, a quite different picture emerges from the above translation. We will deal with the latter problem first. The phrase "the number of mounted troops" is a rather misleading translation of the original Greek, which gives "*kai ho arthimos ton strateumaton tou hippikou*". "*ton strateumaton*" is an articular noun which means "the army", or "of the soldiers". "*tou hippikou*" is a genitive articular noun, and means "of the horsemen", rather giving just "of horsemen" or "mounted troops". So a more faithful translation of this phrase would be "and the number of the army of the horsemen". If we put this more literal translation into context with the rest of the passage, we can shed further light on the identity of the horsemen:

> So the four angels, who had been prepared for the hour, the day, the month and the year, were released to kill a third of mankind. The number of the army of the horsemen was twice ten thousand times

ten thousand; I heard their number.

As we mentioned previously, the fact that the words "four angels" are accompanied by the definite article, giving "*the* four angels" suggests that the reader has already been introduced to these beings. We also argued that the four angels referred to here are the four horsemen of Rev 6. We can find proof of our suggestion by using an alternative rendering of the genitive. Instead of translating this verse as meaning "the army *comprised* of horsemen", it should have the possessive sense "the army *belonging* to the horsemen". This translation is supported by the fact that the second noun is articular giving "the army of *the* horsemen", rather than anathorus, giving "the army of horsemen". Taken in this way, "the horsemen" would refer to the four angels in the preceding verse, whom the author assumes the reader to know. This gives us the following sense:

> So the four [horsemen], who had been prepared for the hour, the day, the month and the year, were released to kill a third of mankind. The number of the army of the horsemen was twice ten thousand times ten thousand; I heard their number.

This sense of the translation is more internally consistent. It explains the expected knowledge of the identity of the angels and also establishes both sets of "horsemen" as the same group of demonic angels. So instead of having a single army of 200 million mounted troops, we have 200 million soldiers of the combined armies of the four horsemen/angels – a figure close to the actual number of combatants who fought in both world wars.

Another feature which suggests that the interpretation of the prophecy must belong to past events is the fact that no army as vast as this can ever be mobilized at any point in the future. The simple truth is that the days of conventional warfare on a global stage are over. With the invention of nuclear weapons, conflicts on the scale and style of the previous world wars will no longer be an option. As the use of atomic weapons on Hiroshima and Nagasaki at the end of the Second World War has already proven, future world wars will be settled with the nuclear option. And once a global nuclear conflict arises, there will be very few people left to fight a conventional war on the ground, let alone 200 million.

The phrase "to kill a third of mankind" is also not entirely consistent with the original Greek of the Apocalypse, which is given as "*hina apokteinosin to triton ton anthropon*". If we look at the last word "*anthropon*", meaning "people" and which is translated above as "mankind", we can see it is preceded by the accusative definite article "*ton*". A more faithful and literal translation of this passage would be "so that they might kill the third of the people". The fact that "*ton anthropon*" here is used in the definite sense suggests that it is a third of *a particular people* that is to be killed. A third part of *the* people, rather than just the broader, generic sense of "people". So which people would this refer to? The most obvious choice of course is the people of Jesus and the Apostles – the Chosen people.

The Holocaust claimed the lives of around five and a half million Jews – which at the time was one third of the world's total Jewish population. The 1946/47 American Jewish Yearbook states that: "The figures reveal that the total Jewish population of the world has decreased by one-third from about 16,600,000 in 1939 to about 11,000,000 in 1946 as the result of the annihilation by the Nazis of more than five and a half million European Jews."[29]

All of a sudden the above, more faithful translation makes perfect sense, giving a startlingly accurate figure of the victims of the Shoah. Shipped en masse from the ghettoes of the occupied territories of the Third Reich to the concentration camps of Eastern Europe, the Jewish people endured the single most prolific act of genocide in human history. Whole families were forced to work in barbaric conditions with little or no nourishment; watching each other waste away until the guards marched them off to be shot, gassed or experimented upon. Indeed no words can ever hope to capture the sheer scope of this evil or the level of despair it instilled in the souls of its victims.

It should be incomprehensible for believing Christians that the scriptures would fail to make any reference to an atrocity on the scale of the Holocaust to the very people God had elected to be the vessel for the world's redemption. The relationship between God and Israel is too long and deep running. Have we found the proof of God's continuing concern for his Chosen people in the pages of the Books of Daniel and the Apocalypse?

The fact that Rev 7 states that these martyrs are descended from the twelve tribes of Israel imparts a distinctly Jewish feel to this portion of the Apocalypse. Importantly for the interpretation outlined above, the passage opens with another reference to four angels who are charged with spoiling the earth. Should these four angels be equated with the horsemen also?

> Then I saw another angel ascending from the rising of the sun, with the seal of the living God, and he called with a loud voice to the four angels who had been given power to harm earth and sea, saying, "Do not harm the earth or the sea or the trees, until we have sealed the servants of our God on their foreheads." And I heard the number of the sealed, 144,000, sealed from every tribe of the sons of Israel. (Rev 7:2-4)

The number 144,000 is highly symbolic for the author. As G.K. Beale elaborates, twelve is the number of completeness "as well as the accompanying idea of unity in diversity".[30] Therefore the figure of 12 x 12,000 represents the totality of God's people. The focus then shifts from the 144,000 to the "innumerable multitude". The innumerable multitude is distinguished from the 144,000, yet also shares in the beatific vision.

So the four angels of this vision, who we argue are the same beings tasked with destroying "a third of the [Jewish] people" in Rev 9:15, are now charged with destroying the earth and the sea. But they are not permitted to do so until the 144,000 have been sealed with the name of God.

It is also interesting to note that 144,000 multiplied by 40 (the biblical number of trial and purification) gives the figure 5,760,000 – a figure very near the closest estimates of the exact number of the victims of the Holocaust. The British historian, Sir Martin Gilbert, estimated the number of the victims of the Shoah at 5,750,000,[31] while others put the figure between 5.29-5.86 million.[32]

---

[29] Schneiderman, H; Maller, J.B. (Eds) *American Jewish Yearbook Vol 48* (Philadelphia: The Jewish Publication Society of America, 1946) p599

[30] Beale, G.K. *The Book of Revelation* p59

[31] Gilbert, M. *Atlas of the Holocaust* (New York: Macmillan, 1982)

[32] Gutman, Y. (Ed.) *Encyclopaedia of the Holocaust* (New York: Macmillan Library Reference USA, 1995)

One of the twenty four elders then explains the vision of the 144,000 to John, with words which become even more poignant in light of their equation with the victims of the Holocaust:

> Then one of the elders addressed me, saying, "Who are these, clothed in white robes, and from where have they come?" I said to him, "Sir, you know." And he said to me, "These are the ones coming out of the great tribulation. They have washed their robes and made them white in the blood of the Lamb. Therefore they are before the throne of God, and serve him day and night in his temple; and he who sits on the throne will shelter them with his presence. They shall hunger no more, neither thirst anymore; the sun shall not strike them, nor any scorching heat. For the Lamb in the midst of the throne will be their shepherd, and he will guide them to springs of living water, and God will wipe away every tear from their eye. (Rev 7:13-17)

Therefore the 144,000 represent the Jewish people, having come through a terrible period of persecution which would claim a third of their number. After the appearance of the horsemen who claim the lives of a third of "the people", the Apocalypse then gives a description of the martyrs killed during this persecution, at the opening of the fifth seal. The fact that this vision occurs after the opening of the first four seals implies that the martyrs of the fifth seal are the people killed during the tumults unfolding at the release of the horsemen of the Apocalypse. Their souls are seen by John under the altar of the heavenly temple at the place of sacrifice, offering up their suffering to God. Like Jesus in Christian thought, by bearing the cruelties perpetrated against them in the Shoah, Israel had become the Suffering Servant of Isaiah. A theme which was also hinted at by Pope John Paul II:

> This extraordinary people continues to bear signs of its divine election. I said this to an Israeli politician once and he readily agreed, but was quick to add: "If only it could cost less!..." Israel has truly paid a high price for its "election." Perhaps because of this, Israel has become more similar to the Son of man, who, according to the flesh, was also a son of Israel.[33]

Does this analogy suggest that the Shoah was the "crucifixion" of the Jews, who like the Christian martyrs, participate and share in the eternal sacrifice of Christ?[34] The

---

[33] John Paul II *Crossing the Threshold of Hope* (London: Jonathan Cape, 1994)

[34] It may be theologically difficult for some Christians to accept that salvation can be attained without belief in Jesus, and there has been some confusion within modern Catholic theology as to the extent of supercessionism (for an excellent take on this subject, see Schoeman, R. *Salvation is from the Jews* (San Francisco: Ignatius Press, 2003). The Mosaic Covenant is not enough to achieve salvation by itself. Even the Jewish patriarchs who preceded Christ could only be saved through Jesus' descent into Hades in the period between his death and resurrection – during the "Harrowing of Hell", when Christ rescued the virtuous dead from the depths of Sheol. We may appeal to Karl Rahner's concept of the "anonymous Christian" here, which influenced the Dogmatic Constitution on the Church *Lumen Gentium* (Vatican City: Libreria Editrace Vaticana, 1964). *Lumen Gentium* states that those "who no fault of their own, do not know the Gospel of Christ or His Church, but who nevertheless seek God with a sincere heart, and moved by grace, try in their actions to do His will as they know it through the dictates of their conscience – those too may achieve eternal salvation" (Paragraph 16). But we must ask how non-Christians can attain salvation, which can only be achieved through Christ? It would follow then that Christ can save even those who have died. Was the Harrowing of Hell confined to those who died before Jesus, or was it an event which stands outside of linear time – meaning that through his descent to the dead Jesus can still rescue those who have died since his death and resurrection?

Jews were indeed "crucified" during the Holocaust; and just as Christ rose from the dead on the third day, the Jewish nation was resurrected from the ashes of Auschwitz three years later in the creation of the state of Israel. An end result which appears to have been predicted by the book of Daniel:

> As I looked, this horn made war with the saints and prevailed over them, until the Ancient of Days came, and judgment was given for the saints of the Most High, and the time came when the saints possessed the kingdom. (Dan 7:21-22)

Note that the "time, times and half a time" may have another layer of meaning in its relation to the duration of the Shoah. In the above passage, the saints of God are given over to the authority of the Little Horn/False Prophet for this set time period. A time period which may be equated with the duration of Hitler's Final Solution, which was brought into effect from January 1942 and was to last until the liberation of Mauthausen and Theresienstadt in May 1945 – just under three and half years.

It is also interesting to note that the word Holocaust is derived from the name of the burnt offering performed at the Temple in Jerusalem, taken from the Greek ολος *holos* "completely" and καυστος *kaustos* "burnt". A sacrifice given for the forgiveness of sin and reconciliation with God. It is striking that the Apocalypse uses the same theme of burnt sacrifice when describing the sacrifice of the martyrs of the four horsemen, who are under the altar of the heavenly throne room:

> When the Lamb opened the seventh seal, there was silence in heaven for about half an hour. Then I saw the seven angels who stand before God, and seven trumpets were given to them. And another angel came and stood at the altar with a golden censer, and he was given much incense to offer with the prayers of all the saints on the golden altar before the throne, and the smoke of the incense, with the prayers of the saints, rose before God from the hand of the angel. Then the angel took the censer and filled it with fire from the altar and threw it on the earth, and there were peals of thunder, rumblings, flashes of lightning, and an earthquake. (Rev 8:1-5)[35]

In the above interpretations of the Books of Daniel and Revelation we seem to have found scriptural proof of the legitimacy of this term, and a justification of some of the conclusions of Holocaust theology in Judaism.[36] Yet the Holocaust does not seem to be the only fulfilment of the prophecy of the great eschatological tribulation. If we study the passage taken from the Apocalypse below, it seems that the Holocaust foreshadows another great persecution during the last years of humankind – a persecution which could only be under the Antichrist himself:

It is surely the event of the Harrowing of Hell that Jesus refers to when he spoke of breaking into the strong man's house: "But no one can enter a strong man's house and plunder his goods, unless he first binds the strong man. Then indeed he may plunder his house." (Mark 3:27) At Jesus' death on the Cross, Satan was "bound for a thousand years" (Rev 20:2), so that Christ could lead the virtuous dead to his Father's house. It is also interesting to note that Jesus' saying "a kingdom divided against itself cannot stand" is found directly in relation to this passage in the synoptics.

[35] These are undoubtedly the same martyrs under the altar at the opening of the fifth seal in Rev 6.

[36] See for example Maybaum, I. *The Face of God After Auschwitz* (Amsterdam: Polak & Van Gennep Ltd, 1965), who perceives a soteriological dimension to the victims of the Holocaust, akin to that of the Suffering Servant in the Book of Isaiah.

When he opened the fifth seal, I saw under the altar the souls of those who had been slain for the word of God and for the witness they had borne. They cried out with a loud voice, "O Sovereign Lord, holy and true, how long before you will judge and avenge our blood on those who dwell upon the earth?" Then they were each given a white robe and told to rest a little longer, until the number of their fellow servants and their brothers should be complete, who were to be killed as they themselves had been. (Rev 6:9-11)

The souls of those martyred by the four horsemen in the above passage are the same as those that wash their robes in the blood of Jesus after being sealed with the name of God in Rev 7. A chilling aspect of the above passage is that it appears to suggest that there is another period of tribulation to follow the one that claimed the lives of these martyrs, who now reside in heaven having been purified in the blood of the Lamb. It appears that the victims of the horsemen were only the first fruits of the eschatological persecution. They are told to wait a while longer for recompense until the persecution still to come has claimed the lives of the final Christian martyrs.

Did the immense suffering of the Jewish people during the course of the Holocaust anticipate the future persecution of the Church – just as the persecution of Jews under Antiochus Epiphanes foreshadowed the violent suppression of Christianity by the Roman Emperors? This future persecution of the Church is not only predicted in Rev 11-13, but also in the Third Secret of Fatima's vision of the systematic murder of the pope and his fellow religious.

Conclusion

It seems that many of the "signs of the times" given by Jesus in the Olivet discourse have already came to pass. We have discussed how the unfolding of some of the major events described in the Apocalypse are accompanied by various astronomical signs. The appearance of such signs were vastly more important to observers in the 1st century than what they are accorded today by modern believers. But given the fact that celestial omens were held with such importance by the writers of the Bible, they should still retain some religious significance for contemporary interpreters.

The greatest of these astronomical omens – the darkening of the Sun and Moon, along with an earthquake, falling stars and the appearance of the sign of the Son of Man, may have been fulfilled in the years 1999-2000 – at exactly the same time we have suggested that the prophecy concerning the mark of the Beast came into fruition. The Apocalypse contains strong indicators that both of these events would unfold conterminously. The astronomical signs that occurred at this crucial juncture in modern history appear to have heralded the fulfilment of the prophecy of the mark of the Beast – at the same time as the opening of the sixth seal, which announces the sealing of the people of God. So the sealing of the saints in heaven is reflected antithetically on earth as the marking with the number of the Beast.

The fact that the Apocalypse explicitly states that the prophecy of the mark of the Beast would be brought about by the machinations of the land-beast/False Prophet suggests that the identity of this figure belongs to a subject in the past, before the prophecy of the number of the Beast reached its fulfilment in the age of the internet. In equating the land-beast of Rev 13 with the little horn of Dan 7-8, we have forwarded the hypothesis that the Book of Daniel predicted that the False Prophet would persecute the Jews before the restoration of Israel – an event which was fulfilled as a result of the Second World War and the Third Reich's Final Solution. If we equate Hitler with the False Prophet, then his actions really did impact and accelerate the development of computer technology which has resulted in the fulfilment of the prophecy of the mark of the Beast.

It appears that the First and Second World Wars were among the signs of the times predicted by Jesus in the Olivet discourse – the great wars that were foretold to occur before the Second Coming (Matt. 24:6-7). They are also the first two woes of the Apocalypse – the plagues of the locusts and the devastation wreaked by the "four horsemen" – who we have equated with the four beasts of Daniel. But it appears that the third woe is still to come in the reign of the Antichrist, persecution of the Church and final battle of Armageddon.

By comparing the Book of Daniel with the text of the Apocalypse, it seems that these eschatological texts predicted a mass religious persecution before the restoration of the Holy Land to the Chosen people. But Rev 6:11 suggests that this event also foreshadows a coming persecution of Christians. Just as Antiochus Epiphanes' persecution of the Jews foreshadowed Nero's persecution of Christians, the Holocaust perpetrated by the Third Reich augurs the impending tribulation of Christians under the Antichrist.

But what can we tell about this coming persecution, or of the reign of the Antichrist and battle of Armageddon? So far in this book we have dealt mostly with interpretations that have already been fulfilled in the past. In this respect, we were in relatively safe territory. The benefit of hindsight is greatly illuminating for any interpreter. Since the events are purported to have happened already, this leaves little room for error. Once we move on to discuss the future however, we are entering into the realms of uncertainty. Therefore any of the conclusions reached in the next part of this book must be made tentatively.

Although the Apocalypse contains a basic framework for the next set of events, exactly how they will unfold is difficult to determine. While we may be able to construct a provisional thesis of how these events will occur, it is impossible to escape from forwarding a certain degree of speculation. In order to limit room for mistake, we will adhere as much as possible to the blueprint provided in the apocalyptic literature of the Bible supplemented by material found in the traditional Catholic prophetic writings.

The sequence of events still to come may be summed up as follows:

The ministry of the Two Witnesses
The spiritual revival/Second Pentecost
The persecution of the Church
The martyrdom of the Two Witnesses
The fall of Babylon
The reign of Antichrist
The Second Coming
The Battle of Armageddon
The General Resurrection and Last Judgment

Given the recapitulatory nature of the Book of Revelation, it is difficult to be sure of the exact chronology of the above sequence; but the above list represents our best guess at the general order of these sequences. According to this scenario, the ministry of the Two Witnesses brings about the great spiritual revival that takes place before the tribulation period. The great persecution includes the period of apostasy the Church is currently experiencing, which will then intensify at a later stage before cumulating in the violence that claims the lives of the Two Witnesses.

Over the course of the next chapter, we shall see that the prophesied "fall of Babylon" – the collapse of the leading world power at the end-time, may create the conditions needed for the next set of events that are to follow. But what exactly is the "whore of Babylon"? How does it suddenly collapse? And what does the author of the Book of Revelation imply will happen as a result of its downfall? As we shall see, the Apocalypse foretells the downfall of the most powerful nation on Earth, caused by an unprecedented cataclysmic event. The political turmoil left in the wake of this disaster may set the stage for the rise to power of the Antichrist and provide the catalyst for Armageddon – the last great war to consume humankind.

CHAPTER FIVE

Babylon Falling

The narrative of the fall of Babylon is one of the most detailed scenes in the Book of Revelation. Over two chapters are dedicated to relating the downfall of this corrupt "whore-city". The first explicit mention of "Babylon" in the Apocalypse occurs in Rev 14:8, which places the fall of Babylon just after the vision of the 144,000 with the Lamb on Mount Zion in Rev 14:1-5, and before the coming of the Son of Man in Rev 14:14:

> Another angel, a second, followed, saying, "Fallen, fallen is Babylon the great, she who made all nations drink the wine of the passion of her sexual immorality."

Babylon is doomed from the very moment of its introduction into the narrative of the Apocalypse. But to what does this symbolic name refer? The preterist meaning of term "Babylon" is usually interpreted by commentators as a cipher for Imperial Rome. As Beale notes, "Rome came to be called 'Babylon' in some sectors of Judaism because it also destroyed the temple in Jerusalem and exiled Israel".[1] In Rev 17, Babylon is depicted as a woman sitting on a scarlet beast with seven heads and ten horns. An angel explains to John in Rev 17:9 that the seven heads of the beast represent seven oρη *ore*, which in Greek can mean either mountains or hills. Aune points out that the phrase "seven hills" was used by writers from the mid-1st century onwards as a symbolic reference to the seven hills on which the ancient city of Rome was seated.[2]

The seven heads of the Beast are also said by the angel to represent seven kings:

> This call for a mind with wisdom: the seven heads are seven mountains on which the woman is seated; they are also seven kings, five of whom have fallen, one is, the other has not yet come, and when he does come he must remain only a little while. As for the beast that was and is not, it is an eighth but it belongs to the seven, and it goes to destruction. (Rev 17:9-10)

Scholars usually interpret the seven kings as seven Roman emperors from Julius Caesar onwards, but are divided over the exact sequence. Some commentators, such as Chilton, use this verse to pin the dating of the Apocalypse to the reign of Nero.[3] This would make the fallen emperors Julius Caesar, Augustus, Tiberius, Caligula and Claudius, putting the composition of Revelation at the extremely early date of the mid-60's AD. Others, such as Smalley, date Revelation towards the end of reign of Vespasian (69-79), making the five kings who have fallen Augustus, Tiberius, Caligula, Claudius and Nero, and glossing over the three short lived reigns of the "caretaker" emperors

---

[1] Beale, G.K. *The Book of Revelation* p755
[2] Aune, D.E. *Revelation 17-22* pp944-945
[3] Chilton, D.C. *The Days of Vengeance* (Fort Worth: Dominion, 1987), p436

Galba, Otho and Vitellius during 68-69AD.[4] Those who wish to follow Ireneaus' dating of the Apocalypse to the reign of Domitian (81-96) either begin with Caligula as the first anti-Christian emperor after the death and resurrection of Jesus and leave out the three caretaker emperors,[5] or view the numbering of seven as purely symbolic.[6] So according to the dating which puts the Apocalypse at the reign of Domitian, the emperor still to come and who reigns for only a short while thus refers to the brief reign of Nerva between 96-98.

Osborne offers a combination of the last two solutions – that the emperor reigning is Domitian, and that the other emperors are glossed over in order to make up a symbolic total of seven.[7] This explanation takes into account the external and internal evidence for a Domitianic date for Revelation, while also giving the symbolic value of the number seven primary importance.

The eighth king, who is said to "belong to the seven" is perhaps another allusion to the *Nero redivivus* myth. This king represents the Antichrist still to come – who, like Nero before him, will be a persecutor of Christians. Nero is thus used as a template by John on which to style the future Antichrist.

The preterist interpretation of the whore of Babylon has been firmly established as a veiled reference to the Roman Empire. So the angelic cry of jubilation: "Fallen, fallen is Babylon the great" foreshadowed the fall of the Roman Empire in the 5th century AD – which rapidly declined after the sack of Rome by the Visigoths in 410. But how are we to identify "Babylon" in a futurist interpretation of Revelation?

The Last Empire

The first and most important key to understanding the futurist meaning of the whore of Babylon can be found in Rev 17:18. Here, the Apocalypse states that the whore of Babylon is the "great city who has dominion over the kings of the earth." Just as the ancient Babylonian Empire was once the world's most powerful nation, the whore of Babylon represents the last great empire to dominate the earth. This leaves us with very few options to choose from. In fact, if we are to equate the whore of Babylon with the world's most powerful nation in the present, then there is only one contender. The only country in existence today that could be said to constitute an "empire" of the stature described in the Book of Revelation is the United States of America.

While in today's nomenclature it is mostly referred to as the world's only remaining superpower, the USA also exhibits various imperialistic characteristics. Although America does not pursue a policy of political domination of foreign states, as is technically required for the definition of "empire", many modern thinkers feel that

---

[4] Smalley, S.S *Thunder and Love* pp40-50
[5] Strobel, A. "Abfassung und Geschichstheologie der Apokalypse nach Kapitel xvii.9-12" *NTS 10*, 439-440
[6] Mounce, R.H. *The Book of Revelation* (Grand Rapids: Eerdmans, 1998), p317. It is almost certain that seven is used here primarily in a symbolic sense.
[7] Osborne, G.R. *Revelation* p620. Although he concludes that Domitian is the reigning emperor based on the other evidence, rather than relying on this passage.

political domination of other countries is no longer required for an "empire" to operate.[8] In the post-modern world, market dominance is the key factor to controlling other societies. In this respect, the United States is undoubtedly the world's market leader, controlling the World Bank, the International Monetary Fund, and the World Trade Organization.

In his book *Imperial Ambitions*, the renowned left-wing political philosopher Noam Chomsky demonstrates how the USA employs regime change as an imperial tool.[9] A basic and pragmatic governmental strategy employed by imperial regimes is to establish puppet states to administrate conquered territories, much like the US has done recently with the interim governments of Afghanistan and Iraq. America has justified itself for military intervention in these cases by invoking the advancement of human rights and prevention of the spread of terrorism.

But history has shown that the US will only intervene if it detects a detrimental effect on its own economic growth. It ignores other cases of atrocities committed by countries that do not impinge on its own selfish interests, such as the Rwandan genocide of 1994, which resulted in the deaths of around one million people. Since any military intervention in Rwanda would not have reaped any worthwhile economic or strategic benefits, America conveniently overlooked the deepening crisis and let the massacres unfold. It seems the "world's policeman" will only act against crimes that will affect itself or its political allies. In the case of the regime change in Iraq, America clearly had imperial interests at heart, with its gaze intently fixed on future oil supplies and the stability of the American economy.

Empires also tend to sponsor the proliferation of their various cultures in conquered territories through the process of cultural imperialism – such as Hellenization under the Greeks, or Latinization under the Romans. Cultural imperialism is used in order to assimilate the conquered populace and thus limit the possibility of rebellion. The USA is similarly involved in this form of psychological conquest, and heavily endorses the spread of American culture. Due to America's dominance in the global market, English is now the *lingua franca* – the international language of commerce. We can travel almost anywhere in the world and come across the names of American conglomerates adorning the shop fronts of local towns, or witness previously traditionally- attired people wearing western-style clothing. By employing these psychological tactics America has used cultural imperialism as a powerful propaganda tool which causes the subject to identify with the subjugator. American culture has spread around the world to such an extent that it has managed to gain the respect of the citizens of many countries who should otherwise view the US in a negative light.

But does all these attributes necessarily mean that America can be described as an empire? Michael Walzer, a leading political philosopher, concludes that "hegemony" is a better term for America's current global dominance; as this is a looser, less authoritarian word.[10] In other words, while it cannot be technically declared to be an empire, since it is not involved in political domination of other countries, America should still be considered to be the world's sole dominant political force due to its current global

---

[8] For example, Michael Hardt and Antonio Negri in their book *Empire* (Massachusetts: Harvard University Press, 2001)

[9] Chomsky, N.   *Imperial Ambitions* (London: Metropolitan Books, 2005)

[10] Walzer, M.   "Is There an American Empire?" *Dissent Magazine* (2003)

hegemony.

For the original author of Revelation, the whore of Babylon represented Rome – the current dominant world-power. However in any eschatological interpretation which posits the end-time to be unfolding in our present age, the USA is the only possible candidate for a modern interpretation of the "whore of Babylon". But how can a country which openly declares itself to be Christian, and which has a healthy population of practicing Christians, be considered to be in need of such vigorous condemnation? To find the answer to this question, we must look back to the pages of the Bible.

The Great Whore

In the Bible, the epithet "whore" was often used for the censure of Israel because of its frequent participation in religious syncretism with the Baal cult. Due to the covenantal nature of the relationship between God and his chosen people, the prophets often portrayed Israel as the wife of Yahweh. In the Song of Solomon for example, the bride preparing herself for her husband was intended to be understood on a metaphorical level as Israel's relationship with Yahweh. This allegory was made even more explicit elsewhere in the Bible. The Book of Isaiah for example, openly describes Israel as the wife of Yahweh.

> For your Maker is your husband, the LORD of hosts is his name; and the Holy One of Israel is your Redeemer, the God of the whole earth he is called. For the LORD has called you like a wife deserted and grieved in spirit, like a wife of youth when she is cast off, says your God. (Isa 54:5-6)

Yet when Israel betrayed its God by worshipping the Baals, the metaphor of the adoring wife was replaced with that of a prostitute. Not only was Israel an adulteress, but it had sold itself to foreign gods in the hope of receiving extra blessings in return.

Before the Babylonian exile, Israel and Judah had often engaged in religious syncretism with the Baal cult. Baal was worshipped in the high places of Israel, and even the Temple in Jerusalem had been periodically used for Baal worship. As the Israelites turned from a pastoral nomadic existence to settle into an agricultural lifestyle, they increasingly adopted the traditions of Canaanite culture. Their new dependency on agriculture allured many Hebrews towards Baal as the Canaanite god of fertility. Before long, Yahweh and Baal were being worshipped side-by-side by a sizeable portion of the Israelite population; and each god was petitioned for their respective perceived attributes. As time progressed, many Israelites failed to differentiate between Yahweh and Baal, viewing them both as different aspects of the same deity. Baalism thus began to become assimilated into Israelite culture, and by the time of Elijah in the 9th century BC, the apostasy had reached such an extent that the number of those who did not engage in such syncreticism numbered only seven thousand.[11]

This spiritual harlotry did not go unheeded. By way of an enacted analogy to Israel's betrayal of Yahweh, the prophet Hosea was commanded to marry the prostitute Gomer (Hos 1:2). As a result of its treachery in following the Baal cult, Hosea declared

---

[11] See 1Kings 19:18

that the covenantal bond between Yahweh and the Northern Kingdom of Israel was dissolved. The Northern Kingdom was no longer under divine protection, and would suffer at the hands of other nations as a result of its transgressions against the Mosaic Law.

The depiction of Israel as the adulterous wife of Yahweh was not solely confined to the Book of Hosea. Isaiah castigates the once faithful city of Jerusalem by using similar corporate terminology which personifies the people of God:

> How the faithful city has become a whore, she who was full of justice! Righteousness lodged in her, but now murderers. (Isa 1:21)

It is directly from such influences that the Book of Revelation develops its concept of the whore of Babylon. But the closest parallels between the whore of Israel and the whore of Babylon can be found in the Book of Ezekiel. Ezekiel states that Jerusalem was once the faithful wife of Yahweh, but became a "whore" by following other gods. As a result of this serious infraction of their exclusive relationship, God's chosen covenantal partner would have to be punished:

> Therefore, O Prostitute, hear the word of the LORD: Thus says the Lord GOD, Because your lust was poured out and your nakedness uncovered in your whorings with your lovers, and with all your abominable idols and because of the blood of your children that you gave to them, therefore, behold, I will gather all your lovers with whom you took pleasure, all those who loved you and all those you hated. I will gather them against you from every side and will uncover your nakedness to them, that they may see all your nakedness. And I will judge you as women who commit adultery and shed blood are judged and bring upon you the blood of wrath and jealousy. And I will give you into their hands, and they shall throw down your vaulted chamber and break down your lofty places. They shall strip you of your clothes and you're your beautiful jewels and leave you naked and bare. They shall bring up a crowd against you, and they shall stone you and cut you to pieces with their swords and they shall burn your houses and execute judgments upon you in the sight of many women. I will make you stop playing the whore, and you shall also give payment no more. (Ezek 16:35-41)

There are many parallels here between the above passage and the whore of Babylon in Rev 17. Both women are prostitutes, adorned with fine clothes and jewellery. Both are overtly blasphemous and desecrate the blood of innocents. And both are punished by their former lovers who turn against them, strip them naked, cut them to pieces and burn them. So the Apocalypse is clearly influenced by Ezekiel in its development of the whore of Babylon imagery.

The parallels between the whores of Revelation and Ezekiel become even more apparent later in Ezek 23, where the "whore" Judah is given a "cup of horror and desolation", which was the same cup her sister Israel drank from before being destroyed by the Assyrians:

> You have gone the way of your sister, therefore I will give her cup into your hand. Thus says the Lord GOD: "You shall drink your sister's cup that is deep and large; you shall be laughed at and held in derision, for it contains much; you will be filled with drunkenness and sorrow. A cup of horror and desolation, the cup of your sister Samaria; and you shall drink it and drain it out, and gnaw its shards, and tear your breasts; for I have spoken, declares the Lord GOD. (Ezek 23:31-34)

By comparing this passage with the whore of Babylon holding a golden cup of abominations, we can see that the whore of Judah in the Book of Ezekiel is the primary inspiration behind the imagery of the whore of Babylon in the Apocalypse:

> The woman was arrayed in purple and scarlet, and adorned with gold and jewels and pearls,
> holding in her hand a golden cup full of abominations and the impurities of her sexual immorality. (Rev
> 17:4)

The term "whore" is thus used in the Bible to denote the betrayal of God by his
covenantal partner. On the transition of this scenario to the Apocalypse, it is now the
Church that is presented as the bride of Christ in the vision of the heavenly Jerusalem
(see Rev 21). So by labelling the entity represented by "Babylon" a whore, the Book of
Revelation is admonishing it for revoking its Christian faith.[12]

The leaders of the Reformation movement in the 16th century equated the whore
of Babylon with the Roman Catholic Church. But by divorcing it from its original
primary context as a cipher for ancient Rome, the reformers missed an essential aspect of
this prophecy. The future manifestation of the whore of Babylon would not be a Church
devoid of temporal power, but like ancient Rome itself, it would be a vastly influential
empire "that has dominion over the kings of the earth" (Rev 17:18).

This means that the whore of Babylon is a nominally Christian entity which has
hegemony over the rest of the world, but at the same time has fallen into a state of
apostasy. A country much like today's United States of America.

The Rise of Secularism

If America is to be equated with the whore of Babylon, then the reason for its
harsh denouncement by the Apocalypse can only be because of its current state of
apostasy. But how exactly has the United States, along with the rest of the Western
world, come to be in the situation where apostasy is so widespread? How can we account
for the loss of faith of millions of Christians worldwide?

Since the rise of the philosophy of secularism during the Enlightenment, there has
been a massive shift away from the Christian faith towards atheism and agnosticism, and
ultimately, away from traditional Christian values. Secularism holds that religion has no
place in the public life, and that the Church should exist separately from the state.
According to this doctrine, the governing powers should remain completely neutral in
matters of faith, and that no religion should be actively promoted by the state. Although
the proponents of secularism claim that this philosophy is not openly atheistic, in
practice, by not actively promoting religion it promotes agnosticism and atheism instead.
Because of their perceived "neutral" religious status, atheism and agnosticism are the
choice of preference for the proponents of secularism.

The philosophy of secularism has been spread with evangelical zeal throughout
Western civilization, and is fervently promoted by many of the world's most powerful
governments. The Western media, which is effectively the various governments' main

---

[12] A similar conclusion is reached by Gordon Campbell in his article "Antithetical Feminine-Urban
Imagery and a Tale of Two Women Cities in the Book of Revelation", *Tyndale Bulletin 55.1* pp81-108

propaganda wing, widely proliferates the philosophy of secularism to the masses.[13] It is through this medium that secular philosophy has been most effectively transmitted.

Due to the ardent promotion of secularization by the various Western governments and media, the Christian Church has been in steady decline during the 20th and 21st centuries. There is a direct correlation between the rise of secularism and the dramatic fall of the number of practicing Christians. Without traditional religious values, public morality has seen a sharp decrease and has been replaced by an increase in hedonism and violent crime.

As a consequence of the shift away from religiosity in the West, the Catholic Church is facing one of its greatest crises in attempting to draw new recruits into the priesthood. In a culture that has become increasingly obsessed with sex, the vows of celibacy demanded of the clergy have become too high a price for today's generation to accept. As the existing clergy grow older, the number of elderly priests who currently make up for these losses is rapidly decreasing. This situation has been exacerbated by the numerous paedophile priest scandals that have rocked the Catholic Church over the last couple of decades. Unfortunately, the celibacy of the priesthood has provided cover for paedophiles to prey on their young victims. The demands of celibacy have also led to a sharp decline in the number of religious vocations after the sexual revolution of the 1960's. In the secular world chastity is not considered a virtue, but a denial of natural human compulsions.

Christianity itself has become a subject of derision in many areas of Western society, and is seen as a symbol of weakness by many young people. Believing in the teachings of Jesus means abiding to a set of rules which appear contrary to what constitutes "normal" modern life. Unfortunately, promiscuity and the hedonistic drug-fuelled lifestyle promoted by contemporary youth culture is now held up as a standard of living to aspire to; while not partaking in such activities can often lead to ostracism from the "in-crowd". Young Christians are thus becoming increasingly hesitant to admit their faith, and many conform to the convictions held by their peers.

The rise in popularity of militant atheist writers such as Richard Dawkins and Christopher Hitchens has provided an intellectual basis for these lifestyle choices. This new breed of militant atheism attacks all forms of religion with an unparalleled level of ferocity, and aims to portray believers as ignorant, superstitious fanatics who are a blight to modern society. Unfortunately, this type of scorn proffered by the adherents of such atheistic propaganda has been widely disseminated by the secular media, and has filtered down to become embedded in popular culture.

So who do we have to blame for the rise of secularism and subsequent rapid decline of Christianity in the West? The Catholic Church has repeatedly cited the influences of Freemasonry as the main cause of its decline in temporal and spiritual power in the age of modernity.[14] The French Revolution, which heralded the beginning

---

[13] As Noam Chomsky notes in his book *Manufacturing Consent: The Political Economy of the Mass Media* (London: Vintage, 2006), although the Western media claims that it autonomous from the state, in reality, they are owned by major corporations which are dependent on the government as a major source of news information. Any news organizations which are fundamentally opposed to the presiding government are usually left out of the loop and subsequently lose readership and advertising revenue. As such, news organizations tend to be pro-government in outlook and policy.

[14] See for example the papal encyclical *Esti Nos* by Leo XIII. *Etsi Multa* issued by Pius IX, utilizes the language of Rev 2:9 to describe the anti-clerical activities of Masons: "Some of you may perchance wonder

of the decline of the Catholic Church's power in Europe, was squarely blamed on the activities of Freemasons.

Before the events that led to the rise of Italian nationalism in the 19th century, the Holy See was still in direct control of the Papal States (which comprised much of the north eastern Italian peninsula). But by the end of the 19th century the papacy was left without any form of temporal authority or political autonomy until the Vatican State was created at the signing of the Lateran Treaty in 1929. Many of the prominent Italian nationalists were Freemasons, including Giuseppe Garibaldi, Camillo di Cavour and Giuseppe Mazzini. The Grand Orient Masonic lodge of France made it their avowed objective to permanently rid religious influences on the affairs of the state, and the 1905 separation of Church and state in France was pushed through largely under the auspices of the interior minister Émile Combes, who was himself a prominent Freemason.

Many of the most influential founding fathers of United States of America were also active Freemasons. When George Washington was sworn in as the first president of the United States, he swore his oath over a Masonic Bible. Washington fully embraced Freemasonry, having served almost 36 years membership by the time he was made President. When he laid the foundation stone of the Capitol building in the new city of Washington D.C in 1793, the first American President and his fellow attendees were kitted out in full Masonic regalia.

Benjamin Franklin is another well-known founding father involved in Freemasonry, and was among six other Masons who signed the Declaration of Independence. Indeed the American Constitution was greatly influenced by the central tenets of Freemasonry.[15] Of the five most instrumental hands in the formulation of the Constitution, three were deeply committed masons. And the Masonic ideal, which is encapsulated by the slogan "Liberty, Equality and Fraternity" is prevalent throughout the constitution.

The secularization of both government and society was one of Freemasonry's primary long-term goals. The spread of Masonic philosophy throughout the intellegista of Europe and North America ensured that the principle of secularism would eventually be realized. And nowhere was this more true than in the United States of America. The separation of Church and state has caused politics in the Western world to be defined by secular, rather than religious ideals; allowing for the legalization of acts that would have been unthinkable under a government which based its laws on the teachings of Christianity. This promotion of moral relativism has since led to a steep decline in ethical values throughout general society. Those who can remember the social order before this cultural revolution lament the loss of a former "golden age", harking back to a time when doors could be left open, children held respect for their elders, and people could walk the streets at night without fear of being accosted by drunken yobs. The demise of this "golden age" can be directly traced back to the decline of the Church and

---

that the war against the Catholic Church extends so widely. Indeed each of you knows well the nature, zeal, and intention of sects, whether called Masonic or some other name. When he compares them with the nature, purpose, and amplitude of the conflict waged nearly everywhere against the Church, he cannot doubt but that the present calamity must be attributed to their deceits and machinations for the most part. For from these the synagogue of Satan is formed which draws up its forces, advances its standards, and joins battle against the Church of Christ.

[15] See Baigent, M; Leigh, R *The Temple and the Lodge* (London: Arrow, 1998), pp346-348

the rise of secularism in the modern age. Without the influence of religion in affairs of the state, society has been robbed of its chief moral bulwark.

The above major societal problems can be directly attributed to the rise to prominence of secular thought in the Western governments – an event which was advanced primarily under the auspices of Freemasonry. The one-time Christian West has now renounced its faith, transforming itself from the bride of Christ to become a godless civilization based on the ideals of secret society that courts Luciferian thought. The Christian West, with America at its helm, has in effect assumed the role of the "whore of Babylon".

Yet the American government does not stand alone in this guilt. The whole of Western civilization itself is culpable in allowing modern society to be founded on the secularist ideals espoused by Freemasonry. If the Apocalypse does indeed refer to the United States in a futurist interpretation of the whore of Babylon, it is not condemning this nation alone. America is merely the symbolic head of the secular West, which has collectively cast off its Christian identity and lapsed into a state of apostasy. It is the entire Western world, engulfed in the current "Great Apostasy" that is represented by the bride-turned-whore.

Mega-tsunami

Throughout the Old Testament the charge of spiritual harlotry is met with a pronouncement of judgment. The Bible frequently adheres to a theology of retribution, where such sins are punished in the present through divine chastisement – a concept which is taken to further extremes for those who have formed an unbreakable covenant with God. The prophet Amos for example, warned that because of its special relationship with Yahweh, Israel would be punished all the more for its sins.[16]

The Bible tells us that Israel was punished in its complete destruction at the hands of the Assyrian Empire due to the Israelite's syncretism with the Baal cult in the Northern Kingdom in the 8th century BC. For the prophets of the Old Testament, the devastation of the Northern Kingdom was considered to be an act of divine retribution against Israel's heterodox spiritual practices. Similarly, the annihilation of Judah by the Babylonian Empire was blamed on its continued participation with the indigenous Canaanite religion.

If we are to extend this proclamation of judgment to the modern era, then we should expect the same principle of retribution to hold today. The Book of Revelation details at considerable length how Babylon will be overthrown in a single, tumultuous event. Although superficially we are not informed of exactly how it is toppled, there are some hints that offer an insight into the catastrophe that brings down this eschatological world empire. Rev 18:21 tells us that John had witnessed an angel performing a symbolic action which alludes to the destruction of Babylon:

> Then a mighty angel took up a stone like a great millstone and threw it into the sea, saying, "So will Babylon the great city be thrown down with violence, and will be found no more...

---

[16] Amos 3:2

This passage contains yet another example of "acted prophecy", similar in form and essence to Jesus' parable of the withered olive tree. Since these symbolic actions point to a specific episode in the eschatological age, does the description of an angel casting a great stone into the sea detail the exact nature in which "Babylon" is to be destroyed? The image of the angel casting a millstone into the sea can be further supplemented by a similar passage found elsewhere in the Apocalypse, which contains the same motif of a large body of material being thrown into the sea. Only this time the symbolic image of the "huge stone" is now replaced with that of "a great mountain burning with fire":

> The second angel blew his trumpet, and something like a great mountain, burning with fire, was thrown into the sea, and a third of the sea became blood. (Rev 8:8)

Could these two passages be describing the same event? Most scholars see a relation between Rev 8:8 and 18:21. G.K. Beale for example, states that "the burning mountain cast into the sea refers to the judgment of a wicked kingdom. This kingdom is to be identified as 'Babylon,' 'the great city' of Revelation 11-18, which holds sway over the evil world system."[17]

But what actual event does the "great mountain burning with fire" being cast into the sea actually refer to? The first, and perhaps most obvious image conjured by the description of "a great mountain burning with fire" is that of a volcano – a mountain which literally spews out smoke and molten rock as if it were on fire. But how could a volcano be thrown into the sea? And why would the modern equivalent of "Babylon" be threatened by such an event? Could a volcano being thrown into the sea really topple a country with the financial and political clout of the US? As we shall see, not only does such a volcano pose a significant threat to the United States, but it may in fact be inevitable that this volcano will someday devastate the eastern coastlines of North and South America.

On the 12th of October 2000, the BBC's flagship documentary series *Horizon* aired a programme that was to cause a considerable amount of controversy in the world of geophysics. Subtitled "Mega-tsunami: Wave of Destruction", the documentary elaborated how the volcano Cumbre Vieja on the Canary island of La Palma poses an enormous risk to the eastern coastline of the Americas. The documentary was based on the combined research of S.N. Ward of the Institute of Geophysics and Planetary Physics at the University of California and S.J. Day of the Benfield Greig Hazard Research Centre at University College, London, who hoped to prove that Cumbre Vieja has the potential to cause one of the greatest natural disasters ever known to human civilisation.

Ward and Day's research shows how the inside of Cumbre Vieja is honeycombed with fissures caused by the rising of molten magma heating and vaporizing water which then erodes the inside of the volcano. This phenomenon has severely weakened the internal structure of the volcano, making it extremely unstable. During its last eruption in 1949, the southern volcano caused a massive crack to appear, and the entire western portion of Cumbre Vieja slipped a few metres towards the Atlantic Ocean.

In 2001, Ward and Day put forward a scientific paper showing how that the entire western flank will eventually give way, possibly even during its next eruption; sending

---

[17] Beale, G.K. *The Book of Revelation* p476

500 thousand million tonnes of rock crashing into the ocean.[18] Ward and Day's research, which took other examples of this phenomenon into account, suggested that the impact of this "lateral collapse" would generate a colossal wave – dubbed a "mega-tsunami", which could reach a local amplitude of between 650-1500 metres. This wave would then rapidly travel westwards reaching a speed of approximately 720kph. Although it would diminish in size by the time it made landfall on the eastern seaboard of America, it could still be as high as 50 metres (to give a sense of perspective, the statue of liberty is 93 metres tall), devastating everything in its wake up to 25km inland.

In comparison with this projected scenario, the Indian Ocean tsunami that occurred on 26th December 2004, reached a height of only 24m at Bandeh Aceh – the region worst affected by the disaster, which was totally obliterated. If this event unfolds in the manner that Ward and Day have projected, then this "mega-tsunami" would be the greatest natural disaster in recorded history.[19]

The portion of the Apocalypse which prophesies the downfall of the eschatological "Babylon" is heavily influenced by Chapter 51 of the Book of Jeremiah, which foretold the destruction of the ancient city of Babylon. It is worth quoting the relevant areas below in comparison with the Book of Revelation to see how the writer of the Apocalypse takes Jeremiah's prophecy of the destruction of Babylon and reinterprets it as the destruction of the leading world power during the eschatological age:

"Flee from the midst of Babylon; let every one save his life! Be not cut off in her punishment, for this is the time of the Lord's vengeance, the repayment he is rendering her. Babylon was a golden cup in the Lord's hand, making all the earth drunken; the nations drank of her wine; therefore the nations went mad. Suddenly Babylon has fallen and been broken; wail for her!... (vv 6-7)[20]

"Behold, I am against you, O destroying mountain, declares the Lord, which destroys the whole earth; I will stretch out my hand against you, and roll you down from the crags, and make you a burnt mountain. No stone shall be taken from you for a corner and no stone for a foundation, but you shall be a perpetual waste, declares the Lord. (vv25-26)[21]

How Babylon is taken, the praise of the whole earth seized! How Babylon has become a horror among the nations! The sea has come up on Babylon; she is covered with its tumultuous waves . (vv41-42)

---

[18] See Ward, S.N; Day, S. "Cumbre Vieja Volcano -- Potential collapse and tsunami at La Palma, Canary Islands", *Geophysical Research Letters 28*, (2001) pp397-400.

[19] In a follow up article in response to criticisms of their mega-tsunami hypotheisis, Ward and Day argue that the figures given of the amplitude of the waves generated were if anything , conservative estimates, suggesting that the actual collapse of the island's flank could in fact be much worse. See McGuire, B; Day, S; Kilburn, C; Ward, S.N. "Volcano collapse-generated megatsunamis: Fact or Fiction?"

[20] Cf. Rev 18:4-5: Then I heard another voice from heaven saying, "Come out of her, my people, lest you take part in her sins, lest you share in her plagues; for her sins are heaped high as heaven, and God has remembered her iniquities. Pay her back as she herself has paid back others, and repay her double for her deeds; mix a double portion for her in the cup she mixed.

Also 17:4-6: The woman was arrayed in purple and scarlet, and adorned with gold and jewels and pearls, holding in her hand a golden cup full of abominations and the impurities of her sexual immorality. And on her forehead was written a name of mystery: "Babylon the great, mother of prostitutes and of earth's abominations." And I saw the woman, drunk with the blood of the saints, the blood of the martyrs of Jesus.

[21] Cf. Rev 11:18 The nations raged, but your wrath came, and the time for the dead to be judged, and for rewarding your servants, the prophets and saints, and those who fear your name, both small and great, and for destroying the destroyers of the earth

A voice! A cry from Babylon! The noise of great destruction from the land of the Chaldeans! For the Lord is laying Babylon waste and stilling her mighty voice. Their waves roar like many waters; the noise of their voice is raised, for a destroyer has come upon her, upon Babylon; (vv54-56)

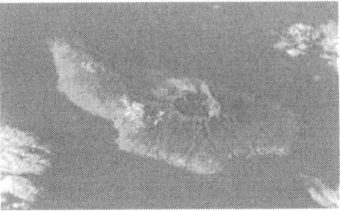

Fig. 18 The island of La Palma, home to the volcano Cumbre Vieja. Could this be the "great mountain burning with fire" that is thrown into the sea, mentioned in the Book of Revelation?

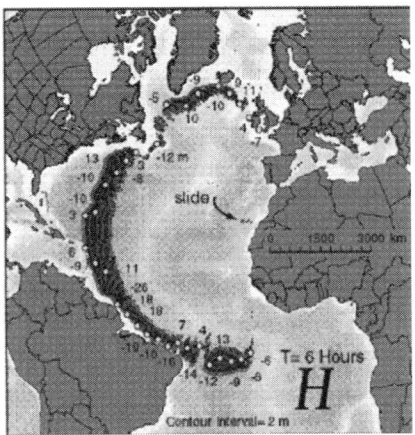

Fig. 19 A computer model developed by geologists S.N. Ward and S.J. Day shows how the collapse of Cumbre Vieja could generate a mega-tsunami that would devastate the eastern seaboard of the Americas. The projected course of the wave is indicated by the dark area.

We can see that the prophecy of the destruction of Babylon in the Book of Jeremiah transcends its immediate context, and echoes the destruction of the eschatological "Babylon" at the end of time – a fact which is established by John's reinterpretation of this event in the Apocalypse. It is also interesting to note that the Book of Jeremiah tells how Babylon will be destroyed by the sea – which would be rather curious indeed, given that the ancient city of Babylon was totally land-locked.

The Inundation of Ireland

There may be another independent prophetic confirmation of the mega-tsunami generated by the collapse of Cumbre Vieja to be found in the prophecies of the destruction of Ireland by flood seven years before the end of the world.[22] The best known version of this prophecy is attributed to St. Columba of Iona (521-597):

I concede a favour to them without exception,
and St Patrick also did concede the same;
that seven years before the last day,
the sea shall submerge Eirin by one inundation.[23]

The above stanza reflects the Irish Antichrist tradition, which as is suggested by the above quatrain, can be traced back to St. Patrick. According to tradition, St. Patrick pleaded with God to spare Ireland from the horrors of the reign of the Antichrist during a 40 day fast on the slopes of Croagh Patrick. God apparently granted St. Patrick's request and told him that the sea would spread over Ireland seven years before the end of the world, thus sparing the Irish from the tribulation of the last days. The earliest version of this prophecy can be found in the writings of Tírechán, which dates back to the 7th century. This in turn is based on the now lost earlier work *The Book of Ultan*. Tírechán's work, along with that of his contemporary Muirchu, and of course the writings of St. Patrick himself (the *Confessio* and the Letter to the soldiers of Coroticus), are the earliest

---

[22] It is perhaps worth also mentioning here a widely circulated prophecy attributed to St. Hildegard (1098-1179) which foretells the destruction of "a great nation in the ocean" by a tidal wave, cited by Yves Dupont in his book *Catholic Prophecy* (Rockford, Il.: TAN, 1970). However Dupont's work contains many spurious prophecies with no references to his original source material. It is highly unlikely that this prophecy is an authentic oracle of Hildegard. There were many spurious prophecies attributed to Hildegard in the Middle Ages, such as by the anti-mendicant movement (See Kerby-Fulton, K. *Reformist Apocalypticism and Piers Plowman* (Cambridge: Cambridge University Press, 1990) pp156ff), and it is more likely that this prophecy originates from such pseudo-Hildegardian literature. Note the anachronistic references to 'colonies', supposedly made centuries before modern colonialism began in the 16th century: *Before the comet comes, many nations, the good excepted, will be scourged by want and famine. The great nation in the ocean that is inhabited by people of different tribes and descent will be devastated by earthquake, storm, and tidal wave. It will be divided and, in great part submerged. That nation will also have many misfortunes at sea and lose its colonies. [After the] great comet, the great nation will be devastated by earthquakes, storms and great waves of water, causing much want and plagues. All coastal cities will live in fear, and many of them will be destroyed by tidal waves, and most living creatures will be killed, and even those who escape will die from horrible diseases. For in none of those cities does a person live according to the laws of God.*
[23] Cited in O'Kearney, N. *The Prophecies of Ss. Columbkille, Maeltamlacht, Ultan, Seadhna, Coireall, Bearcan, Malachy, &tc* (Dublin: John O'Daly, 1856), pp41-42. There is a vita on St. Columba written by Adamnan, the ninth abbot of Iona who died around 704, which frequently tells of the prophetic abilities of Colmcille, although no mention is made of the above particular prophecy here. (Interestingly Adamnan's vita is most famous for containing the first known reference to the Loch Ness monster!) O'Kearney lists the source of this prophecy in his book as *Colum Cille cecinit* ("Colmcille sang"). The *Colum Cille cecinit* is a collection of old poems attributed to the saint which can be dated back as far as the ninth or tenth centuries, but most likely is not the version quoted in full in O'Kearney's book, which is a later forgery based on rhetoric for the 1798 Irish rebellion. See Madden, R.R. *Exposure of literary frauds and forgeries concocted in Ireland: spurious predictions designated prophecies of Columbkille etc., etc., etc.* (Dublin: John F. Fowler, 1866)

reliable sources on the saint's life. The account of St Patrick's life given by Tírechán outlines three prayers made by Patrick for the people of Ireland.

> These are the three prayers of Patrick, as they were delivered to us by the Hibernians, entreating that all should be received on the day of judgment, if we should repent even in the last days of our life. That he should not be shut up in hell. That barbarian nations should never have the rule over us. That no one shall conquer us, that is the Scots, before seven years previous to the day of judgment, because seven years before the judgment we shall be destroyed in the sea, this is the third.[24]

Could this inundation which threatens to engulf Ireland shortly before the end of the world be the same as the mega-tsunami that will be generated by the collapse of Cumbre Vieja? The fact that this prophecy predicts that Ireland would be struck with a colossal ocean-surge seven years before the last day is a rather striking parallel to our own conclusions. If Cumbre Vieja collapses into the Atlantic, then Ireland would be one of the countries in Western Europe that will be affected by the resulting mega-tsunami.[25]

The Fall of Babylon

The economic repercussions of such a large scale catastrophic event, which would see the losses of major cities such as New York, Washington D.C, Boston, Philadelphia and Miami, would plunge America into economic meltdown. It could even topple the US from its status as the world's only remaining superpower. With the American economy crippled, the United States government would no longer have the capacity to dominate the world market, or intervene in foreign affairs. A political vacuum could be created in the wake of this disaster, leaving other countries clamouring to fill America's position as the leading role.

In an even worse case scenario, America's enemies could use such a devastating natural disaster to permanently dispose of the threat presented by this superpower. Indeed Rev 17:16 suggests that "Babylon" would be destroyed when its former companion – the beast with ten horns, turns against it:

> And the ten horns that you saw, they and the beast will hate the prostitute. They will make her desolate and naked, and devour her flesh and burn her up with fire…

But what could the beast with ten horns represent in this scenario? If, as Revelation suggests, the sea-beast is a close ally of the whore, then we would have to conclude that the ten horns somehow represent Europe. As we discussed earlier, the ten horns appear to have represented the nations of the Axis coalition during the Second World War. Could they continue to represent Europe even after the collapse of Nazism?

The Beast with seven heads and ten horns is commonly interpreted by modern prophecy teachers as representing Europe.[26] This is largely due to Europe's geographical

---

[24] Betham, W. (Ed) "Tírechán's Collections Concerning St. Patrick" *Book of Armagh* (Irish Antiquarian Researches. Vol. 2. Dublin: William Curry, Jun. and Co., 1827), pp348-402

[25] Although it is unlikely that the entire island would be submerged as a result of this disaster – the threat would most likely be limited to the western and southern coastal regions.

[26] Following Hal Lindsey. See *The Late Great Planet Earth* pp88ff

connection with the principle territory of the Ancient Roman Empire – which was the original meaning of the Beast with seven heads (which represented the seven hills of Rome). So there is somewhat of a modern futurist consensus that the sea-beast represents a revived Roman Empire – a new Europe united under a single presidency, much akin to the European Union of today.

But what could cause Europe to turn against its greatest ally? At present, it seems unthinkable that such an event could take place. Europe has many strong historical ties with the United States that have developed into a unique bond of fellowship. Yet in twenty or thirty years from now the world could be a very different political landscape. Increased global warming will eventually lead to a massive loss of agricultural land due to large areas of flooding. Combined with a rising world population and the depletion of natural resources such as oil, political tensions will be greatly increased in the years to come. Even old allies such as America and Europe could be pitted against each other in direct economic and political competition. If the relationship between America and Europe had soured by the time of this prophesied disaster, then it could be an ideal opportunity for the European Union to dispose of its new found political opponent. Europe could seek to curb America's recovery by depriving it of much needed financial aid, thus hindering any attempt at economic recovery and ensuring that it remained politically defunct.

The collapse of America as a world power would send the world into economic turmoil. The Apocalypse appears to hint at such an economic depression in Rev 18:

> And the merchants of the earth weep and mourn for her, since no one buys their cargo anymore, cargo of gold, silver, jewels, pearls, fine linen, purple cloth, silk, scarlet cloth, all kinds of scented wood, all kinds of articles of ivory, all kinds of articles of costly wood, bronze, iron and marble, cinnamon, spice, incense, myrrh, frankincense, wine, oil, fine flour, wheat, cattle and sheep, horses and chariots, and slaves, that is, human souls. (Rev 18:11-13)

History has shown that at times of great political and economic stress people look to strong leadership to guide them out of danger. Hitler rose to power in Germany after the sanctions imposed against the Weimar Republic by the Treaty of Versailles meant that Germany was hit particularly hard by the Great Depression. Inflation spiralled out of control, plunging the German people into severe hardship. Hitler's strong personality appealed to the Germans in this time of distress. He appeared to be a leader with enough conviction to resolve their economic difficulties and restore pride in the German nation once again. A similar depression could arise worldwide if the market leader collapsed as a world power. Could the Antichrist use the desperation caused by such an event to seize control over world politics?

As we have noted above, it is frequently suggested by interpreters of biblical prophecy that the Antichrist will assume the presidency of a European super-state as the head of a revived (symbolic) Roman Empire. Of course, this does not necessarily mean that the Antichrist's seat of power would be literally centred on the modern city of Rome. Rather it symbolizes a Europe unified under a single leader like the Roman Empire of old. According to the Book of Revelation (when taken from a futurist, eschatological perspective), the state this Beast represents once existed and did not anymore, but would be revived toward the end of the world before heading into its ultimate destruction:

The beast that you saw *was, and is not, and is about to rise* from the bottomless pit and go to destruction. And the dwellers on earth whose names have not been written in the book of life from the foundation of the world will marvel to see the beast, because it was and is not and is to come. This calls for a mind with wisdom: the seven heads are seven mountains on which the woman is seated… (Rev 17:8-9)

So the crux of this prophecy is that the empire of the seven hills (symbolising Rome) would cease to exist for a period of time, but would eventually be restored during the eschatological age. The Beast would then be controlled for a time by the whore of Babylon, who triumphantly rides upon its back as if it were some form of demonic animal of burden which can be steered in any direction she chooses. But the ten kings represented by the ten horns of the Beast with seven heads would eventually turn upon their mistress, leaving her desolate after she succumbs to a cataclysm symbolized by the powerful angel throwing a large boulder into the sea.

If America's economy buckled under the pressure of such a catastrophic natural disaster, then it would be logical to assume that Europe would one of the main contenders to fill the political vacuum left in its wake. The presidency of the EU would become the most pivotal position of power in the Western world.

But what exactly will be the main role of the Antichrist when he does come into power, as the Book of Revelation predicts? If Christ came to save the world, then it follows that the Antichrist will come to destroy it. A role which is hinted at by an alternative name for the Devil/Antichrist in the Apocalypse:

They have as king over them the angel of the bottomless pit. His name in Hebrew is Abaddon, and in Greek he is called Apollyon. (Rev 9:11)

The Hebrew word אבדון *'abaddon* means "destruction", while the Greek term Ἀπολλύων *Apollyon* means "Destroyer". The title "Apollyon" appears to allude to the Greek god Apollo on one level, whilst also calling to mind the angel of death of the Exodus plagues, who took the lives of the Egyptian firstborn (Exod 12:23). The angel of death was also referred to as the "destroyer" in the Book of Exodus by the Hebrew word המשחית *ha-mashchit*.

In order to fulfil this role of "destroyer", the Antichrist, working together with the Dragon and False Prophet, incites humankind to annihilate themselves by dividing them against one another. Pitting them against each other in a battle which will eventually consume the world:

And I saw, coming out of the mouth of the dragon and out of the mouth of the beast and out of the mouth of the false prophet, three unclean spirits like frogs. For they are demonic spirits, performing signs, who go abroad to the kings of the whole world, to assemble them for battle on the great day of God the Almighty. ("Behold, I am coming like a thief! Blessed is the one who stays awake, keeping his garments on, that he may not go about naked and be seen exposed!") And they assembled them at the place that in Hebrew is called Armageddon. (Rev 16:13-16)[27]

---

[27] The three demonic spirits that issue out of the mouths of the Dragon, Beast and False prophet to gather the armies of the world for battle may represent three world wars. The First World War would be represented by the spirit that came out of the mouth of the Dragon, who in Rev 9, was cast to earth to release the locust plague from the abyss – an event we have previously compared with the Tunguska event and the rise of military aircraft. The Second World War would be associated with the spirit that proceeds

Armageddon

The Book of Revelation repeatedly states that the role of the Beast, or Antichrist, is to gather the nations of the world together and assemble them for battle. A battle which will ultimately destroy humankind before the inauguration of the General Resurrection and Last Judgment. The battle of Armageddon is recapitulated a number of times in the Apocalypse. The first mention of this great war is in Rev 16 above, with other references found in Rev 19:11-21 and Rev 20:7-10.

Dispensationalists tend to take the chronology of the Apocalypse literally, and assert that the battle of Armageddon in Rev 19 is followed by a literal millennial reign of Christ on earth. According to dispensationalist teaching, this thousand year reign will be followed by one last satanically-inspired insurrection by the countries of "Gog"and "Magog" during the battle depicted in Rev 20.[28]

However there is a consensus in the scholarly world that the eschatological battles described in Rev 16, 19 and 20 all refer to the same event – the battle of Armageddon. G.K. Beale, for example argues that the recapitulatory accounts of the battle of Armageddon in Rev 19 and 20 is based on the description of the battle of Gog and Magog in Ezekiel 38-39, which also recapitulates itself.[29]

As we argued in the introduction, the thousand year reign of Christ is best understood as either the symbolic of the period of the Church, or if a more literal understanding is required, then on another level it could also represent the first thousand years of Christian unity which ended with the Great Schism of 1054. There will not be any literal future thousand year reign of Christ, nor any battle after it.

The various battles described in Rev 16, 19 and 20 all refer to the same great war – a conflict that will consume humankind before the commencement of the Last Judgment. But what kind of conditions could bring about such a devastating war? Could the cataclysmic events caused by the collapse of Cumbre Vieja into the Atlantic ocean and subsequent downfall of America create the conditions which will bring about this final eschatological battle? If American hegemony was to disintegrate as a result of the ensuing mega-tsunami, not only would it affect the world's economy, but it would also have repercussions in the wider political world. Countries that relied on the US for military protection would now be under threat from their neighbouring enemies. None more so than the fledging state of Israel.

The Israeli problem is currently one of the greatest threats to world security. The existence of the state of Israel lies at the very heart of the crisis in the Middle East. It is the main source of contention between the Arab and Western worlds today. Apart from the Israeli military's current possession of a nuclear deterrent, the only thing preventing another attempted invasion of Israel by its Arab neighbours is the threat posed by the support of its staunchest ally – the United States of America. Without the protection of the American government, Israel would quickly become the focus of attention for the

---

from the mouth of the False Prophet, who we previously identified as Adolf Hitler. The final world war would then be caused by the spirit that comes out of the mouth of the Beast, or Antichrist.

[28] See for example, Haggith, D. *Prophets of the Apocalypse* pp389ff, or the dispensationalist chronology outlined in Tim LaHaye and Jerry Jenkin's fictional *Left Behind* series.

[29] Beale, G.K. *The Book of Revelation* pp974ff

Muslim world, triggering global political instability and providing a catalyst for another world war.

This scenario is exactly what the Bible predicts for the instigation of the last war. The Apocalypse foretells that the final battle of humankind will be caused by an invasion of Israel on the plain of Megiddo. The word Armageddon is derived from the Hebrew *Har-megiddon*, which literally means "mount of Megiddo" and most probably relates to Mount Carmel, which is close to the vicinity of the plain of Megiddo.[30] The plain of Megiddo is situated in a valley in Northern Israel on the border with the Lebanon. If a military invasion of Israel was launched from the Lebanon, it would have to first pass through the valley of Megiddo, which has long been used as a natural invasive position.

Although Rev 16:16 states that the armies will be gathered at the valley of Megiddo, it makes plain elsewhere in the Bible that the primary focus of the eschatological battle is an invasion of Jerusalem. John may have been particularly influenced in this instance by Zech 12, which describes an invasion of Jerusalem during the end-time, after the appearance of Christ as the "one whom they have pierced":

> Behold, I am about to make Jerusalem a cup of staggering to all the surrounding peoples. The siege of Jerusalem will also be against Judah. On that day I will make Jerusalem a heavy stone for all the peoples. All who lift it will surely hurt themselves. And all the nations of the earth will gather against it...
>
> And on that day I will seek to destroy all the nations that come against Jerusalem. "And I will pour out on the house of David and the inhabitants of Jerusalem a spirit of grace and pleas for mercy, so that, when they look on me, on him whom they have pierced, they shall mourn for him, as one mourns for an only child, and weep bitterly over him, as one weeps over a firstborn. On that day the mourning in Jerusalem will be as great as the mourning for Hadad-rimmon in the plain of Megiddo. (Zech 12:2-3; 8-11)

The Apocalypse shows the influences of this passage elsewhere in Rev 1, which also alludes to the Second Coming:

> Behold, he is coming with the clouds, and every eye will see him, even those who pierced him, and all tribes of the earth will wail on account of him. (Rev 1:7)

These passages seem to indicate that the eschatological battle is connected in some way with the Second Coming of Jesus. The Book of Joel contains yet another description of the eschatological battle, as well as its relationship to the Second Coming and Last Judgment. Here, the events are concentrated in the Valley of Jehoshaphat outside Jerusalem:

> "For behold, in those days and at that time, when I restore the fortunes of Judah and Jerusalem, I will gather all the nations and bring them down to the Valley of Jehoshaphat. And I will enter into judgment with them there, on behalf of my people and my heritage Israel, because they have scattered them among the nations and have divided up my land...
>
> Proclaim this among the nations: Consecrate for war; stir up the mighty men. Let all the men of war draw near; let them come up. Beat your plowshares into swords, and your pruning hooks into spears; let the weak say, "I am a warrior." Hasten and come, all you surrounding nations, and gather yourselves there. Bring down your warriors, O Lord. Let the nations stir themselves up and come up to the Valley of Jehoshaphat; for there I will sit to judge all the surrounding nations. Put in the sickle, for the harvest is ripe. Go in, tread, for the winepress is full. The vats overflow, for their evil is great. Multitudes,

---

[30] See Beale, G.K *The Book of Revelation* p839.

multitudes, in the valley of decision! For the day of the Lord is near in the valley of decision. (Joel 3:1-2, 9-14)

The phrase "valley of decision" is a Hebrew word play on the word **שפט** *shophet* meaning "to judge". The meaning of the name Jehoshaphat in Hebrew is "Yahweh judges". So the "Valley of Jehoshaphat" literally means "the valley where God judges" The Apocalypse alludes to this passage from Joel in Rev 14 – which contains the parallel motifs of harvesting with a sickle and the trampling of a winepress, combined with the appearance of the Danielic Son of Man at the Second Coming:

> Then I looked, and behold, a white cloud, and seated on the cloud one like a son of man, with a golden crown on his head, and a sharp sickle in his hand. And another angel came out of the temple, calling with a loud voice to him who sat on the cloud, "Put in your sickle, and reap, for the hour to reap has come, for the harvest of the earth is fully ripe." So he who sat on the cloud swung his sickle across the earth, and the earth was reaped. Then another angel came out of the temple in heaven, and he too had a sharp sickle. And another angel came out from the altar, the angel who has authority over the fire, and he called with a loud voice to the one who had the sharp sickle, "Put in your sickle and gather the clusters from the vine of the earth, for its grapes are ripe." So the angel swung his sickle across the earth and gathered the grape harvest of the earth and threw it into the great winepress of the wrath of God. And the winepress was trodden outside the city, and blood flowed from the winepress, as high as a horse's bridle, for 1,600 stadia. (Rev 14:14-20)

The account of the final battle in the Apocalypse also borrows heavily from Ezekiel 38-39. Here, the prophet describes how Gog, the prince of the land of Magog in the "uttermost north" will attack the land of Israel during the "latter years" (a term which is related to the biblical "end of days") before being met with God's judgment:

> After many days you will be mustered. In the latter years you will go against the land that is restored from war, the land whose people were gathered from many peoples upon the mountains of Israel, which had been a continual waste. Its people were brought out from the peoples and now dwell securely, all of them…
> You will come up against my people Israel, like a cloud covering the land. In the latter days I will bring you against my land, that the nations may know me, when through you, O Gog, I vindicate my holiness before their eyes…
> But on that day, the day that Gog shall come against the land of Israel, declares the Lord GOD, my wrath will be roused in my anger. For in my jealousy and in my blazing wrath I declare, On that day there shall be a great earthquake in the land of Israel. The fish of the sea and the birds of the heavens and the beasts of the field and all creeping things that creep on the ground, and all the people who are on the face of the earth, shall quake at my presence. And the mountains shall be thrown down, and the cliffs shall fall, and every wall shall tumble to the ground. I will summon a sword against Gog on all my mountains, declares the Lord GOD. Every man's sword will be against his brother. With pestilence and bloodshed I will enter into judgment with him, and I will rain upon him and his hordes and the many peoples who are with him torrential rains and hailstones, fire and sulfur. So I will show my greatness and my holiness and make myself known in the eyes of many nations. Then they will know that I am the LORD. (Ezek 38: 8, 16,18-23)

This portion of Ezekiel also lies behind Rev 20:7-10 – a passage which contains scenes that strongly resemble modern warfare:

> And when the thousand years are ended, Satan will be released from his prison and will come out to deceive the nations that are at the four corners of the earth, Gog and Magog, to gather them for battle; their number is like the sand of the sea. And they marched up over the broad plain of the earth and

surrounded the camp of the saints and the beloved city, but fire came down from heaven and consumed them, and the devil who had deceived them was thrown into the lake of fire and sulfur where the beast and the false prophet were, and they will be tormented day and night forever and ever. (Rev 20:7-10)

Is there a possibility that an invasion of Israeli territory would be met with the option of a nuclear retaliation, thus precipitating the onslaught of a nuclear war? Modern Israel is undoubtedly a member of the "nuclear club" – a fact which was widely publicised when former Israeli nuclear plant worker Mordechai Vanunu handed over a description and photographs of Israel's nuclear warheads to a British newspaper during the eighties. This revelation forced a revision of the estimation of Israel's nuclear arsenal, putting the figure at around 100-200 warheads. If such an attack on Israel was ever launched by the surround Arab states, there is a strong possibility that it would respond by launching a tactical nuclear strike. Could this act of desperation provoke a similar reaction from other countries? Zech 14 relates to the eschatological battle as well, and also appears to contain imagery evocative of nuclear warfare:

And this shall be the plague with which the LORD will strike all the peoples that wage war against Jerusalem: their flesh will rot while they are still standing on their feet, their eyes will rot in their sockets, and their tongues will rot in their mouths. And on that day a great panic from the LORD shall fall on them, so that each will seize the hand of another, and the hand of the one will be raised against the hand of the other. (Zech 14:12-13)

So what kind of reaction could we expect if Israel did launch a nuclear weapon, even if in a limited strategic use? Some military experts feel that such limited use of nuclear weapons would be acceptable in extreme circumstances in order to curtail the proliferation of weapons of mass destruction (WMD) or to act as a powerful psychological deterrent.[31] Yet such an action could provide the catalyst for a wider nuclear conflict, even if used tactically or pre-emptively.

Of all the Muslim countries of the Middle East, only Pakistan is currently known to have any nuclear capabilities. Iran is also presently at the threshold of becoming a nuclear power, and in twenty years' time other Arab nations, such as Syria, could also have the capacity to build nuclear weapons. It is inevitable that such countries will eventually develop nuclear technology. If some of the above nations formed an Arab coalition against Israel, then we could almost certainly expect them to retaliate by launching a nuclear warhead at one of Israel's predominantly Jewish cities, such as Tel Aviv. (As home to the third holiest shrine in Islam and a large population of Palestinians,

---

[31] Amy F. Woolf, a US government specialist in nuclear weapons policy, outlines the current American and Russian nuclear strategic doctrines in her article *Nonstrategic Nuclear Weapons*. Woolf describes the American policy as follows: 'Assistant Secretary of Defense Edward Warner testified that "the U.S. capability to deliver an overwhelming, rapid, and devastating military response with the full range of military capabilities will remain the cornerstone of our strategy for deterring rogue nation ballistic missile and WMD proliferation threats".'

The Russian nuclear weapons policy is even less stringent still. As Woolf further states: 'In mid-2009, when discussing the revision of Russia's defense strategy that was expected late in 2009 or early 2010, Nikolai Patrushev, the head of Russia's Presidential Security Council, indicated that Russia would have the option to launch a "pre-emptive nuclear strike" against an aggressor "using conventional weapons in an all-out, regional, or even local war".' Woolf, A.F. "Nonstrategic Nuclear Weapons" *Congressional Research Service* (2011)

Jerusalem would most likely not be included among the potential targets for a nuclear strike). This could then start a nuclear counter-exchange that could spill over to other countries bordering the target centres.

Given his role of "destroyer", it is likely that the Antichrist would exploit such diplomatic tensions in an attempt to bring about a war which would annihilate humanity. The act of gathering the nations together for battle is mentioned in Rev 16:14, and again in Rev 19:19-21 and 20:7-9. Each time either Satan, or his agent the Antichrist, is responsible for deceiving them into warring with each other. If the Antichrist managed to heighten tensions between other rival powers at the time of the prophesied invasion of Israel through the Valley of Megiddo, then there is every possibility that this event could ignite a Third World War.

But what is the actual probability that such a war could completely obliterate humankind? The Bible repeatedly affirms that humanity will one day draw to a close. Revelation alerts us to this looming threat a number of times, but never *explicitly* states how this will happen. However a number of key junctures, the Apocalypse hints that it is the battle of Armageddon which is responsible for bringing about the end of the world. The eschatological battle is directly followed by the Last Judgment in both Rev 19 and Rev 20. And after the battle of Armageddon is mentioned in Rev 16, the angel with the seventh plague bowl announces rather climatically that God's plan for the world is finished. Since the Last Judgment occurs after the destruction of the old world and the resurrection of the dead, the placement of it after the eschatological battle suggests that this war has destroyed humankind.

Descriptions of how the end unfolds is detailed elsewhere in the Bible. One of the most frightening visions of the end of the world is given in the second epistle of St. Peter:

> ...scoffers will come in the last days with scoffing, following their own sinful desires. They will say, "Where is the promise of his coming? For ever since the fathers fell asleep, all things are continuing as they were from the beginning of creation." For they deliberately overlook this fact, that the heavens existed long ago, and the earth was formed out of water and through water by the word of God, and that by means of these the world that then existed was deluged with water and perished. But by the same word the heavens and earth that now exist are stored up for fire, being kept until the day of judgment and destruction of the ungodly. But do not overlook this one fact, beloved, that with the Lord one day is as a thousand years, and a thousand years as one day. The Lord is not slow to fulfill his promise as some count slowness, but is patient toward you, not wishing that any should perish, but that all should reach repentance. But the day of the Lord will come like a thief, and then the heavens will pass away with a roar, and the heavenly bodies will be burned up and dissolved, and the earth and the works that are done on it will be exposed. Since all these things are thus to be dissolved, what sort of people ought you to be in lives of holiness and godliness, waiting for and hastening the coming of the day of God, because of which the heavens will be set on fire and dissolved, and the heavenly bodies will melt as they burn! But according to his promise we are waiting for new heavens and a new earth in which righteousness dwells. (2Pet 3:4-13)

The theme of judgment by fire foretold in the second Petrine epistle is repeated elsewhere in the Bible. In Rev 20:9, fire comes down from heaven to consume the combatants in the eschatological battle :

> And they marched up over the broad plain of the earth and surrounded the camp of the saints and the beloved city, but fire came down from heaven and consumed them...

This vision is remarkably similar to another passage in the Bible concerning the earth's judgment by fire. The Book of Zephaniah also appears to connect the eschatological battle with the judgment of the earth by fire:

> "Therefore wait for me," declares the Lord, "for the day when I rise up to seize the prey. For my decision is to gather nations, to assemble kingdoms, to pour out upon them my indignation, all my burning anger; for in the fire of my jealousy all the earth shall be consumed. (Zeph 3:8)

Do these passages suggest that the world will be destroyed in a cataclysmic world war? When viewed together, it certainly seems that the Bible is warning us of this approaching threat. But what are the chances that all human life could be completely extinguished by a nuclear war? The possibility that humankind could destroy itself with its own weapons has been the subject of much discussion since the invention of the atom bomb at the close of the Second World War. But how feasible is this claim? While Earth would undoubtedly suffer billions of lives lost, along with years of nuclear winter and radioactive fallout after thermo-nuclear warfare; is it really possible that such an event could completely wipe out the human race? Humankind has after all proven itself to be highly adaptable to almost every sort of environment, from the Ice Ages and the various polar expeditions, to the colonization of the desert and other hostile landscapes. Surely we could adapt and survive even from the extremely hostile weather conditions caused by nuclear war?

The exact long-term effects of a nuclear war are still a matter of debate among environmentalists and geophysicists. A recent study published in the *Journal of Geophysical Research* has concluded that the effects of a nuclear winter may be a lot worse than previously thought.[32] This study models its hypothesis on a war using most or all of the world's current nuclear arsenals, which have fallen by around a third since the end of the Cold War. It calculates that the smoke and dust projected into the atmosphere by the explosion of the world's current nuclear stockpiles would cool the earth's surface by an average of -7°C to -8°C for a sustained number of years. In comparison, the cooling caused by the last Ice Age dropped the global average by -5°C. This would see the total collapse of global agriculture for an indeterminate number of years, and the cessation of food production would ensure that the vast majority of survivors would die of starvation within a year.

However this study only factored the world's current nuclear stockpiles, which due to a period of relative peace, is at a fairly low capacity. If there was an increased period of political tension (such as the scenario we have already postulated at the fall of America), then we could expect the world's nuclear arsenals to increase accordingly, and the world's combined nuclear stockpiles could easily be pushed back up to Cold War levels or beyond. We also have to take into consideration nuclear proliferation amongst a number of other smaller, less stable countries in the years to come. This increased aggregate of nuclear weaponry would further compound the catastrophic model proposed by the above survey. Therefore the complete destruction of humankind by nuclear war is still a very real and frightening possibility.

The Bible teaches that humanity will be totally destroyed before the general resurrection and Last Judgment. A number of passages indirectly affirm this outcome, such as the passing away of the old heaven and the old earth in Rev 21. Others are more

---

[32] Robock, A; Oman, L; Stenchikov, G.L. "Nuclear winter revisited with a modern climate model and current nuclear arsenals: Still catastrophic consequences" *Journal of Geophysical Research Vol 112* (2007)

openly explicit. Zephaniah for example, tells us that the earth will be completely devastated by the judgment of fire:

> I will utterly sweep away everything from the face of the earth," declares the Lord. "I will sweep away man and beast; I will sweep away the birds of the heavens and the fish of the sea, and the rubble with the wicked. I will cut off mankind from the face of the earth," declares the Lord. (Zeph 1:2-3)

> I will bring distress on mankind, so that they shall walk like the blind, because they have sinned against the Lord; their blood shall be poured out like dust, and their flesh like dung. Neither their silver nor their gold shall be able to deliver them on the day of the wrath of the Lord. In the fire of his jealousy, all the earth shall be consumed; for a full and sudden end he will make of all the inhabitants of the earth. (Zeph 1:17-18)

Jeremiah also had a vision of the world as utterly bereft of life:

> I looked on the earth, and behold, it was without form and void; and to the heavens, and they had no light. I looked on the mountains, and behold, they were quaking, and all the hills moved to and fro. I looked, and behold, there was no man, and all the birds of the air had fled. I looked, and behold, the fruitful land was a desert, and all its cities were laid in ruins before the Lord, before his fierce anger. (Jer 4:23-26)

This passage in Jeremiah is part of a wider sequence of events which parallel the prophecy of the whore of Babylon. It immediately turns from this apocalyptic vision to imagery which clearly influenced the scarlet clad prostitute of the Book of Revelation:

> And you, O desolate one, what do you mean that you dress in scarlet, that you adorn yourself with ornaments of gold, that you enlarge your eyes with paint? In vain you beautify yourself. Your lovers despise you; they seek your life. (Jer 4:30)

Could this be a further connection with the fall of Babylon and the subsequent demise of humanity? The proximity of this image to the scene of devastation depicted just moments earlier would not have escaped the attention of the author of Revelation. John obviously saw the relation between the "desolate one" of Jeremiah and the destruction of humankind, since the fall of Babylon and the battle of Armageddon are similarly tied together in the Apocalypse.

Conclusion

The Apocalypse foretells that the fall of the last world empire will bring about the conditions needed for the rise of the Antichrist and the cause of the battle of Armageddon. Today, the only possible country that could be said to dominate world politics to the extent of constituting an "empire" is the United States of America. If the next eruption of the volcano Cumbre Vieja sends the western flank of the island cascading into the sea, then it would result in a colossal tidal wave that could sweep away the eastern coast of the Americas. This event would almost certainly spell the end of the USA as a superpower, and the economic repercussions could cause immense political instability. Perfect conditions for the rise to power of charismatic leader promising to have the solution to the world's problems.

If this individual happened to be the Antichrist, bent on leading humanity to its destruction, then his ascension to power will be undoubtedly be accompanied by political machinations designed to deepen tensions between existing enemies and creating fresh disputes between old allies – gathering the nations of the world together for their ultimate destruction. The final straw which will see these strains tipping over into full-scale nuclear conflict will be the invasion of Israel by a coalition of Arab countries exploiting the demise of its chief ally.

But if the Bible does predict this calamitous fate for our future, then when can we expect these events to take place? Constructing fixed dates in some sort of "doomsday clock" to oblivion is an extremely precarious venture. The recurring failure of past interpreters in setting a precise date for the end-time should act to serve as a warning against being so presumptuous as being able to determine God's plan for humanity in advance. Nonetheless, Jesus frequently mentions in Scripture that the people living during the end of the age should take note of the signs of the times in which they live, so they can repent and reconcile themselves with God. So even if we can't establish an exact date for the end of the world, it is prudent to take note of key eschatological markers so that we may know the time is drawing near.

CHAPTER SIX

Dating the End-time

Attempting to establish a precise date for the Second Coming of Jesus and the inauguration of the eschaton has been a matter of serious contention since the earliest days of Christianity. Christ had warned the disciples that no one, including Jesus himself, knew the day and hour of his Coming, and that he would come at the very time it would least be expected:

> But concerning that day and hour no one knows, not even the angels of heaven, nor the Son, but the Father only. (Matt 24:36)

> But know this, that if the master of the house had known at what hour the thief was coming, he would not have left his house to be broken into. You also must be ready, for the Son of Man is coming at an hour you do not expect. (Luke 12:39-40)

> Just as it was in the days of Noah, so will it be in the days of the Son of Man. They were eating and drinking and marrying and being given in marriage, until the day when Noah entered the ark, and the flood came and destroyed them all. Likewise, just as it was in the days of Lot - they were eating and drinking, buying and selling, planting and building, but on the day when Lot went out from Sodom, fire and sulfur rained from heaven and destroyed them all - so will it be on the day when the Son of Man is revealed. (Luke 17:26-30)

However in his apocalyptic discourse, Jesus explicitly stated that the signs of his Coming would be openly recognizable to those who sought for them in the last days. He even urges believers to take note of such signs and be careful to take heed of them when they appear:

> Now when these things begin to take place, straighten up and raise your heads, because your redemption is drawing near. (Luke 21:28)

As we have already seen, the Book of Daniel also suggests that the hidden meaning of its visions would be revealed during the last days. In Dan 12, the angel Gabriel tells Daniel that the words he was commanded to write would be sealed until the approach of the end-time. These verses imply that the true meaning of Daniel's visions would finally be revealed at the close of history:

> But you, Daniel, shut up the words and seal the book, until the time of the end. Many shall run to and fro, and knowledge shall increase...

> "Go your way, Daniel, for the words are shut up and sealed until the time of the end...." (Dan 12:4, 9)

While no one could hope to determine the exact date of the end-time, Jesus made clear that the approach of his Second Coming would be announced by various omens; and that these signs could be recognizable by the faithful in the last days. Daniel was also told that the mysterious words of his prophecy was only to be sealed until the time of the end, implying that their true meaning would be eventually revealed during the end of days. In addition, Christ also promised that the hidden meaning of such portions of Scripture would eventually be revealed by the Holy Spirit:

> I still have many things to say to you, but you cannot bear them now. When the Spirit of truth comes, he will guide you into all the truth, for he will not speak on his own authority, but whatever he hears he will speak, and he will declare to you the things that are to come. He will glorify me, for he will take what is mine and declare it to you. (John 16:12-14)

So while no one can know the exact time of the end, it seems that there is enough scriptural evidence to suggest that the people living at the end of the age would be able to recognize that the time was drawing near. As we have argued throughout this book, many of these portents appear to have already been fulfilled, and consequently, we should be able to establish that the end-time is very close indeed. We still cannot determine an exact date, for it is not for us "to know times or seasons that the Father has fixed by his own authority" (Acts 1:7). The end may come at any time – be it within a year or the next hundred. But by examining the most relevant data outlined in the Scriptures, we may able to extract some vital clues that may provide us with enough information to roughly approximate our place in the history of salvation.

The Sabbath Millennium

One of the major pointers used by modern prophecy watchers to determine that we are living during the end-times is the concept of a "sabbath millennium".[1] The writers of the Talmud, along with many early Christians, believed that history would come to completion in seven thousand years – a week of millennia. Just as God finished the work of creation in seven days, so the history of humankind would find its completion after seven thousand years. The early church father Hippolytus (d.235), followed by Lactantius (d.320), expected the sabbath millennium/thousand year reign of Christ to begin about the year 500AD – 6000 years after what they had reckoned to be the date of creation.[2] The Babylonian Talmud also taught that the world would exist for six thousand years.[3] Since the Hebrew calendar puts the date of creation at the year 3760 in the common era, this would date the end of days to around 2240AD – the Hebrew year 6000 Anno Mundi. These sources seem to have drawn from a common tradition concerning a sabbath millennium which dates from before the 3rd century AD.

However the biblical date of creation was subject to major revision during the 17th century, when James Ussher the Anglican archbishop of Armagh compiled what is perhaps the definitive chronology of the Bible in his work *Annales veteris testamenti, a*

---

[1] See Haggith, D. *Prophets of the Apocalypse* pp379-389
[2] Hippolytus *In Dan.* 4.; Lactantius *Inst.* 7.25.
[3] Avodah Zarah 9a

prima mundi origine deducti (*Annals of the Old Testament, deduced from the first origins of the world*). In this revised biblical chronology, Ussher attempted to date the creation of the world by calculating the length of time given in the various genealogies and regnal lengths of the Bible in comparison with other Ancient Near Eastern historical records. In doing so, he determined that the world came into existence in 4004BC.

While we know that the universe is in fact several billion years old, the account given in Genesis may be understood as reflecting a prophetic understanding of history. As such, it may contain a prophetic timescale which is symbolically portrayed as consisting of seven millennia. If this is correct, then it may be of some significance that by using the anchor date provided by Genesis, we can establish that the seventh millennium began around the year 1996 – two thousand years after the birth of Christ, circa 4BC.

The idea of a sabbath millennium can be found in some apocryphal writings dating back to the early Christian era. When the protocanon was finally closed during the 4th century AD, a number of writings were excluded due to the contested nature of their divinely-inspired status. Among these were two other works which forwarded the concept of a sabbath millennium. The most widely known of these books is the Secrets of Enoch, otherwise known as 2 Enoch, which was most probably written during the first century AD at Alexandria.[4] This book is to be distinguished from 1 Enoch, which was written by several different hands at various stages throughout the 2nd to 1st centuries BC, and quoted by St. Jude in the New Testament (Jude 1:14-15).

2 Enoch 33:1 asserts that the full span of history will last for seven thousand years. In an early example of millennialism, the author of 2 Enoch holds that the seventh millennium will be a sabbath millennium, after which time itself will come to an end:

> And I appointed the eighth day also, that the eighth day should be the first-created after my work, and that *the first seven* revolve in the form of the seventh thousand, and that at the beginning of the eighth thousand there should be a time of not-counting, endless, with neither years nor months nor weeks nor days nor hours.

The Epistle of Barnabas also forwards the concept of a sabbath millennium. Some of the early Church fathers were willing to ascribe authorship of this letter to Barnabas the companion of Paul. However modern scholarship prefers to regard it as a pseudepigraphical work written by an Alexandrian Gentile Christian circa 130AD. The Epistle of Barnabas differs from 2 Enoch, in that it posits that the end would come after six thousand years were completed, instead of seven thousand:

> Elsewhere he says, If your children will keep my Sabbaths, then will I put my mercy upon them. And even in the beginning of the creation he makes mention of the Sabbath: And God made in six days the works of his hands; and he finished them on the seventh day, and he rested the seventh day, and sanctified it. Consider, my children, what it signifies, that he finished them in six days. The meaning of it is this: that in six thousand years the Lord God will bring all things to an end. For with him one day is a thousand years, as he himself testifies, saying, Behold this day will be as a thousand years. Therefore, children, in six days, that is, in six thousand years, will all things be accomplished. And he rested the seventh day, means this: that when his Son will come, and abolish the season of the Wicked One, and judge the ungodly, and will change the sun and the moon and the stars, then he will gloriously rest in that seventh day.

---

[4] Myers, A.C (Ed) *The Eerdmans Bible Dictionary* (Grand Rapids: Eerdmans, 1987), p337

(Barn 13:2-6)

Barnabas' placement of the sabbath millennium after six thousand years reflects the same tradition that influenced Hippolytus, Lactantius and the Talmud. As such, this should perhaps be considered to be the more authentic version of this concept. An important feature in the above passage is that according to Barnabas, the apocalyptic "changing" of the Sun, Moon and stars occurs at the end of the sixth millennium. As we have already suggested, the eschatological astronomical phenomena appears to have taken place between the years 1999-2000 – right at the beginning of the sabbath millennium, which according to Ussher's chronology, began in 1996. So it appears that the Epistle of Barnabas predicted the eschatological darkening of the Sun and Moon and the falling of stars to occur at the turn of the last millennium – the precise moment we postulated that these phenomena occurred.

The fact that the world did not come to an end in 1996 would put the concept of the sabbath millennium into some doubt. But the beginning of the sabbath millennium is perhaps better understood as the date at which the end-time commences, rather than the date of a sudden and abrupt climax. As we shall argue below, it seems that the start of the sabbath millennium is a period when the Devil is cast from heaven to begin his reign on earth.

If the true beginning of the sabbath millennium was heralded by the eschatological astronomical phenomena at the turn of the last millennium, this would place it as beginning in the year 1999 rather than 1996. The real significance of the sabbath millennium is primarily symbolic. The Gregorian calendar in use today was based on the calculations of Dionysius Exiguus, a 6th century monk who dated Christ's birth to the year 1AD. It is this date which holds the most symbolic value for Christians. As such, the symbolic significance of the sabbath millennium should probably be rounded off to conform with the date used by Christians to determine the calendar year. This would mean that the true start of the sabbath millennium occurred around the years 1999-2000, and that it was announced by the appearance of the astronomical and geophysical signs given in the Bible – namely a tight grouping of solar and lunar eclipses together with a meteor shower and an earthquake.

As we shall see, the appearance of these signs also seems to be associated in the Bible with the fall of Satan. The Book of Revelation suggests that Satan's reign on earth begins after he is cast out of heaven – a subject which is covered in some detail in Rev 12. If we can establish that the reign of Satan began at the beginning of the sabbath millennium in the year 1999, and that this event was heralded by the astronomical phenomena of at the turn of the last century, then it is perhaps more than coincidence that the prophecy of the mark of the Beast was also fulfilled in the same year. By studying the content of Rev 12 in closer detail, we may be able to strengthen our proposal that the astronomical and geophysical events of 1999 marked the fall of Satan and the subsequent inauguration of his reign on earth.

The Fall of Satan

It is a commonly believed that the account of the fall of Satan in Rev 12 solely relates to the primordial expulsion of Satan from the angelic hierarchy at the beginning of creation. While this event is certainly reflected in this passage, it cannot be confined to the primordial fall alone. As the writer of Revelation is aware, whilst Satan is in a fallen state, he is still allowed to pass between the heavenly and earthly spheres at will and is permitted to stand in the heavenly court to accuse mankind of its sins. The Book of Revelation tells us that at some point towards the eschaton, Satan will no longer be tolerated to stand in the heavenly court accusing humanity of its sinfulness; but will be ejected from the heavenly sphere completely, and cast to earth by the archangel Michael. This event will limit the Devil's existence to the earthly sphere alone.

This leads us to question what happens when there is no longer any place for Satan in heaven and the earth becomes his sole dwelling place? Is this the beginning of the event of the Antichrist?

Many theologians believe Rev 12 describes a second, eschatological fall of Satan during the last days. G.K Beale states "Just as Satan and his hosts fell at the beginning of the first creation, so he had to fall at the start of the second, new creation."[5] After the primordial rebellion and subsequent fall of Lucifer at the beginning of creation, Satan still had access to the heavenly court, where he would act in the capacity of the accuser of humanity (see Job 1:6-9; 2:1-6; Zech 3:1-2). In Rev 12:10 Satan "accuses [our brothers] day and night before our God". S.S Smalley informs us that "To some extent, Satan had a place in heaven, and access to God's presence; and this may have inspired the expectation of a final celestial battle before the end-time."[6] Aune enlightens us further:

> The myth of the heavenly battle between Michael and Satan resulting in the defeat and expulsion of Satan and his angels from heaven is narrated as an *eschatological* event in 12:9, but as an exclusively *primordial* or *protological* event in early Jewish and Islamic literature, a motif based on Isa 14:12-15. It is of course possible that the tradition of Satan's presence before the heavenly throne of God as an adversary of the righteous on earth led to a reinterpretation of the tradition of his primordial expulsion from heaven, resulting in a tale of his eschatological expulsion.[7]

The Cosmic Drama

Immediately prior to the narrative which details the fall of Satan in chapter twelve of the Apocalypse, the text seems to allude yet again to the motif of the darkening of the Sun and Moon, and stars being cast to earth:

> And a great sign appeared in heaven: a woman clothed with the sun, with the moon under her feet, and on her head a crown of twelve stars. She was pregnant and was crying out in birth pains and the agony of giving birth. And another sign appeared in heaven: behold, a great red dragon, with seven heads and ten horns, and on his heads seven diadems. His tail swept down a third of the stars of heaven and cast them to

---

[5] Beale, G.K. *The Book of Revelation* p658
[6] Smalley, S. *The Revelation to John* p324
[7] Aune, D.E. *Revelation* p694

the earth. And the dragon stood before the woman who was about to give birth, so that when she bore her child he might devour it. She gave birth to a male child, one who is to rule all the nations with a rod of iron, but her child was caught up to God and to his throne, and the woman fled into the wilderness, where she has a place prepared by God, in which she is to be nourished for 1,260 days. (Rev 12:1-11)

The image of the Woman adorned with the Sun in the travail of childbirth has long been interpreted as symbolizing the end-time tribulation of the Church before it gives birth to the Messiah. This particular passage is rich in background inspiration, and contains allusions to several biblical passages. But it is also influenced by the mythology of the ancient Mediterranean. Most scholars agree that John incorporated elements of the combat myth in this portion of the Apocalypse, and seems to have used this highly popular story-form as a template for the prophecy of the Woman adorned with the Sun.

The combat myth was a widely prevalent literary form in the ancient world, made of separate stories which all converged on a similar theme. This theme usually incorporated a reference to an evil usurper who "is doomed to be vanquished by a yet unborn prince".[8] In the Greek rendition of this story, the goddess Leto, being pregnant with Apollo the son of Zeus, was attacked by the dragon Python. Python was forewarned by the oracle at Delphi that left unchecked, the unborn Apollo would be the cause of its eventual demise. The serpent then attempted to prevent this fate by killing the pregnant Leto and her unborn child. But its efforts failed and Apollo eventually grew up to slay the monster with his legendary arrows.

Other versions of the combat myth can be found in the Osiris and Isis legend of ancient Egypt, or Marduk, the chief god of Babylon slaying the seven-headed water dragon Tiamat.

In Rev 12 the unfolding drama of the combat between the Woman adorned with the Sun and her unborn child against the Red Dragon is played out in the sky as a sign which could be seen in heaven – "a great sign appeared in heaven" The Greek word ουρανος (*ouranos*) can mean both "heaven" and "sky"; while the word σεμειον

(*semeion*) is often used to translate the Hebrew word אות ('oth), which as well as meaning "sign" or "mark" can also mean "omen". So the first part of Rev 12:1 may also be translated as "a great omen appeared in the sky".

S.S. Smalley elaborates on the word *semeion* further, and states that "In the New Testament the word is used with reference to a celestial portent which carries a warning for the future".[9] Therefore it appears that the author is signifying that while these events are acted out in a separate plane of existence by the principal characters of the Dragon and the Woman adorned with the Sun, they will also be visible in the earth's sky as some form of celestial omen. Events which are played out in the spiritual, heavenly realm are thus reflected on the earthly sphere by a series of related astronomical prodigies.

As we shall see, the image of the Dragon standing by the Woman clothed with the Sun in order to devour her child, appears to be a mythological dramatization of the cosmic events described in Rev 6:12-13; 8:12. Rare celestial events were accorded with a great deal of significance in antiquity,[10] and were often considered to be a reflection of

---

[8] Beale, G.K. *The Book of Revelation* p624
[9] Smalley, S.S. *The Revelation to John* p313
[10] For a broader outline of the importance of astrology/astronomy in the first century Mediterranean and its usage in the Apocalypse see Malina, B.J; Pilch, J.J *Social-Science Commentary on the Book of Revelation*

events which were occurring in the realm of the gods. Signs in the sky were believed to be physical manifestations of the actions of the gods; and such actions were believed have repercussions for those that inhabited the earthly plane.

In the Apocalypse we are told that a sign appeared in the heavens – that of a Woman adorned with the Sun accompanied by the Moon at her feet, with twelve stars in her crown. This is undoubtedly a symbolic representation of events occurring in the sky. The Woman represents the Sun itself, and the twelve stars are thought to symbolize the twelve constellations.[11] The imagery of the Moon being at the woman's feet is strikingly reminiscent of the position of the Moon during a solar eclipse.

The next sign that appears in the sky is that of a "great Red Dragon", with seven heads and ten horns. Could this Red Dragon symbolize the Moon during a total lunar eclipse? If so, then the Red Dragon may represent the Moon itself. We are told that the Dragon stood in front of the Woman (at her feet?) as she was in the throes of childbirth, in order to devour her Child as soon as he was born. If the Dragon/Moon stood in front of the Woman/Sun, this would produce a total solar eclipse.

The idea that eclipses were caused by a ferocious dragon intent on consuming the Sun can be found in many early cultures. The ancient Chinese for example, attempted to frighten off the eclipse dragon by banging on pots and drums; while in India ascetics would immerse themselves in water in an act of worship which they believed would aid the Sun in its cosmic struggle against this ravenous mythical creature. The author could certainly have been aware of such traditions, as the Middle East was known to have trade links with India and the Far East even at this early stage. Ancient trade routes carried more than just commercial produce; they were also a conduit for transmitting culture and ideas. As such, the myth of the eclipse dragon could have easily been carried to Asia Minor by the 1st century.

So the two signs that appear in the sky in Rev 12 appear to be pictorial representations of the solar and lunar eclipses mentioned in Rev 6:12-13. A further connection to this passage can be found in the Dragon sweeping "a third of the stars" with his tail and dragging them to earth – which is clearly an allusion to the stars falling to earth in Rev 6:13. Once again, we have all the elements of a solar eclipse, lunar eclipse and meteor shower combined together in one passage; only this time the events are played out by what can only be described as actors in a cosmic drama. It is helpful to compare the similarities of Rev 12:1-4 with 6:12-13 as well as 8:12 when viewed side by side in table form:

(Fortress Press: Minneapolis, 2000)
[11] See Beale, G.K. *The Book of Revelation* pp626-627

Rev 6:12-13	Rev 8:12	Rev 12:1-4
Sun becomes black	Third of Sun struck	Moon/Dragon at the feet of woman adorned with the sun
Moon becomes like blood	Third of Moon struck	Moon/Dragon is red in appearance
Stars fall to earth	Third of stars struck Rev 12:1-4	Dragon sweeps down a third of the stars and casts them to earth.

If the divine drama in Rev 12 is a recapitulation of the celestial phenomena described in Rev 6:12-13; 8:12, then these phenomena may also be related to the astronomical events of 1999-2000. As the primary focus of Rev 12 is the casting of Satan from heaven, it would appear that the eschatological astronomical phenomena were the outwardly visible signs of the fall of Satan and the beginning of his worldly reign. Did the astronomical events which began to occur in the year 1999 herald the casting of Satan to earth? If so, then we may be able to further posit an astronomical symbolism behind the seven heads of the Dragon mentioned in Rev 12:3, and connect this with the planetary alignment of 5th May 2000.

As we have noted previously, the Book of Revelation states that the signs of the Woman adorned with the Sun and the Red Dragon with seven heads could be seen in the sky. If the seven heads of the Dragon could be seen in the heavens, then they must relate to some form of celestial bodies visible in the night skies – either stars or planets. The most likely point of reference to seven heavenly bodies may be found in the seven classical "planets" that were known to the ancients. Only five of the solar system's eight planets are visible to the naked eye – Mercury, Venus, Mars, Jupiter and Saturn. It was thus only these observable planets that were included in ancient mythology and astrology. Because these five planets had no fixed place in the firmament, they were grouped together by the ancients with the only other wandering bodies in the sky – the Sun and Moon, which were known collectively as the "seven planets".

If we are maintain that the seven heads of the Dragon symbolize the seven classical planets, this would explain why Rev 13:1 states that the seven heads of the Dragon had "blasphemous names". When John wrote the Book of the Apocalypse, the seven classical planets were named after the Roman gods Mercury, Venus, Mars, Jupiter, Saturn, Sol and Luna – names which are considered blasphemous by the monotheistic religion of Christianity. So if the sign of the Dragon with seven heads is a celestial omen concerning the seven classical planets, then the planetary alignment of the year 2000, which involved the massing of the five classical planets together with the Earth, Sun and Moon, would have fulfilled this prophecy perfectly.

We can further establish that the fall of Satan is associated with the eschatological astronomical phenomena by looking at the arrangement of the material given in Rev 8:12-9:2. It has long been acknowledged that this passage contains a veiled reference to the fall of Satan. But importantly, it is also connected to the eschatological darkening of the Sun:

> And the fifth angel blew his trumpet, and I saw a star fallen from heaven to earth, and he was given the key to the shaft of the bottomless pit. He opened the shaft of the bottomless pit, and from the shaft rose smoke like the smoke of a great furnace, and the sun and the air were darkened with the smoke from the shaft.[12]

The imagery of the "star" falling from heaven to open the abyss is usually identified by scholars with the fall of Satan. Stars are often presented in the Apocalypse as representations of angelic beings. And the above verses contain strong echoes of a similar passage in Isaiah that has been associated with the fall of Satan:

> How you are fallen from heaven, O Day Star, son of Dawn! How you are cut down to the ground, you who laid the nations low! You said in your heart, 'I will ascend to heaven; above the stars of God I will set my throne on high; I will sit on the mount of assembly in the far reaches of the north; I will ascend above the heights of the clouds; I will make myself like the Most High." But you are brought down to Sheol, to the far reaches of the pit. (Isa 14:12-15)

As Beale states: "The expression in Rev 9:1 may be another way of saying that "Satan… was cast to the earth, and his angels with him were cast".[13] Not only does the fall of Satan occur in Rev 9:1 immediately after a reference to the darkening of the Sun, Moon and stars; but the Sun is darkened as a result of the impact of the star/Satan falling to earth. So the fall of Satan is clearly associated with the eschatological signs that we previously connected to the astronomical and geophysical events which marked the beginning of the sabbath millennium around the years 1999-2000.

Another important factor we have to take into consideration is the fact that the Apocalypse describes the rising of the Beast from the sea and the sealing of the inhabitants of the earth with his mark directly after Satan is cast to earth in Rev 12. The motif of the Beast rising from the sea in Rev 13 is held in deliberate contrast to Satan being cast to earth in Rev 12. Satan falls to earth only to rise again in the person of the Beast/Antichrist. He rises from the sea, which symbolises the primordial chaos, because this is the location of the abyss or "bottomless pit" – the place to which the fallen angel in 9:1 was given the key to unlock.

As G.R Osborne notes:

> 'The "abyss" stems from the imagery originally associated with the fathomless depths of the ocean, as in the "surface of the deep" in Gen 1:2… In several places it speaks of "the waters of the great deep" (Ps. 42:7; Isa. 51:10. The "abyss" became an idiom for the place of the dead and possibly because the dead were unclean, it came to be used for the "pit" or "prison house" in which fallen angels were imprisoned'.[14]

---

[12] As we noted earlier in chapter six, this portion of the Apocalypse can be linked to the events of Tunguska and the rise of modern aviation. However it also functions on another level which specifically relates to the fall of Satan.

[13] Beale, G.K. *The Book of Revelation* p492

[14] Osborne, G.R. *Revelation* p363

Elsewhere in the Apocalypse, we are specifically told that this is the place from which the Beast will emerge:

> 'And when they have finished their testimony, the beast that rises from the bottomless pit will make war on them and conquer them and kill them'. (Rev 11:8)

> 'The beast that you saw was, and is not, and is about to rise from the bottomless pit and go to destruction.' (Rev 17:8)

So according to Rev 9; 12-13 the fall of Satan to earth is the primary and immediate cause of the Beast to emerge from the sea/abyss and subsequently to bring into effect the prophecy of the mark of the Beast. This would therefore suggest that the eschatological fall of Satan directly coincides with the timing of the implementation of the mark of the Beast on earth (which in turn parallels the sealing of the saints in heaven). As we shall see, there are a number of other prophecies which seem to link the fall of Satan with the turn of the millennium, thus placing the date for the mark of the Beast in this same time-frame.

The Year of the Dragon

Many extra-biblical prophecies have predicted the coming of either Satan or the Antichrist at the turn of the millennium. We should take the time here to survey the most important of these prophecies in order to further strengthen our hypothesis that the fall of Satan is connected to the astronomical events of the years 1999-2000.

Prior to their eventual publication in 2002, many commentators believed that the reason the secrets of La Salette were being withheld from public consumption was because they contained a scathing attack on the Church hierarchy. But now we are able to examine this contention in retrospect, it seems that the main reason the secrets of La Salette were suppressed by the Church until their eventual release in 2002 was primarily because that they had contained a specific date. A date which could have generated mass hysteria had they been released beforehand.

The secret given to Maximin by Our Lady of La Salette in 1846 contained a date prophesying the arrival of a "monster" that would come to disturb the peace – the year 2000:[15]

> Then, after [that], a great peace will come, but it will not last a long time. A monster will come to disturb it. All that I tell you here will arrive in the other century, at the latest in the year two thousand.

If the Vatican had released the secrets before the date contained in Maximin's secret it would have been accused by critics of creating sensationalism. So as a matter of prudence, the secrets were withheld until the date mentioned in Maximin's secret had

---

[15] Maximin's mention of a monster coming to disturb the peace brings to mind the Dragon of Revelation, who goes off to make war on the woman's offspring (Rev 12:17). Elsewhere in the Apocalypse, we are told that the Devil's role is to gather the armies of the world together for battle, and thus to take away peace from the earth (see Rev 16:14-16; 20:8).

finally passed. So the original secrets of La Salette appear to indicate the coming of the monster/Antichrist by the year two thousand at the latest. Yet with the benefit of retrospect, we can determine that the only possible way this prophecy could have been fulfilled at the date specified is if we accept the above hypothesis that the fall of Satan occurred at the turn of the last millennium.[16]

Another well-known prophecy that could be used to support the hypothesis of the fall of Satan at the end of the second millennium is a popular prophecy concerning a vision attributed to Pope Leo XIII. We can trace the story behind the origins of this prophecy back to Pope Leo XIII's inauguration of the St. Michael Prayer in 1884, which was requested to be said after low mass:

Saint Michael the Archangel,
defend us in battle;
be our protection against the wickedness and snares of the devil.
May God rebuke him, we humbly pray:
and do thou, O Prince of the heavenly host,
by the power of God,
thrust into hell Satan and all the evil spirits
who prowl about the world seeking the ruin of souls.
Amen

Writing in 1947, Fr. Domenico Pechenino, a priest who worked at the Vatican during the time of Leo XIII, states that he had witnessed the moment that inspired the pope to take this action:

I do not remember the exact year. One morning the great Pope Leo XIII had celebrated a Mass and, as usual, was attending a Mass of thanksgiving. Suddenly, we saw him raise his head and stare at something above the celebrant's head. He was staring motionlessly, without batting an eye. His expression was one of horror and awe; the colour and look on his face changing rapidly. Something unusual and grave was happening in him.

"Finally, as though coming to his senses, he lightly but firmly tapped his hand and rose to his feet. He headed for his private office. His retinue followed anxiously and solicitously, whispering: 'Holy Father, are you not feeling well? Do you need anything?' He answered: 'Nothing, nothing.' About half an hour later, he called for the Secretary of the Congregation of Rites and, handing him a sheet of paper, requested that it be printed and sent to all the ordinaries around the world. What was that paper? It was the prayer that we recite with the people at the end of every Mass. It is the plea to Mary and the passionate request to the Prince of the heavenly host, (St. Michael: Saint Michael the Archangel, defend us in battle) beseeching God to send Satan back to hell."[17]

At some stage in the 20th century, rumours began to circulate about the contents of Pope Leo's vision, and a prophecy was attributed to him concerning this event. There are several variants of this prophecy (suggesting it first circulated in oral form), all with the

---

[16] It is perhaps worth mentioning at this point that Yves Dupont cites a prophecy by one "St John of the Cleft Rock" supposedly dating back to the 14th century, which predicts the coming of the Antichrist at the turn of the millennium. Although it must be noted that Dupont does not cite the original source for this prophecy, and "St John of the Cleft Rock" appears to be unknown to history. So this prophecy is almost certainly fraudulent and is of unknown date or origin. "It is said about twenty centuries after the Incarnation of the Word, the Beast in its turn shall become man. About the year 2000 AD, Antichrist will reveal himself to the world." Cited in Dupont, Y. *Catholic Prophecy* p23

[17] *Ephemerides Liturgicae* V. LXIX, pp 54–60.

same general theme of the pope hearing a conversion between Jesus and the Devil styled after the dialogues in the Book of Job, where Satan is permitted greater power for a period of 75 or 100 years.

> "When asked what had happened, he explained that, as he was about to leave the foot of the altar, he suddenly heard voices – two voices, one kind and gentle, the other guttural and harsh. They seemed to come from near the tabernacle. As he listened, he heard the following conversation:
> The guttural voice, the voice of Satan in his pride, boasted to Our Lord: "I can destroy your Church."
> The gentle voice of Our Lord: "You can? Then go ahead and do so."
> Satan: "To do so, I need more time and more power."
> Our Lord: "How much time? How much power?"
> Satan: "75 to 100 years, and a greater power over those who will give themselves over to my service."
> Our Lord: "You have the time, you will have the power. Do with them what you will."[18]

Other variants of this prophecy (which are admittedly later in origin and thus less authentic, but perhaps may still reflect a certain truth) specifically identify this time period as the 20th century. This would imply that the Devil would face some form of opposition, restriction or expulsion at the end of the allotted time:

> Pope Leo XIII (d. 1903) had a prophetic vision of the coming century of sorrow and war. After celebrating Mass, the Holy Father was conferring with his cardinals. Suddenly, he fell to the floor. The cardinals immediately called for a doctor. No pulse was detected, and the Holy Father was feared dead. Just as suddenly, Pope Leo awoke and said, 'What a horrible picture I was permitted to see!' In this vision, God gave Satan the choice of one century in which to do his worst work against the Church. The devil chose the 20th century. So moved was the Holy Father from this vision that he composed the prayer to St. Michael the Archangel.[19]

Perhaps the most famed prophecy dating the coming of the Antichrist to the turn of the last millennium was made by Nostradamus. Michel de Nostradame was born in 1503 to Jewish parents who had converted to Catholicism. Although Nostradamus professed to be a lifelong adherent to the Catholic faith, the means by which he made his divinations were far from orthodox. Nostradamus was clearly influenced by astrology and occult wisdom, and employed a divination technique that echoed the pagan Delphic oracle. We should therefore be aware that the prophecies of Nostradamus are not divinely inspired, and should be held separately from the other Church approved prophecies mentioned in this book. Yet this particular prophecy of Nostradamus compliments our above hypothesis so perfectly that it deserves to at least be mentioned.

The Bible teaches that prophecies made even by unclean spirits can still prove to be accurate. In the Book of Acts for example, Paul and Silas were confronted with a slave-girl possessed by a spirit which could tell the future:

> As we were going to the place of prayer, we were met by a slave girl who had a spirit of divination and brought her owners much gain by fortune-telling. She followed Paul and us, crying out, "These men are servants of the Most High God, who proclaim to you the way of salvation." And this she kept doing for

---

[18] The earliest version of this story to appear in print can be traced back to a 1934 German Sunday newspaper article *Theol-Prakt. Quartalschrift 87*. This would suggest that Fr. Pechenino had knowledge of the rumours circulating about the institution of the St. Michael prayer when he first gave the above testimony to the Italian journal *La Settimana del Clero* 1947. If so, then his testimony would appear to bolster the rumours, rather than refute them.

[19] Saunders, W. "Archangels and Guardian Angels", *Arlington Catholic Herald* (1st January 1997).

many days. Paul, having become greatly annoyed, turned and said to the spirit, "I command you in the name of Jesus Christ to come out of her." And it came out that very hour. But when her owners saw that their hope of gain was gone, they seized Paul and Silas and dragged them into the marketplace before the rulers. (Acts 16:16-19)

The Church Fathers recognised the various pagan messianic prophecies (e.g. Virgil's *Fourth Eclogue*) as legitimate predictions of Christ. And St. Thomas Aquinas uses the example of the Sibyls to prove that the heathens were capable of true prophecy.[20] So while we can accept that non-Christians can have the ability to be able to discern the future, we cannot be sure of the source of their inspiration – which may or may not emanate from genuine spiritual vision, or from unclean spirits with the intent to deceive. Pope Benedict XIV sums up this position as follows:

> "The recipients of prophecy may be angels, devils, men, women, children, heathens, or gentiles; nor is it necessary that a man should be gifted with any particular disposition in order to receive the light of prophecy provided his intellect and senses be adapted for making manifest the things which God reveals to him. Though moral goodness is most profitable to a prophet, yet it is not necessary in order to obtain the gift of prophecy."[21]

The Church therefore teaches that we should never actively seek such heterodox knowledge by consulting soothsayers or fortune tellers.[22]

Despite his extremely questionable religious orthodoxy, Nostradamus is regarded by many as one of history's greatest prognosticators. Nostradamus had managed to establish a reputation for himself during his own lifetime, having gained acceptance in the French royal court and famously predicting the death of King Henry II of France as a result of a mounted dual. But it is for forecasting events after his own lifetime that Nostradamus is most celebrated for; such as the emergence of the British Empire, Napoleon Bonaparte, the French Revolution and Adolf Hitler.

However not all of Nostradamus' prophecies have been fulfilled in the manner they were expected to. One of the most famous examples of a supposedly failed prophecy of Nostradamus is that found in Century 10 Quatrain 72.

L'an mil neuf cens nonante neuf sept mois,	The year 1999 seven months
Du ciel viendra un grand Roy d'effrayeur,	From the sky will come a great King of Terror:
Resusciter le grand Roy d'Angolmois,	To bring back to life the great King of the Angolmois,
Avant apres, Mars regner par bon heur.	Before and after Mars to reign by good luck.

The fact that nothing of such note seemed to happen throughout the duration of

---

[20] Aquinas, Thomas, *Summa Theologica* SS 172:6
[21] Benedict XIV *Heroic Virtue: On the Beatification and Canonization of the Servants of God* III (Prato: 1840)
[22] "All forms of divination are to be rejected: recourse to Satan or demons, conjuring up the dead or other practices falsely supposed to "unveil" the future. Consulting horoscopes, astrology, palm reading, interpretation of omens and lots, the phenomena of clairvoyance, and recourse to mediums all conceal a desire for power over time, history, and, in the last analysis, other human beings, as well as a wish to conciliate hidden powers. They contradict the honor, respect, and loving fear that we owe to God alone." *Catechism of the Catholic Church*, 2116

1999, let alone anything of such universal significance, led many to assume that this much- hyped verse was a failed prophecy.[23] It has since become a source of major embarrassment for Nostradamus enthusiasts, and has tarnished the reputation of a seer renowned for the accuracy of his predictions. However we may be able to rescue this quatrain if we interpret it in light our findings concerning the year 1999 discussed above.

If we were to propose that Nostradamus' prophecy of the "great King of Terror" descending from the sky was related to the fall of Satan, then this quatrain would suddenly become abundantly clear. Satan is often depicted as falling from the sky to the earth after being cast out of the heavenly court. We have already discussed such imagery detailed in Rev 12:7-12 above, or other passages such as Luke 10:18: "And [Jesus] said to them, 'I saw Satan fall like a star from heaven.'" Nostradamus' prediction of the tyrant descending from the sky is obviously in line with the fall of Satan. The title "great King of Terror" meets this interpretation, as it seems to contain some Satanic connotations, and recalls the king of the abyss who descends from the sky in Rev 9:1 (cf. Rev 9:11).

The second verse of Nostradamus' quatrain, where the great King of Terror restores "the great King of the Angolmois" to life, is reminiscent of Rev 9:1, where the fallen angel unlocks the abyss from which the sea-beast will emerge, and also 13:1-4, where the Dragon delegates his authority to the sea-beast who has recovered from a mortal wound:

> One of its heads seemed to have a mortal wound, but its mortal wound was healed, and the whole earth marveled as they followed the beast. And they worshiped the dragon, for he had given his authority to the beast, and they worshiped the beast, saying, "Who is like the beast, and who can fight against it?"

As we can see from the latter half of this passage, the Dragon is credited with the Beast's restoration to life. Nostradamus' phrase "the great King of the Angolmois" is widely recognized to be a reference to the Antichrist. Nostradamus, along with most other seers and prophets, believed in the cyclical nature of time, and that history was destined to repeat itself. It is recognized by the vast majority of Nostradamus scholars that this quatrain most likely alludes to a second coming of the Mongolian warlord Genghis Khan, since the word *Angolmois* is an anagram of *Mongolois*. It appears that Nostradamus believed that an Antichrist-type figure, moulded in the spirit of Genghis Khan (who was a fierce and ruthless world emperor), would be revived by this fearsome entity that descended from the sky. Therefore if Nostradamus' "great King of Terror" brings the Antichrist to life, then it stands to reason that he could well be identified with the Dragon of Revelation.

The "seven months" mentioned by Nostradamus in the above quatrain is remarkably close to the date of the eclipse on 12th August 1999. If we were to interpret the first line of this quatrain as meaning after the seven months had elapsed, rather than the seventh month itself, this would take us directly into the month of August. Understood in this manner, this controversial quatrain turns out to be yet another incredibly accurate prediction made by the esteemed soothsayer.

---

[23] The various attempts to link this quatrain to the 9/11 terrorist attacks are feeble at best.

There is another interesting component of the prophecies of St. Malachy which may further confirm our above findings. Although it may not provide us with an *exact* date, it does seem to place the eschatological astronomical phenomena during the reign of the correct pontiff. St. Malachy's title for John Paul II is *De labore solis* – "from the labour of the Sun". As we draw nearer to the end of St. Malachy's list of popes, the pontifical titles become increasingly apocalyptic in tone. We noted earlier in chapter two how this phrase was particularly apt for John Paul II, given the fact that he was both born and buried during a partial solar eclipse. However the appellation *De labore solis* is also an unmistakable reference to Rev 12 and the Woman adorned with the Sun suffering the pains of childbirth. Does St. Malachy's list of future popes therefore suggest that the prophecy of the Woman adorned with the Sun in Rev 12 would be fulfilled during the pontificate of John Paul II? If so, this would further confirm our suggestion that the astronomical events of 1999-2000 were foretold by Rev 12, since they occurred towards the close of John Paul II's papacy.

So if we take a brief overview of the supportive evidence which suggests that the eschatological astronomical and geophysical phenomena occurred at the turn of the last millennium, we can see that when combined it constitutes a persuasive argument indeed:

The beginning of the sabbath millennium has been calculated at around the year 1996. If we are to go by the symbolic value of the Christian calendar, then the sabbath millennium could be said to have begun at the turn of the last century around the year 2000.

The Book of Revelation links the occurrence of the eschatological astronomical phenomena with the fall of Satan and the implementation of the mark of the Beast. Astronomical phenomena exactly matching that described in the Apocalypse occurred between the years 1999-2000.

The secrets of La Salette foretold that a monster would come to disturb the peace by the year 2000 at the latest.

Nostradamus predicted that the Antichrist would be brought to life by the great King of Terror who descends from the sky in the year 1999 plus seven months.

St. Malachy seems to have foretold that the prophecy of the Woman adorned with the Sun would be fulfilled during the pontificate of Pope John Paul II – between 1978 and 2005.

The supporting facts may not end here however. There is a weight of evidence to suggest that the vision of the Third Secret of Fatima revealed to the public on 26th June 2000 was actually not the full text of the secret. Various Fatima experts have shown that there was an accompanying "attachment" to the visionary portion of the Third Secret that has been withheld by the Congregation for the Doctrine of the Faith. This "attachment" is thought to contain the words of Our Lady explaining the meaning of the vision of the assassination of the pope. And according to some sound detective reasoning, it has been adduced that this portion of the secret also concerns the struggle between the Dragon and the Woman adorned with the Sun in Rev 12. This as yet undisclosed part of the secret of Fatima has been dubbed by the Italian press as the "Fourth Secret".

The "Fourth" Secret of Fatima?

When Pope John Paul II announced in a homily delivered during the beatification ceremony of Francisco and Jacinta Marto on 13th May 2000 that he would reveal the contents of the Third Secret of Fatima to the world, he ominously chose Rev 12 as the first reading for the mass. During his homily, John Paul II stated that the message of Fatima was specifically linked with this portion of scripture:

> The message of Fatima is a call to conversion, alerting humanity to have nothing to do with the "dragon" whose "tail swept down a third of the stars of heaven, and cast them to the earth".[24]

The timing for this homily and its subject material is either a striking coincidence, or the Vatican was more informed than what it was revealing in public. A number of commentators have noted how that while Pope John Paul II compared the message of Fatima to Rev 12, there is no direct allusion to this particular piece of scripture in any of the original secrets. At least not in any of the secrets that have been revealed *so far*.[25]

When the contents of the Third Secret were first published in the summer of 2000, some of the most prominent Fatima experts questioned whether the Church had fully disclosed its entire content. The "official" interpretation which confined the vision to past events was perceived in many quarters to be a major anti-climax to the hype that had surrounded the Third Secret. It raised a host of questions from both the public and researchers alike. One of the most controversial aspects of presentation was that Cardinal Sodano had attempted to limit the interpretation of the vision of the Third Secret to the assassination attempt on John Paul II in 1981:

> According to the interpretation of the "little shepherds", which was also recently confirmed by Sister Lucia, the "Bishop clothed in white" who prays for all the faithful is the Pope. As he makes his way with great effort towards the Cross amid the corpses of those who were martyred (Bishops, priests, men and women religious and many lay persons), he too falls to the ground, apparently dead, under a burst of gunfire.
> After the assassination attempt of 13 May 1981, it appeared evident to His Holiness that it was "a motherly hand which guided the bullet's path", enabling the "dying Pope" to halt "at the threshold of death" (Pope John Paul II. *Meditation with the Italian Bishops from the Policlinico Gemelli, Insegnamenti*, vol XVII/1, 1994, p. 1061). On the occasion of a visit to Rome by the then Bishop of Leiria-Fatima, the Pope decided to give him the bullet which had remained in the jeep after the assassination attempt, so that it might be kept in the Shrine. At the behest of the Bishop, the bullet was later set in the crown of the statue of Our Lady of Fatima.
> The successive events of 1989 led, both in the Soviet Union and in a number of countries of Eastern Europe, to the fall of the Communist regime which promoted atheism. For this too His Holiness offers heartfelt thanks to the Most Holy Virgin. In other parts of the world, however, attacks against the Church and against Christians, together with the burden of suffering which they involve, tragically continue. Even if the events to which the third part of the Secret of Fatima refers now seem part of the past, Our Lady's call to conversion and penance, issued at the beginning of the twentieth century, remains timely and urgent today.[26]

---

[24] John Paul II, *Beatification of Francisco and Jacinta Marto, Shepherds of Fatima* (Vatican City: Libreria Editrace Vaticana, 2000)

[25] See Kramer, P. (Ed.) *The Devil's Final Battle* (Terryville: The Missionary Association, 2002), p102

[26] Sodano, A. "Address of Cardinal Angelo Sodano regarding the "Third Part" of the Secret of Fatima at the conclusion of the solemn mass of John Paul II" (Vatican City: Libreria Editrace Vaticana, 2000)

But if its interpretation belonged to the past, why was there such a prolonged reluctance to reveal its contents? Why was the Third Secret still kept hidden from the public for over twenty years after the assassination attempt if the Vatican really believed that it was fulfilled by the events of 1981? This "official" presentation and interpretation of the Third Secret of Fatima did not conform to the expectations of the many people who had spent years scrutinising and analysing every aspect of the secret.

The contents of the secret were privy to central members of the Vatican hierarchy from the moment it had been first opened by Pope John XXIII in 1959. Throughout the course of the forty years from when the secret was first opened until its eventual publication in 2000, separate pieces of information on the secret had trickled down from various Vatican officials that had allowed Fatima scholars to build a basic framework of its central subject matter. This extensive knowledge about the subject material of the secret, as well as the recorded data concerning its physical attributes, appeared to conflict with the version of the secret published in the year 2000 – a fact which suggested to many Fatima experts that the entire contents of the secret had not been fully divulged.

In his now famous interview with the Catholic magazine *Jesus* published in 1984, the then Prefect for the Congregation for the Doctrine of the Faith, Cardinal Joseph Ratzinger, stated that the Third Secret corresponded to what was announced already in Scripture and time and again in the other Marian apparitions. Ratzinger, who was privy to the contents of the secret at this time, declared that it referred to the *Novissimi* (Latin for the "last things"), and that to reveal it now would confuse religious prophecy with "sensationalism".[27]

This description was quite different from Cardinal Sodano's interpretation that the secret predicted the assassination attempt on John Paul II. Sodano's explanation of the secret's contents could hardly be described as "sensational". On the contrary, this understanding of the secret perplexed many of the highly expectant Catholic faithful. In a climb-down from his comments about "sensationalism" in 1984, Cardinal Ratzinger admitted in *The Message of Fatima* that the content of secret being published was somewhat of an anti-climax to the hype that had been generated by the Vatican's initial refusal to publish the secret at the date chosen by Sr. Lucia:

"Those who expected exciting apocalyptic revelations about the end of the world or the future course of history are bound to be disappointed. Fatima does not satisfy our curiosity in this way, just as Christian faith in general cannot be reduced to an object of mere curiosity".[28]

Given that the publication of the secret was withheld for forty years past the date specified by Sr. Lucia, Catholics were led to the belief that the secret contained an insight into future apocalyptic events which was too frightening for public consumption. They most certainly did not expect it to predict a failed assassination attempt that held little or no contemporary significance at the time of the secret's release, or that it would be presented by Vatican officials as having nothing to do with the end-times. There was simply nothing in this version of the secret that would merit the secret's suppression for forty years after the date specified for publication.

These reservations about the version of the secret published in 2000 were

---

[27] Ratzinger, J. *Jesus* (November 11, 1984) p79
[28] Ratzinger, J. "Theological Commentary" *The Message of Fatima*

compounded by the fact that long after its publication, Sr. Lucia was still forbidden to talk about the secret without prior approval from the Vatican; and that her private cell in the convent at Coimbre in Portugal was sealed off after her death in 2005. No one but appointed officials were granted access to this room, which contained many of Lucia's personal writings – documents which may have contained material relating to the Third Secret.

There were many glaring omissions that *The Message of Fatima* document failed to address. In Lucia's Fourth Memoir, a brief sentence was appended to the end of the Second Secret which many commentators interpreted as the first words of the Third Secret. When the Second Secret was first revealed in Sr. Lucia's Third Memoir it had concluded with the words: "The Holy Father will consecrate Russia to me, and she will be converted, and a period of peace will be granted to the world."[29] But when the Second Secret was included in Lucia's Fourth Memoir, it contained a new ending which stated: "In Portugal the dogma of the Faith will always be preserved, etc."[30] The addition of this material was considered to be highly significant, as it seemed to indicate that this sentence would in fact be the first words of the Third Secret, and that the rest of the secret would follow on from the highly suggestive "etc."

It appeared to many investigators that it was highly unlikely that the Virgin Mary would end a sentence in such an abrupt manner. The use of the word "etc." had implied that there was a continuation here which had deliberately been left out, and that this "etc." was a bridge leading to the Third Secret. Yet the text of the secret released in June 2000 omitted any explanation of this sentence, relegating its inclusion in Sr. Lucia's Fourth Memoir to a footnote in the accompanying official document *The Message of Fatima*.

The nuggets of information concerning the Third Secret that were leaked by Vatican officials prior to its publication in 2000 seemed to fit in with the implications of this "lost verse" perfectly. The statement that "in Portugal …. the faith will always be preserved" suggested to many commentators that the faith would be lost elsewhere,[31] and the Third Secret was therefore regarded by most Fatima scholars as a prediction of a mass apostasy of the Church.[32] This was in line with insights provided by those few individuals within the Catholic hierarchy who had already read the secret prior to its publication.

During a speech in Vienna, Austria on September 10, 1984, Alberto Amaral, the third Bishop of Fatima, stated that the content of the Third Secret related to mass apostasy:

> "Its content concerns only our faith. To identify the Secret with catastrophic announcements or with a nuclear holocaust is to deform the meaning of the message. *The loss of faith of a continent is worse than the annihilation of a nation*; and it is true that faith is continually diminishing in Europe."[33]

Cardinal Ratzinger also seemed to confirm that the secret related to apostasy in his 1984 interview with *Jesus* magazine, by announcing that it concerned "the dangers

---

[29] De Jesus, L. *Fatima in Lucia's Own Words* p109
[30] Ibid. p167
[31] Following Fr Joaquin Alonso. See Kramer, P. *The Devil's Final Battle* p32
[32] Ibid. pp31ff.
[33] Cited in Kramer, P. *The Devil's Final Battle* p169

threatening the faith and life of the Christian, and therefore the life of the world."[34]

Other key figures who had read the secret also publicly stated that it related to an apostasy of the Church. During an interview for the journal *Il Sabato* in 1990, Cardinal Oddi had stated "It [the Third Secret] has nothing to do with Gorbachev. The Blessed Virgin was alerting us against apostasy in the Church."[35] It also appears to have been alluded to by Pope John Paul II. During a sermon at Fatima on May 13, 1982, John Paul II hinted at the content of the secret by asking his audience: "Can the Mother who, with all the force of the love that She fosters in the Holy Spirit and desires everyone's salvation, can She remain silent when She sees the very bases of Her children's salvation *undermined*?" He then went on to answer his own question: "No, She cannot remain silent."[36] The theme of the undermining of faith again recalls the subject of apostasy.

Sr. Lucia herself issued some revelations concerning the Third Secret to Fr. Fuentes, a priest writing about Fatima in 1957. In this interview, Lucia connected the Third Secret to Rev 12 and suggested that it concerned an apostasy in the Church:

> Father, the devil is in the mood for engaging in a decisive battle against the Blessed Virgin. And the devil knows what it is that most offends God and which in a short space of time will gain for him the greatest number of souls. *Thus, the devil does everything to overcome souls consecrated to God, because in this way, the devil will succeed in leaving souls of the faithful abandoned by their leaders, thereby the more easily will he seize them.* That which afflicts the Immaculate Heart of Mary and the Heart of Jesus is *the fall of religious and priestly souls.* The devil knows that *religious and priests who fall away from their beautiful vocation drag numerous souls to hell… The devil wishes to take possession of consecrated souls.* He tries to corrupt them in order to lull to sleep the souls of laypeople and thereby lead them to final impenitence.[37]

As we can see, there are some obvious connections between this statement and Rev 12, which are primarily encapsulated in the reference to a battle for souls between the Devil and the Virgin. The above words of Sr. Lucia concerning a battle between the Virgin and the Devil recall the struggle between the Woman adorned with the Sun and the Red Dragon. And her statement that the Devil drags numerous souls to hell clearly alludes to the Dragon dragging the stars from the sky and throwing them to the earth in Rev 12:4. Traditional Catholic interpretation has always held that the Dragon sweeping a third of the stars from the sky refers to the Devil leading a third of the clergy into apostasy.[38] In her above statement, Sr. Lucia reveals that by drawing the religious away from their vocation, the Devil also leads the laity into apostasy. This was yet another strong indication to pre-2000 Fatima researchers that the contents of the Third Secret related to the Great Apostasy foretold in the New Testament.

Due to the combined weight of such leaked information concerning the contents of the Third Secret, almost every Fatima researcher before its release in June 2000 concluded that the secret had prophesied an apostasy in the Church. This expectation, coupled with the Church's previous reluctance to publish the secret, led many observers to suspect that the full text of the secret had not been released.

Evidence has emerged since the secret's publication which appears to have

---

[34] Ibid.

[35] Ibid p33

[36] Pope John Paul II, cited in Kramer, P. *The Devil's Final Battle* p170

[37] Sr. Lucia's interview with Fr. Fuentes, cited in Kramer, P. *The Devil's Final Battle* p168

[38] See for example, Kramer, H.B. *The Book of Destiny* pp280-284

vindicated this conviction. Various Fatima scholars gave a detailed critique of the Vatican's handling of the Third Secret in a 2002 book edited by Fr. Paul Kramer called *The Devil's Final Battle*. This book forcefully argues (in a regrettably harsh critique of the Vatican hierarchy) that the secret actually consists of two separate parts – a visionary element, which was the part of the secret revealed in 2000; and a separate letter which contains the words of the Virgin Mary explaining the visionary section. Kramer et al point out that previous studies of the physical characteristics of the Third Secret during the 1950's showed that it was written on a single sheet of paper, while the part of the secret released in 2000 was comprised of four pages of text.[39]

When the Holy Office requested that Bishop of Fatima should send the Third Secret to the Vatican in 1957, the secret was entrusted to the auxiliary Bishop Venancio. Venancio meticulously recorded every detail of the Bishop of Fatima's envelope, right down to measuring the exact size of its dimensions. Venancio stated that when he held the Bishop's envelope up to the light, it could be seen to contain Sr. Lucia's smaller envelope, with a single sheet of paper inside. The sheet was estimated by Venancio to contain around 25 lines of text, with margins of three quarters of a centimetre; while the version published in 2000 is made up of 62 lines with no margins.

In 1967, the Prefect of the Congregation for the Doctrine of the Faith, Cardinal Ottaviani, independently confirmed that the secret was written on a single sheet of paper, stating "She wrote on *a sheet of paper*, in Portuguese, what the Holy Virgin *had asked her* to tell ...."[40]

Kramer et al, quoting from earlier sources, notes that Sr. Lucia stated in a covering letter she sent to the Bishop of Fatima that the secret was sealed in an envelope which was then placed inside notebooks that contained another part of the secret:

> I have written what you asked me; God willed to try me a little, but finally this was indeed His will: [the text] is sealed in an envelope and it [the sealed envelope] is in the notebooks ... Examination of the original Portuguese reveals that Sister Lucy means to say that the Secret proper is in the envelope, and that the envelope is in one of her notebooks which she also consigned to Archbishop Manuel Maria Ferreira da Silva (the Archbishop of Gurza) for carrying to Bishop da Silva of Fatima in June of 1944. As Frère Michel further states:
>> The seer discreetly handed the Bishop of Gurza *the notebook* in which she had slipped the *envelope* containing the Secret. That same evening, the bishop placed the envelope into the hands of Bishop da Silva..."[41]

Kramer et al go on to quote Fr. Joseph Schweigl (a Jesuit priest sent by Pope Pius XII in 1952 to interrogate Sr. Lucia on the Third Secret), as learning from the celebrated Portuguese nun during his investigation that the secret has two parts: "one concerns the Pope; the other logically (although I must say nothing) would have to be the continuation of the words: 'In Portugal, the dogma of the Faith will always be preserved.'"[42]

According to Kramer, the two parts of the secret were then stored separately – the words of Our Lady were kept in a safe by the pope's bedside in the Papal Apartments,

---

[39] Kramer, P. *The Devil's Final Battle* p152
[40] Cited in Ibid. (Emphasis Kramer's) p152
[41] Ibid. p148. Kramer's first quote is Sr. Lucia herself, quoted by Father Alonso in *Fatima 50*, October 13, 1967, p. 11. His second is Frère Michel de la Sainte Trinité, *The Whole Truth About Fatima - Vol III: The Third Secret*, p. 47
[42] Kramer, P. *The Devil's Final Battle* p31

and the other four page account of the vision was stored in the Secret Archives of the Holy Office. This appears to be confirmed by conflicting reports regarding the location of where the secret is stored. Some high ranking Vatican dignitaries, including Archbishop Capovilla, the personal secretary to John XXIII, have publicly stated that the secret resides in the Papal Apartments;[43] while other official documents, including those released to accompany the publication of the Third Secret, state that the secret was permanently kept in the Secret Archives of the Holy Office.[44]

Kramer et al single out the *Washington Post* report which highlights the conflicting accounts as to when John Paul II first read the secret. The newspaper noticed a discrepancy between some of the official statements issued by the Vatican. Vatican spokesman Joaquin Navarro-Valls announced on May 13th 2000 that John Paul II first read the secret in 1978 a few days after assuming the papacy. This statement apparently contradicted the claim made by another key architect of *The Message of Fatima* – Archbishop Bertone (who has since been elevated to cardinal by Benedict XVI and is now Vatican Secretary of State), when he declared that the Pope first read the text of the Third Secret after his assassination attempt in 1981.

Kramer et al then go on to point out that the Pope could read the secret the first a few days after ascending the throne of St. Peter because it was kept in a bedside cabinet in the Papal Apartments – as was confirmed by a number of sources, including Archbishop Capovilla. As such the Pope could read this letter with relative ease, and there was no need to involve a third party to acquire it. However Bertone states in *The Message of Fatima* that after the assassination attempt the Pontiff had to request that the secret be delivered to him from the Archives of the Holy Office.[45] A number of prominent Fatima experts feel that these inconsistencies can only be explained by the existence of two texts of the secret – one which was kept in the Papal Apartments and another in the Secret Archives.[46]

Fr. Kramer's contentions, which are shared by many Catholics worldwide, appeared to be sensationally confirmed in 2006 at the publication in Italy of Antonio Socci's *Il Quarto Segreto di Fatima (The Fourth Secret of Fatima)* on 22nd Nov, 2006. Socci, a highly respected Italian journalist and TV anchorman, who had previously conducted interviews at the request of the Vatican itself, originally began his investigation convinced that the entire secret had been released in June 2000.[47] But during the course of his research, Socci was ultimately left to conclude that part of the secret had been withheld. After he had studied the issues raised by Kramer and the work of Solideo Paolini, a young Italian author who had also written extensively on the subject, Socci became convinced of the legitimacy of these claims.[48] During a series of discussions with Paolini, Socci was shocked when the author turned over to him some startling revelations about the Third Secret, coming from a source no less than the aforementioned Archbishop Loris Francesco Capovilla – the former secretary of Pope

---

[43] Capovilla, L.F. "A Reserved Note of L.F. Capovilla" *Fatima Crusader* (17 May 1967).

[44] "To ensure better protection for the "secret" the envelope was placed in the Secret Archives of the Holy Office on 4 April 1957." *The Message of Fatima*

[45] Ibid.

[46] See Kramer, P. *The Devil's Final Battle* pp147ff

[47] Socci, A. *The Fourth Secret of Fatima* pp1-5

[48] A brief article by John Vennari summarizing the works of Socci and Paolini can be found at http://www.cfnews.org/Socci-FourthSecret.htm

John XXIII who was present when the secret was originally opened in 1959.

After making initial contact with the 91 year-old Archbishop on 5th July, 2006, Paolini managed to get Capovilla to agree to respond in writing to a list of questions concerning the existence of an unpublished text of the Third Secret. In reply, Capovilla sent Paolini a number of papers from his personal archive, suggesting that he should compare them with the text of the official 26th June 2000 *Message of Fatima* booklet. After scrutinizing the official documents Capovilla had sent him, Paolini noticed that the Archbishop's papers certified that Pope Paul VI had read the Secret on June 27th, 1963, six days after assuming the papacy.[49] Yet the official *Message of Fatima* booklet stated that Paul VI did not read the secret until 27th March 1965.[50]

Paolini decided to question Capovilla about the implications of this discrepancy:

"I brought to his attention the contrast between his 'confidential notes' and what is asserted in The Message of Fatima, to which he himself had directed me. He answered: 'Ah, but I have spoken the truth. Look, I am still lucid!' 'My goodness, Your Excellency, but how can one explain this evident discrepancy?' At this point he responded with considerations that seemed to refer to eventual lapses of memory, interpretations of what he had intended to say, to the fact that we are not speaking of Holy Scripture... I objected: 'Yes, Excellency, but my reference is to a clear written text [the official Vatican document, namely The Message of Fatima] which is based on the notes in the Archive!' Monsignor Capovilla: 'But I am right; perhaps the Bertone envelope is not the same as the Capovilla envelope...' Immediately, I interrupted him: 'Therefore, both dates are correct because there are two texts of the Third Secret?' Here there was a brief silent pause. Then Monsignor Capovilla responded: 'Precisely so!'"[51]

---

[49] Thursday the 27th of June 1963, I was on duty in the Anticamera in the Vatican [the outer office where the Pope meets various persons]. Paul VI in the early morning received among others, Cardinal Fernando Cento (who had been Papal Nuncio to Portugal) and shortly afterwards the Bishop of Leiria Monsignor Joao [John] Pereira Venancio. Upon leaving, the Bishop asked for "a special blessing for Sister Lucy". It is evident that during the audience, they spoke about Fatima. In fact in the afternoon the Sostituto [the Substitute Secretary of State] Monsignor Angelo Dell'Acqua telephoned me on Via Casilina (I was a temporary guest of the Sisters of the "Poverelle"):
"I am looking for the package [plico] of Fatima. Do you know where it is kept?"
"It was in the drawer on the right hand side of the desk, named 'Barbarigo', in the [Papal] bedroom." One hour later Dell'Acqua called me back: "Everything is okay. The envelope [plico] has been found." Friday morning (28 June) between one meeting and another Paul VI asked me:
"How come on the envelope there is your (Capovilla's) name?"
"John XXIII asked me to write a note regarding how the envelope arrived in his hands with the names of all those to whom he felt he should make it known."
"Did he make any comment?"
"No, nothing except what I wrote on the outer file [involucro]: 'I leave it to others to comment or decide.'"
"Did he later ever return to the subject?"
"No, never. However the devotion of Fatima remained alive in him."
"A Reserved Note of L.F. Capovilla"
 Writing in 1985, Frere Michel de la Sainte Trinite also refers to this episode: "Paul VI adopted straight away the same attitude. Elected on June 21, 1963, some time afterwards he asked for the text of the Secret. This proves his lively concern for this subject. Since no one knew what Pope John XXIII had done with it, they questioned his secretary, Mgr. Capovilla, who indicated the place where the manuscript had been put. Pope Paul VI surely read it at that point but he did not speak about it." De la Sainte Trinite, M. "The Secret of Fatima... Revealed" *La Contre Reforme Catholique No 222*(May 1986)
[50] "Paul VI read the contents with the Substitute, Archbishop Angelo Dell'Acqua, on 27 March 1965, and returned the envelope to the Archives of the Holy Office, deciding not to publish the text." *The Message of Fatima*
[51] Paolini, S. Cited in Socci, A. *The Fourth Secret of Fatima* p132

Here for the very first time was confirmation of two texts coming from a uniquely placed source – the only living witness to the original opening of the envelope in 1959.

In his book, Socci forwards the hypothesis that only one part of the text of the Third Secret was published due to the result of a power struggle within the Vatican. He claims that while Pope John Paul II and Cardinal Ratzinger wanted to publish the text in its entirety, they were opposed by certain members of the Roman Curia.[52] Socci postulates that by way of compromise, John Paul II would allude to the content of the other part of the secret in his sermon at Francisco and Jacinta's beatification ceremony on 13th May 2000. A sermon which was based on a reading from Rev 12.

Much to the delight of Socci and the "Fatimist" movement, on May 11th 2010, Pope Benedict XVI decided to reverse the "official" relegation of the secret to past events advanced by the *Message of Fatima* document. During a prepared interview aboard his plane whilst making a pilgrimage to Fatima, the Holy Father stated that the vision of the suffering of the pope had on-going significance for the Church and should not be solely confined to the 1981 assassination attempt, as was suggested by Cardinal Sodano. During the flight to Portugal, the Vatican Press Officer, Fr. Federico Lombardi put forward this question to the Pope:

"Thank you, and now come to Fatima, in some way the culmination, even spiritually, of this visit. Your Holiness, what meaning do the Fatima apparitions have for us today? In June 2000, when you presented the text of the third secret in the Vatican Press Office, a number of us and our former colleagues were present. You were asked if the message could be extended, beyond the attack on John Paul II, to other sufferings on the part of the Popes. Is it possible, to your mind, to include in that vision the sufferings of the Church today for the sins involving the sexual abuse of minors?

Pope Benedict replied:

I would say that, here too, beyond this great vision of the suffering of the Pope, which we can in the first place refer to Pope John Paul II, an indication is given of realities involving the future of the Church, which are gradually taking shape and becoming evident. So it is true that, in addition to moment indicated in the vision, there is mention of, there is seen, the need for a passion of the Church, which naturally is reflected in the person of the Pope, yet the Pope stands for the Church and thus it is sufferings of the Church that are announced. The Lord told us that the Church would constantly be suffering, in different ways, until the end of the world. The important thing is that the message, the response of Fatima, in substance is not directed to particular devotions, but precisely to the fundamental response, that is, to ongoing conversion, penance, prayer, and the three theological virtues: faith, hope and charity. Thus we see here the true, fundamental response which the Church must give – which we, every one of us, must give in this situation. As for the new things which we can find in this message today, there is also the fact that attacks on the Pope and the Church come not only from without, but the sufferings of the Church come precisely from within the Church, from the sin existing within the Church. This too is something that we have always known, but today we are seeing it in a really terrifying way: that the greatest persecution of the Church comes not from her enemies without, but arises from sin within the Church, and that the Church thus has a deep need to relearn penance, to accept purification, to learn forgiveness on the one hand, but also the need for justice. Forgiveness does not replace justice. In a word, we need to relearn precisely this essential: conversion, prayer, penance and the theological virtues. This is our response, we are realists in expecting that evil always attacks, attacks from within and without, yet that the forces of good are also ever present and that, in the end, the Lord is more powerful than evil and Our Lady is for us the visible, motherly guarantee of God's goodness, which is always the last word in history.[53]

---

[52] Socci, A. *The Fourth Secret of Fatima* pp82-89
[53] Benedict XVI *Interview of the Holy Father Benedict XVI with the Journalists During the Flight to Portugal* (Vatican City: Libreria Editrace Vaticana, 11th May 2010)

The combined evidence which suggests that part of the secret of Fatima has been withheld is certainly compelling. But this would lead us to question why some individuals within the Vatican hierarchy would be so opposed to the publication of the entire Third Secret? What exactly could it contain that would warrant its suppression by the Church hierarchy for over fifty years after its recommended date of release?

An Apocalyptic Date Contained in the Third Secret?

If Socci, Paolini, Kramer, Fr. Gruner, Vennari et al are correct, and there really is another part of the Third Secret that has not yet been revealed, then it immediately begs the question: "why not?" Many Fatima experts suggest either that the Vatican wishes to avoid spreading panic over the apocalyptic content of the secret, or that it is seeking to suppress a critique of the Vatican apparatus that was communicated by Our Lady of Fatima.

However both of the above explanations for the suppression of the second part of the Third Secret can be easily countered. Firstly, we can respond to the proposal that the secret is being hidden to protect the laity by asking what could be more frightening than the horrors depicted by the Book of Revelation and the other eschatological parts of the Bible? The Second Epistle of St. Peter predicts that the world will be destroyed by fire, and the Book of Zephaniah states that all life will be swept off the face of the planet. Can there possibly be anything even more unsettling than this in the Third Secret? Besides, the apocalyptic tone of the content of the Third Secret released in June 2000, with flaming swords threatening humanity and a city representing the Church lying half in ruins during a mass religious persecution, is frightening enough in its own right. Yet the Church has determined that this subject matter is fit enough for presentation to the public.

The Catholic Church could also hardly be accused of shrinking from preaching fire and brimstone in the past. It was only after the Second Vatican Council that the Church began to change direction and forward a more positive, optimistic outlook. Before this a focus on the apocalyptic chastisement of humankind was a staple of many Sunday morning sermons. So the Church could scarcely be accused of attempting to spare the sensitivities of the laity.

The second reason cited by some "Fatimists" for the suppression of the secret is because it supposedly contains a critique of the post-conciliar Church, or that it warns that Rome would become the seat of the Antichrist. We can meet this hypothetical explanation for the suppression of the secret by asking why the Virgin Mary would decide to entrust a secret to the very institution she was lambasting? The fact that the Church was chosen to be the custodian of the secret surely suggests Divine sanction and approval of the institution she bequeathed it to. And Christ himself promised that the gates of hell would not prevail against the Church (Matt 16:18).

We should also take into account the fact that the Vatican has also approved the message of Our Lady of Akita, which among other things, warns of a schism or some other form of conflict within the Church which sounds remarkably like the divisions caused by the current paedophile scandal:

"If men do not repent and better themselves, the Father will inflict a terrible punishment on all humanity. It will be a punishment greater than the deluge, such as one will never have seen before. Fire will fall from the sky and will wipe out a great part of humanity, the good as well as the bad, sparing neither priests nor faithful. The survivors will find themselves so desolate that they will envy the dead. The only arms which will remain for you will be the Rosary and the Sign left by My Son. Each day recite the prayers of the Rosary. With the Rosary, pray for the Pope, the Bishops and the priests.

"The work of the devil will infiltrate even into the Church in such a way that one will see Cardinals opposing Cardinals, Bishops against other Bishops. The priests who venerate Me will be scorned and opposed by their confreres (other priests). Churches and altars will be sacked. The Church will be full of those who accept compromises, and the demon will press many priests and consecrated souls to leave the service of the Lord.

"The demon will be especially implacable against the souls consecrated to God. The thought of the loss of so many souls is the cause of My sadness. If sins increase in number and gravity, there will no longer be pardon for them.

"...Pray very much the prayers of the Rosary. I alone am able to still save you from the calamities which approach. Those who place their confidence in Me will be saved."[54]

If the Church is willing to approve a private revelation which contains a horrific prediction of nuclear holocaust and a division within the Church, then there is no reason it would be fearful of releasing a prediction of Rome becoming the seat of the Antichrist if it was included in the Third Secret. If Rome, or even more specifically, the Vatican, ever became the seat of the Antichrist, then it could only be under the rule of an antipope. The true Church would still exist. Why would the Vatican be afraid of a prediction of a future antipope? There have been plenty of antipopes in the past, and it is a possibility that such a scenario could occur again in the future.

Perhaps the main reason the Third Secret was not published before the year 2000, and the real explanation as to why the alleged second part of the secret remains hidden, was because the second part contains a specific date at some point in the future after 1960. If that were the case, it would seriously restrict the Vatican's ability to publicly endorse the secret before the predicted date had come to pass.

We may be able to find some evidence that the second part of the Third Secret gave an exact date by some rather telling words of Pope John XXIII. When he first read the Third Secret, Pope John decided not to publish it, as it "does not concern the years of my pontificate".[55] How else would Pope John know that it did not relate to his pontificate, unless there was a specific date mentioned in the text itself that was well beyond his expected life span? A date which is closer to our own time than to the 1960s.

If the alleged second part of the Third Secret did contain an exact date, then it would not be unprecedented in the Fatima literature. Sr. Lucia had previously set the date of 1960 for the release of the secret because "it would be better understood" at this point.[56] So it is not altogether unthinkable that the Third Secret may have contained a date also.

---

[54] The messages of Akita were given to Sr. Agnes Sasagawa amidst a series of supernatural phenomena in 1973. Sr. Agnes was afflicted with stigmata, and the statue where she received her visions of the Virgin Mary secreted blood and water, which was watched live on Japanese television. Sr. Agnes was miraculously cured of deafness in 1982, as promised by Our Lady during her first message in 1973. See Fukushima, F. *Akita: Mother of God As Coredemptrix Modern Miracles of Holy Eucharist* (Goleta CA: Queenship Publishing, 1997)

[55] Cited in De la Sainte Trinite, M. *The Whole Truth About Fatima Vol. III* p557

[56] *The Message of Fatima*

The inclusion of a date in the "hidden" part of the Third Secret would explain why the Vatican was (and still is) so reluctant to release it. The Holy Office could not afford to publicly endorse a prophecy containing a precise date, as it would promote sensationalism and suffer a serious loss of credibility if it did not reach fulfilment at the specified date. This would explain the Vatican's otherwise bizarre act of distancing itself from the secret in the Vatican communiqué of 8th Feb, 1960 stating that the secret would not be revealed:

> "Although the Church recognizes the Fatima apparitions She does not desire to take the responsibility of guaranteeing the veracity of the words that the three shepherd children said that the Virgin Mary had addressed to them."[57]

What else could be contained in the secret that the Church would be so unwilling to publicly sanction? If the secret simply contained vague and symbolic language that could be fulfilled in a number of different ways, it would not present much of a problem. If it contained something specific such as a date however, then the Church would have to be able to absolutely guarantee that the prophecy would unfold by the appointed time. It would be unprecedented for the Church to guarantee in advance that an exact prophecy would come to pass by a precise date.

The Book of Deuteronomy states that to be able to determine the difference between true and false prophecy, we must wait until the prophesied event unfolds. If the words of the prophecy are fulfilled, it is true prophecy, if not, it is false:

> And if you say in your heart, 'How may we know the word that the Lord has not spoken?'— when a prophet speaks in the name of the Lord, if the word does not come to pass or come true, that is a word that the Lord has not spoken; the prophet has spoken it presumptuously. You need not be afraid of him. (Deut 18:21-22)

It makes perfect sense for the Vatican to follow the recommendations laid down in Deuteronomy, and withhold approval until after the date had passed and the prophecies had been either vindicated or falsified.

If the alleged second part of the Third Secret does concern the Great Apostasy and the struggle between the Dragon and the Woman adorned with the Sun, as a number of researchers have suggested, then this hypothetical date would most likely predict when the above circumstances were to take place. And if this date referred to the end of the millennium, as we have already suggested above, then it would account for the Vatican's chosen release date in the jubilee year 2000, and would also explain the other popes' refusal to publish the secret even though Sr. Lucia's recommended publication date of 1960 had long since passed.[58]

---

[57] Cited in De la Sainte Trinite, M. *The Whole Truth About Fatima Vol. III* pp578-586

[58] It is perhaps worth mentioning here the popular tradition that Sr. Lucia prophesied that she would live to see what is variously described as the fulfilment of the prophecy contained in the Third Secret, or the beginning of the chastisement mentioned in it. If Sr. Lucia did make such a claim, then our hypothesis that the remaining part of the secret may have contained a reference to Rev 12 and a date relating to the end of the millennium, would explain the purported fulfilment of a prophecy made in the Third Secret during her lifetime. However so far, it has not been possible to find any mention of this prophecy in Sr. Lucia's published writings. It may be a popular misconception based on Our Lady's 1917 prophecy detailed in Sr. Lucia's Fourth Memoir that Jacinta and Francisco would soon die, but that Lucia would survive them to spread the message of Fatima. "I will take Jacinta and Francisco soon. But you are to stay here some time

We can gain an insight into official Vatican policy on the matter of prophecies containing a specific date by examining the case of the secrets of La Salette.

Before their eventual publication in 2002, conspiracy theorists held that the secrets were being suppressed due to their controversial subject matter. In claims similar to those concerning the suppression of the Third Secret, critics forwarded the notion that the secrets had prophesied that Rome would become the seat of the Antichrist, or that they contained a message which was simply too frightening to reveal. If we look at how the secrets were conveniently "discovered" in October 1999 – towards the end of the latest date by which Maximin stated the prophecy would be fulfilled; it becomes apparent that the real reason the Vatican withheld the secrets for so long was because they had contained a specific date. There was no mention of any sort of condemnation of the papacy, nor was the secret "too frightening". With the benefit of hindsight, we can now see that the real reason the secrets of La Salette were left undisclosed was because the Church could not afford to engage in sensationalism by endorsing a prophecy which contained an exact date in the future. If there were no dates, then they would have been a lot safer to publicly endorse, as the time limit for such prophecies to be fulfilled is effectively endless, and there would be no mass hysteria generated in the lead up to the appointed date.

Meeting a self-imposed prophetic deadline is an immensely different scenario altogether. If the secret, along with its advancement of an exact date, was officially sponsored and turned out to fail at the appointed time (which La Salette seemingly did, unless we follow the interpretation offered earlier in this book), then it would have been a source of major embarrassment to the Vatican. So judging by this comparison, if an officially approved prophecy contains a specific date, then as a completely logical matter of policy, the Vatican withholds its publication until the date has passed.

We can find some evidence of the secret containing elements of a precise nature in Mgr. Capovilla's reasons why John XXIII decided not to release the text:

"Pope John imposed the silence for two reasons: (1) it did not seem to him 'to consist entirely of things supernatural,' (2) he did not dare to risk an immediate interpretation, in the midst of the complex 'Fatima phenomenon,' prescinding from *minute precisions*...."[59] (Emphasis added)

So, could the date of publication for the Third Secret of Fatima also have been postponed until the date given in the alleged second part had passed? The secrets of La Salette were arranged to be "discovered" almost simultaneously with the arrival of the expiration date contained in Maximin's secret. Gauging by this standard, if the alleged second part of the Third Secret did contain a date, then it would be natural to assume that the first visionary element was published within a year of the date specified in the second interpretive portion.

It is unlikely that anyone in the Vatican would have linked the astronomical phenomena at the turn of the millennium with the the fall of Satan described in the Apocalypse, or with the prophecy of the mark of the Beast. Therefore the date may have

---

longer. Jesus wishes to make use of you to make me known and loved." Santos, L. *Fatima in Lucia's Own Words* p191. No mention is made here of Lucia living until the fulfilment of a specific prophecy however.
[59] Cited in Socci, A. *The Fourth Secret of Fatima* p154

passed without the physical, earthly signs which the Bible stated would accompany the fall of Satan and implementation of the mark of the Beast having been noticed. This would explain Cardinal Sodano's attempts to equate the visionary element of the Third Secret with past events, and Cardinal Bertone's continued reluctance to reveal the alleged second part. Perhaps some people at the Vatican feel that there is not enough evidence to support the claim that the prophecy had been fulfilled by the secret's specified date.

It would also explain why the other great Marian secrets revealed to the shepherd children of La Salette were released "through the back door". Despite also having been authenticated by the Church, these secrets were released with none of the pomp and ceremony accorded to the Third Secret during its release. Instead, they were "re-discovered" by Fr. Michel Corteville in 1999, and working together with Fr. Rene Laurentin, they were eventually published in 2002. We can be sure that the Church would never have permitted these secrets to be published before the turn of the millennium, since both secrets restricted themselves to specific dates by which they were to be fulfilled (before 1946 for part of Melanie's and before 2000 for Maximin's). When these dates passed without any apparent form of fulfilment, they were conferred with a low-key release.

No such low-profile release would be possible for the Third Secret however. If this highly publicized prophecy contained a date – a date which appeared not to have been fulfilled at the appointed time, there would be widespread media attention to highlight this failure. The various anti-Catholic establishments would be sure to disseminate these failings as far and wide as possible. But if it contained two separate and independent parts, one of which did not contain a date, then it would be possible to satisfy public curiosity with the publication of the "safe" version, and ensure its unfalsifiability by confining the interpretation to past events. The seemingly failed element of the second part of the secret could then be left to fade into obscurity without ever having to be made public.

We can perhaps find a hint at what date this may have been was in the words of John Paul II in his book *Crossing the Threshold of Hope*:

"Therefore, when I was shot by the assassin in St. Peter's Square, I did not pay any heed at first to the fact that it was precisely the anniversary of the day on which Mary had appeared to the three shepherds in Fatima, in Portugal, revealing to them those words which, by the end of the century, seemed to be moving toward their fulfilment."[60]

Here the Pope specifically mentions that the prophecy of the Third Secret contains words that seemed to be moving toward their fulfilment *by the end of the century*.

Upon returning from celebrating the funeral mass of Sr. Lucia in February 2005, Cardinal Bertone was asked about the interpretation of the Third Secret in the journal *La Repubblica*. As part of his response, he gave the following statement: "prophecy must always be interpreted: It is enough to think of the Apocalypse, of the signs in heaven. Have these perhaps not already been seen with the airplanes that toppled the Twin Towers?"[61] It is highly unlikely that Cardinal Bertone would think that the "signs in

---

[60] Pope John Paul II *Crossing the Threshold of Hope*, p243
[61] *La Republica* (Feb 17 2005). Cited in Socci, A. *The Fourth Secret of Fatima* p119

heaven" spoken of in the Apocalypse would symbolise the plane attacks on 9/11 alone. As we have already seen, the "signs in heaven" described in the Book of Revelation are unmistakably astronomical in character, and would undoubtedly be recognized as such by an expert in theology. There is simply nothing in the Apocalypse that would even remotely describe the attacks on 9/11. Yet the timing of the events of 9/11 in the year 2001 are remarkably close to the "signs in heaven" we have already suggested occurred between the years 1999-2000. Could these musings of the Cardinal Secretary of State contain an insight into the content of the hidden part of the Third Secret?

If the Third Secret did openly explicate that the fall of Satan or struggle between the Dragon and the Woman adorned with the Sun would occur at the turn of the millennium, it would be extremely difficult to maintain that such an event had occurred without some form of physical evidence. And unless someone knew what kind of evidence they were looking for, it would be easy to overlook the astronomical and geophysical events which occurred around this time. It would therefore be natural to connect such phenomena with 9/11, which was undoubtedly the most significant event of that general time period.

During a speech given at a General Papal Audience at the Vatican on 12th January, 2005, just two months before his death, John Paul II once again turned to comment on Rev 12:

> Thus, let us move on to the second part of our Canticle. After the dramatic scene of the woman with child "clothed with the sun" and the terrible red dragon (cf. 12: 1-9), a mysterious voice intones a hymn of thanksgiving and joy. The joy derives from the fact that Satan, the ancient enemy whose role at the heavenly court was that of the "accuser of our brethren" (12: 10), as we see in the Book of Job (cf. 1: 6-11; 2: 4-5), was "thrown down" from heaven. Henceforth, therefore, he no longer possesses such great power. He knows "that his time is short" (Rv 12: 12), for history is nearing the radical turning point of liberation from evil and he consequently reacts with "great wrath".
>
> On the other side towers the risen Christ, whose blood is the principle of salvation (cf. 12: 11). He has received from the Father a royal authority over the entire universe; in him are fulfilled "the salvation and the power and the kingdom of our God" (12: 10).
>
> Associated with Christ's victory are the Christian martyrs who chose the way of the Cross, neither succumbing to evil nor giving in to its virulence but keeping themselves for the Father, united with the death of Christ through a witness of self-giving and courage that has brought them to "[love] not their lives even unto death" (12: 11). We seem to hear an echo of Christ's words: "He who loves his life loses it, and he who hates his life in this world will keep it for eternal life" (Jn 12: 25).[62]

Note that in the latter part of this passage, the Pope comments on the theme of martyrdom couched in language which reflects the vision of the Third Secret. He also refers to a "turning point" which sounds remarkably similar to the spiritual revival and period promised by numerous prophecies, including Fatima (at the promise conversion of Russia in the Second Secret). As the Pope quoted from the same portion of the Apocalypse when he announced that the Third Secret would be revealed, it is highly likely that the two would have become intimately bound in his mind. The similarities in this speech with the imagery of the Third Secret are striking. Just as in the Third Secret, Christian martyrs take the path of the cross and contribute to the sacrificial death of Jesus.

---

[62] Pope John Paul II, "By the blood of the Lamb", *General Audience 12th January 2005*, (Vatican City: Libreria Editrace Vaticana, 12th January 2005)

Do these words of the late pope contain yet another glimpse into the connections between the Third Secret and Rev 12? If the alleged second part of the Third Secret does concern a mass apostasy and references to chapter 12 of the Apocalypse as is expected, then it may corroborate our other findings in this chapter.

Since Sr. Lucia specifically stated that the Third Secret related to chapters 8 to 13 of the Apocalypse, there is also the possibility that the secret may refer to the threat of a future mega-tsunami, and perhaps also to the Antichrist or the mark of the Beast.[63] Chapter 8 of the Book of Revelation is where we find the reference to the "mountain on fire" being thrown into the sea, while chapter 13 concerns the rise of the Beast and the execution of the need of his mark in order to engage in commerce. The portion of the Third Secret released in the year 2000 certainly does not appear to contain any direct references to Rev 13, which leaves us to wonder if there is something missing from the secret.

Concerning the Third Secret's links to Rev 8, it is interesting to note the comments that were attributed to Pope John Paul II by the magazine *Stimme des Glaubens*. This Catholic journal reported that during a conference in Fulda, Germany, in November 1980, John Paul II addressed a private audience concerning the contents of the Third Secret. In the course of this discussion, the Pope is said to have suggested that the Third Secret contains depictions of a cataclysmic event where "the oceans will flood entire sections of the earth":

"Because of the seriousness of its contents, in order not to encourage the world wide power of Communism to carry out certain coups, my predecessors in the chair of Peter have diplomatically preferred to withhold its publication. On the other hand, it should be sufficient for all Christians to know this much: if there is a message in which it is said that the oceans will flood entire sections of the earth; that, from one moment to the other, millions of people will perish... there is no longer any point in really wanting to publish this secret message. Many want to know merely out of curiosity, or because of their taste for sensationalism, but they forget that 'to know' implies for them a responsibility. It is dangerous to want to satisfy one's curiosity only, if one is convinced that we can do nothing against a catastrophe that has been predicted."[64]

So the combined evidence suggests that there is a portion of the Third Secret not revealed which contains references to a great apostasy, the conflict between the Woman adorned with the Sun and the Red Dragon in Rev 12 and a date for this event, and possibly (although by no means certain) allusions to the mark of the Beast and a hugely destructive flooding of several countries by the ocean.

If the alleged second part of the Third Secret has been held back due to a seemingly erroneous dating of the events it describes, then it is understandable that the Vatican would wish to avoid confusing the laity or leading them into error. This is not to suggest that if the second part or "attachment" to the Third Secret really does exist, this means that the Vatican was deliberately setting out to deceive the public in order to hide

---

[63] De la Sainte Trinite, M. *The Whole Truth About Fatima, Volume III* p533
[64] Although it is disputed whether these words can be directly attributed to John Paul II. Cardinal Bertone suggests that these comments were indeed made by the Pope. See Bertone, T. *The Last Secret of Fatima*, (New York: Doubleday, 2008), p48. The Vatican Press Office and Cardinal Ratzinger however denied that it took place. See Socci, A. "Dear Cardinal Bertone: Who between me and you is deliberately lying?" *The Fatima Crusader 86* (2007)

Divine objection to the reforms made by the Second Vatican Council (as is forwarded by many Traditionalist groups). It may be, as Paolini suggests, due to the view by some individuals within the Vatican that the attachment it is not actually part of the secret itself, but rather Sr. Lucia's own interpretation of the vision, which could theoretically be flawed.[65] If the Third Secret contained a date relating to the millennium, as did the secrets of La Salette, then it is possible that members of the Vatican hierarchy believe that this part of the secret was tainted by personal intuition of Sr. Lucia and not the actual words of Our Lady.

While the secrets of Fatima may perhaps be the most important direct heavenly messages outside of Divine Revelation, they still belong to the sphere of private revelation, and as such are subject to the discretion of the Magesterium. If the teaching authority of the Church decides that it would be harmful to publish such private revelations, then we can only trust in its superior judgment.

As we shall see, another apparition of the Virgin Mary occurred shortly after the release of the Third Secret in June 2000, in the city of Assiut in Upper Egypt. This apparition, which was captured on film and witnessed by thousands of individuals, appears to have fulfilled another aspect of the prophecy of the Woman adorned with the Sun in Rev 12. The apparitions at Assiut may provide further confirmation that the events of Rev 12 were fulfilled at the turn of the millennium, and can be used to support our theory that we are currently living in the age of Satan's reign on earth.

The Apocalyptic Nativity: A New Slaughter of the Innocents?

In traditional Roman Catholic theology, the Woman adorned with the Sun is equated with the Virgin Mary – an interpretation that has been held by the Church since the first millennium AD. Despite numerous objections from Protestant commentators, there remains an extremely good case for adhering to this understanding. Rev 12 has many parallels to the story of the birth of Christ, and appears to recount an apocalyptic version of the nativity. In verse 4, we are told that the Dragon positions itself at the Woman's feet in order to devour her Child as soon as He is born.[66] However the Dragon is thwarted in this attempt on the Child's life when the Woman flees into the desert, where God has prepared a place for her:

> His tail swept down a third of the stars of heaven and cast them to the earth. And the dragon stood before the woman who was about to give birth, so that when she bore her child he might devour it. She gave birth to a male child, one who is to rule all the nations with a rod of iron, but her child was caught up to God and to his throne, and the woman fled into the wilderness, where she has a place prepared by God, in which she is to be nourished for 1,260 days. (Rev 12:4-6)

---

[65] Paolini, S. "My Meetings with Archbishop Capovilla and the Socci-Cardinal Bertone Struggle", *The Fatima Network* (2007). Private revelation is fraught with such obstacles, given the difficulties in distinguishing between the material that is truley inspired from the personal convictions of the seer.

[66] Verse 5 can be a little misleading, as we are told the Child was "caught up to God and to his throne", which suggests that he was taken into heaven as an infant. However the real event that this verse is alluding to is the ascension of Jesus into heaven after his death and resurrection. So the text is referring to the destiny of the Child rather than narrating an event which immediately takes place after his birth.

The Woman's flight into the wilderness is recapitulated again in vv13-14:

> And when the dragon saw that he had been thrown down to the earth, he pursued the woman who had given birth to the male child. But the woman was given the two wings of the great eagle so that she might fly from the serpent into the wilderness, to the place where she is to be nourished for a time, and times, and half a time.

The Dragon's pursuit of the Woman and his intent to devour the Child upon his birth is clearly based on King Herod's attempt to kill the infant Jesus during the slaughter of the Holy Innocents. When Herod learned from the Magi that a star seen in the east had heralded the birth of the Messiah, the tyrant immediately made plans to dispose of his potential usurper by killing every infant under the age of two in the vicinity of Bethlehem. However Joseph was warned of Herod's intentions in a dream, and the Holy Family fled into the Egyptian wilderness to escape this impending danger.[67] So the flight of the Woman adorned with the Sun into the wilderness can be understood as an apocalyptic retelling of the story of the flight of the Holy Family into Egypt. However the Apocalypse's use of the nativity story here sits uncomfortably with the book's futurist perspective. What message has this story to convey in an eschatological context?

The vision of the labour of the Woman clothed with the Sun appears to represent the future Church waiting to give birth to the Messiah at the end of time, as some commentators suggest.[68] But it also invites us to link the events of Christ's birth in some way with the fall of Satan. The first stage in Satan's downfall did after all take place at the birth of the Messiah. But while Satan's defeat was guaranteed by Christ's victory over death on the Cross, his ultimate downfall would not occur until the end-time, when he is finally cast from the heavenly throne room to the earth. Could the dating of the fall of Satan exactly two thousand years after the traditional date of the birth of Jesus be symbolically conveyed by this passage? After all a key component of Satan's role in the Apocalypse and elsewhere in the Bible is the fact that he seeks to imitate God. The Holy Trinity is aped by the Unholy Trinity; the Lamb is mimicked by the anti-Lamb; and the resurrection of Jesus is parodied by the wounded head of the sea-beast that is miraculously healed. Could the fall of Satan and inauguration of his earthly reign two thousand years after the birth of Christ be an extension of this use of parody?

The Book of Revelation's re-imagining of the story of the nativity in an eschatological context is used to symbolize events that are unfolding on the spiritual plane. The earth is yet again caught up in the birth-pangs of the Messiah, who is coming to usher in the Last Judgment and finally vanquish the enemy of humankind. But the Devil is unhappy with this situation and attempts to cause as much damage as possible before he meets his eventual fate. The story of the nativity acts as a perfect template from which the story of the struggle between the Woman and the Dragon could expand, thus firmly connecting the events leading up to the Second Advent with those surrounding the First Coming of Christ.

We have argued that the cosmic struggle between the Dragon and the Woman adorned with the Sun was reflected by a series of related phenomena on the earthly plane at the turn of the millennium. As we shall see, it appears that the eschatological flight of

---

[67] Matt 2:1ff
[68] E.g. Osborne, G.R. *Revelation* pp457-458

the Woman into the wilderness of Egypt may also have been reflected visibly on earth around this same time period.

On 17th August 2000, exactly one year to the day after the earthquake in Izmit, Turkey,[69] a series of remarkable apparitions of the Virgin Mary began to appear on the roof of St. Mark's Coptic cathedral in the Egyptian city of Assiut – the place where the Holy Family are traditionally said to have sojourned during their escape from the wrath of King Herod. According to Coptic tradition, Assiut was the furthest point south in Egypt that the Holy Family had journeyed to before making their way back to Palestine.

The phenomena reported at Assiut were given limited coverage by newsgroups such as CNN, ABC and the BBC at the time, and are officially recognized as authentic by the Egyptian Coptic Church.[70] But they have since fallen out of common public knowledge in the West. The apparitions began to occur around the time of the Coptic feast commemorating the arrival of the Holy Family in Assiut, which is celebrated annually in the town during the month of August. Starting on 17th August, and appearing on several occasions thereafter, the apparitions at Assiut were witnessed by crowds numbering into the tens of thousands. Eyewitnesses reported seeing large luminous doves in the night sky before, during and after the apparitions. The apparitions themselves were accompanied by an aroma of incense and strong flashes of light which would illuminate the crosses on the cathedral.

It is perhaps of some significance that the Greek word used for "place" in Rev 12 (τοπος *topos*) is known elsewhere in the New Testament as a synonym for "temple"; and in the LXX it has the meaning of "sanctuary".[71] So the passage in Rev 12 could also be translated as "But the woman was given the two wings of the great eagle so that she might fly from the serpent into the wilderness, to the temple where she is to be nourished for a time, and times, and half a time".

Some of the witnesses to the apparitions at Assiut reported seeing visions of Mary with light pouring out from her hands; while others say they could only see the strobe-like lights that had illuminated the cathedral from various angles. Journalists present at the scene failed to establish the source of the lights, which came both from the sky and from between the domes where the apparitions had occurred. Thousands of people, both Christians and Muslims, turned out each night to witness the spectacle, singing, chanting and praying; and there were numerous reports of miraculous healings by some of those who had attended the events.

---

[69] It is perhaps worth noting here that Turkey also has close associations with the Virgin Mary, as it is to here, the site of ancient Ephesus, that tradition tells us Our Lady journeyed with the Apostle John after Jesus' entreaty for the Beloved Disciple to take his mother into his care in John 19:25-27. A particularly strong tradition places John at Ephesus, from where he was exiled to the island of Patmos – the place where the Book of Revelation was written.
[70] See for example, Hawley, C. "Virgin Mary 'appears' in Egypt" *BBC News* (2000), or Abdel-Hamid, H. "Virgin Mary Said to Appear in Southern Egypt" *ABC News* (2000)
[71] See Beale, G.K. *The Book of Revelation* p648

... وماتزال التجليات النورانية فوق قباب كنيسة مار مرقس باسيوط

Figs. 20-21 Some images of the unexplained lights that appeared over the Coptic Cathedral of St. Mark's in Assiut. Thousands of witnesses at the scene claimed that these lights were accompanied by apparitions of the Virgin Mary.

The fact that the apparitions occurred on a church roof and were accompanied by luminous doves recalls the other famous Egyptian apparitions of Our Lady at Zeitoun. These apparitions, which are officially approved by the Egyptian Coptic Church, and recognized by the local Catholic patriarch, Cardinal Stephanos I, appeared over St. Mary's Coptic Church between 1968 and 1971.[72] The Zeitoun apparitions were witnessed by hundreds of thousands of people across every religious denomination, including Egypt's Marxist president Abdul Nasser, and are one of the few modern apparitions recognized as authentic by the Catholic Church.[73] These apparitions are remarkable in the fact that they correspond with a category of visions defined in Catholic theology as *visio sensibilis* – apparitions that have a spatial existence exterior to the body which can be perceived by the bodily senses. This is unlike any of the other approved modern apparitions such as Lourdes and Fatima, which are classed as *visio imaginativa* – interior visions of supernatural origin which can be seen by the visionary but do not have an objective existence.[74]

---

[72] Johnston, F. *When Millions Saw Mary* (Chumleigh: Augustine Publishing Co., 1980), pp13-14

[73] Cardinal Bertone, the Vatican Secretary of State, lists the authentic (Church approved) apparitions as those of Rome, 1842; La Salette, 1846; Lourdes, 1858; Pontmain, France, 1871; Gietrzwald, Poland, 1877; Fatima, 1917; Beauraing, Belgium, 1932-1933; Banneaux, Belgium, 1933; Zaytun (Zeitoun), 1968; Akita, Japan, 1973; Kibeho, Rwanda, 1981-1989. See Bertone, T. *The Last Secret of Fatima* (New York, Doubleday, 2008) pp10-11. One may add here the apparitions at Knock, Ireland.

[74] See Cardinal Ratzinger's Theological Commentary in *The Message of Fatima*. Cf. St. Teresa of Avila's

Zeitoun, which is a district in the Egyptian capital Cairo, is traditionally held to be the first place in Egypt to which the Holy Family fled. Since local tradition holds that Assiut was their furthest point before returning home, some commentators have suggested that these apparitions were a heavenly re-enactment of the Holy Family's flight into Egypt. As the Assiut apparitions are a continuation of those seen at Zeitoun, the Church approval accorded the first apparitions should theoretically extend to cover these latest apparitions also.

The appearances of Our Lady at Assiut seem to be rather timely in relation to the astronomical phenomena of the years 1999-2000. And as we shall see, the appearance of the Virgin Mary at Assiut may even make a more direct connection between the fall of Satan and the implementation of the prophecy of the mark of the Beast.

Fig. 22 One of the most famous photographs taken of the apparitions at Zeitoun, which much like Assiut, were accompanied by the appearance of luminous doves and appeared on the top of a church roof in Egypt.

Although the apparitions of Our Lady at Assiut were not accompanied by the revelation of a message (unlike those at Fatima or La Salette), there is some evidence which suggests that the Virgin Mary may have been attempting to communicate a message through the vision itself. Some of the people present at the apparitions stated that Our Lady made some mysterious gestures. One witness, Ishaq Malti Sourial, reported seeing a light taking the form of the Virgin Mary "holding a square shaped sparkling object in her right hand".

"I will never forget the night of the 28 September when my family and I stood on a rooftop on the eastern side of the church at 3:30am. It was just before dawn. At 4am a gleam of light appeared on the dome and moved on to the church spire. After about 25 minutes, the light began to take on the form of the Virgin Mary holding a square-shaped sparkling object in her right hand. She then appeared in the eastern and western church windows."[75]

Was Our Lady trying to convey a message in this vision? As we noted earlier, 1st

---

The Interior Castle The Sixth Mansions.

[75] Reported in the Egyptian newspaper article "Our Lady of Assiut", *Watani International* (18th Feb 2001).

century Jews wore square-shaped boxes known as phylacteries in their hands as a literal observation of Exod 13 and Deut 6. It seems likely that the square-shaped box in this vision may have represented a heavenly *tefillin* – the seal of God which mirrors the inauguration of the diabolic phylactery bearing the mark of the Beast. It is possible that this vision was a warning that the prophecy concerning the number of the Beast had reached fulfilment in the event of the internet enabled mobile phone; antithetically reflecting the sealing of the saints in heaven.

The latest appearances of the Virgin Mary in 2009 at Warraq, Cairo, may also confirm that these apparitions are related to the prophecy of the Woman adorned with the Sun. The apparitions at Warraq have provided some of the most detailed images captured on film of this phenomenon.[76] While there have been no direct messages revealed during these apparitions, the symbolism of their location seems to be of utmost importance, centring on sites connected with the Holy Family's flight into Egypt. The names of the churches involved also seem to be of some significance. The first appearances at Zeitoun occurred at St. Mary's Coptic church – a building named after the Virgin herself. Another of these apparitions, also approved by the Coptic Church occurred over the church of St. Demiana in the Shoubra district of Cairo between the years 1986-1991. The life of St. Demiana tells of another "slaughter of the innocents", where the martyr-virgin of the late 3rd/early 4th century was executed along with forty other young Christian virgins during the persecution under Diocletian. The Assuit apparitions took place at St. Mark's Coptic church, and it has been noted that the Zeitoun apparitions coincided with the return of the relics of St. Mark (who is the patron saint of Egypt) to Alexandria in 1968 by Pope Paul VI.[77]

The site of the latest appearances at Warraq may hold the most telling aspect of these apparitions, as they were located at the Virgin Mary and Archangel Michael Coptic Church. The only place in Scripture which links the Virgin Mary with the Archangel Michael is contained in Rev 12.

Each of these apparitions have been subject to police investigation. At Zeitoun, the entire district's electric supply was cut in order to rule out any fakery using some form of sophisticated lighting technology. The apparitions continued during the blackouts however, suggesting that any alleged hoaxers would have to be incredibly well-organised. The very nature of the lights themselves, judging by both eyewitness testimony and the images captured on film, would be impossible to fake with contemporary technology however. The radiant, human-like figure of light recorded at Warraq moves around the domes of the church, and appears and disappears on camera without any visible electrical apparatus. An image of this level of luminosity would be impossible to create without some rather bulky electrical equipment which would be immediately apparent before and after the light display. The human-like light form could only possibly be faked by light being emitted from a life-size human-shaped light bulb, given that the figure itself is the primary light-source. This hypothetical equipment would then have to be moved to another area of church unseen by the crowd of thousands of spectators gathered below.

The only feasible way that an image such as this could be faked without visible equipment would be by light being projected onto the church roof from a remote location.

---

[76] Hassan, A. "Egypt: Is it the Virgin Mary or just a curious flash of light?" *LA Times* (2009)
[77] Johnston, F. *When Millions Saw Mary*, p3

But again, it would be impossible to create a projection of a human-like figure of light unless the hoaxers have had access to holographic projectors akin to that proposed by the "Project Blue Beam" conspiracy theory.[78] Holographic technology that could theoretically produce a human like figure composed of light has recently been unveiled. Although modern holographic technology could not achieve anywhere near this level of brightness, and is still very much cutting-edge today. It would not have been available at the turn of the millennium, and could only be dreamed of in the late 1960's when the apparitions of Our Lady first began to occur in Egypt.

This has led most sceptics to argue that the lights were produced by a natural phenomenon such as St Elmo's fire, or so-called "earthquake lights", and that the human-like figure is simply a case of religious pareidolia. But this would not explain why the only recorded instances of these phenomena in Egypt are confined to appearing over church buildings at places associated with the flight of the Holy Family into Egypt. The odds of such rare natural weather phenomena occurring over a religious building just once would be staggering in itself, never mind on several different occasions.

If these apparitions are related to the prophecy of the Woman clothed with the Sun in Rev 12, then they may explain the timing of their first occurrence in 1968. As we noted earlier, this portion of the Apocalypse is based to a large extent on the story of the nativity. The sole reason for the Holy Family's flight into Egypt was in order to escape Herod's slaughter of the innocents:

> Now when they had departed, behold, an angel of the Lord appeared to Joseph in a dream and said, "Rise, take the child and his mother, and flee to Egypt, and remain there until I tell you, for Herod is about to search for the child, to destroy him." And he rose and took the child and his mother by night and departed to Egypt and remained there until the death of Herod. This was to fulfill what the Lord had spoken by the prophet, "Out of Egypt I called my son." Then Herod, when he saw that he had been tricked by the wise men, became furious, and he sent and killed all the male children in Bethlehem and in all that region who were two years old or under, according to the time that he had ascertained from the wise men. (Matt 2:13-16)

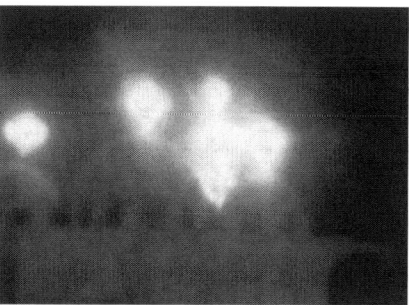

Fig. 23 A photograph of the apparition of Our Lady above the Virgin Mary and Archangel Michael Coptic church at Warraq, Cairo in December 2009.

---

[78] "Project Blue Beam" is a conspiracy theory forwarded by Serge Monast, who suggested that NASA, together with the United Nations, were planning to establish a one-world religion by staging a fake Second Coming of Christ using holographic projection technology. Monast, S. *Project Blue Beam* (Presse Libre Nord-Américaine, 1994)

Fig. 24 A second photograph taken at Warraq shows that the radiant figure of light has moved to the central dome.

The parallels here with Rev 12 are quite evident. The Woman who has given birth to the Messiah flees into the wilderness to escape from the pursuing Dragon, who intends to devour her child as soon as he is born, and issues forth a flood which threatens to sweep them away:

And the dragon stood before the woman who was about to give birth, so that when she bore her child he might devour it....
And when the dragon saw that he had been thrown down to the earth, he pursued the woman who had given birth to the male child. But the woman was given the two wings of the great eagle so that she might fly from the serpent into the wilderness, to the place where she is to be nourished for a time, and times, and half a time. The serpent poured water like a river out of his mouth after the woman, to sweep her away with a flood. (Rev 12:5, 13-15)

We can further identify the location of the "wilderness" here with Egypt by this passage's allusion to the Exodus wanderings. The Woman being gifted "the two wings of the great eagle" in Rev 12 reflects portions of Scripture associated with the Exodus of the Israelites from Egypt:

You yourselves have seen what I did to the Egyptians, and how I bore you on eagles' wings and brought you to myself. (Exod 19:4)

He found him in a desert land, and in the howling waste of the wilderness; he encircled him, he cared for him, he kept him as the apple of his eye. Like an eagle that stirs up its nest, that flutters over its young, spreading out its wings, catching them, bearing them on its pinions, the Lord alone guided him, no foreign god was with him. (Deut 32:10-12)

It is perhaps more than coincidence that the story of the Exodus begins with another episode of a slaughter of innocents – when the Egyptian Pharaoh decrees that in order to curtail their population growth, every male infant born to the Hebrew slaves should be cast into the Nile (Exod 1:15-2:10). And the Israelites escape only after the "Destroyer" takes the lives of the Egyptian first-born during the Passover (Exod 11:1-12:32). So the association between the slaughter of innocents and the land of Egypt occurs in the Bible on a number of different levels.

Just as the original flight of the Holy Family into Egypt was necessitated by an act of mass infanticide, these apparitions of the Virgin Mary in Egypt began to appear amidst the backdrop of what was the beginning of the greatest act of infanticide the world has ever known – the legalisation of abortion.[79] The year in which the apparitions in Zeitoun first occurred was a pivotal moment in process behind the legalisation of abortion. The Abortion Act in the UK came into effect during April 1968, the same month the apparitions began to take place. This year also saw President Lyndon Johnson's Committee on The Status of Women publishing a report calling for a repeal of all abortion laws in the US. The implementation of the UK Abortion Act was the major turning point in international abortion law, and was soon to be followed by a host of other nations. By mid-1969 ten US states had loosened their abortion laws, including Colorado, North Carolina, California, Georgia, Maryland, Arkansas, Kansas, Delaware, Oregon and New Mexico. Abortion on demand was eventually established after the US Supreme Court deemed individual state bans on abortion to be unconstitutional following the Roe v Wade case in 1973.

In France, women seeking an abortion began to travel to the UK to have the procedure after the Abortion Act came into effect in 1968. The relative ease of travelling to the UK to procure an abortion would lead to France revising its own abortion laws, and abortion was finally legalised in France in 1975.

Therefore the appearances of the Virgin Mary in Egypt occurred at the exact moment the floodgates in abortion law had been opened. Was this a heavenly response to the blood of millions of innocents crying from the ground?

The Date for the Mark of the Beast Foretold

There is another more recent prophecy concerning the turn of the millennium, which completely independently of the conclusions drawn in this book, explicitly connects this event with the timing of the implementation of the mark of the Beast. This remarkable parallel to the hypothesis we have presented thus far was made by Fr. Stefano Gobbi, an Italian Catholic priest who claimed to have received interior locutions of the Virgin Mary between the years 1972-1997.[80] Fr. Gobbi states that his interior locutions began during a pilgrimage to Fatima whilst praying at the little Chapel of the Apparitions. Some priests were gathering themselves against "the authority of the Church", which was presumably in opposition to the reforms made during the Second Vatican Council. In reaction to this, Fr. Gobbi states that an "interior force" urged him to gather priests who were willing to consecrate themselves to the Immaculate Heart of Mary and be "powerfully united to the pope". He prayed for confirmation of this interior voice to Our Lady, and claimed to have received a response whilst on pilgrimage at the Shrine of the

---

[79] See Pope John Paul II's statement in *Evangelium Vitae* – "I declare that direct abortion, that is, abortion willed as an end or as a means, always constitutes a grave moral disorder, since it is the deliberate killing of an innocent human being." (Vatican City: Libreria Editrace Vaticana, 1995)

[80] An interior locution differs from an apparition in that the recipient receives thoughts and ideas that are believed to emanate from a supernatural source, rather than related directly through a vision or external voice. Many mystics claim to have experienced this phenomena, such as St. Teresa of Avila and Mother Teresa of Calcutta. See St. Teresa of Avila's *The Interior Castle* Sixth Mansions Chap 3.

Annunciation in Nazareth during the same month.[81]

From these humble beginnings, Fr. Gobbi formed the Marian Movement of Priests, whose membership now numbers around 400 cardinals and bishops, more than 100,000 priests, and millions of religious and laypeople around the world. Fr. Gobbi recorded the locutions he received between 1972-1997, and they were eventually published together in his book *To the Priests, Our Lady's Beloved Sons*, which has the imprimatur of three Roman Catholic cardinals – Bernardino Ruiz, Ignatius Dauod and John Baptist Wu. Whilst the Congregation for the Doctrine of the Faith has yet to take an official position on the authenticity of Fr. Gobbi's locutions, he has a groundswell of support from key figures in the Church hierarchy. Pope John Paul II celebrated mass with Fr. Gobbi on an annual basis in his private chapel in the Vatican for several years.

The most overtly prophetic part of the book consists of the messages revealed to him in the year 1989. Here, Fr. Gobbi warns that Freemasonry seeks to establish an idol in place of the Church:

> Ecclesiastical Masonry goes as far as even building a statue in honor of the beast and forces all to adore this statue.
>
> But, according to the first commandment of the holy law of the Lord, only God is to be adored and to Him alone must every form of worship be rendered. And so they substitute for God a strong, powerful and dominating idol. An idol so powerful that it puts to death all who do not adore the statue of the beast. An idol so strong and dominating as to cause all, small and great, rich and poor, freemen and slaves, to receive a mark on the right hand and on the forehead, and that no one can buy or sell without having this mark, that is to say, the name of the beast or the number of its name. This great idol, built to be served and adored by all, as I have already revealed to you in the preceding message, is a false christ and a false church.
>
> But what is its name?
>
> In the thirteenth chapter of the Apocalypse it is written, 'This calls for wisdom. Let him who has understanding reckon the number of the beast: it represents a human name. And the number in question is 666 (six hundred and sixty-six).' With intelligence, illumined by the light of divine Wisdom, one can succeed in deciphering from the number, 666, the name of a man and this name, indicated by such a number, is that of the Antichrist.
>
> Lucifer, the ancient serpent, the devil or Satan, the Red Dragon, becomes, in these last times, the Antichrist. The Apostle John already affirmed that whoever denies that Jesus Christ is God, that person is the Antichrist. The statue or idol, built in honour of the beast to be adored by all men, is the Antichrist.
>
> Calculate now its number, 666, to understand how it indicates the name of a man. The number, 333, indicates the divinity. Lucifer rebels against God through pride, because he wants to put himself above God. 333 is the number which indicates the mystery of God. He who wants to put himself above God bears the sign, 666, and consequently this number indicates the name of Lucifer, Satan, that is to say, of him who sets himself against Christ, of the Antichrist.
>
> 333 indicated once, that is to say, for the first time, expresses the mystery of the unity of God. 333 indicated twice, that is to say, for the second time, indicates the two natures, that of the divine and the human, united in the divine Person of Jesus Christ. 333 indicated thrice, that is to say, for the third time, indicates the mystery of the Three Divine Persons, that is to say, it expresses the mystery of the Most Holy Trinity. Thus the number, 333, expressed one, two and three times, expresses the principal mysteries of the Catholic faith, which are: (1) the Unity and the Trinity of God, (2) the incarnation, the passion and death, and the resurrection of our Lord Jesus Christ.
>
> If 333 is the number which indicates the divinity, he who wants to put himself above God himself is referred to by the number 666.
>
> 666 indicated once, that is to say, for the first time, expresses the year 666, six hundred and sixty-six. In this period of history, the Antichrist is manifested through the phenomenon of Islam, which directly denies the mystery of the divine Trinity and the divinity of our Lord Jesus Christ. Islamism, with its

---

[81] Gobbi, S. *To the Priests, Our Lady's Beloved Sons* (Milan: Marian Movement of Priests, 1998), p15

military force, breaks loose everywhere, destroying all the ancient Christian communities, and invades Europe and it is only through my extraordinary motherly intervention, begged for powerfully by the Holy Father, that it does not succeed in destroying Christianity completely.

666 indicated twice, that is to say, for the second time, expresses the year 1332, thirteen hundred and thirty-two. In this period of history, the Antichrist is manifested through a radical attack on the faith in the word (Parola) of God. Through the philosophers who begin to give exclusive value to science and then to reason, there is a gradual tendency to constitute human intelligence alone as the sole criterion of truth. There come to birth the great philosophical errors which continue through the centuries down to your days. The exaggerated importance given to reason, as an exclusive criterion of truth, necessarily leads to the destruction of the faith in the word (Parola) of God. Indeed, with the Protestant Reformation, Tradition is rejected as a source of divine revelation, and only Sacred Scripture is accepted. But even this must be interpreted by means of the reason, and the authentic Magisterium of the hierarchical Church, to which Christ has entrusted the guardianship of the deposit of faith, is obstinately rejected. Each one is free to read and to understand Sacred Scripture according to one's personal interpretation. In this way, faith in the word (Parola) of God is destroyed. The work of the Antichrist, in this period of history, is the division of the Church and the consequent formation of new and numerous christian confessions which gradually become driven to a more and more extensive loss of the true faith in the word (Parola) of God.

666 indicated thrice, that is to say, for the third time, expresses the year 1998, nineteen hundred and ninety-eight. In this period of history, Freemasonry, assisted by its ecclesiastical form, will succeed in its great design: that of setting up an idol to put in the place of Christ and of his Church. A false christ and a false church. Consequently, the statue built in honor of the first beast, to be adored by all the inhabitants of the earth and which will seal with its mark all those who want to buy or sell, is that of the Antichrist. You have thus arrived at the peak of the purification, of the great tribulation and of the apostasy. The apostasy will be, as of then, generalized because almost all will follow the false christ and the false church. Then the door will be open for the appearance of the man or of the very person of the Antichrist![82]

Here, we have an explicit prophecy dating the implementation of the mark of the Beast to an era beginning in the year 1998. This is incredibly close to our proposed dating of the fulfilment of this prophecy to the turn of the millennium. The slight discrepancy can be reconciled with our own date when we take into account the symbolic nature of the year 1998 as 3 x 666. Besides, the prophecy states that it would be in this "period of history" rather than in that exact year, giving a wider scope for its precise fulfilment. It is even more remarkable that Fr. Gobbi places this prophecy in the context of the struggle of the Woman adorned with the Sun with the Red Dragon.

The fact that the heavenly signs which occurred between the years 1999-2000 correspond to the astronomical, geophysical and visionary phenomena described in the Book of Revelation, and that they are all concentrated around the same general time period (at the exact time which Our Lady of La Salette, Fr. Gobbi and Nostradamus foretold) cannot be easily put down to coincidence. If we look at the table on the next page we can see exactly how well these events all tie in together with the Book of Revelation:

---

[82] Gobbi, S. *To the Priests, Our Lady's Beloved Sons* pp497-499

Rev 6	
Sun becomes black	Aug. 11th 1999 – Total eclipse of the sun visible over Turkey – the location of the seven churches of Rev 1-3.
Stars fall to earth	Eclipse happens during the Peresid meteor shower which peaks annually between 11th – 13th of August. Then three months later a rare meteor storm which is recognized to be the most spectacular such event of its kind occurs at the same time as the launch of the first internet enabled mobile phone.
Earthquake	Aug. 17th 1999 – Earthquake measuring 7.5 on the Richter scale strikes Izmit in North-western Turkey, killing over 17,000 people
Moon becomes like blood	21st Jan. 2000 – Total lunar eclipse gives the moon a blood red hue.
Rev 7; 13	
The sealing of the saints in heaven occurs at the opening of the sixth seal and is heralded by the above astronomical and geophysical phenomena. This act of sealing appears to mirror the marking of the inhabitants of the earth with the number of the Beast.	Nov. 1999 – The world's first internet enabled mobile phone goes on sale, thus merging the letters www with a handheld phylactery-like device. This occurs within a year of the date Fr. Gobbi gave for the era in which the mark of the Beast would be implemented.
Rev 12	
Dragon is cast out of heaven and begins his reign on earth. The language used in this chapter suggests that the fall of Satan would coincide with the above phenomena. The Dragon pursues the Woman adorned with the Sun, who flees into the desert in an apocalyptic version of the story of the nativity.	May 13th 2000 -- Pope John Paul II reads from Rev 12, in the beatification ceremony of Jacinta and Francisco, apparently alluding to the contents of the second part of the Third Secret. 17th Aug. 2000 – Our Lady appears in Assiut, Egypt – the site in the desert tradition tells us the Holy Family sought refuge in. This apparition occurs on the Christian jubilee year commemorating the two thousandth anniversary of this event. Some witnesses report that Our Lady held a square shaped box in her hand.

We have thus accumulated a wealth of evidence which indicates that the fall of Satan coincided with the astronomical and geophysical phenomena of the years 1999-2000. This evidence, once pooled together, perfectly complements the numerous end-time prophecies dealing with this exact time period, allowing us to develop a comprehensive argument which cannot be easily dismissed. Was this the precise moment in history in which the eschatological element of the protoevangelium was finally fulfilled?:

> "I will put enmity between you and the woman, and between your offspring and her offspring; he shall bruise your head, and you shall bruise his heel." (Gen 3:18)

Parousia

The appearance of these numerous "signs of the times" emphatically suggest that the event of the Second Coming is rapidly approaching. Christ himself stated during the Olivet discourse that:

> "when you see all these things, you know that he is near, at the very gates. Truly, I say to you, this generation will not pass away until all these things take place." (Matt 24:33).

But what exactly will the Second Coming of Jesus entail? And to what extent will this event effect the close of history? Although the end-time Paraousia of Jesus is a central tenet of the Christian faith, its precise nature remains a mystery. Many questions still surround this pivotal eschatological event, and we simply cannot determine the exact manner in which the Second Coming will manifest itself.

We can establish certain aspects of the nature of the Second Coming from the few details given in Scripture. The Bible tells us that Jesus will return from heaven in a manner similar to his miraculous departure from the Earth during the Ascension:

> And when he had said these things, as they were looking on, he was lifted up, and a cloud took him out of their sight. And while they were gazing into heaven as he went, behold, two men stood by them in white robes, and said, "Men of Galilee, why do you stand looking into heaven? This Jesus, who was taken up from you into heaven, will come in the same way as you saw him go into heaven." (Acts 1:9-11)

This description of the return of Christ in a manner similar to his departure during the Ascension parallels Jesus' presentation of himself as the apocalyptic Son of Man in the gospels – a saying which directly alludes to Dan 7:13:

> "I saw in the night visions, and behold, with the clouds of heaven there came one like a son of man, and he came to the Ancient of Days and was presented before him. And to him was given dominion and glory and a kingdom, that all peoples, nations, and languages should serve him; his dominion is an everlasting dominion, which shall not pass away, and his kingdom one that shall not be destroyed. (Dan 7:13-14)

Modern scholarship generally recognizes that when Jesus referred to himself as the Son of Man in the Gospels, he was alluding to this mysterious piece of Scripture which describes a messianic-like being coming with the clouds of heaven at the end of days.[83] Although it contains numerous other symbolic elements, Jesus' use of the Son of Man title is derived mostly from this particular biblical passage. If we look at the Son of Man saying taken from the Olivet discourse below for example, we can see that it contains a description of Jesus in near-verbatim language to that used in Dan 7:13:

> Then will appear in heaven the sign of the Son of Man, and then all the tribes of the earth will mourn, and they will see the Son of Man coming on the clouds of heaven with power and great glory. (Matt 24:30)

The vision of Jesus as the apocalyptic Son of Man, descending from the sky with the clouds of heaven, is therefore the single most enduring image of the Second Coming. But how close is this image of Jesus descending from the sky to the real event of the Parousia? The New Testament repeatedly states that the Second Coming will be a miraculous event, which given its parallels to Jesus' Ascension into heaven, cannot be taken any other way but literally. So the Parousia will be a miraculous event similar in nature to the ascension, and not a metaphor as some preterists suggest,[84] or an invisible event which takes place in heaven, as some other Christian groups advocate.[85] Nor will there be any "reincarnation" of Jesus, as is commonly believed among various doomsday cults and in popular culture.[86]

The Bible is unequivocally clear that upon his return, Jesus will physically appear in the sky in power and glory, in what will be the singularly most important event of the eschatological age. While the miraculous nature of this doctrine may prove difficult to accept for those inclined towards a critical or liberal interpretation of scripture, it is no more problematical a belief than is say, the Resurrection or Ascension of Jesus. If one accepts the miraculous nature of these events, as is necessary for all orthodox Christians, then it should be just as easy to accept the miraculous nature of the Second Coming.

Another point on which the Scriptures appear to agree is that the return of Jesus will also somehow inaugurate the Last Judgment. Since the Last Judgment can only take place after the final demise of humanity, this would suggest that the Second Coming is connected in some way with the end of the world itself. Is it possible that the end-time Parousia of Christ will somehow bring about the events that will lead to the ultimate destruction of the world?

In a passage which can only make sense when applied to the eschatological age, Jesus tells the disciples that the ultimate result of his mission would be to bring war rather than peace:[87]

---

[83] See for example Wright, N.T. *Jesus and the Victory of God* (London: SPCK Publishing,1996) pp510-519

[84] For a Preterist account of the Second Coming see McKenzie, D.W. *The Antichrist and the Second Coming* (Longwood, FL: Xulon Press, 2009).

[85] Such as the beliefs of the Jehovah's Witnesses.

[86] For example, some members of the Branch Davidians came to believe that David Koresh was the Messiah before the siege at Waco. The Rastafarians believe that the Ethiopian Emperor Haile Selassie was the Second Advent of Jesus. Of the myriad other cult leaders who have claimed to be reincarnations of Jesus, some of the most notable include Jim Jones, leader of the People's Temple, Marshall Applewhite, leader of Heaven's Gate, and Charles Manson, leader of the Family. The idea that Jesus would be reincarnated is also perpetuated in popular culture by films such as *The Omen III: The Final Conflict* and by an erroneous interpretation of Rev 12.

[87] Davies and Allison give a list of ancient texts in which the sword specifically represents eschatological

Do not think that I have come to bring peace to the earth. I have not come to bring peace, but a sword. (Matt 10:34)

The theme of Jesus coming to bring a sword to the world in the eschatological age is carried over in the Apocalypse. Here, a double-edged sword projects from the mouth of the risen Christ, who is now depicted as the Warrior-Messiah coming to bring war to the earth. A sword which symbolizes divine proclamations of judgment:

Then I saw heaven opened, and behold, a white horse! The one sitting on it is called Faithful and True, and in righteousness he judges and makes war. His eyes are like a flame of fire, and on his head are many diadems, and he has a name written that no one knows but himself. He is clothed in a robe dipped in blood, and the name by which he is called is The Word of God. And the armies of heaven, arrayed in fine linen, white and pure, were following him on white horses. From his mouth comes a sharp sword with which to strike down the nations, and he will rule them with a rod of iron. He will tread the winepress of the fury of the wrath of God the Almighty. On his robe and on his thigh he has a name written, King of kings and Lord of lords. Then I saw an angel standing in the sun, and with a loud voice he called to all the birds that fly directly overhead, "Come, gather for the great supper of God, to eat the flesh of kings, the flesh of captains, the flesh of mighty men, the flesh of horses and their riders, and the flesh of all men, both free and slave, both small and great." And I saw the beast and the kings of the earth with their armies gathered to make war against him who was sitting on the horse and against his army. And the beast was captured, and with it the false prophet who in its presence had done the signs by which he deceived those who had received the mark of the beast and those who worshiped its image. These two were thrown alive into the lake of fire that burns with sulfur. And the rest were slain by the sword that came from the mouth of him who was sitting on the horse, and all the birds were gorged with their flesh. (Rev 19:11-21)

The imagery of this passage is obviously symbolic. Jesus will not come as some sort of Divine general at the head of an angelic army, but rather will in some way contribute to the coming eschatological battle. A passage in the Pauline epistles contains a similar theme of Jesus leading an angelic horde in the eschatological battle, exacting fiery vengeance upon the enemies of God. But it also contains a message of hope, where the believers at the end-time marvel at the glory of the Second Coming of Jesus:

This is evidence of the righteous judgment of God, that you may be considered worthy of the kingdom of God, for which you are also suffering — since indeed God considers it just to repay with affliction those who afflict you, and to grant relief to you who are afflicted as well as to us, when the Lord Jesus is revealed from heaven with his mighty angels in flaming fire, inflicting vengeance on those who do not know God and on those who do not obey the gospel of our Lord Jesus. They will suffer the punishment of eternal destruction, away from the presence of the Lord and from the glory of his might, when he comes on that day to be glorified in his saints, and to be marveled at among all who have believed, because our testimony to you was believed. (2Thes 1:5-10)

The above passages inform us that the Second Coming will be an extremely divisive event. Somehow, it seems that the Parousia of Christ will lead to the eschatological battle of Armageddon, where his vengeance will be inflicted through "flaming fire". But if the Second Coming is to provide the catalyst for the final war of humankind, then we are forced to conclude that there will be a duration of time between the event of the Parousia and the Last Judgment. Enough time to allow for a period between the actual event of Jesus' coming and the gathering together for the battle of

---

judgment in their work *A Critical and Exegetical Commentary on the Gospel according to Saint Matthew* (Edinburgh: T&T Clark, 1991) p218

Armageddon.

But if Jesus is to make a spectacularly triumphant return as is depicted in the Bible, why would there still be reason to doubt that it ever happened? Surely all peoples would believe in the truth of Christianity in light of this event? Both Rev 1:7 and Matt 24:27-28 state that the return of Jesus will be fully visible to all:

> Behold, he is coming with the clouds, and every eye will see him, even those who pierced him, and all tribes of the earth will wail on account of him. Even so. Amen.

> For as the lightning comes from the east and shines as far as the west, so will be the coming of the Son of Man. Wherever the corpse is, there the vultures will gather.[88]

But if the whole world will observe the Second Coming of Jesus, how will there remain so many unbelievers? Not only does the Book of Revelation suggest that some people will be unconvinced of the reality of the Second Coming, but that it would in some way be the cause of the most troubling period in human existence. Even the greatest of miracles can be met with a great deal of scepticism and doubt. We need only to take the events Fatima as an example. Although the miracle of the Sun was witnessed by over 70,000 people (including anti-Clerical journalists who were present with the sole purpose of debunking the children's claims), it is still either completely ignored or regarded with extreme scepticism by the secular media. This is in spite of the fact that no satisfactory alternative explanation for these events has ever been offered by sceptical investigators. In the absence of the continuing presence of Jesus after the Second Coming, there will still be room for doubters to deny that the Parousia had ever taken place, and perhaps even accuse the event as being a pious fraud perpetrated by hoaxers using state of the art technology.[89] The fact that it will be witnessed by large numbers like that of the miracle of the Sun at Fatima or the modern apparitions of the Virgin Mary in Egypt, will count for very little.

It is precisely this unbelief that will eventually lead to the battle of Armageddon. But while the Apocalypse indicates that Jesus himself will provide the catalyst for Armageddon, it is Satan and his minions who gather the nations of the world together to be destroyed (Rev 16:14). The Devil will exploit the circumstances that lead to this last war, causing the final rebellion of humankind against Christ.

So what exactly takes place at the Parousia that will bring about the circumstances which contribute to this last world war? Can the Second Coming be linked to the other catalyst for the battle of Armageddon which we discussed in chapter six – the collapse of

---

[88] Note that the phrase "Wherever the corpse is, there the vultures will gather" evokes the language of the eschatological banquet in Ezek 39:17-20 and the previously mentioned passage in Rev 19:11-21. So it appears that this phrase contains another link between the Second Coming and the eschatological battle.

[89] In fact such a scenario is already being primed by some New World Order conspiracy theorists. We have already noted how some Fundamentalist Christians believe that the New World Order elite will attempt to deceive the world's inhabitants into accepting a one-world religion in an operation known as "Project Blue Beam". According to this theory, the Second Coming will be faked by using hologram technology that has been developed by scientists at NASA, and be used to promote the new one-world religion. (See Monast, S. *Project Blue Beam*). Holographic technology that can project 3D images is already a scientific reality; and may reach such an advanced stage in twenty years' time. So the Project Blue Beam conspiracy theory could in turn be inverted by atheists, and be used to suggest that the Second Coming was faked by Fundamentalist Christians.

the United States? Could Cumbre Vieja's next eruption coincide with the Second Advent of Christ?

The Eschatological Earthquake

The Second Coming has been linked with catastrophic events elsewhere in the Bible. The Book of Zechariah, for example, states that a great earthquake will accompany the arrival of the Messiah on the Mount of Olives – a passage which is framed by the background context of the gathering together for the eschatological battle:

> Behold, a day is coming for the LORD, when the spoil taken from you will be divided in your midst. For I will gather all the nations against Jerusalem to battle, and the city shall be taken and the houses plundered and the women raped. Half of the city shall go out into exile, but the rest of the people shall not be cut off from the city. Then the LORD will go out and fight against those nations as when he fights on a day of battle. On that day his feet shall stand on the Mount of Olives that lies before Jerusalem on the east, and the Mount of Olives shall be split in two from east to west by a very wide valley, so that one half of the Mount shall move northward, and the other half southward. And you shall flee to the valley of my mountains, for the valley of the mountains shall reach to Azal. And you shall flee as you fled from the earthquake in the days of Uzziah king of Judah. Then the LORD my God will come, and all the holy ones with him. (Zech 14:1-5)

According to Acts 1:11-12, the Mount of Olives was the place of the Ascension of Jesus. As this passage in the Book of Acts states that Jesus will return in exactly the same way he left, many interpreters have held that the Parousia will be centred on this particular location. Due to a literal understanding of the above passage in Zechariah, there presently exists a large number of Jewish, Christian and Muslim cemeteries on or near the Mount of Olives. Throughout history, many people have wished to be interred near Mount Olivet so they would be among the first to be resurrected from the dead at the coming of the Messiah.

Zechariah's theme of the great earthquake on the Mount of Olives was also adapted by the Apocalypse. The eschatological earthquake is a stock motif in apocalyptic writings, and references to this future event can be found in the teachings of Jesus as well as in the Book of Revelation.[90] But there seems to be a particularly striking parallel between the above Zechariah quotation and a passage in the Apocalypse which is specifically associated with the fall of Babylon:

> And there were flashes of lightning, rumblings, peals of thunder, and a great earthquake such as there had never been since man was on the earth, so great was that earthquake. The great city was split into three parts, and the cities of the nations fell, and God remembered Babylon the great, to make her drain the cup of the wine of the fury of his wrath. (Rev 16:18-19)

A theme common to both passages is that Jerusalem, or the "great city" is split into a number of parts by this earthquake. Curiously, Revelation further states that God remembers to punish Babylon at the occurrence of this eschatological earthquake. There appears to be some connection between the punishment of the whore of Babylon and the

---

[90] See Bauckham, R. "The Eschatological Earthquake in the Apocalypse of John," *Novum Testamentum* 19 (1977) pp224-233.

occurrence of this earthquake in Jerusalem. Could the great earthquake that accompanies the event of the Second Coming coincide with, or even cause a particularly violent eruption of Cumbre Vieja? If so, then this would explain how the "cities of the nations" would fall as the result of one earthquake. The only way an earthquake could cause such widespread destruction would be if it set in motion a series of other related natural disasters. If this earthquake in some way triggered an eruption of Cumbre Vieja, which in turn generated a mega-tsunami, this would explain how the "cities of the nations" would be destroyed by this one event.

Scientists have recently theorized that seismic events of a strong magnitude can lead to wider geological instability around the world, and may even cause a chain reaction that can trigger volcanic eruptions.[91] Volcanic eruptions have followed high magnitude earthquakes in the past, and academics are still debating whether a link can be established between the two. If such a link does exist, then a particularly strong earthquake centred on or near Jerusalem may theoretically trigger a volcanic eruption on the Canary Islands.

The city of Jerusalem lies very close to the seismic fault line of the Jordan Rift Valley, which borders the unstable region between the African and Arabian tectonic plates. The Jordan Rift Valley, which is home to the Dead Sea – the lowest geographical point on dry land, has been particularly active in the past. Some major seismic events in this area have even been recorded in the Bible. The prophets Amos and Zechariah for example, inform us that a major earthquake struck the region of Judah during the reign of Uzziah in the mid-8th century BC (Amos 1:1; Zech 14:5).

But the Apocalypse tells us that the eschatological earthquake that will strike "the great city" (which Zechariah specifically identifies as Jerusalem) will be the greatest such event in human history (Rev 16:18). In order for an event such as this to occur, there would have to be a massive slippage of either the African or Arabian tectonic plates, or a collision between the two. If the African plate shifted as a result of this colossal earthquake, then it could theoretically cause a surge of magmatism in the volcanic hotspot at the other end of the same plate in the Canary Islands. This could then trigger an eruption of Cumbre Vieja which would cause a lateral collapse of its western flank, generating a mega-tsunami that would devastate the eastern shorelines of North and South America. If this brought about the demise of the USA as the world's leading superpower, then as we proposed earlier, it would leave a political vacuum that could be exploited by the Antichrist, who will then set about creating the conditions for the battle of Armageddon. Thus the earthquake that accompanies the Second Coming seems to set in motion a series of events that will eventually lead to a Third World War – the third woe of the Apocalypse which threatens to destroy humankind:

> The second woe has passed; behold, the third woe is soon to come. Then the seventh angel blew

---

[91] For a brief overview of this phenomenon see Noserale, D; Larson, T. "Chain Reaction: Earthquakes that Trigger other Natural Hazards" *People, Land & Water* (2006). Cf. Bettwy, M. "NASA Data Show Earthquakes May Quickly Boost Regional Volcanoes" *Nasa* (2007)
Although for the time being, scientists are only willing to concede that this phenomenon occurs among volcanoes within a 500km radius of the earthquake. A wider impact zone is decidedly more difficult to prove, but this doesn't rule out the possibility that it would increase magmatism over a wider area altogether. Also the greatest earthquake "since man was on the earth" as described by Rev 16:18, may have a significantly increased chance of boasting volcanic activity over a wider range.

his trumpet, and there were loud voices in heaven, saying, "The kingdom of the world has become the kingdom of our Lord and of his Christ, and he shall reign forever and ever." And the twenty-four elders who sit on their thrones before God fell on their faces and worshiped God, saying, "We give thanks to you, Lord God Almighty, who is and who was, for you have taken your great power and begun to reign. The nations raged, but your wrath came, and the time for the dead to be judged, and for rewarding your servants, the prophets and saints, and those who fear your name, both small and great, and for destroying the destroyers of the earth." (Rev 11:14-18)

This Third Woe of the Apocalypse, where the raging nations are destroyed by the wrath of God, ushers in the Last Judgment and New Creation.

We can find a direct connection between the battle of Armageddon and the eschatological earthquake elsewhere in the Bible, in Ezekiel 38:

But on that day, the day that Gog shall come against the land of Israel, declares the Lord GOD, my wrath will be roused in my anger. For in my jealousy and in my blazing wrath I declare, on that day there shall be a great earthquake in the land of Israel. The fish of the sea and the birds of the heavens and the beasts of the field and all creeping things that creep on the ground, and all the people who are on the face of the earth, shall quake at my presence. And the mountains shall be thrown down, and the cliffs shall fall, and every wall shall tumble to the ground. I will summon a sword against Gog on all my mountains, declares the Lord GOD. Every man's sword will be against his brother. (Ezek 38:18-23)

The above passage directly associates the advancement of "Gog" against Israel (who the Apocalypse depicts as the principal character of the battle of Armageddon) with the occurrence of the eschatological earthquake and the throwing down of "mountains". Could this be further confirmation that the eschatological earthquake is connected to the Apocalypse's vision of the volcano being thrown into the sea, which in turn destroys "Babylon"?

The fall of Babylon is also closely connected to the Second Coming of Christ in Rev 14. Both events are mentioned within close proximity of each other:

Another angel, a second, followed, saying, "Fallen, fallen is Babylon the great, she who made all nations drink the wine of the passion of her sexual immorality."
.... Then I looked, and behold, a white cloud, and seated on the cloud one like a son of man, with a golden crown on his head, and a sharp sickle in his hand. And another angel came out of the temple, calling with a loud voice to him who sat on the cloud, "Put in your sickle, and reap, for the hour to reap has come, for the harvest of the earth is fully ripe." So he who sat on the cloud swung his sickle across the earth, and the earth was reaped. (Rev 14:8;14-16)

Here, the vision of Christ, who is one again portrayed as the Danielic Son of Man, is revealed to John just after the theme of the fall of Babylon is first introduced. So there is also a link in this passage between the Second Coming (and by implication the earthquake that accompanies it) and the fall of Babylon.

The Gospel of Luke also links the Second Coming with a great calamity concerning the sea and the "powers of heaven" being shaken:

And there will be signs in sun and moon and stars, and *on the earth distress of nations in perplexity because of the roaring of the sea and the waves*, people fainting with fear and with foreboding of what is coming on the world. For the powers of the heavens will be shaken. And then they will see the Son of Man coming in a cloud with power and great glory. (Luke 17:25-27)

If the Second Coming coincides with the greatest earthquake in recorded history which is predicted to be centred on Jerusalem, it may also explain Jesus' enigmatic words concerning the Parousia: "Wherever the corpse is, there the vultures will gather" (Matt 24:28). The eschatological armies, led by the Antichrist, will gather over the corpse of Jerusalem in the aftermath of these disasters in an attempt to seize control of the Holy Land:

> Then I saw an angel standing in the sun, and with a loud voice he called to all the birds that fly directly overhead, "Come, gather for the great supper of God, to eat the flesh of kings, the flesh of captains, the flesh of mighty men, the flesh of horses and their riders, and the flesh of all men, both free and slave, both small and great." And I saw the beast and the kings of the earth with their armies gathered to make war against him who was sitting on the horse and against his army. (Rev 19:17-19)

But it is in achieving this destiny as the "Destroyer" of humanity that the Antichrist will meet with his ultimate defeat in death. The war that claims the collective lives of humanity also proves to be the final and eternal undoing of the unholy trinity at the General Resurrection:

> And the beast was captured, and with it the false prophet who in its presence had done the signs by which he deceived those who had received the mark of the beast and those who worshiped its image. These two were thrown alive into the lake of fire that burns with sulfur. And the rest were slain by the sword that came from the mouth of him who was sitting on the horse, and all the birds were gorged with their flesh. (Rev 19:20-21)

Conclusion

The combined prophetic evidence suggests that we are currently approaching the end of the age. While the exact date for the Second Coming of Jesus remains elusive, we can establish its proximity by reading the signs of the times. Many of the most famous prophecies made for the end-time in the Bible have either already been fulfilled, or are in the process of completion. The Jews have returned to the Holy Land; there has been a massive departure from the faith in Western Christendom; visions of the Woman adorned with the Sun have appeared in the very place depicted in the Bible at a time when a new slaughter of the innocents was inaugurated by modern society. Signs which point to the Second Advent of Christ.

The most pressing matter however is the manner in which Christians as a whole will deal with the possibility that the prophecy of the number of the Beast has reached fulfilment in the age of the internet. Is there any way we can know for sure that the internet provides the ultimate realisation of the prophecy of the number of the beast? Catholics are protected from error in such matters in the chair of St. Peter. Ultimately, the final and definitive pronouncement on this subject resides in the infallible hands of the Holy See, and how we react to this discovery can be dictated only by the Magisterium. For the time being, we must confine ourselves to exploring hypothetical answers to this problem.

We can begin working towards an answer to the problem presented by the number of the Beast's apparent relationship with modern technology by studying the Church's current teaching on this subject. In his 2009 encyclical *Caritas in veritate* Pope Benedict XVI analyses the role of technology in the light of the Book of Genesis, linking its applications for good or evil in the freewill of humanity:

> Technology — it is worth emphasizing — is a profoundly human reality, linked to the autonomy and freedom of man. In technology we express and confirm the hegemony of the spirit over matter....
>
> For this reason, technology is never merely technology. It reveals man and his aspirations towards development, it expresses the inner tension that impels him gradually to overcome material limitations. *Technology, in this sense, is a response to God's command to till and to keep the land* (cf. Gen 2:15) that he has entrusted to humanity...[1]

Does this mean that technology is neutral in itself, and its capacity for good or evil lies solely within how it is applied by the user? Adrian Walker, a Catholic theologian, has questioned the neutrality of technology, concluding that we must take into account the fact that various pieces of technology have their own a priori purposes which negate this "neutral" aspect:

> It is worth noting that the latest gadgets sometimes provoke an ill-defined sense of unease in us.

---

[1] Benedict XVI *Caritas in Veritate* (Vatican City: Libreria Editrace Vaticana, 2009)

The latest gadgets tend to change our lives in massive ways, and often rather more quickly than we are prepared for. Think of the sudden ubiquity of the personal computer and then, on its heels, of the internet. A whole generation ("generation Y") has grown up "wired", before we have had a chance to ask what being wired means and whether it is a good thing or not. And so, amidst all of the celebration over the latest life-changing technological breakthrough, there is also a good deal of head shaking, too. Somehow, we feel dimly, something is being lost. The machine has won another victory over nature. Are we altogether sure that it is good for the machine to be so invincible?...

The machines we build have the technological mind-set built into them. The hawkers of these machines seek to assure us, of course, that they have no purposes other than the ones we give them – that we, not the machines, are the masters. But the fact is that the machines do have purposes of their own, purposes hidden from most of us by the pervasiveness of the mind-set those purposes express. And so we begin to wonder: are we really are the masters after all, or might not the machines be pulling the strings? I'm not suggesting, of course, that anyone (in his right mind) actually believes that there are, say, gremlins in his refrigerator or computer. My point is just that there is a logic to the development and spread of technological gadgetry – a logic partly fuelled, of course, by the market – that seems to stride forward with an increasingly irresistible momentum. Most professionals, I daresay, are now hooked up to the internet in their homes and/or offices. Was this the result of a sovereign choice? Or of a more or less willing capitulation to the inevitable?[2]

Another Catholic theologian, Stratford Caldecott, further develops Walker's conception of the neutrality of technology:

Sitting in a meeting recently with a group of people each of whom was staring down into one or other electronic gadget, the following quotation came to mind:

"In our contemporary world it may be said that the more a man becomes dependent on the gadgets whose smooth functioning assures him of a tolerable life at the material level, the more estranged he becomes from an awareness of his inner reality. I should be tempted to say that the centre of gravity of such a man and his balancing point tend to become external to himself: that he projects himself more and more into objects, into the various pieces of apparatus on which he depends for his existence. It would be no exaggeration to say that the more progress 'humanity' as an abstraction makes towards the mastery of nature, the more actual individual men tend to become slaves of this very conquest." – Gabriel Marcel, *Men against Humanity* (London: Harvill Press, 1952)

Technology is far from neutral, as it is frequently assumed to be in both popular and scholarly writings on this subject. "The medium is the message" (McLuhan), and a technology is not simply a technique that may be employed for good or ill. It bears within itself a value system and a worldview – perhaps even a metaphysics and a theology. Telephone, television and the internet, for example, change our sense of space and time, and have a variety of effects on the relationships within the family and the wider social community. Some of these effects will be humanly beneficial, others less so, but an assessment of the technology is not possible without paying attention to the overall pattern of these effects, and to the purpose or function of the technology in relation to the purpose of human life itself. In what respect is a given tool actually serving the true end of man?[3]

We can address these concerns in light of Pope Benedict's above assessment of technology as a necessary extension of man's commandment to keep and till the land in the Book of Genesis:

"Because you have listened to the voice of your wife and have eaten of the tree of which I commanded you, 'You shall not eat of it,' cursed is the ground because of you; in pain you shall eat of it all

---

[2] Walker, A. "Not Neutral: Technology and the 'Theology of the Body'" *Second Spring 7*
[3] Caldecott, S. "Regenerate Science" *Beauty for Truth's Sake Blog* (1st December 2009)

the days of your life; thorns and thistles it shall bring forth for you; and you shall eat the plants of the field. By the sweat of your face you shall eat bread, till you return to the ground, for out of it you were taken; for you are dust, and to dust you shall return." (Gen 3:17-19)

It seems that God's original intention for man was to be at one with the environment, being sustained harmoniously by nature. This mutually sustaining relationship with nature is complicated by humankind's development of technology when man begins to manipulate his surroundings through agriculture in order to find sufficient nourishment. It is here, in the growth of agriculture that we find the birth of technology that will inevitably lead to the development of civilisation itself, symbolised through the story of Cain and Abel. Abel the pastoral nomad favoured by God is murdered by his agrarian brother. In a precursor to the mark of the Beast, Cain is then marked by God to set him apart from other peoples, and his descendants go on to build the first cities.

Genesis offers an unrelenting critique of civilisation. The civic *modus operandi* is held in juxtaposition with the pastoral nomadic existence led by Abraham and the rest of the patriarchs. From the haughty attempts to build the tower of Babel, to the destruction of the wicked Sodom and Gomorrah, civilisation is seldom held in a sympathetic light. Civilisation, and the technology that allows it to develop, is created through the artifice of man.

The Book of Genesis thus depicts civilisation and technology as a necessary evil resulting from humankind's development of wisdom. The promises of the Serpent that the gift of wisdom would be imparted through the consumption of the fruit of the Tree of Knowledge of Good and Evil, ring true. It is exactly this wisdom that enables the creation of technology and civilisation. But the Serpent in his jealousy knows that it is this same knowledge and technology that will lead to the ultimate demise of humanity itself:

Now the serpent was more crafty than any other beast of the field that the Lord God had made. He said to the woman, "Did God actually say, 'You shall not eat of any tree in the garden?'" And the woman said to the serpent, "We may eat of the fruit of the trees in the garden, but God said, 'You shall not eat of the fruit of the tree that is in the midst of the garden, neither shall you touch it, lest you die.'" But the serpent said to the woman, "You will not surely die. For God knows that when you eat of it your eyes will be opened, and you will be like God, knowing good and evil." So when the woman saw that the tree was good for food, and that it was a delight to the eyes, and that the tree was to be desired to make one wise, she took of its fruit and ate, and she also gave some to her husband who was with her, and he ate. (Gen 3:1-6)

The other unseen consequence of the imparting of wisdom to humanity at the behest of the Serpent is eschatological in character, and will eventually lead to the destruction of humanity at its own hands – a theme touched upon by Cardinal Ratzinger in his commentary on the Third Secret of Fatima:

The angel with the flaming sword on the left of the Mother of God recalls similar images in the Book of Revelation. This represents the threat of judgement which looms over the world. Today the prospect that the world might be reduced to ashes by a sea of fire no longer seems pure fantasy: man himself, with his inventions, has forged the flaming sword.[4]

The "flaming sword" which threatens to consume the planet described in the

---

[4] *The Message of Fatima*

Third Secret finds its origins in the same part of the Book of Genesis. Genesis states that a flaming sword was placed at the gates of Eden to protect the Tree of Life:

> Then the Lord God said, "Behold, the man has become like one of us in knowing good and evil. Now, lest he reach out his hand and take also of the tree of life and eat, and live forever—therefore the Lord God sent him out from the garden of Eden to work the ground from which he was taken. He drove out the man, and at the east of the garden of Eden he placed the cherubim and a flaming sword that turned every way to guard the way to the tree of life." (Gen 3:22-24)

The English poet William Blake perceived the eschatological role of the flaming sword described in the Book of Genesis in his poem *The Marriage of Heaven and Hell*:

> The ancient tradition that the world will be consumed in fire at the end of six thousand years is true... For the cherub with his flaming sword is hereby commanded to leave his guard at the tree of life, and when he does, the whole creation will be consumed...[5]

The irony is that the flaming sword that threatens human existence was forged by man himself. Like Damocles of legend, this sword hangs above the head of humanity, and we are waiting for its inevitable descent. However the sword was set in place by humanity itself due to its development of modern innovations such as climate-changing industrialisation and thermo-nuclear weapons.

The "mark of Cain" first appeared at the birth of technology and civilisation to distinguish the first murderer from the rest of humankind. In a way, this mark was an externalised representation of humanity's rebellion itself. Now a new "mark of Cain" has resurfaced at the end of history as a symbol which thoroughly encapsulates modern technology and globalization in the form of the mark of the Beast – the brand of Satan, who was "was a murderer from the beginning" (John 8:44). A mark which is the ultimate consequence of humanity's development of technology, and which ultimately augurs its own self-destruction.

The threat posed by the flaming sword described in the Book of Genesis and the Third Secret of Fatima can only be in response to a perceived threat to the "Tree of Life". In this allusion to the Book of Genesis, does the Third Secret suggest that humanity will make a Promethean attempt to use technology to (figuratively speaking) bypass the flaming sword guarding the Tree of Life and eat of its fruit? If so, then what sort of threat could humanity pose towards the "Tree of Life"? Since the Tree of Life represents immortality, it seems that Genesis is warning against humanity attempting to achieve "immortality" through technology.

Some futurists believe that the first person to live to the age of a thousand is already living among us.[6] There are others who believe that it will become possible to "upload" human consciousness directly to a computer, and "download" it again into a humanoid robot, the mind of artificially created clone, or a new body physically reconstructed through nano-technology; thus giving the potential for "eternal" life.[7] Adrian Walker warns of the inevitability of science's attempt to achieve this goal:

---

[5] Blake, W. *The Marriage of Heaven and Hell* (1790)
[6] Cambridge geneticist Dr. Aubrey de Grey has famously commented "I think the first person to live to 1,000 might be 60 already". De Grey, A. "We will be able to live to 1,000" *BBC News* (2004)
[7] See for example Ray Kurzweil's *The Age of the Spiritual Machine* (London: Penguin, 2000)

Not surprisingly, a culture that thinks it can reshape the physical world technologically is also prone to think, sooner or later (especially when the cultural influence of Christianity begins to wane), that it can extract human consciousness from its given embodiment, rearrange this embodiment, and then reinsert consciousness when the rearrangement is satisfactorily completed. A technological culture is committed, in principle, to the view that our consciousness can be downloaded into any old embodiment just as the consciousness of the characters in The Matrix is downloaded into computer-generated bodies.[8]

Pope Benedict XVI also anticipates this frivolous ambition in his encyclical *Caritas in veritate*:

Our freedom is profoundly shaped by our being, and by its limits. No one shapes his own conscience arbitrarily, but we all build our own "I" on the basis of a "self" which is given to us. Not only are other persons outside our control, but each one of us is outside his or her own control. *A person's development is compromised, if he claims to be solely responsible for producing what he becomes.* By analogy, the development of peoples goes awry if humanity thinks it can re-create itself through the "wonders" of technology, just as economic development is exposed as a destructive sham if it relies on the "wonders" of finance in order to sustain unnatural and consumerist growth. In the face of such Promethean presumption, we must fortify our love for a freedom that is not merely arbitrary, but is rendered truly human by acknowledgment of the good that underlies it. To this end, man needs to look inside himself in order to recognize the fundamental norms of the natural moral law which God has written on our hearts.[9]

Yet it is not even necessary for humankind to reach the stage of recreating himself through technology before it desecrates the fruit of the Tree of Life. This process has already begun in the work of embryonic stem cell research and science's foray into human cloning and creating human/animal hybrids. Just as eating the fruit of the Tree of Knowledge of Good and Evil resulted in the introduction of human mortality, so too may tampering with the fruit of the Tree of Life bring about the collective death of humanity.

We can see in retrospect that Sr. Lucia's instruction for the Third Secret to be released by 1960 as it would then be "better understood", was that it was precisely at this time that humankind began its assault on life itself. The year 1961 saw the release of the first contraceptive pill, thus inaugurating the "sexual revolution". It is no coincidence that the cultural revolution which began in the 1960's correlated directly with the decline of the Church in the West, paving the way for the current state of mass apostasy the Church is enduring today. This same cultural revolution also directly led to the worldwide legalisation of abortion. As the Catholic social scientist D.R. Carlin notes:

"....abortion was the keystone of the entire sexual revolution. If abortion is not allowable as a kind of insurance policy, then a cultural policy of maximising sexual freedom becomes impractical... Do away with abortion and the entire sexual revolution collapses, and do away with the sexual revolution and the whole personal-liberty revolution collapses."[10]

The 1960's also saw major breakthroughs in scientific research into the very fabric of life itself, which paved the way for the development of cloning and stem cell research. It is during this moment in history that what John Paul II described of as the "culture of death" was born, which would in turn lead to the current state of apostasy the

---

[8] Walker, A. "Not Neutral: Technology and the 'Theology of the Body'" *Second Spring 7*
[9] Benedict XVI *Caritas in Veritate*
[10] See Carlin, D.R. "The Sudden Decline of the Catholic Church in America" *The Catholic Social Science Review 10* (2005)

Church is enduring today. In an *ad limina* address to the bishops of America in 1998, the Pope summarised the repercussions of the sexual revolution of the 1960's as forewarned by Paul VI's landmark encyclical *Humanae Vitae*:

> Thirty years after *Humanae Vitae* we see that mistaken ideas about the individual's moral autonomy continue to inflict wounds on the consciences of many people and on the life of society. Paul VI pointed out some of the consequences of separating the unitive aspect of conjugal love from its procreative dimension: a gradual weakening of moral discipline; a trivialization of human sexuality; the demeaning of women; marital infidelity, often leading to broken families; state-sponsored programs of population control based on imposed contraception and sterilization (cf. *Humanae Vitae,* 17). The introduction of legalized abortion and euthanasia, ever increasing recourse to in vitro fertilization, and certain forms of genetic manipulation and embryo experimentation are also closely related in law and public policy, as well as in contemporary culture, to the idea of unlimited dominion over one's body and life.[11]

Already at this stage in history, humankind was foraging in the Tree of Life so that it may exploit the benefits of its fruit. If we continue on the path paved by the "culture of death" to despoil the Tree of Life, then we should expect to be met with the "flaming sword" that protects it. Could this ultimate destiny of destruction for humankind have been part of the Devil's true goal, as reflected in the mythology of this ancient biblical text?

If Satan's primeval intention for technology does lead to the cessation of human existence, then once again his plan will be thwarted by the work inaugurated in Christ's sacrificial death on the Cross and his glorious Resurrection. The Church, as the mystical body of Christ, will emulate its master in the eschatological resurrection after the collective crucifixion of humanity at the end of time, which leads to the creation of the New Heaven and the New Earth. The Bible is unambiguously clear that the world will end in an age of anarchy and pandemonium. Yet despite the Book of Revelation's depiction of a chaotic and tumultuous future, it concludes with a surprisingly optimistic climax. The unmitigated violence of the preceding chapters is turned completely on its head. The author is as pains to emphasize that after the battle of Armageddon there will be a general resurrection of the dead before the Last Judgment, where everyone will be recompensed for their actions on earth.

While Armageddon will bring history to a close, the reader is urged not to despair, as the "former things" was an imperfect existence that had deviated from the original paradisal setting of the Divine plan as outlaid in Genesis. Everything has now turned full circle. Paradise is created anew and restored to humankind, who have been resurrected in the flesh to dwell in the beatific vision of God. The closing hortatory statement of Revelation – "Come, Lord Jesus", stresses that the event of the Second Coming is not to be feared, but should rather be looked forward to with expectant hope. It is this last act of Divine mercy that will draw humankind closer to God.

In what is perhaps the greatest grace to come, we are promised that this age of

---

[11] John Paul II *Address of the Holy Father Pope John Paul II to the Bishops of the Episcopal Conference of the United States of America* (Vatican City: Libreria Editrace Vaticana, 1998)

unbelief and disorder will eventually give way to a new spiritual awakening of humanity before the end of the world is to take place. Like a terminal penitent on his deathbed, humankind will be granted a last sacrament – the extreme unction of the Second Pentecost; and will be given the chance to be strengthened, repent and turn from its sins before its inevitable demise. Our judgment has already been decided – a fate which we have collectively brought upon ourselves. But the hand of judgment has been stayed for the sake of the elect, until the fullness of God's people have been brought into the fold. It is this last sign of hope and the final vision of Our Lord Jesus that will be God's parting gift to humanity:

> Then I saw a new heaven and a new earth, for the first heaven and the first earth have passed away, and the sea was no more. And I saw the holy city, new Jerusalem, coming down out of heaven from God, prepared as a bride adorned for her husband. And I heard a loud voice from the throne saying, "Behold, the dwelling place of God is with man. He will dwell with them, and they will be his people, and God himself will be with them as their God. He will wipe away every tear from their eyes, and death shall be no more, neither shall there be mourning nor crying nor pain anymore, for the former things have passed away." And he who was seated on the throne said, "Behold, I am making all things new." (Rev 21:1-5)

Appendix I

Chronology

BC

598	First deportation of Jewish exiles to Babylon. Jerusalem is sacked and the Temple is stripped of its treasures
587/586	Destruction of Solomon's Temple. Second deportation of exiles
c.538	Return from exile
445	Edict of Artaxerxes I approving the rebuilding of Jerusalem
168	Antiochus IV Epiphanes desecrates the Temple igniting the Maccabaean revolt
c.4	Birth of Jesus Christ and flight of the Holy Family to Egypt

AD

c.33	Death, resurrection and ascension of Jesus
64	Neroian persecution
70	Destruction of the Herodian Temple
c.90	St. John writes the Apocalypse
132-5	Bar Kochba rebellion
312	Conversion of the Roman Emperor Constantine
638	Muslim conquest of Jerusalem
688	Construction of the Dome of the Rock begins on the Temple Mount in Jerusalem
692	Construction of the Dome of the Rock is completed
1054	Great Schism between the Eastern Orthodox and Catholic Churches
1139	St Malachy travels to Rome, where he is reputed to have received his vision of the list of popes
1517	Beginning of the Protestant Reformation
1846	Virgin Mary appears to shepherd children at La Salette

1908:

June 30th	Tunguska event
September 3rd	Public demonstrations of powered flight at Fort Myer leads to the development of the world's first military airplane
1914	Outbreak of World War One

1917:	
May 13th	Apparitions of the Virgin Mary begin to appear to the shepherd children of Fatima.
October 13th	The last appearance of the Virgin Mary at Fatima, during which the miracle of the sun is witnessed by over 70,000 people.
November 7th	Bolshevik Revolution
1918	End of World War One
1938	Aurora Borealis lights the skies of the Northern Hemisphere, a sign which Our Lady of Fatima foretold would herald another world war
1939	Outbreak of World War Two
1942	Hitler's "Final Solution" begins to be fully implemented
1945	End of World War Two
1948	Creation of the modern state of Israel
1967	Six Day War and the beginning of the Israeli occupation of East Jerusalem
1968:	
April 2nd	Apparitions of the Virgin Mary begin to appear over the roof of St Mary's Coptic Church at Zeitoun, Egypt.
April 27th	The UK Abortion Act comes into effect, which was the major turning point in abortion law throughout the world.
1978	John Paul II ascends the papacy - St. Malachy's 'Labour of the sun'
1986:	
February 9th	Perihelion of Halley's Comet
April 26th	Chernobyl disaster
1989:	Fr. Stefano Gobbi predicts the year 1998 (3 x 666) would inaugurate an era during which the prophecy of the mark of the Beast would be implemented.
1999:	Nostradamus' date of the descent of the 'King of Terror' from the sky
July 28th	Partial lunar eclipse
August 11th	Total eclipse of the sun
August 12th	Peak of Perseid meteor shower
August 17th	Large earthquake in Izmit, Turkey, kills around 45,000 people
November 17th	Peak of Leonid meteor storm
	Launch of first WAP mobile phone
2000:	Latest date given in the secrets of La Salette for the arrival of a monster that would 'disturb the peace'
	Latest possible date for the end of Satan's power in the prophecy attributed to Pope Leo XIII
January 21st	Total Lunar Eclipse
May 5th	Alignment of the planets Mercury, Venus, Earth, Mars, Jupiter and Saturn together with the sun and moon
May 13th	Beatification ceremony of Jacinta and Francisco Marto. Pope John Paul II announces that the text of the Third Secret of Fatima will

	be released to the public. He then uses Rev 12 to form the basis of his sermon
August 17th	Apparitions of the Virgin Mary begin to appear in Assiut, Egypt
2005	Death of Pope John Paul II.
	Benedict XVI ascends the papacy – St. Malachy's 'Glory of the Olives'
2009	Apparitions of the Virgin Mary appear in Warraq

Appendix II

The Ionic numeral system used by the ancient Greeks required 27 letters, while there was only 24 in the Greek alphabet. To make up 27 letters, the ancient Greeks used three letters that had dropped out of everyday use - digamma, qoppa and sampi. As we can see below, the number six in Greek is still equivalent to the letter W when transliterated into the Roman alphabet. The digamma, or Fαυ (*wau*) as it was originally known, would later come to represent the sixth letter of the Roman alphabet – F. The Greek numerals and their transliteration are given below:

A α	alpha	A	1
B β	beta	B	2
Γ γ	gamma	G	3
Δ δ	delta	D	4
E ε	epsilon	E	5
F ϝ	digamma	W	6
Z ζ	zeta	Z	7
H η	eta	E	8
Θ θ	theta	Th	9
I ι	iota	I	10
K κ	kappa	K	20
Λ λ	lambda	L	30
M μ	mu	M	40
N ν	nu	N	50
Ξ ξ	xi	X	60
O o	omicrion	O	70
Π π	pi	P	80
Ϙ ϙ	qoppa	Q	90
P ρ	rho	R	100
Σ σ	sigma	S	200
T τ	tau	T	300
Y υ	upsilon	Y	400
Φ φ	phi	Ph	500
X χ	chi	Ch	600
Ψ ψ	psi	Ps	700
Ω ω	omega	O	800
ϡ ϡ	sampi	Ss	900

Bibliography

Abdel-Hamid, H.   "Virgin Mary Said to Appear in Southern Egypt", *ABC News*, 2000, http://abcnews.go.com/International/story? id=82658&page=1

Anderson, B.W.   *The Living World of the Old Testament* (4th Ed), Harlow, Longman, 1988

Andrews, R.   *Blood on the Mountain*, London, Weidenfeld & Nicholson, 1999

Anon.   "Over 5 billion mobile phone connections worldwide" *BBC News*, 9th July 2010, http://www.bbc.co.uk/news/10569081

Anon.   "Our Lady of Assiut", *Watani International*, 2001. Available online at http://www.zeitun-eg.org/watani_ international.htm

Anon.   "The Great Leonid Meteor Storm of 1833" *Nasa Science News*, 1999 http://science.nasa.gov/newhome/headlines/ast22jun99_2.h tm

Armstrong, K.   *A History of God*, London, Vintage, 1999

_____.   *A History of Jerusalem*, London, HarperCollins, 1996

_____.   *The Battle for God*, London, HarperCollins, 2000

Ashe, G.   *The Book of Prophecy*, London, Orion, 1999

Augustine.   *The City of God*, London, Penguin, 2003
Bettenson, H. (Trans)

Aune, D.E.   *Revelation* 1-5, Dallas, Word, 1997

_____.   *Revelation* 6-16, Dallas, Word, 1998

_____.	*Revelation* 17-22, Dallas, Word, 1998
Bacchiarello, J. (Ed)	*Forty Dreams of St. John Bosco*, Rockford, TAN, 1996
Baigent, M; Leigh, R.	*The Temple and the Lodge*, London, Arrow, 1998
Ball, B.W; Brill, E.J.	*A Great Expectation - Eschatological Thought in English Protestantism to 1660*, Leiden, 1975
Barlow, F. (Ed.)	*Life of King Edward the* Confessor, New York, Thomas Nelson, 1962
Barry, K.	*The Greek Qabalah*, York Beach, Weiser, 1999
Batten, D. (Ed.)	*The Creation Answers Book*, Brisbane, Creation Book Publishers, 2007
Bauckham, R.	*The Climax of Prophecy*, London: Continuum, 1998
_____.	"The Eschatological Earthquake in the Apocalypse of John", *Novum Testamentum* 19, 1977.
Beale, G.K.	*The Book of Revelation,* Carlisle, Paternoster, 1999
Benedict XIV	*Heroic Virtue: On the Beatification and Canonization of the Servants of God* III, Prato, 1840
Benedict XVI	*Anglicanorum Coetibus*, Vatican City, Libreria Editrace Vaticana, 2009 http://www.vatican.va/holy_father/benedict_xvi/apost_constitutions/documents/hf_ben-xvi_apc_20091104_anglicanorum-coetibus_en.html
_____.	*Caritas in Veritate*, Vatican City, Libreria Editrace Vaticana, 2009 http://www.vatican.va/holy_father/benedict_xvi/encyclicals/documents/hf_ben-xvi_enc_20090629_caritas-in-veritate_en.html
_____.	*Homily of His Holiness Pope Benedict XVI Palm Sunday* Vatican City, Libreria Editrace Vaticana, 2011
_____.	*Interview of the Holy Father Benedict XVI with the Journalists During the Flight to Portugal* (Vatican City, Libreria Editrace Vaticana, 11th May 2010) http://www.vatican.va/holy_father/benedict_xvi/speeches/2

226   Bibliography

                              010/may/documents/hf_ben-
                              xvi_spe_20100511_portogallo-interview_en.html

        _____.   *Jesus of Nazareth Vol. 2*, London, CTS, 2011

        _____.   *Lecture of the Holy Father: Faith, Reason and the
                              University Memories and Reflections*, Vatican City,
                              Libreria Editrice Vaticana, Sept 12th 2006
                              http://www.vatican.va/holy_father/benedict_xvi/speeches/2
                              006/september/documents/hf_ben-
                              xvi_spe_20060912_university-regensburg_en.html

Berners-Lee, T.   *Weaving the Web: Origins and Future of the Worldwide
                              Web*, London, Orion, 1999

Bertone, T.   *The Last Secret of Fatima*, New York, Doubleday, 2008

Betham, W. (Ed)   "Tírechán's Collections Concerning St. Patrick" *Book of
                              Armagh*, Irish Antiquarian Researches. Vol. 2. Dublin,
                              William Curry, Jr. and Co., 1827

Bettwy, M.   "NASA Data Show Earthquakes May Quickly Boost
                              Regional Volcanoes", *NASA*, 2007,
                              http://www.nasa.gov/centers/goddard/news/topstory
                              /2007/earthquake_volcano.html

Biggs, J.   "Bill Gates wants to help the Third World with cellphone
                              banking", *Crunchgear*, 2009
                              http://www.crunchgear.com/2009/02/17/bill-gates-wants-
                              to-help-the-third-world-with-cellphone-banking/

Blake, W.   *The Marriage of Heaven and Hell*, 1790

Bolton, R.   *The Order of the Ages: World History in the Light of a
                              Universal Cosmogony*, San Rafael, Sophia Perennis, 2001

Bosco, J;   *Forty Dreams of St. John Bosco*, Rockford, TAN, 1969
Bacchiarello, J (Ed)

Boudreaux, R.   "Catholic Church Unveils 'Third Secret of Fatima'" *LA
                              Times*, 27th June 2000
                              http://articles.latimes.com/2000/jun/27/news/mn-45242

Bourmaud, D.   "Discovery of the Secrets of La Salette: A Book Review",
                              Newsletter of the District of Asia, 2003,

	http://www.sspxasia.com/Newsletters/2003/Jul-Dec/Secret_of_La_Salette.htm
Bouw, G.	*Geocentricity*, Cleveland, Association for Biblical Astronomy, 1992
Bradley, M.	*The Secret Societies Handbook*, London, Cassell, 2005
Bullinger, E.W.	*Number in Scripture*, New York, Cosimo Classics, 2005
Caldecott, S.	*Beauty for Truth's Sake: On the Re-enchantment of Education*, Grand Rapids, Brazos, 2009
_____.	*Companion to the Book of Revelation*, London, Catholic Truth Society, 2008
_____.	Caldecott, S. "Regenerate Science" *Beauty for Truth's Sake Blog* (1st December 2009) http://beauty-in-education.blogspot.com/search?updated-max=2009-12-04T07%3A59%3A00Z&max-results=3
_____.	*The Seven Sacraments: Entering the Mysteries of God*, New York, Crossroad, 2006
Campbell, G.	"Findings, Seals, Trumpets and Bowls: Variations upon the Theme of Covenant Rupture and Restoration in the Book of Revelation." *Westminister Theological Journal* 66, 2004
_____.	"Feminine-Urban Imagery and a Tale of Two Women-Cities in the Book of Revelation" *Tyndale Bulletin*, 55.1, 2005
_____.	"How to say what. Story and Interpretation in the Book of Revelation" *Irish Biblical Studies* 23, 2001
_____.	*L'Apocalypse de Jean. Une Lecture Thematique*, Excelsis, 2007
_____.	"Pour Lire L'Apocalypse de Jean L'Interet D'une Approche Thematique" *Revue Réformée* 224, 2003
Capovilla, L.F.	"A Reserved Note of L.F. Capovilla", *The Fatima Network*, 1967. http://www.fatima.org/news/newsviews/092707capovilla.asp
Carlin, D.R.	"The Sudden Decline of the Catholic Church in America"

	The Catholic Social Science Review 10. 2005 http://www.docstoc.com/docs/34864969/The-Sudden-Decline-of-the-Catholic-Church-in-America
Carlo, G.	"Dr. George Carlo's Response to the Danish Study" *Safe Wireless Initiative*, 2006, http://www.emf-health.com/reports-drcarlo-danishstudy.htm
Carlo, G; Schram, M.	*Cell Phones: Invisible Hazards in the Wireless Age*, New York, Carroll & Graf Publishers, Inc., 2001
Carr, N.	"Is Google Making Us Stupid? What the Internet is doing to our brains." *The Atlantic*, 2008
_____.	*The Shallows: What the Internet Is Doing to Our Brains*, New York, W.W. Norton, 2010
Carson, D.A.	*The Gospel According to John*, Grand Rapids, Eerdmans, 1991
Cassius Dio, Cary, E. (Trans)	*Roman History* Vol. VIII, Massachusetts, Loeb Classical Library, 1925
Charles, R.H.	*A Critical and Exegetical Commentary on the Revelation of St. John* Vol 1, Edinburgh, T&C Clark, 1920
Chidester, D.	*Christianity: A Global History*, London, Penguin, 2000
Chilton, D.C.	*The Days of Vengeance: An Exposition of the Book of Revelation*, Fort Worth, Dominion, 1987
Chomsky, N.	*Hegemony or Survival: America's Quest for Global Dominance*, London, Penguin, 2004
_____.	*Imperial Ambitions*, London, Metropolitan Books, 2005
_____.	*Manufacturing Consent: The Political Economy of the Mass Media*, London, Vintage, 2006
Clement XII	*In Eminenti*, 1738, Papal Encyclicals Online, http://www.papalencyclicals.net/Clem12/c15inemengl.htm
Congregation for the Doctrine of the Faith	*The Message of Fatima*, Vatican City, Libreria Editrace Vaticana, 2000, http://www.vatican.va/roman_curia/congregations/cfaith/

documents/rc_con_cfaith_doc_20000626_message-fatima
_en.html, 2000

Cowan, R.B.   "NXP Says Demand for NFC Chips to Soar" *Reuters*, 11th
                          May 2011, http://www.reuters.com/article/2011/05/19/us-
                          summit-nxp-idUSTRE74I4HC20110519

Dart, J.   "'Beam me up' Theology - The Debate Over 'Left
                          Behind'", *Christian Century*, 2002,
                          http://findarticles.com/p/articles/mi_m1058/is_20_119/ai_9
                          2589345

Davies, W.D.   *A Critical and Exegetical Commentary on the Gospel*
Allison, D.C.   *according to Saint Matthew* Vol 2, Edinburgh, T&T Clark,
                          1991

Davis, J.J.   *Biblical Numerology*, Grand Rapids, Baker, 1968

Dawkins, R.   *The Blind Watchmaker*, London, Penguin, 1988

_____.   *The God Delusion*, London, Transworld, 2006

De Grey, A.   "We will be able to live to 1,000" *BBC News*, 2004
                          http://news.bbc.co.uk/1/hi/uk/4003063.stm

De Jesus, L.   *Fatima in Lucia's Own Words*, Fatima, Postulation Centre,
                          1976

De la Sainte Trinite, M. "The Secret of Fatima… Revealed" *La Contre Reforme
                          Catholique No 222*, May 1986
                          http://www.fatima.org/crusader/crthird/sfrpg12.asp#1

_____.   *The Whole Truth About Fatima Vol. III*, Buffalo,
                          Immaculate Heart Publications, 1990

De Marchi, J.   *The True Story of Fatima*, St. Paul, Catechetical Guild
                          Educational Society, 1956

Draper, G;   "Childhood cancer in relation to distance from high voltage
Vincent, T;   power lines in England and Wales: a case-control study"
Kroll, M.E;   *British Medical Journal vol. 330* p1290, June 2nd 2005
Swanson, J.

Drosnin, M.   *The Bible Code*, London, Orion, 1997

Dupont, Y.   *Catholic Prophecy*, Rockford, Il., TAN, 1970

Eusebius,   *Eusebius: The Church History*, Grand Rapids,
Maier, P.L. (Trans)   Kregel Academic & Professional, 2007

Fazekas, A.   "2009 Leonid Meteor Shower: 'Strong Outburst' Expected"
                              National Geographic News, 2009
                              http://news.nationalgeographic.com/news/2009/11/091113-
                              2009-leonids-meteor-shower-peak.html

Fideler, D.   *Jesus Christ, Sun of God*, Wheaton, Quest Books, 1993

Fiorenza, E.S.   "Composition and Structure of the Book of Revelation"
                              Catholic Biblical Quarterly 39, 1977

Foschini, L.   "Probable asteroidal origin of the Tunguska Cosmic Body"
                              Astronomy and Astrophysics, 2001 http://www-
                              th.bo.infn.it/tunguska/aah2886.pdf

Frend, W.H.C   *The Early Church*, London, SCM Press, 2003

Frost, M.   *Desert Storm: The 1999 Leonid Meteor Shower*, 1999,
                              http://www.britastro.org /sinai_leonids99/reports/frost.html

Fukushima, F.   *Akita: Mother of God As Coredemptrix Modern Miracles of
                              Holy Eucharist*, Goleta CA, Queenship Publishing, 1997

Gilbert, A.   *Signs in the Sky*, London, Corgi, 2001

Gilbert, M.   *Atlas of the Holocaust*, New York, Macmillan, 1982

Gobbi, S.   *To the Priests, Our Lady's Beloved Sons*, Milan, Marian
                              Movement of Priests, 1998

Goldingay, J.E.   *Daniel*, Nashville, Word, 1989

Gouin, P.   *Sister Mary of the Cross. Shepherdess of La Salette.
                              Melanie Calvat*, New Jersey, The 101 Foundation, 1968

Gutman, Y. (Ed.)   *Encyclopedia of the Holocaust*, New York, Macmillan
                              Library Reference USA, 1995

Hagger, N.   *The Secret Founding of America*, London, Watkins
                              Publishing, 2007

Haggith, D.   *Prophets of the Apocalypse*, London, HarperCollins, 2001

Ham, S.   "GO-Tags May Replace Cash and Credit Cards",
                               Bloomberg Businessweek, August 28th 2008,
                               http://www.businessweek.com/magazine/content/08_36/b4
                               098058931873.htm

Hassan, A.   "Egypt: Is it the Virgin Mary or just a curious flash of
                               light?" *LA Times*, 2009
                               http://latimesblogs.latimes.com/babylonbeyond/2009/12/eg
                               ypt-people-turn-to-holy-phenomenon-in-times-of-crisis-
                               .html

Hardt, M; Negri, A.   *Empire*, Massachusetts, Harvard University Press, 2001

Hartley, D.   *Observations on Man, His Frame, His Duty and his
                               Expectations*, 2 vols, London, J. Johnson, 1801

Haussleiter, J. (Ed)   "Victorinus of Pettau", *Victorini Epscopi Petavionses
                               Opera*, CSEL 49, Vienna, 1916

Hawley, C.   "Virgin Mary 'appears' in Egypt", *BBC News 24*, 2000,
                               http://news.bbc.co.uk/1/hi/world/middle_east/912026.stm

Hippolytus,   *The Extant Works and Fragments of Hippolytus*,
Salmond, S.D.F (Trans)   http://www.earlychristianwritings.com/text/hippolytus-
                               exegetical.html

Hogue, J.   *The Last Pope*, Shaftesbury, Element Books, 2000

Holzhauser, B.   *Interpretatio Apocalypsis usque ad cap. XV, v. 5*, Bamberg,
                               1784

S. L. Jaki.   *God and the Sun at Fatima*, New Hope KY, Real View
                               Books, 1999

James, J.   "Are Smartphones taking over credit card payments?",
                               Credit Karma Blog, 6th August 2010,
                               http://blog.creditkarma.com/credit-cards/are-smartphones-
                               taking-over-credit-card-payments/

John Paul II   *Address of the Holy Father Pope John Paul II to the
                               Bishops of the Episcopal Conference of the United States of
                               America (California, Nevada, Hawaii)*, Vatican City,
                               Libreria Editrace Vaticana, 1998,

232   Bibliography

http://www.vatican.va/holy_father/john_paul_ii/speeches/1
998/october/documents/hf_jp-ii_spe_19981002_ad-limina-
usa_en.html

_____.   *Beatification of Francisco and Jacinta Marto, Shepherds of
Fatima*, Vatican City, Libreria Editrace Vaticana, 2000,
http://www.vatican.va/holy_father/john_paul_ii/travels/doc
uments/hf_jp-ii_hom_20000513_beatification-
fatima_en.html

_____.   "By the blood of the Lamb", *General Audience* 12th
January 2005, Vatican City, Libreria Editrace Vaticana,
http://www.vatican.va/holy_father/john_paul_ii/audiences/
2005/documents/hf_jp-ii_aud_20050112_en.html

_____.   *Crossing the Threshold of Hope*, London, Jonathan Cape,
1994

_____.   *Evangelium Vitae*, Vatican City, Libreria Editrace
Vaticana, 1995,
http://www.vatican.va/holy_father/john_paul_ii/encyclicals
/documents/hf_jp-ii_enc_25031995_evangelium-
vitae_en.html

_____.   *General Audience*, Vatican City, Libreria Editrace Vaticana
12th January 2005
http://www.vatican.va/holy_father/john_paul_ii/audiences/
2005/documents/hf_jp-ii_aud_20050112_en.html

Johnston, F.   *When Millions Saw Mary*, Chumleigh, Augustine
Publishing Co., 1980

Josephus, F.   *Josephus: The Complete Works*, Nashville,
Whiston, W. (Trans)   Thomas Nelson, 2004

Keener, C.S.   *A Commentary on the Gospel of Matthew*, Grand Rapids,
Eerdmans, 1999

_____.   *Revelation*, Grand Rapids, Zondervan, 2000

Kepler, J.   *De vero Anno, quo aeternus Dei Filius humanam naturam
in Utero benedictae Virginis Mariae assumpsit*, 1613

Kerby-Fulton, K.   *Reformist Apocalypticism and Piers Plowman*, Cambridge,
Cambridge University Press, 1990

Kramer, H.B.	*The Book of Destiny*, Rockford, TAN, 1955
Kramer, P. (Ed)	*The Devil's Final Battle*, The Missionary Association, Terryville, 2002
Kurzweil, R.	*The Age of the Spiritual Machines*, London, Penguin, 2000
LaSor, W.S; Hubbard, D.A; Bush, F.W.	*Old Testament Survey* (2nd Ed), Grand Rapids, Eerdmans, 1996
Laurentin, R; Corteville, M.	*Découverte du Secret de la Salette*, Fayard, Paris, 2002
Leo XIII	*Esti Nos*, The Papal Library, 1882, http://www.saint-mike.org/Library/Papal_Library/LeoXIII/Encyclicals/Etsi_Nos.html
Lightfoot, J.B	*St. Clement of Rome*, London, Macmillan, 1869
Linsey, H.	*The Late Great Planet Earth*, Grand Rapids, Zondervan, 1970
_____.	*There's a New World Coming*, Grand Rapids, Zondervan, 1974
Lombardi, F.	"Don't Let Wi-Fi Leave Your Prayer Life Dry" *Zenit*, 23rd Nov 2008, http://www.zenit.org/article-24341?l=English
Luard, H R. (Ed.)	*Lives of Edward the Confessor*, London, 1858
Madden, R.R.	*Exposure of literary frauds and forgeries concocted in Ireland: spurious predictions designated prophecies of Columbkille etc., etc., etc.* Dublin, John F. Fowler, 1866
Malina, B.J; Pilch, J.J.	*Social-Science Commentary on the Book of Revelation*, Fortress Press, Minneapolis, 2000
Marshall, I.H.	*Luke*, Carlisle, Paternoster, 1978
Maybaum, I.	*The Face of God After Auschwitz*, Amsterdam, Polak & Van Gennep Ltd, 1965
McCoy, B.	"Chiamus: An Important Structural Device Commonly Found in Biblical Literature" *Chafer Theological Seminary*

	Journal 9, 2003
McGinn, B. (Ed)	*Apocalyptic Spirituality: Treatises and Letters by Lactantius, Adso of Montier-en-Derl, Joachim of Fiore, the Spiritual Franciscans and Savonarola*, Mahwah, Paulist Press, 1979
McGinn, B.	*Antichrist: Two Thousand Years of the Human Fascination with Evil*, San Francisco, HarperCollins, 1994
_____.	*Visions of the End: Apocalyptic Traditions in the Middle Ages*, New York, Columbia University Press, 1979
McGrath, A.	*The Twilight of Atheism*, London, Rider, 2004
_____.	*Dawkins' God*, Oxford, Blackwell, 2005
_____.	*The Dawkins Delusion?*, London, SPCK, 2007
McGuire, B; Day, S; Kilburn, C; Ward, S.N.	"Volcano collapse-generated megatsunamis: Fact or Fiction?" http://www.es.ucsc.edu/~ward/papers/EOSCumbreVieja.pdf
McKenzie, D.W.	*The Antichrist and the Second Coming*, Xulon Press, 2009
Michell, J.	*City of Revelation*, London, Abacus, 1972
Monast, S.	*Project Blue Beam*, Presse Libre Nord-Américaine, 1994
Morris, L.	*Revelation* (Revised Edition), Leicester, IVP, 1987
Mounce, R.H.	*Revelation* (2nd Ed.), Grand Rapids, Eerdmans, 1998
Myers, A.C (Ed)	*The Eerdmans Bible Dictionary*, Grand Rapids, Eerdmans, 1987
Newman, J.H.	*The Second Spring*, 1852 http://users.stargate.net/~elcore/2ndsprng.htm
Noserale, D; Larson, T.	"Chain Reaction: Earthquakes that Trigger other Natural Hazards" *People, Land & Water*, 2006 http://www.usgs.gov/homepage/science_features/docs/plw1906/chain_reaction.pdf.
Oberweis, M.	"Die Bedeutung der neutestamentlichen 'Raetzelzahlen'

666 (Apk 13:18) und 153 (Joh 21:11)." *Zeitschrift fur die neutestamentliche Wissenschaft* 77 pp226-241.

O'Kearney, N.	*The Prophecies of Ss. Columbkille, Maeltamlacht, Ultan, Seadhna, Coireall, Bearcan, Malachy, &tc*, Dublin, John O'Daly, 1856
Osborne, G.R.	*Revelation,* Grand Rapids, Baker Academic, 2002
Paolini, S.	"My Meetings with Archbishop Capovilla and the Socci-Cardinal Bertone Struggle", *The Fatima Network*, 2007 http://www.fatimapeaceconferences.com/solideo_paolini_2007_en.asp
Pius IX	*Etsi Multa*, 1873, Papal Encyclicals Online, http://www.papalencyclicals.net/Pius09/p9etsimu.htm
Pliny the Elder, Healey, J. (Trans)	*Natural History*, London, Penguin, 1991
Pritchard, J.B. (Ed.)	*Ancient Near Eastern Texts Relating to the Old Testament* (3rd Ed), Princeton, Princeton University Press, 1969
Prevost, J.P	*How to Read the Apocalypse*, London, SCM, 1991
Rainsford, S.	"Belarus cursed by Chernobyl" *BBC News*, April 26th 2005 http://news.bbc.co.uk/1/hi/world/europe/4485003.stm
Ratzinger, J.	*Jesus*, November 11th 1984
Reeves, M.	*The Influence of Prophecy in the Later Middle Ages*, Notre Dame, University of Notre Dame Press, 1993
Relfe, M.S.	*When Your Money Fails*, Montgomery, AL: Ministries, 1981
Roberts, A. (Ed)	*The Ante-Nicene Fathers Vol III*, New York, Cosimo, 2007
_____.	*The Ante-Nicene Fathers Vol VII*, New York, Cosimo, 2007
Robertson, P.	*The New World Order*, Nashville, W Publishing Group, 1991

Robock, A;
Oman, L;
Stenchikov, G.L.

"Nuclear winter revisited with a modern climate model and current nuclear arsenals: Still catastrophic consequences" *Journal of Geophysical Research* Vol. 112, 2007, http://climate.envsci.rutgers.edu/pdf/RobockNW2006 JD008235.pdf

Rogers, S.

Toils and Struggles of the Olden Times, Cincinnati, Standard Publishing Company, 1880

Satinover, J.

The Truth Behind the Bible Code, London, Sidgwick & Jackson, 1997

Saunders, W.

"Archangels and Guardian Angels", *Arlington Catholic Herald*, 1st January 1997

Schemann, S.

"Chernobyl Fallout: Apocalyptic Tale" *New York Times*, 25th July 1986

Schneiderman, H;
Maller, J.B. (Eds.)

American Jewish Yearbook Vol 48 (Philadelphia, The Jewish Publication Society of America, 1946)

Schoeman, R.

Salvation is from the Jews, San Francisco, Ignatius Press, 2003

Schüz, J;
Jacobsen, R;
Olsen, J.H;
Boice, J.D;
McLaughlin, J.K;
Johansen, C.

"Cellular Telephone Use and Cancer Risk: Update of a Nationwide Danish Cohort". *Journal of the National Cancer Institute 98* (December 2006) pp1707–1713.

Seward, D.

The Dancing Sun, London, Macmillan, 1993

Short, M.

Inside the Brotherhood, London, Harpercollins, 1993

Smalley, S.S.

The Revelation to John, Downers Grove, IVP, 2005

_____.

Thunder and Love: John's Revelation and John's Community, Milton Keynes, Nelson Word, 1994

Snobelen, S.

"The mystery of this restitution of all things": Isaac Newton on the return of the Jews, *Millenarianism and Messianism in Early Modern European Culture: The*

Millenarian Turn, Dordrecht, Kluwer Academic, 2001.

Socci, A.   "Dear Cardinal Bertone: Who between me and you is deliberately lying?" *The Fatima Crusader 86*, 2007
http://www.fatimacrusader.com/cr86/cr86pg35.asp

———.   *The Fourth Secret of Fatima*, Fitzwilliam, Loreto Publications, 2009

Stanton, G.   *Gospel Truth? New Light on Jesus and the Gospels*, Valley Forge, Trinity Press, 1995

Stevenson, J. (Ed)   *A New Eusebius*, London, SPCK, (revised edition) 1987

Stewart, D; Missler, C.   *The Coming Temple*, Orange, Dart Press, 1991

Strack, H.L.
Stemberger, G.   *Introduction to the Talmud and Midrash*, Edinburgh, T.&T. Clark, 1991

Strobel, A.   "Abfassung und Geschichstheologie der Apokalypse nach Kapitel xvii.9-12" *New Testament Studies 10*, 1964

Suetonius
Graves, R. (Trans)   *The Twelve Caesars*, London, Penguin, 2007

Tavo, F.   "The Structure of the Apocalypse. Re-examining a Perennial Problem" *Novum Testamentum* XLVII, 2005

Teresa of Avila   *The Interior Castle*, 1577, New York, Cosimo Inc

Terry, M.S.   *The Sibylline Oracles*, Whitefish, Kessinger Publishing, 2007

Tyconius;
Babcock, W.S. (Trans)   *Tyconius: The Book of Rules*, Atlanta, Society of Biblical Literature, 1989

Various;   *Catechism of the Catholic Church*, Vatican City, Libreria Editrace Vaticana, 1993
http://www.vatican.va/archive/ENG0015/_INDEX.HTM

———.   *Catholic Encyclopaedia*,
http://www.newadvent.org/cathen/

———.   *Lumen Gentium*, Vatican City, Libreria Editrace Vaticana, 1964
http://www.vatican.va/archive/hist_councils/ii_vatican_cou

ncil/documents/vat-ii_const_19641121_lumen-
gentium_en.html

Vennari, J.   "The Fourth Secret of Fatima", *Catholic Family News*,
                               2007, http://www.cfnews.org/Socci-FourthSecret.htm

Wainwright, A.W.   *Mysterious Apocalypse*, West Broadway, Wipf and Stock
                               Publishers, (reprint) 2001

Walker, A.   "Not Neutral: Technology and the 'Theology of the Body'"
                               Second Spring 7

Walvoord, J.F;   *Armageddon: Oil and the Middle East Crisis*,
Walvoord, J.E.   Grand Rapids, Zondervan, 1974

Walzer, M.   "Is There an American Empire?", *Dissent Magazine*, 2003
                               http://www.dissentmagazine.org/article/?article=455

Ward, S.N;   "Cumbre Vieja Volcano -- Potential collapse and tsunami
Day, S.J.   at La Palma, Canary Islands", *Geophysical Research
                               Letters 28*, 2001 pp397-400
                               http://www.es.ucsc.edu/~ward/papers/La_Palma_grl.pdf

Woolf, A.F.   "Nonstrategic Nuclear Weapons" *Congressional Research
                               Service*, 2011
                               http://www.fas.org/sgp/crs/nuke/RL32572.pdf

Wright, N.T.   *Jesus and the Victory of God*, London, SPCK
                               Publishing,1996

Wynne-Jones, J.   "Facebook and MySpace can lead children to commit
                               suicide, warns Archbishop Nichols", *The Telegraph*, 1st
                               Aug 2009
                               http://www.telegraph.co.uk/news/newstopics/religion/5956
                               719/Facebook-and-MySpace-can-lead-children-to-commit-
                               suicide-warns-Archbishop-Nichols.html

Index

Printed in Great Britain
by Amazon